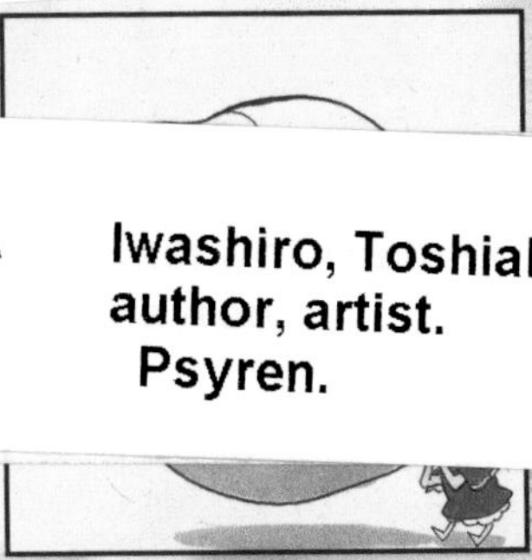

Toshiaki Iwashiro

I just finished reading a book of sci-fi manga short stories by Fujiko F. Fujio. When I was a child, I simply enjoyed them for their entertainment value, but now that I'm an adult working in the same field, I can appreciate how incredible they really are.

Toshiaki Iwashiro was born December 11, 1977, in Tokyo and has the blood type of A. His debut manga was the popular *Mieru Hito*, which ran from 2005 to 2007 in Japan in *Weekly Shonen Jump*, where *Psyren* was also serialized.

PSYREN VOL. 7
SHONEN JUMP Manga Edition

STORY AND ART BY TOSHIAKI IWASHIRO

Translation/Camellia Nieh
Lettering/Annaliese Christman
Design/Matt Hinrichs
Editor/Joel Enos

PSYREN © 2007 by Toshiaki Iwashiro
All rights reserved.
First published in Japan in 2007 by SHUEISHA Inc., Tokyo.
English translation rights arranged by SHUEISHA Inc.

Printed in the U.S.A.

Published by VIZ Media, LLC
P.O. Box 77010
San Francisco, CA 94107

10 9 8 7 6 5 4 3 2 1
First printing, November 2012

www.viz.com

THE WORLD'S
MOST POPULAR MANGA
SHONEN JUMP
www.shonenjump.com

SHONEN JUMP MANGA EDITION

7

THE DECEMBER 2ND REVOLUTION

Story and Art by
Toshiaki Iwashiro

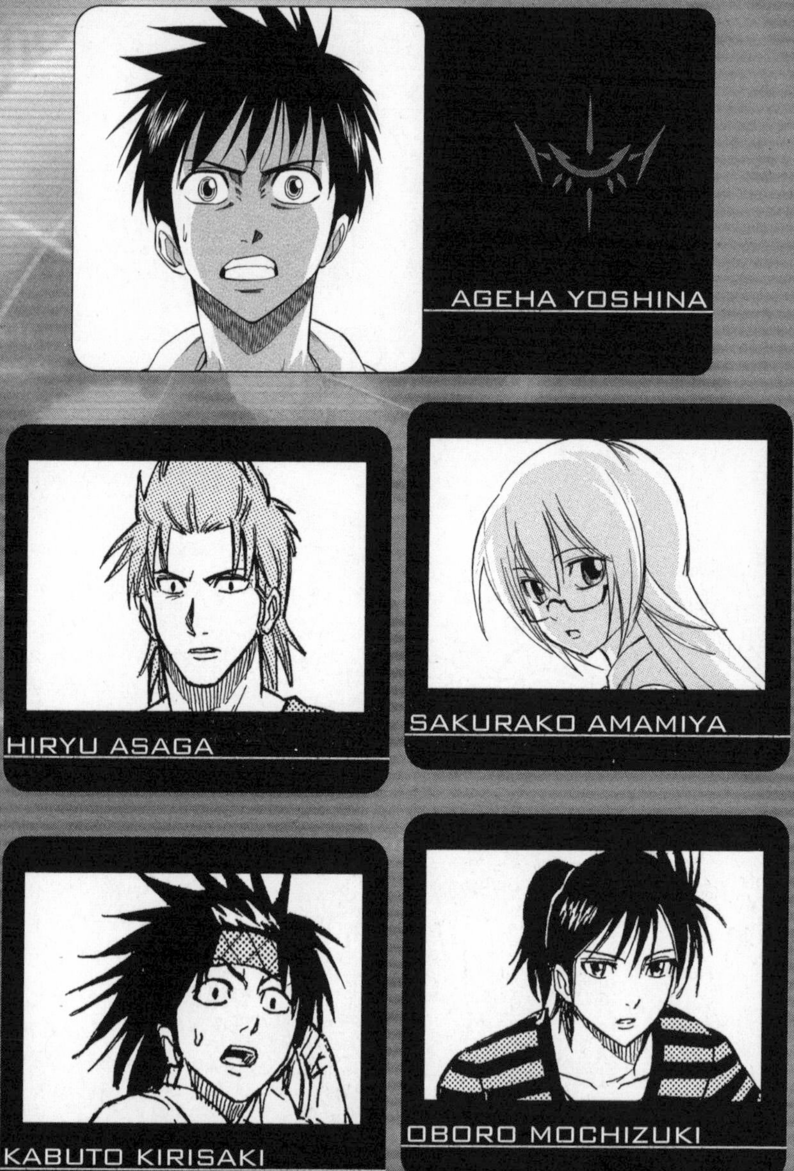
AGEHA YOSHINA
SAKURAKO AMAMIYA
HIRYU ASAGA
OBORO MOCHIZUKI
KABUTO KIRISAKI

Characters

KIYOTADA INUI

THE ELMORE WOOD GANG

SABURO INUI

KAGETORA HYODO

Story

WHILE SEARCHING FOR HIS MISSING FRIEND SAKURAKO AMAMIYA, HIGH SCHOOLER AGEHA YOSHINA HAPPENS UPON A RED TELEPHONE CARD EMBLAZONED WITH THE WORD *PSYREN* THAT TRANSPORTS HIM INTO A LIFE-OR-DEATH GAME IN A BIZARRE WORLD.

AGEHA TRIES TO WARN HIS ELDERLY FRIEND ELMORE OF THE DISASTER IN HER FUTURE, BUT THE MYSTERIOUS NEMESIS Q WHISKS HIM OFF TO THE PSYREN TIMELINE. THERE, HE LEARNS THAT NEMESIS Q IS A PSIONIC PROGRAM CREATED TO CHANGE THE PAST. MEANWHILE, KAGETORA PURSUES THE PERPS BEHIND A STRING OF THEFTS TARGETING LOAN SHARKS, BUT INSTEAD HIS TARGETS CAPTURE HIM. WITH THE HELP OF THE ELMORE WOOD GANG, THE KIDS WHO LIVE AT THE TRAINING HOUSE THAT ELMORE RUNS, AGEHA MANAGES TO OVERCOME KIYOTADA INUI AND HIS TWO PSIONIST HENCHMEN.

VOL. 7
THE DECEMBER 2ND REVOLUTION
CONTENTS

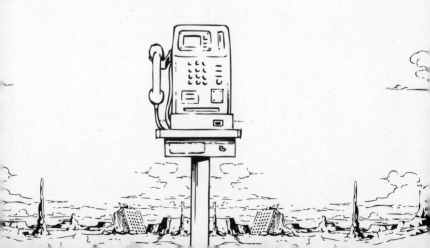

CALL.54: BROTHERS

WHY IS THIS HAPPENING?

WHAT NOW?

THERE'S SOMEBODY UPSTAIRS.

WHY? I DON'T UNDERSTAND...

...

HOW DID THEY FIND US?

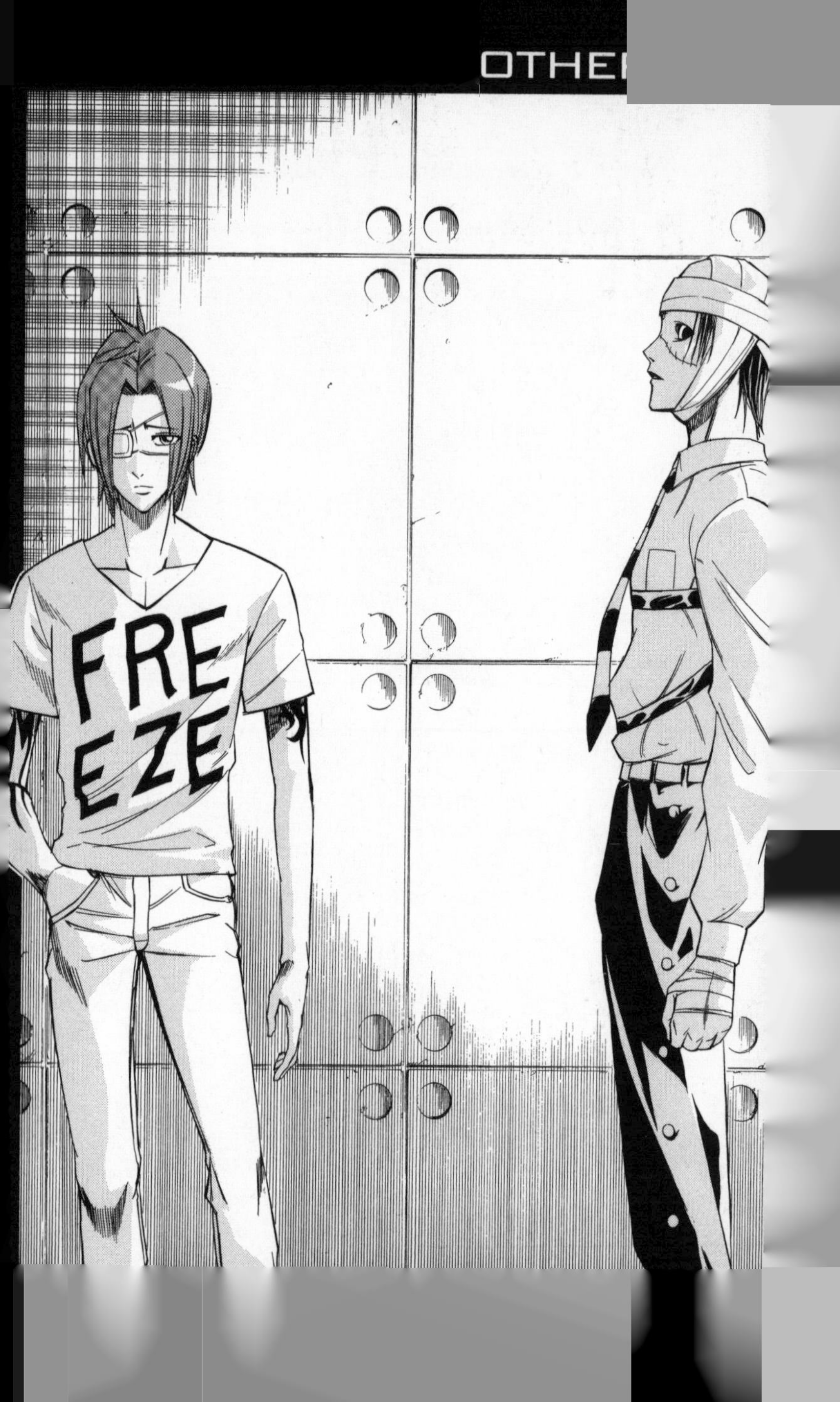
OTHE
FRE
EZE

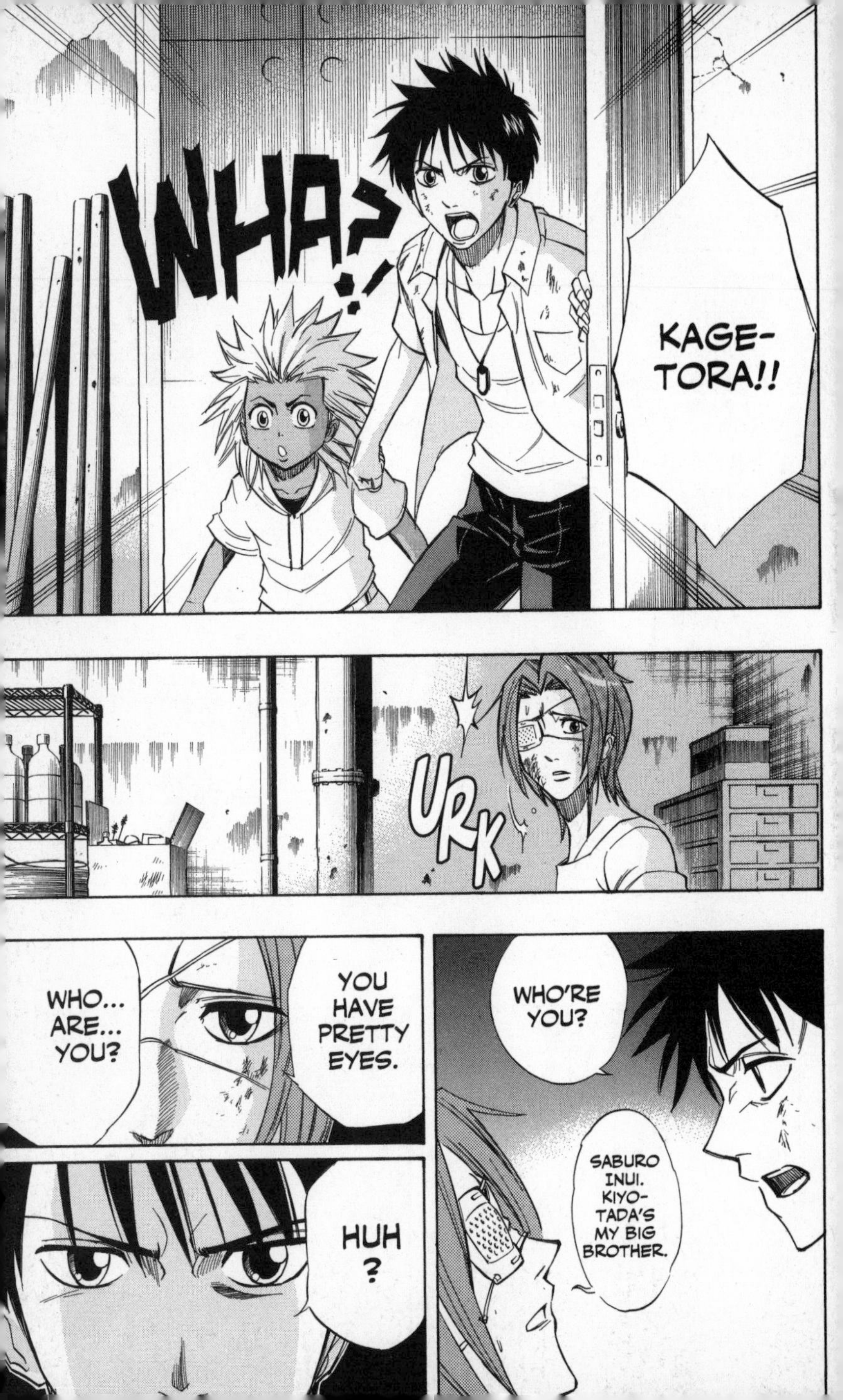
KAGE-TORA!!
WHA?!
URK
WHO'RE YOU?
SABURO INUI. KIYO-TADA'S MY BIG BROTHER.
YOU HAVE PRETTY EYES.
WHO... ARE... YOU?
HUH?

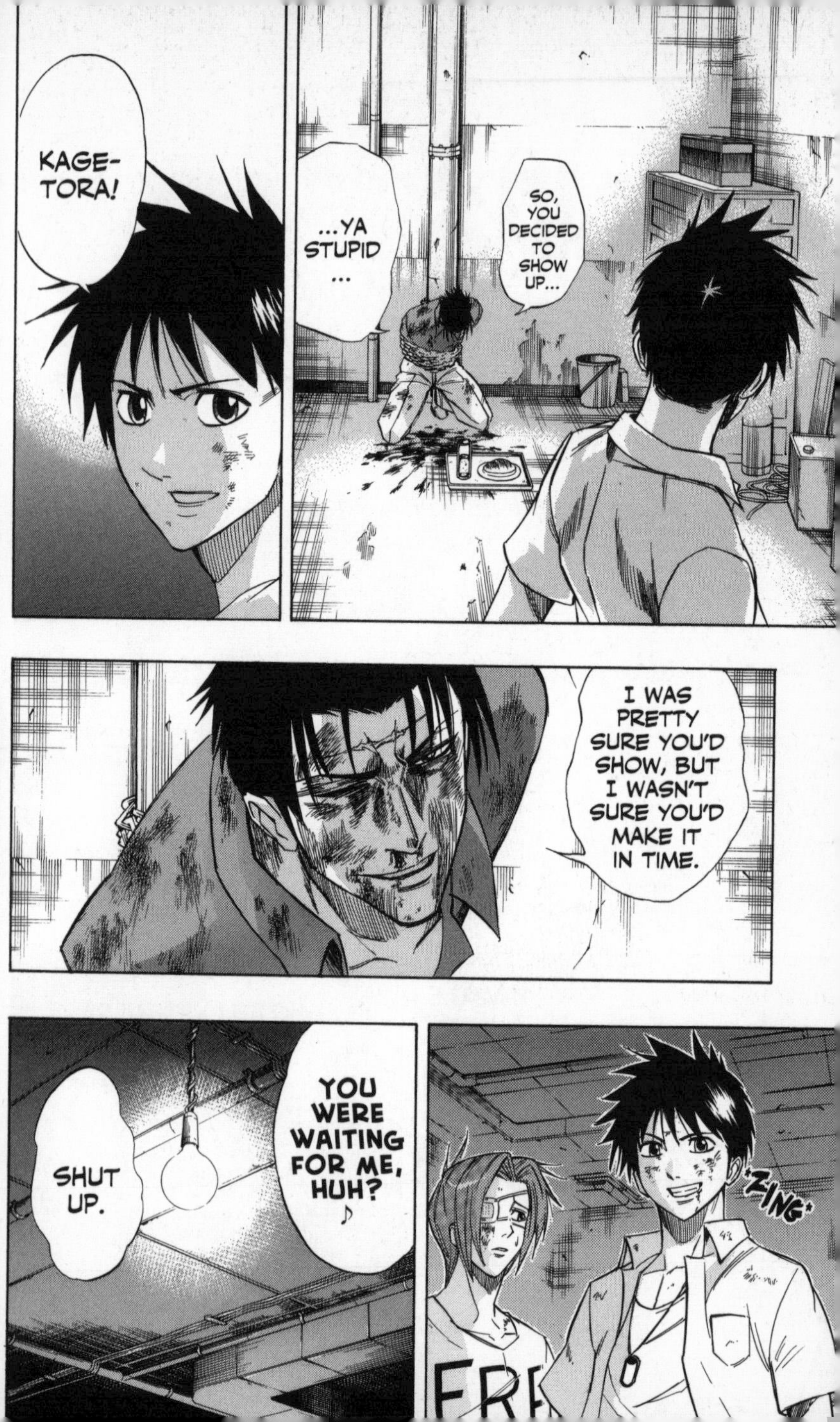
SO, YOU DECIDED TO SHOW UP...
...YA STUPID...
KAGE-TORA!
I WAS PRETTY SURE YOU'D SHOW, BUT I WASN'T SURE YOU'D MAKE IT IN TIME.
ZING
YOU WERE WAITING FOR ME, HUH? ♪
SHUT UP.

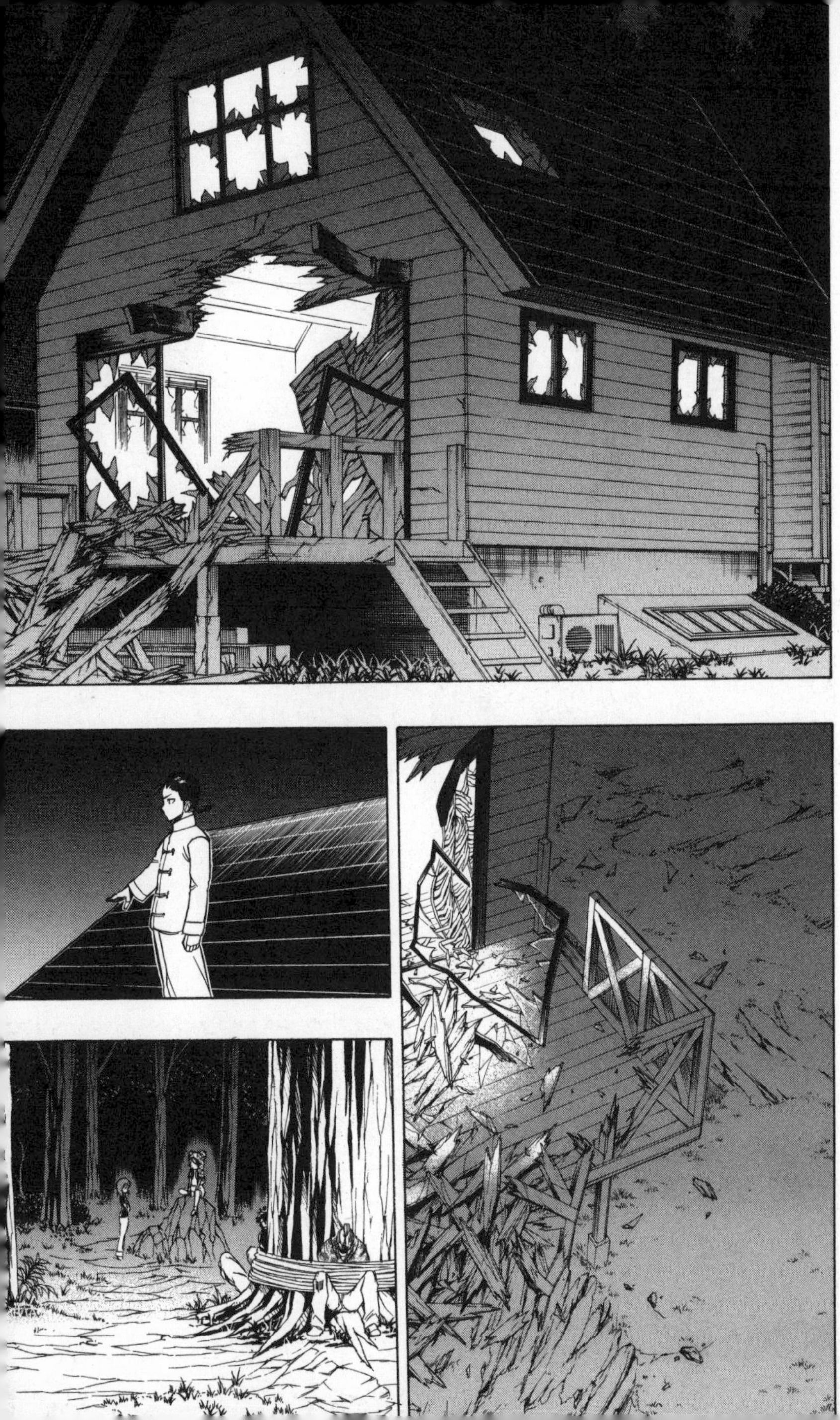

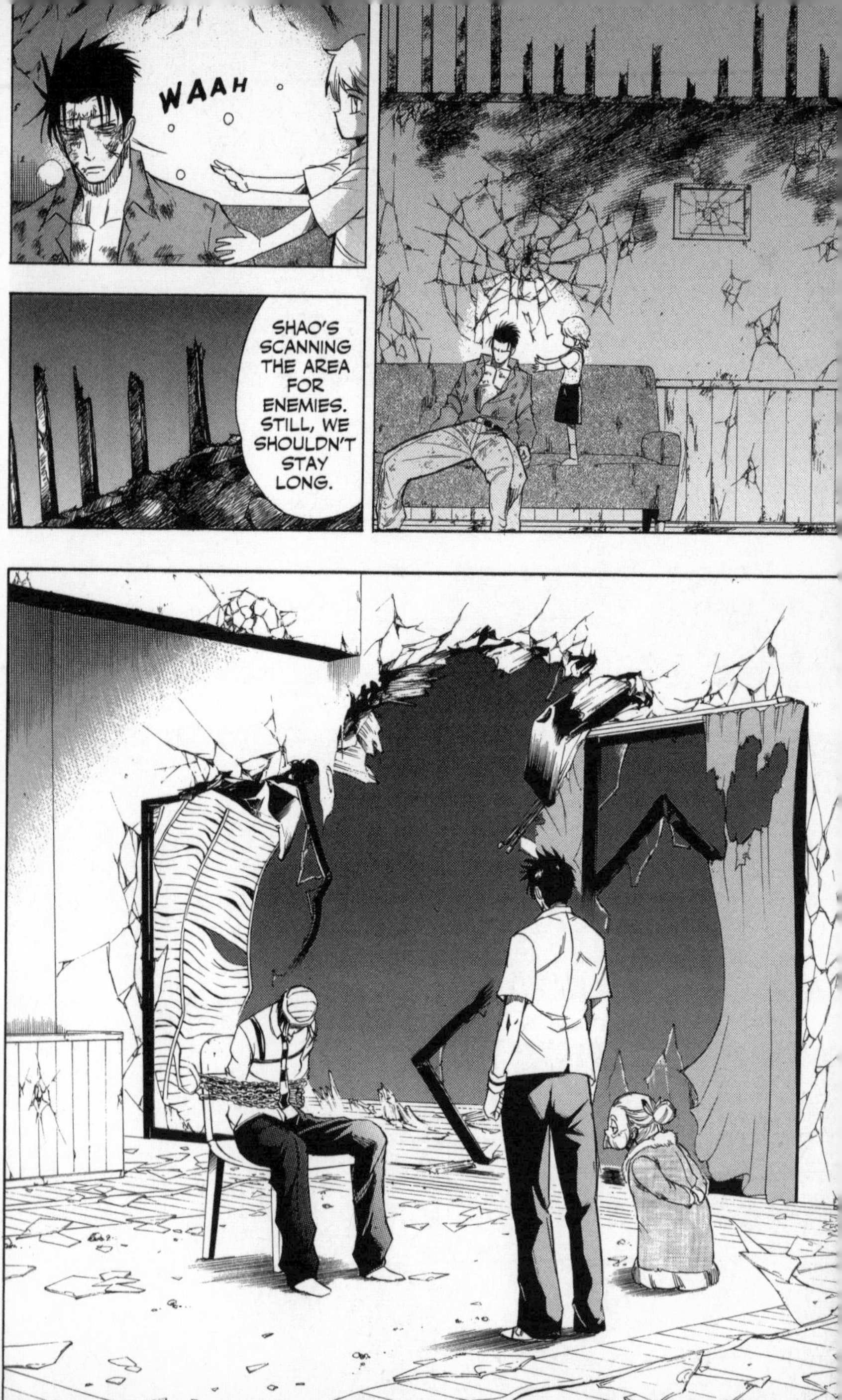
WAAH
SHAO'S SCANNING THE AREA FOR ENEMIES. STILL, WE SHOULDN'T STAY LONG.

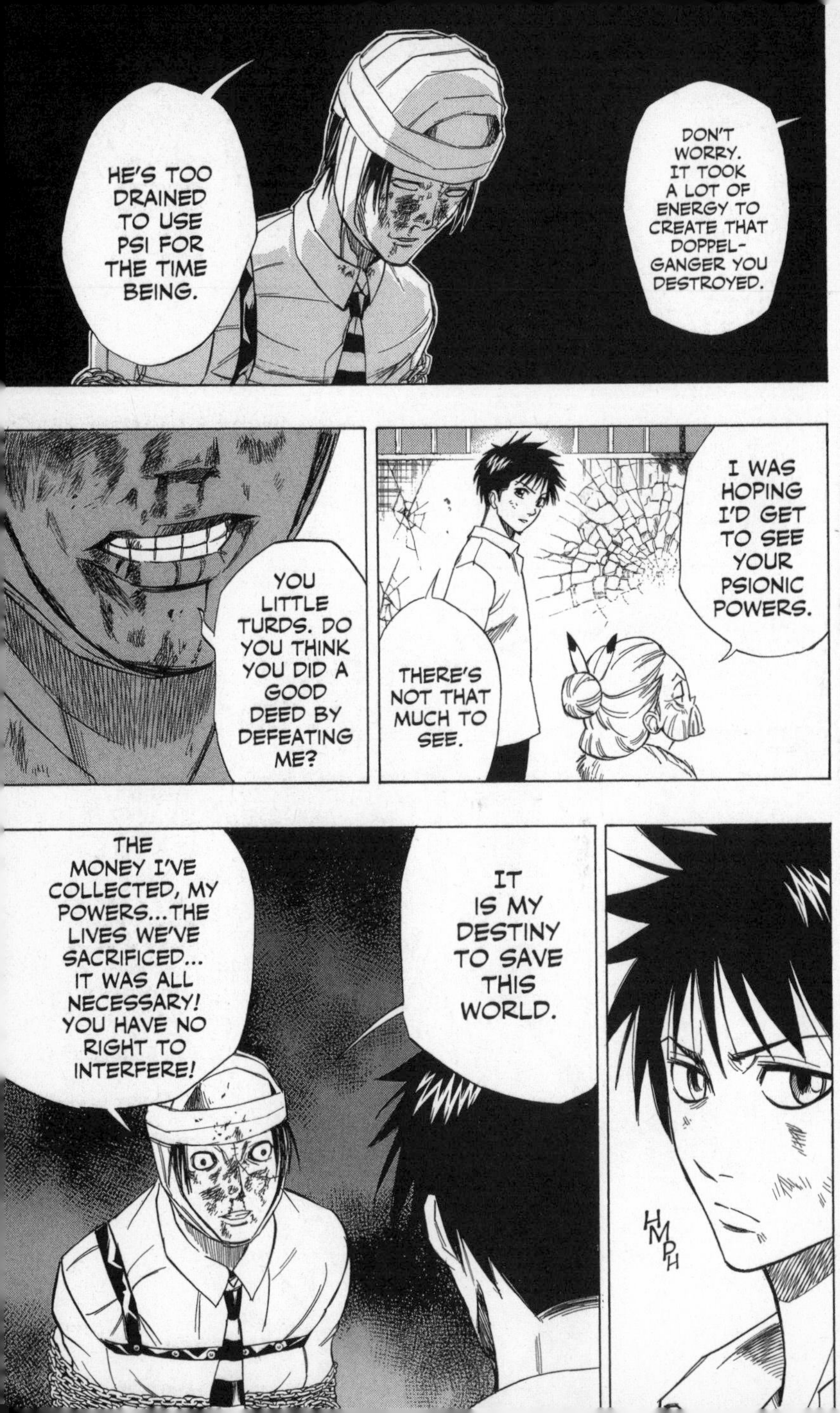
DON'T WORRY. IT TOOK A LOT OF ENERGY TO CREATE THAT DOPPEL-GANGER YOU DESTROYED.
HE'S TOO DRAINED TO USE PSI FOR THE TIME BEING.
I WAS HOPING I'D GET TO SEE YOUR PSIONIC POWERS.
THERE'S NOT THAT MUCH TO SEE.
YOU LITTLE TURDS. DO YOU THINK YOU DID A GOOD DEED BY DEFEATING ME?
HMPH
IT IS MY DESTINY TO SAVE THIS WORLD.
THE MONEY I'VE COLLECTED, MY POWERS...THE LIVES WE'VE SACRIFICED... IT WAS ALL NECESSARY! YOU HAVE NO RIGHT TO INTERFERE!

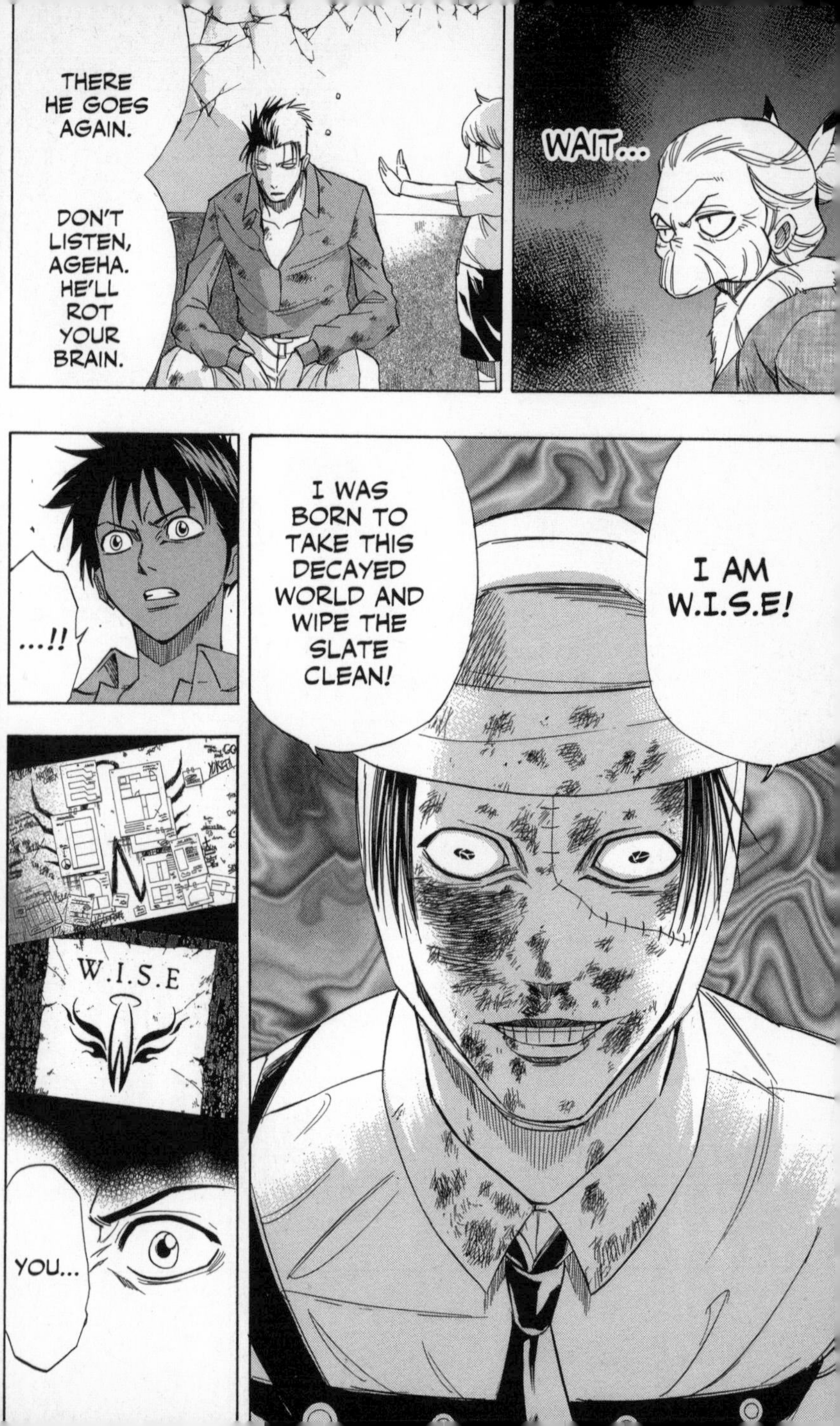
WAIT...
THERE HE GOES AGAIN.
DON'T LISTEN, AGEHA. HE'LL ROT YOUR BRAIN.
I AM W.I.S.E!
I WAS BORN TO TAKE THIS DECAYED WORLD AND WIPE THE SLATE CLEAN!
...!!
W.I.S.E
YOU...

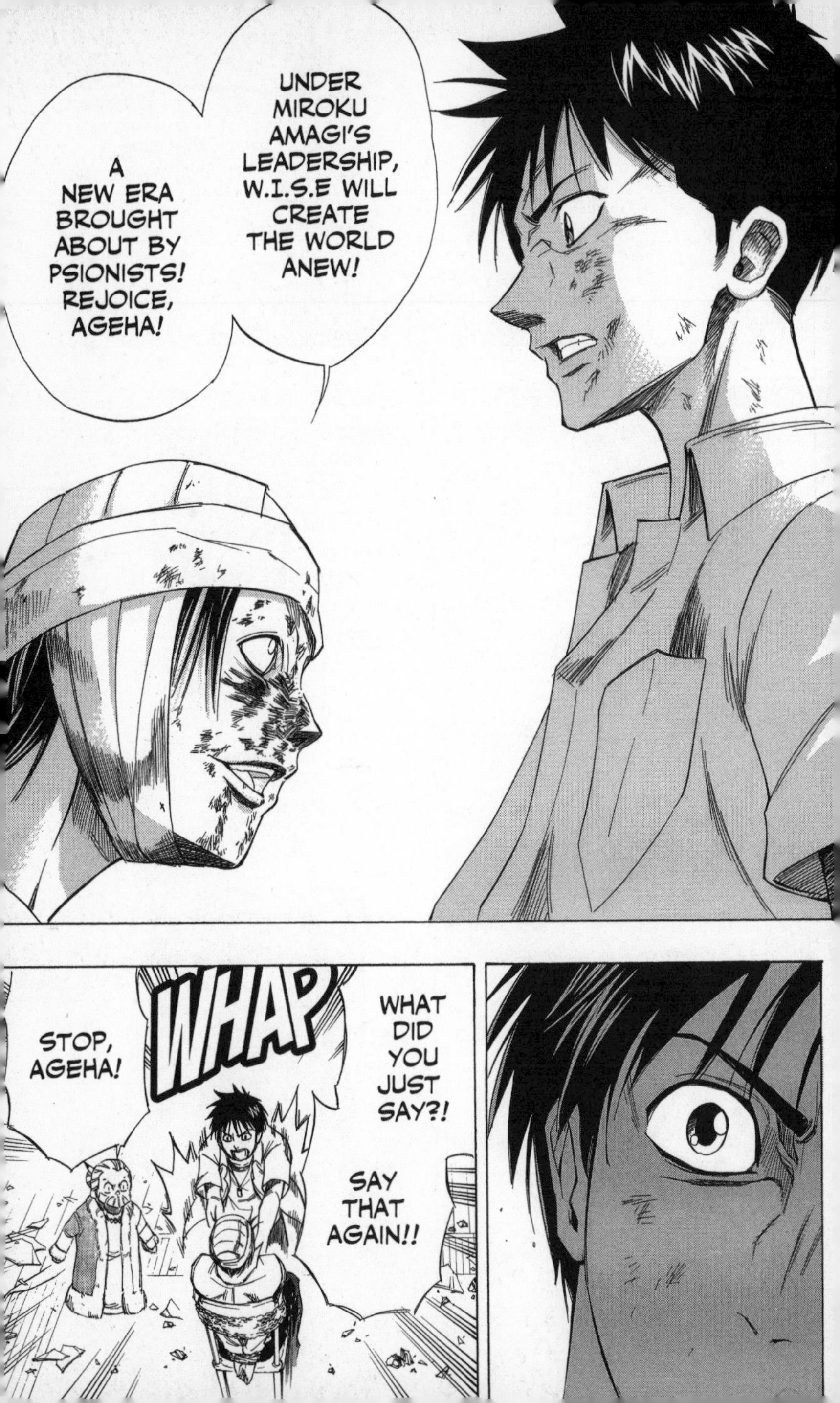
UNDER MIROKU AMAGI'S LEADERSHIP, W.I.S.E WILL CREATE THE WORLD ANEW!
A NEW ERA BROUGHT ABOUT BY PSIONISTS! REJOICE, AGEHA!
WHAT DID YOU JUST SAY?!
SAY THAT AGAIN!!
WHAP
STOP, AGEHA!

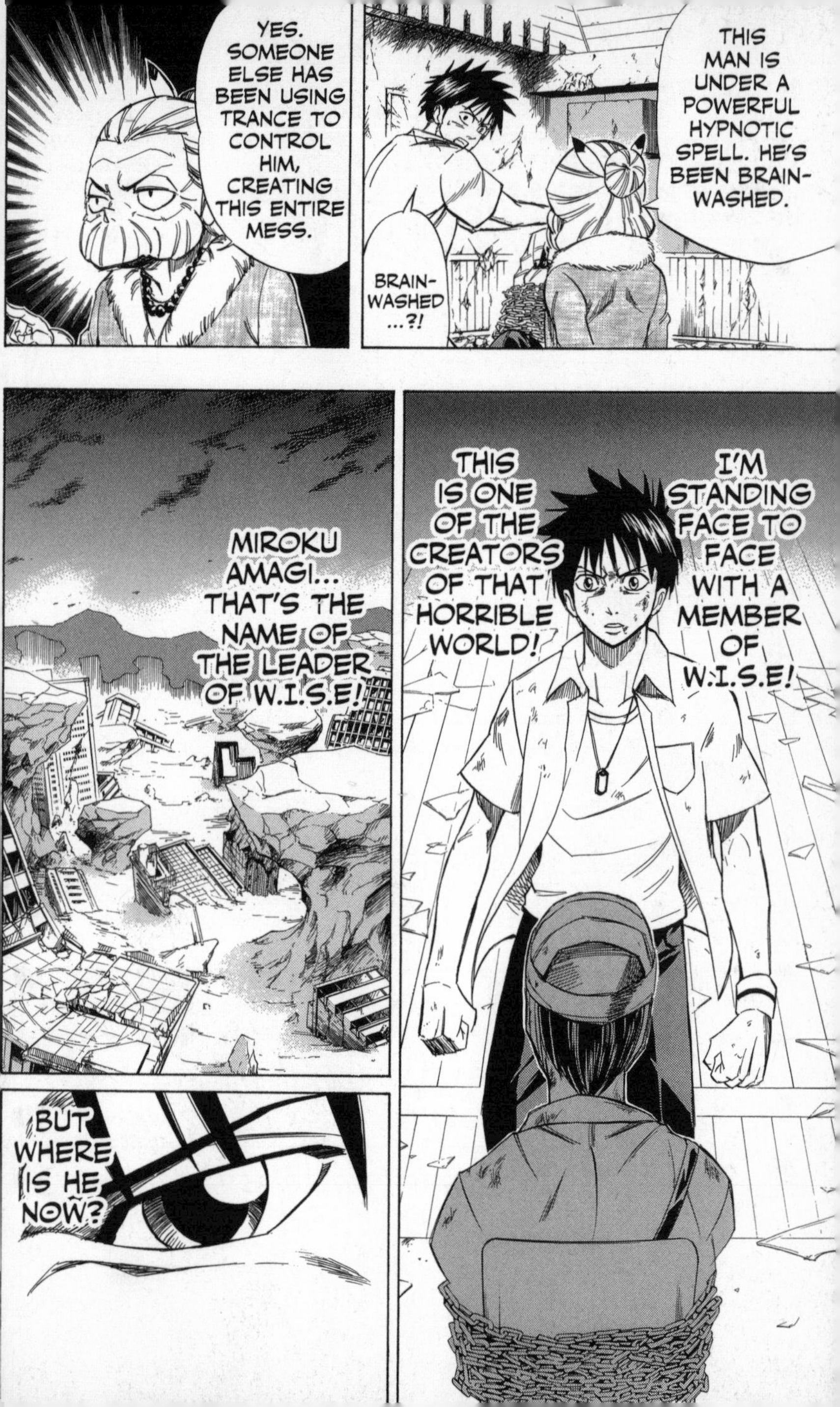
THIS MAN IS UNDER A POWERFUL HYPNOTIC SPELL. HE'S BEEN BRAIN-WASHED.
BRAIN-WASHED ...?!
YES. SOMEONE ELSE HAS BEEN USING TRANCE TO CONTROL HIM, CREATING THIS ENTIRE MESS.
I'M STANDING FACE TO FACE WITH A MEMBER OF W.I.S.E!
THIS IS ONE OF THE CREATORS OF THAT HORRIBLE WORLD!
MIROKU AMAGI... THAT'S THE NAME OF THE LEADER OF W.I.S.E!
BUT WHERE IS HE NOW?

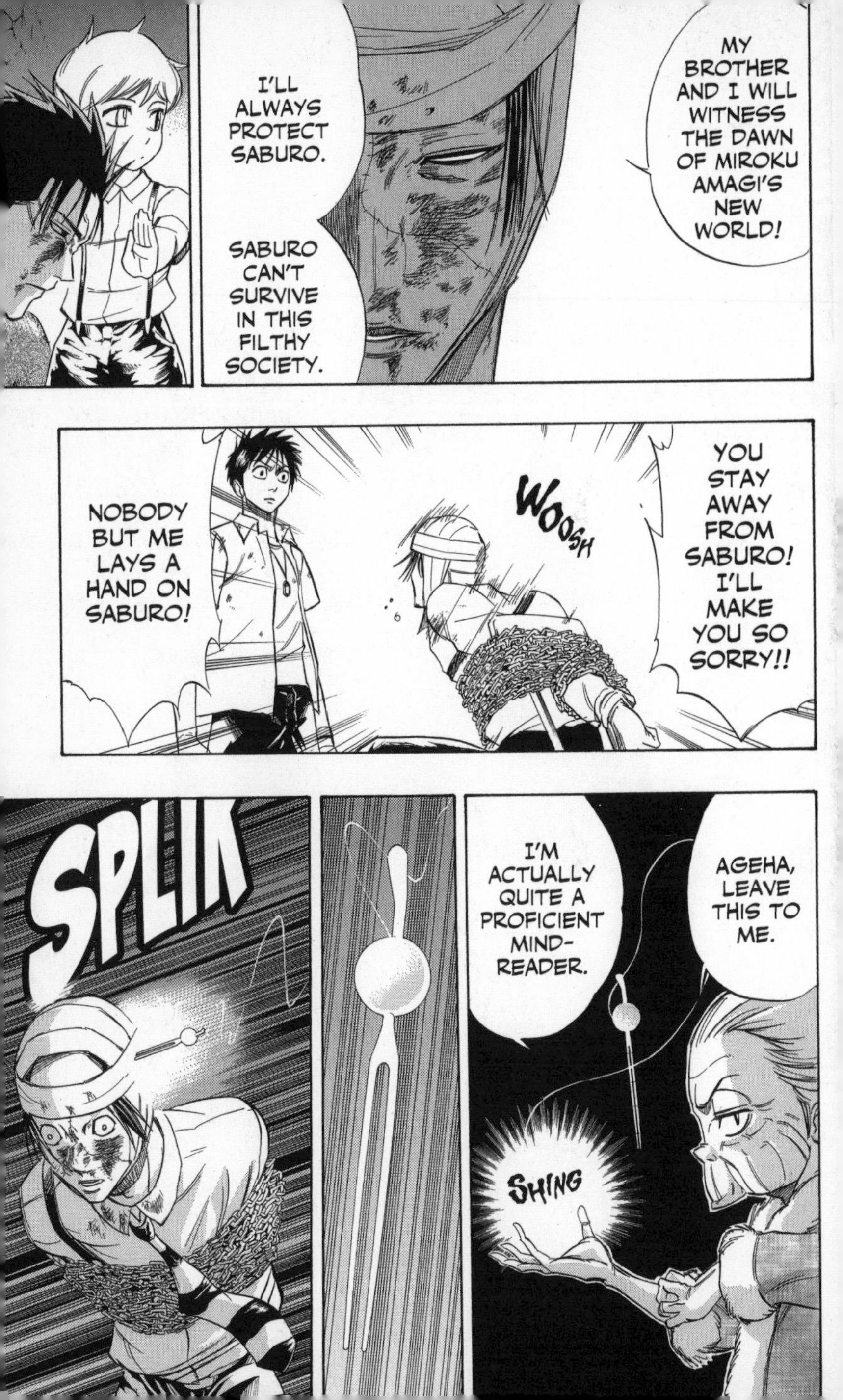
MY BROTHER AND I WILL WITNESS THE DAWN OF MIROKU AMAGI'S NEW WORLD!
I'LL ALWAYS PROTECT SABURO.
SABURO CAN'T SURVIVE IN THIS FILTHY SOCIETY.
YOU STAY AWAY FROM SABURO! I'LL MAKE YOU SO SORRY!!
WOOSH
NOBODY BUT ME LAYS A HAND ON SABURO!
AGEHA, LEAVE THIS TO ME.
I'M ACTUALLY QUITE A PROFICIENT MIND-READER.
SHING
SPLIK

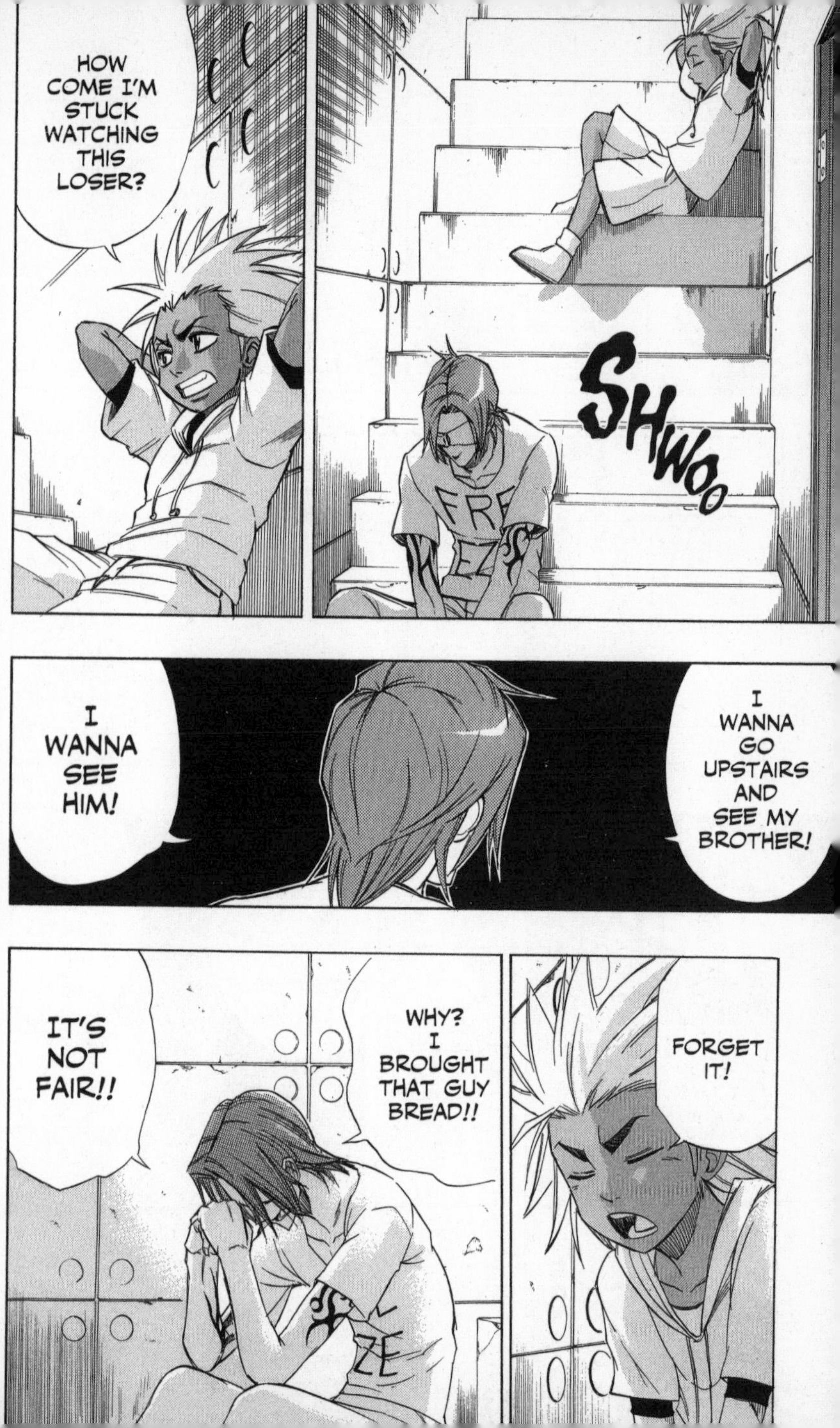
SHWOO
HOW COME I'M STUCK WATCHING THIS LOSER?
I WANNA GO UPSTAIRS AND SEE MY BROTHER!
I WANNA SEE HIM!
FORGET IT!
WHY? I BROUGHT THAT GUY BREAD!!
IT'S NOT FAIR!!

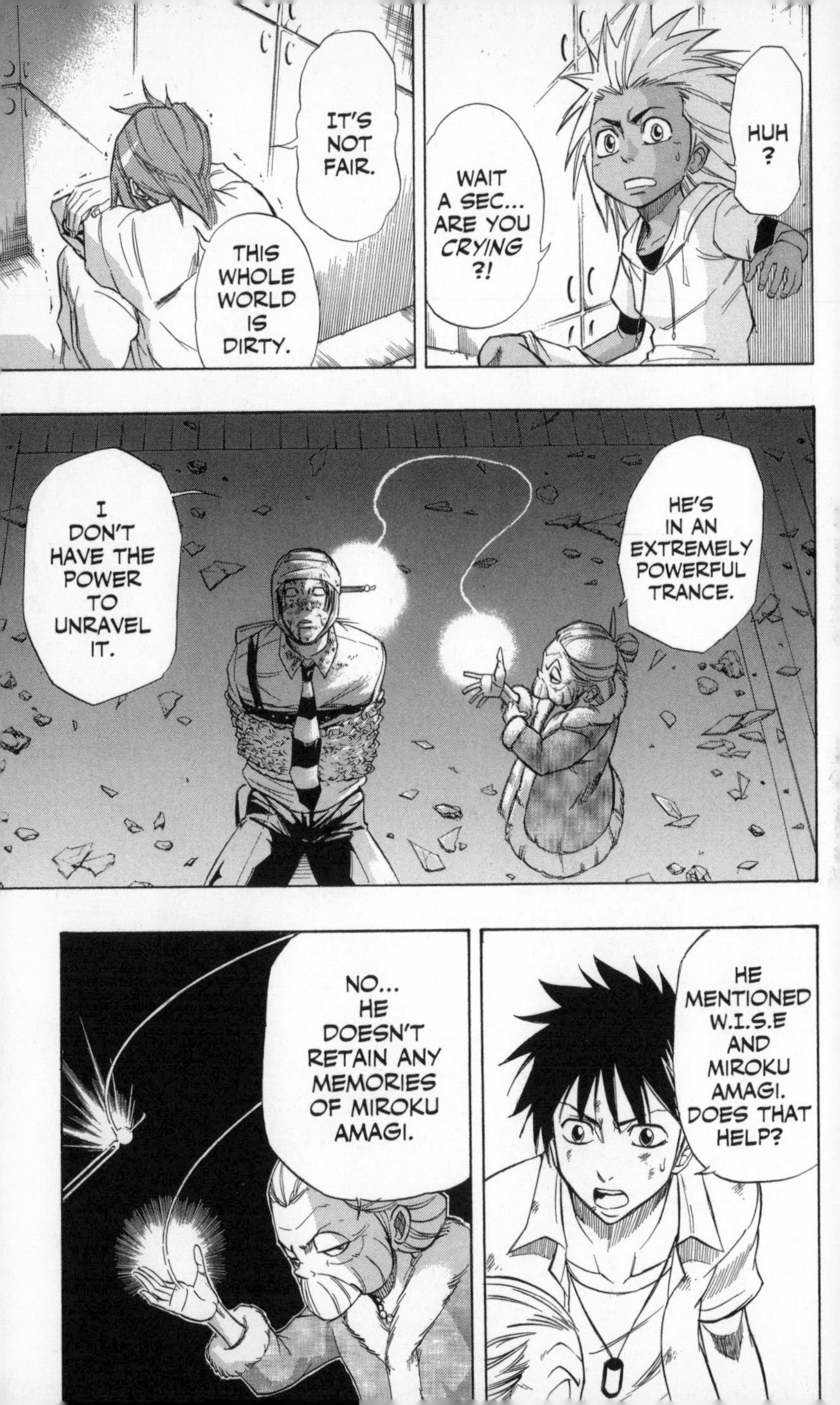
HUH ?
WAIT A SEC... ARE YOU CRYING ?!
IT'S NOT FAIR.
THIS WHOLE WORLD IS DIRTY.
HE'S IN AN EXTREMELY POWERFUL TRANCE.
I DON'T HAVE THE POWER TO UNRAVEL IT.
HE MENTIONED W.I.S.E AND MIROKU AMAGI. DOES THAT HELP?
NO... HE DOESN'T RETAIN ANY MEMORIES OF MIROKU AMAGI.

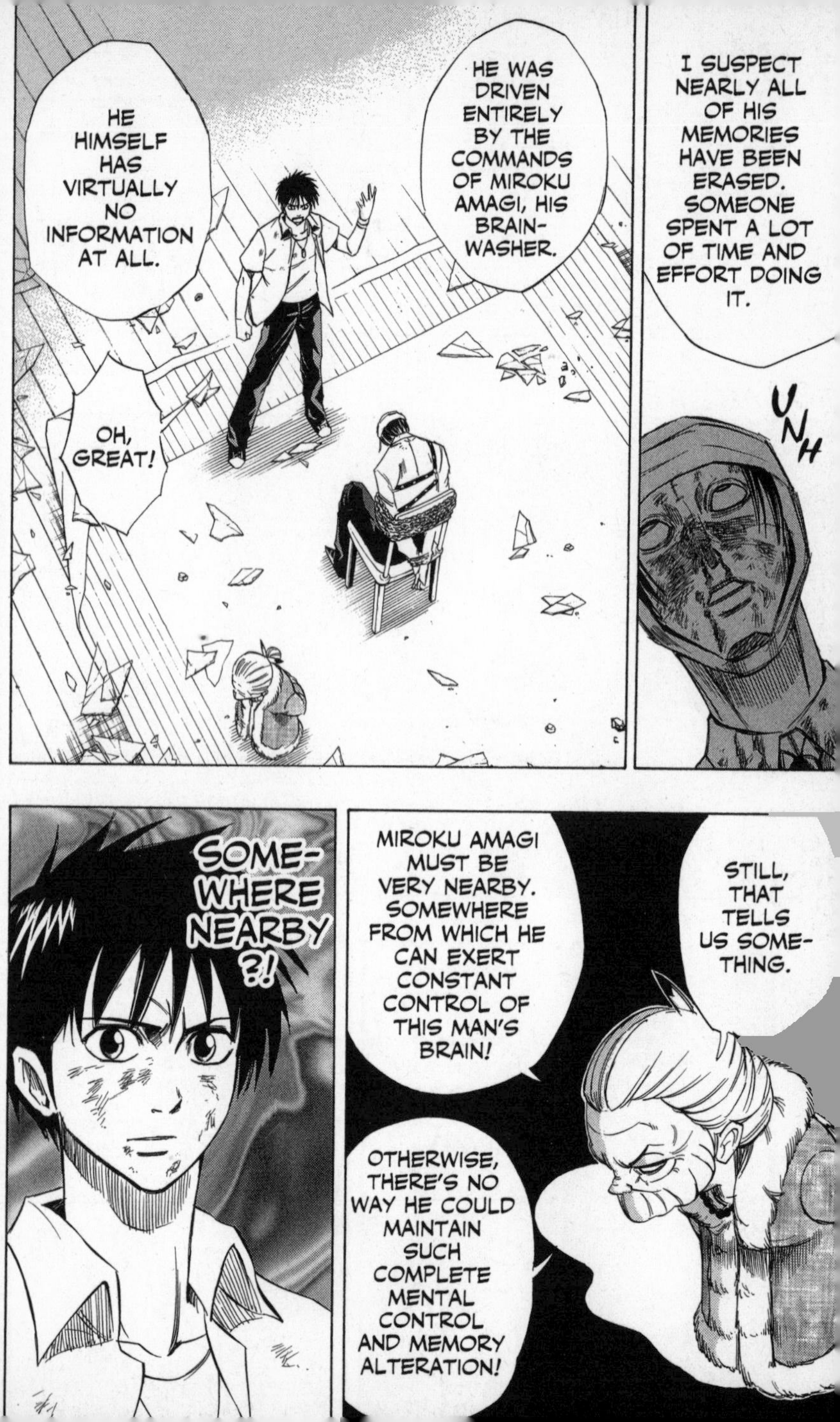
I SUSPECT NEARLY ALL OF HIS MEMORIES HAVE BEEN ERASED. SOMEONE SPENT A LOT OF TIME AND EFFORT DOING IT.
UNH
HE WAS DRIVEN ENTIRELY BY THE COMMANDS OF MIROKU AMAGI, HIS BRAIN-WASHER.
HE HIMSELF HAS VIRTUALLY NO INFORMATION AT ALL.
OH, GREAT!
STILL, THAT TELLS US SOME-THING.
MIROKU AMAGI MUST BE VERY NEARBY. SOMEWHERE FROM WHICH HE CAN EXERT CONSTANT CONTROL OF THIS MAN'S BRAIN!
OTHERWISE, THERE'S NO WAY HE COULD MAINTAIN SUCH COMPLETE MENTAL CONTROL AND MEMORY ALTERATION!
SOME-WHERE NEARBY ?!

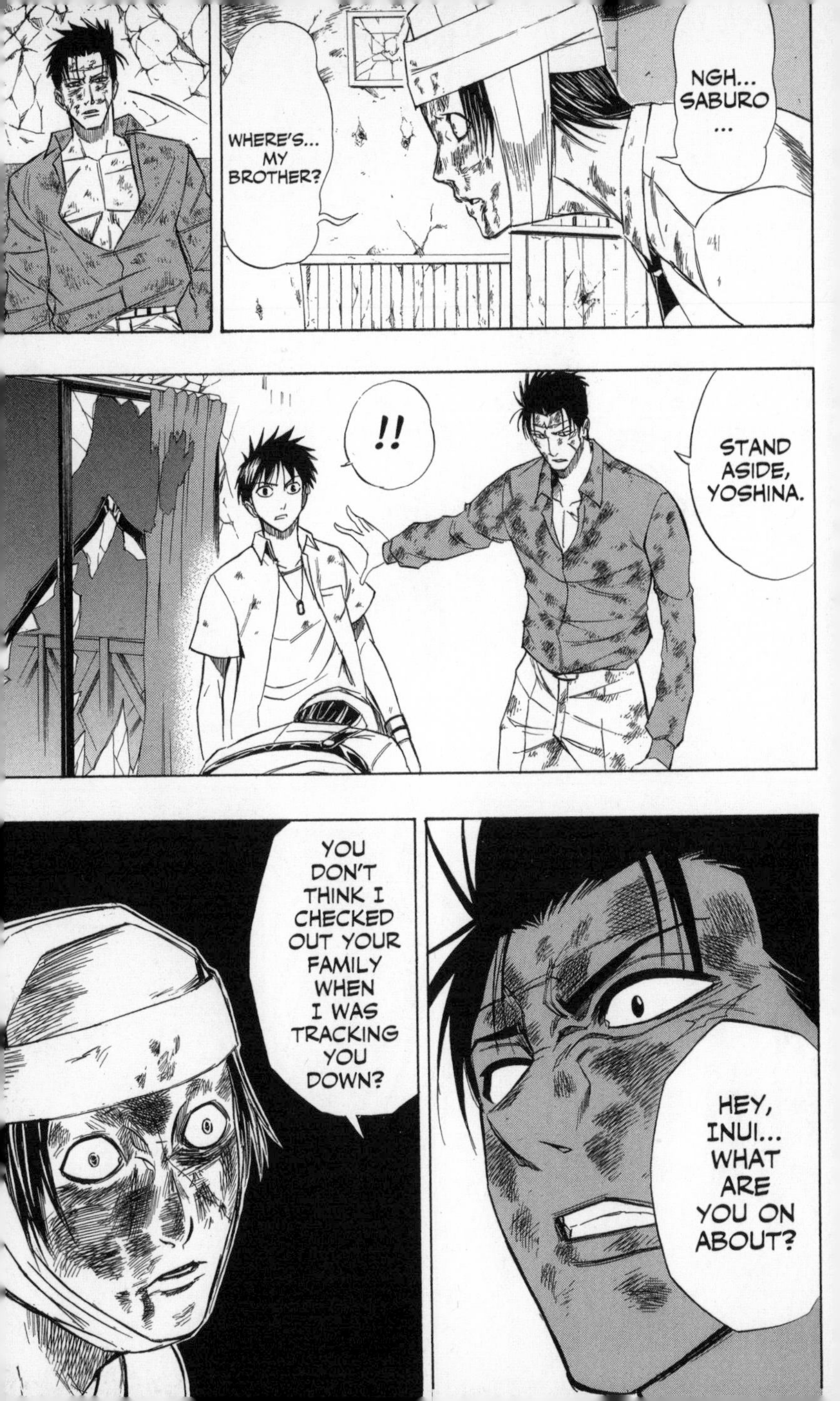
NGH... SABURO ...
WHERE'S... MY BROTHER?
STAND ASIDE, YOSHINA.
!!
HEY, INUI... WHAT ARE YOU ON ABOUT?
YOU DON'T THINK I CHECKED OUT YOUR FAMILY WHEN I WAS TRACKING YOU DOWN?

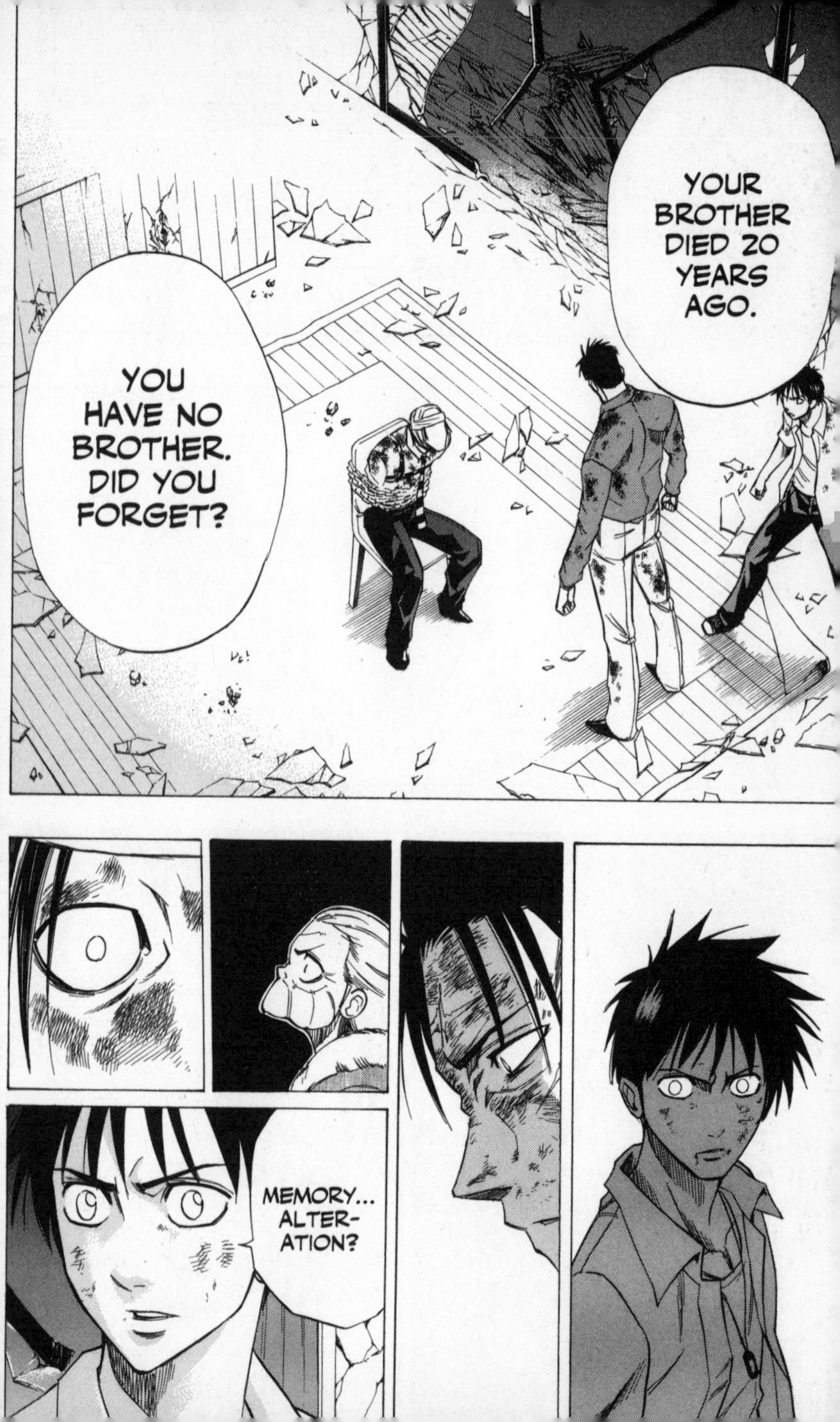
YOUR BROTHER DIED 20 YEARS AGO.
YOU HAVE NO BROTHER. DID YOU FORGET?
MEMORY... ALTER- ATION?

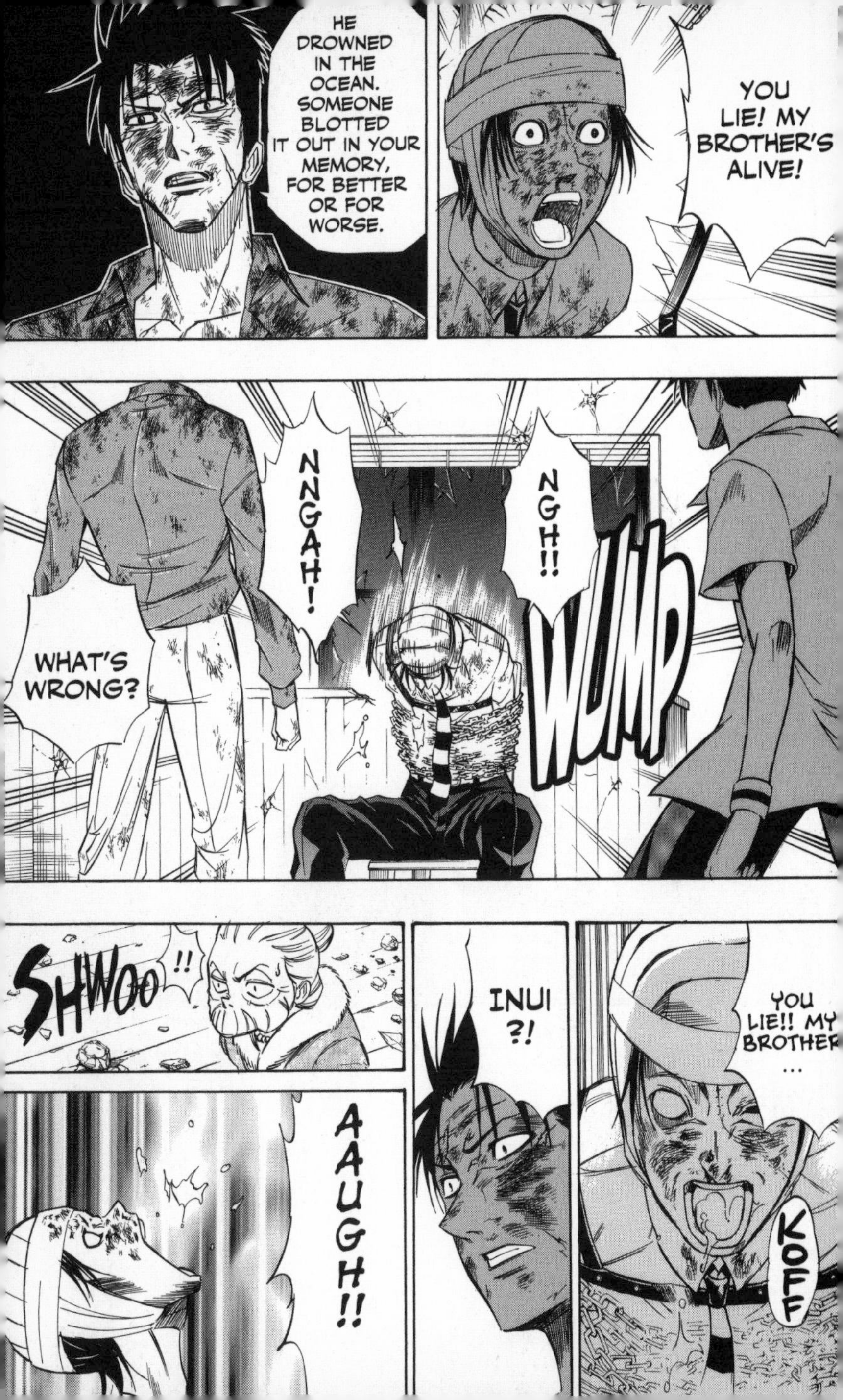
YOU LIE! MY BROTHER'S ALIVE!
HE DROWNED IN THE OCEAN. SOMEONE BLOTTED IT OUT IN YOUR MEMORY, FOR BETTER OR FOR WORSE.
NGH!!
WUMP
NNGAH!
WHAT'S WRONG?
YOU LIE!! MY BROTHER...
KOFF
INUI ?!
SHWOO!!
AAAUGH!!

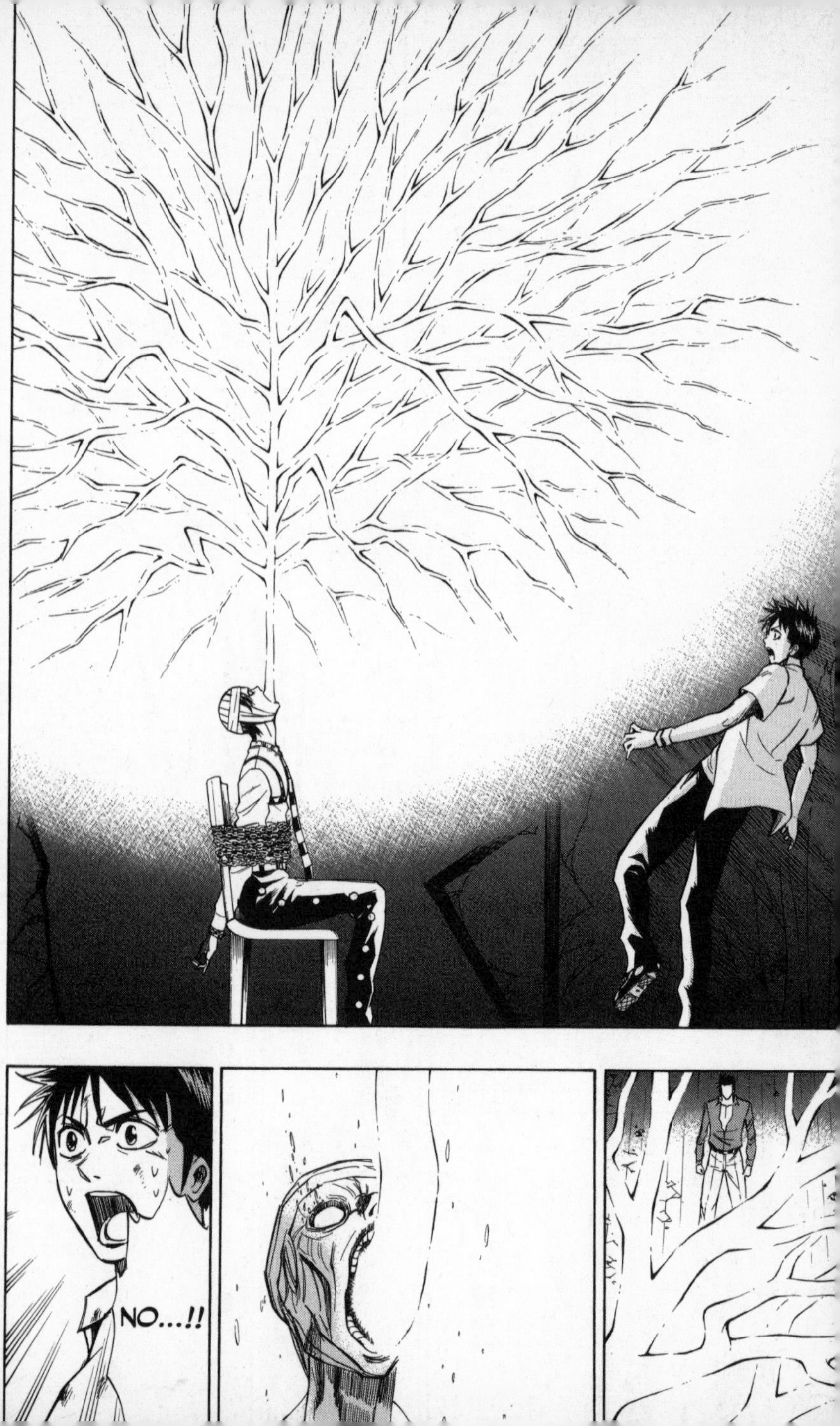
NO...!!

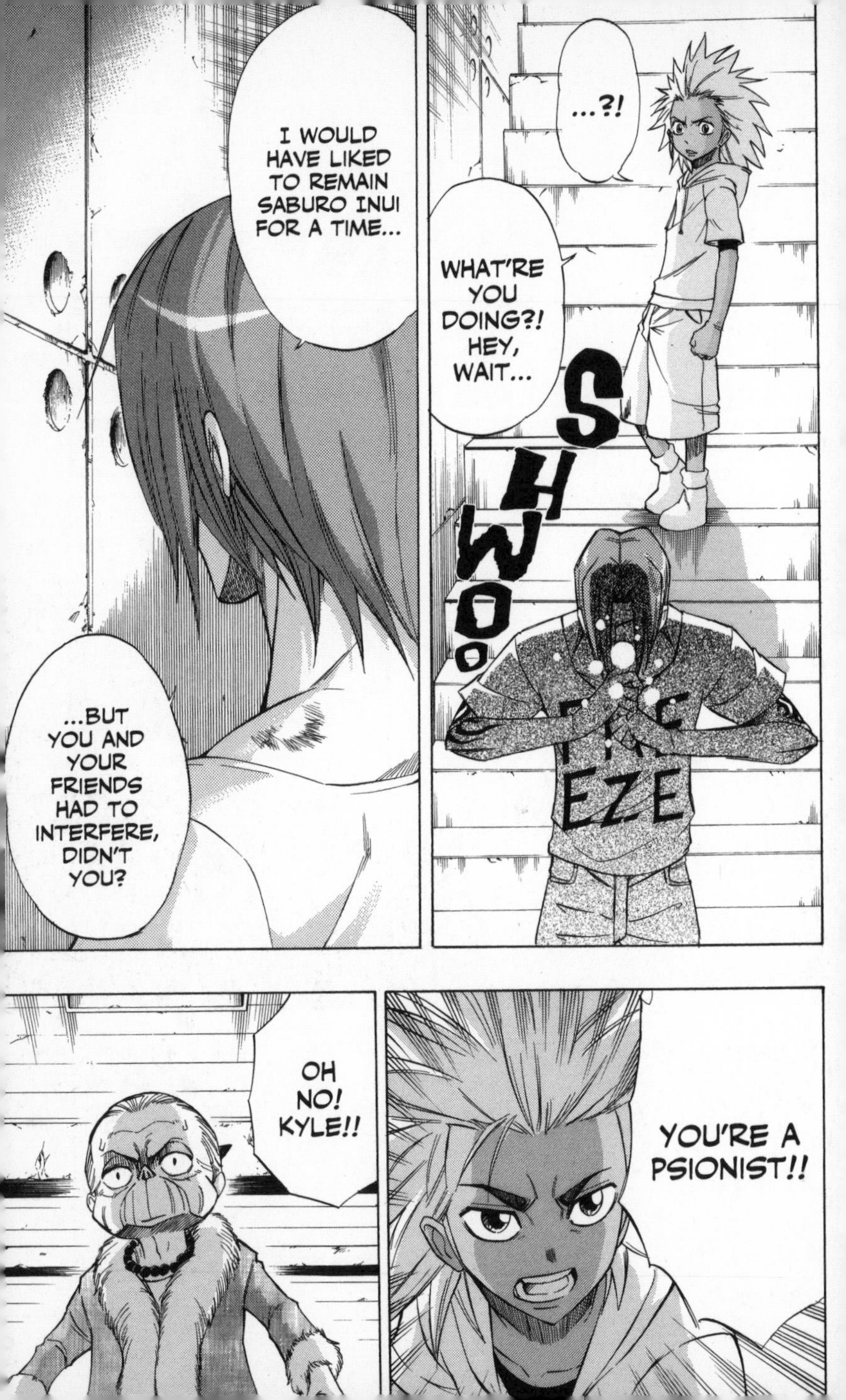
...?!
WHAT'RE YOU DOING?! HEY, WAIT...
SHWOO
I WOULD HAVE LIKED TO REMAIN SABURO INUI FOR A TIME...
...BUT YOU AND YOUR FRIENDS HAD TO INTERFERE, DIDN'T YOU?
YOU'RE A PSIONIST!!
OH NO! KYLE!!

NEW YEAR'S PRAYERS
DING
LET TATSUO BE OKAY...
NO PARTIC-ULAR PRAYERS
MONEY!!
PLEASE MAKE MY SISTER NICER! AND MY ALLOWANCE BIGGER!
AND MAY SAKURAKO ACCEPT MY LOVE!
MAY AGEHA NOT BE QUITE SO DUMB...

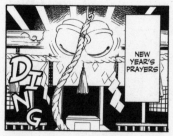

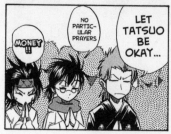

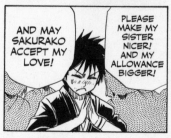

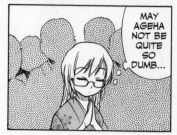

CALL.55: MIROKU

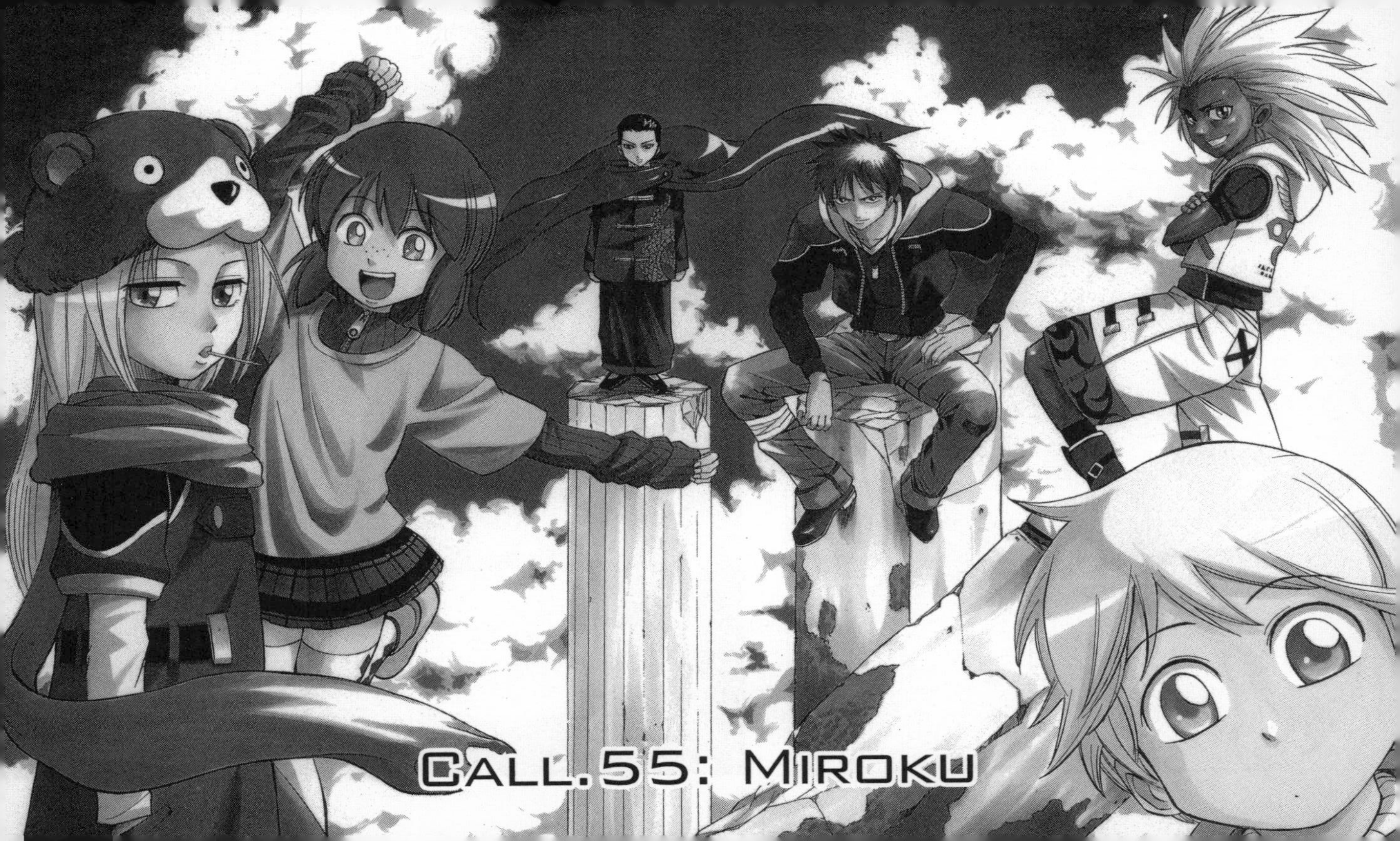

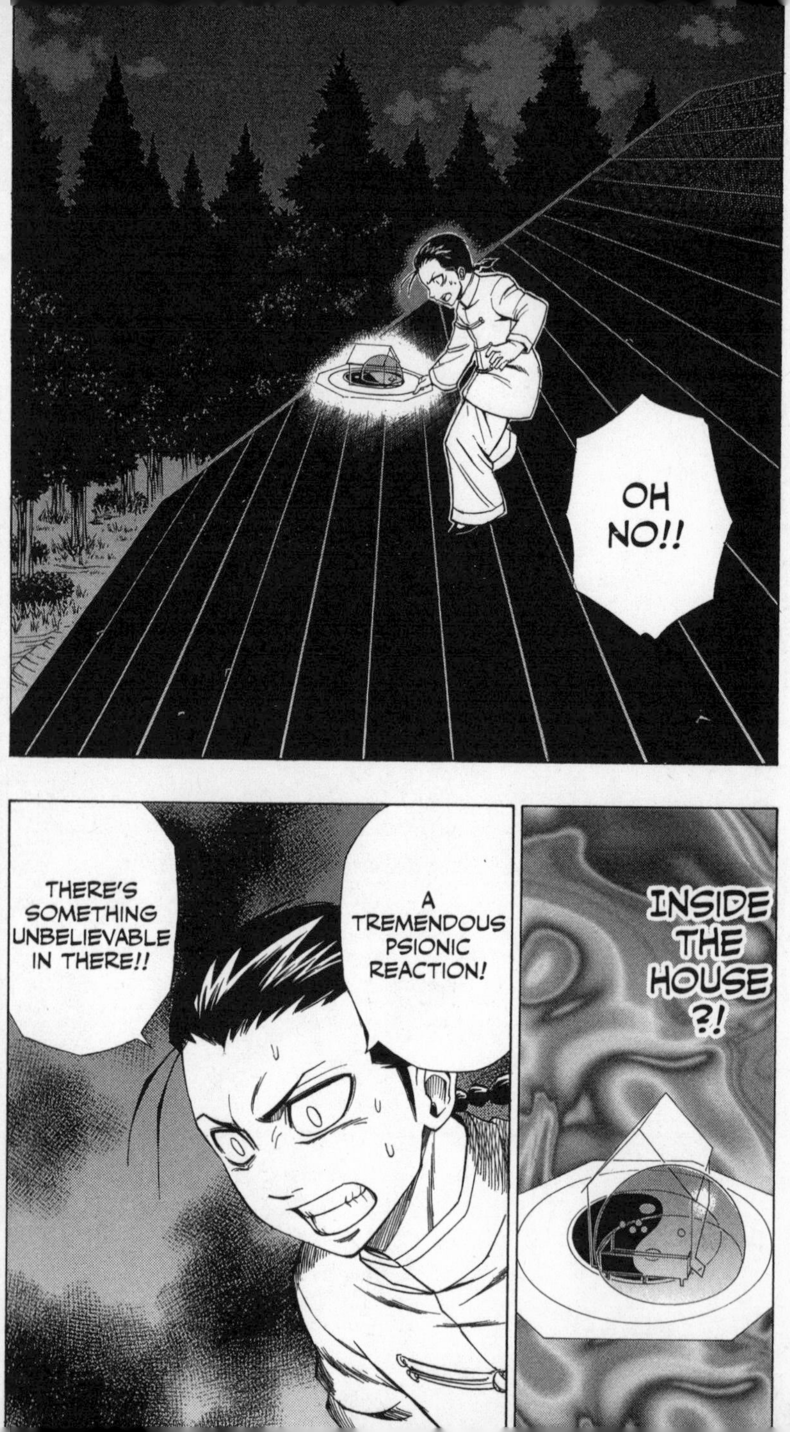
OH NO!!
INSIDE THE HOUSE ?!
A TREMENDOUS PSIONIC REACTION!
THERE'S SOMETHING UNBELIEVABLE IN THERE!!

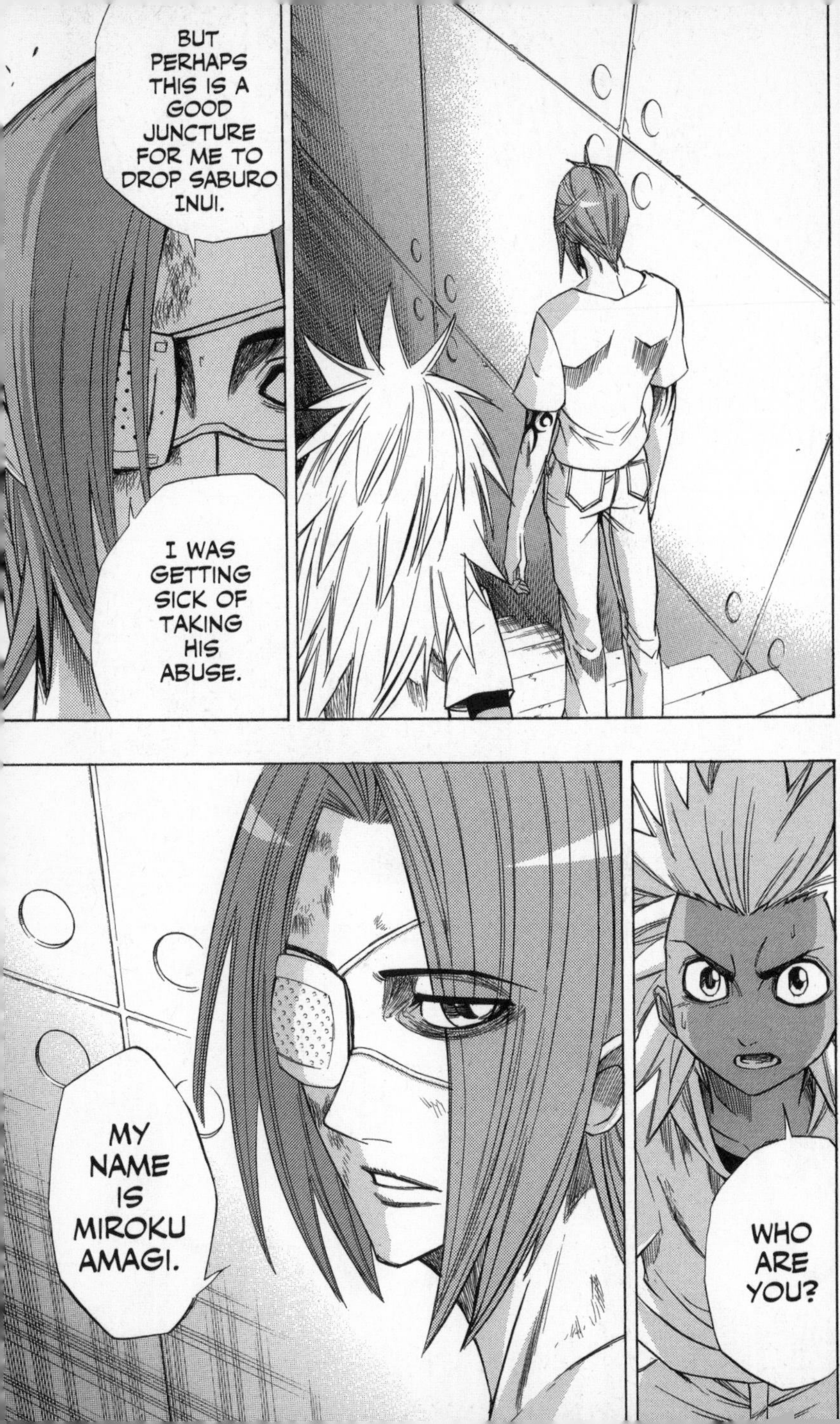
BUT PERHAPS THIS IS A GOOD JUNCTURE FOR ME TO DROP SABURO INUI.
I WAS GETTING SICK OF TAKING HIS ABUSE.
WHO ARE YOU?
MY NAME IS MIROKU AMAGI.

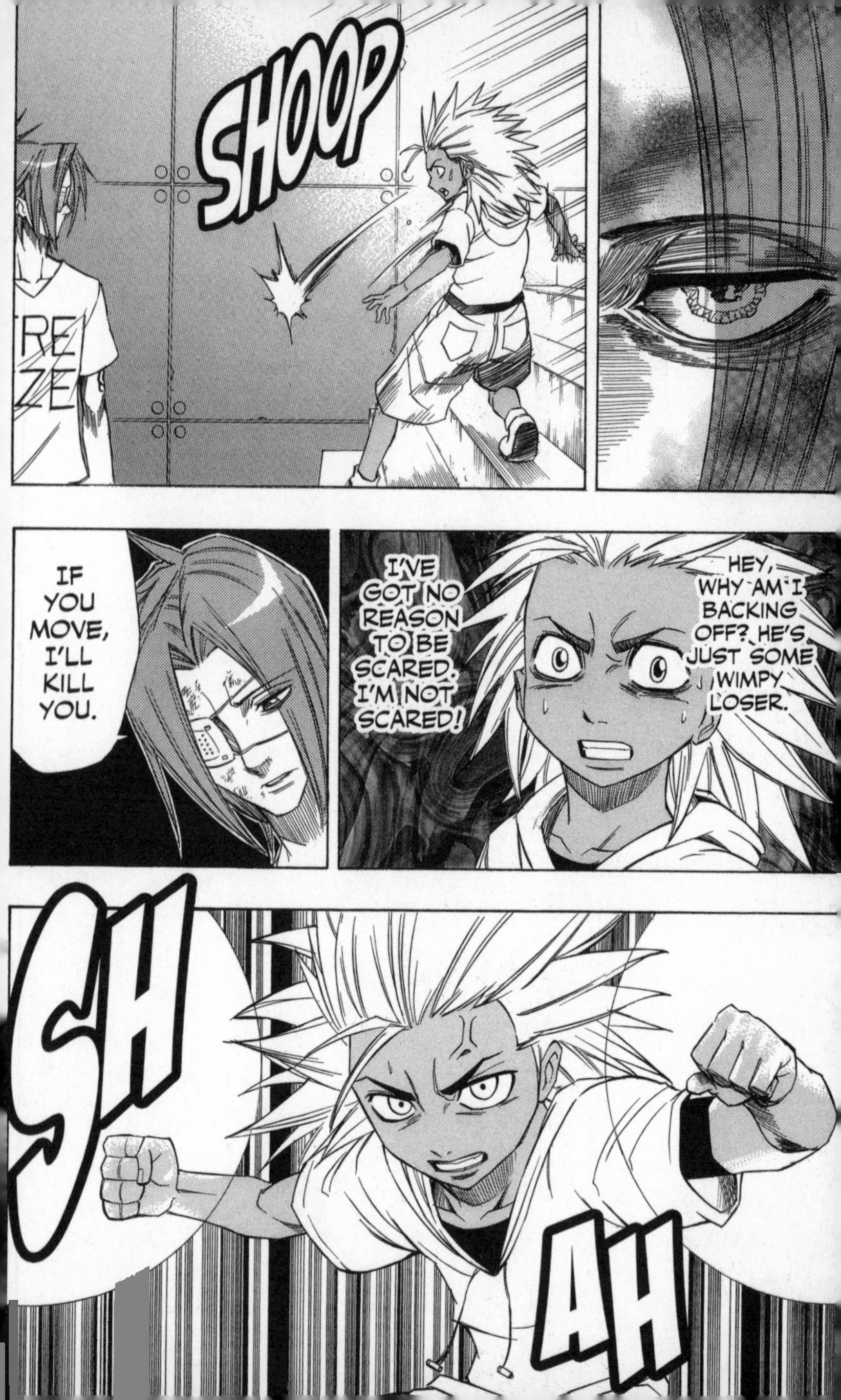
SHOOP
HEY, WHY AM I BACKING OFF? HE'S JUST SOME WIMPY LOSER.
I'VE GOT NO REASON TO BE SCARED. I'M NOT SCARED!
IF YOU MOVE, I'LL KILL YOU.
SH
AH

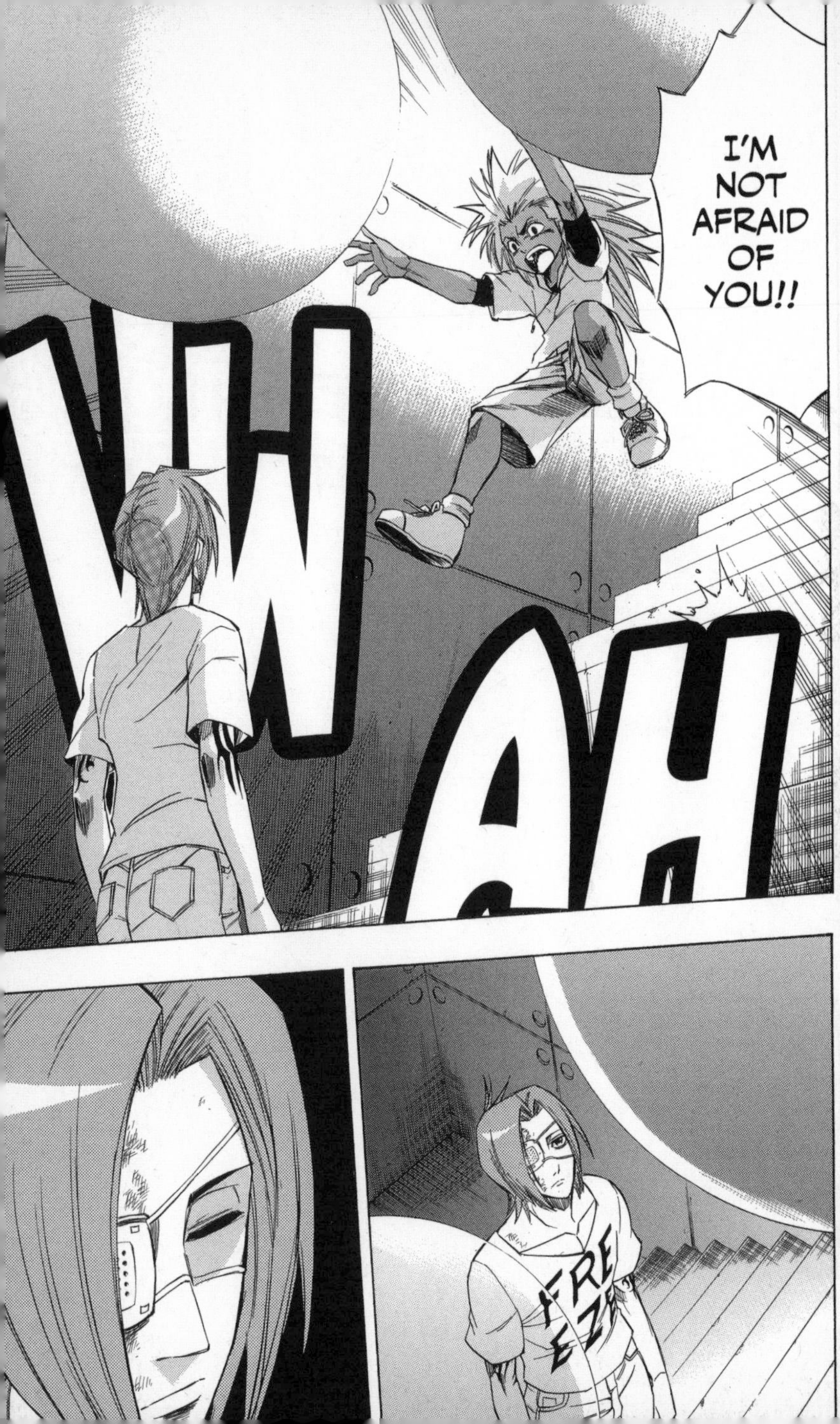
I'M NOT AFRAID OF YOU!!
WAH

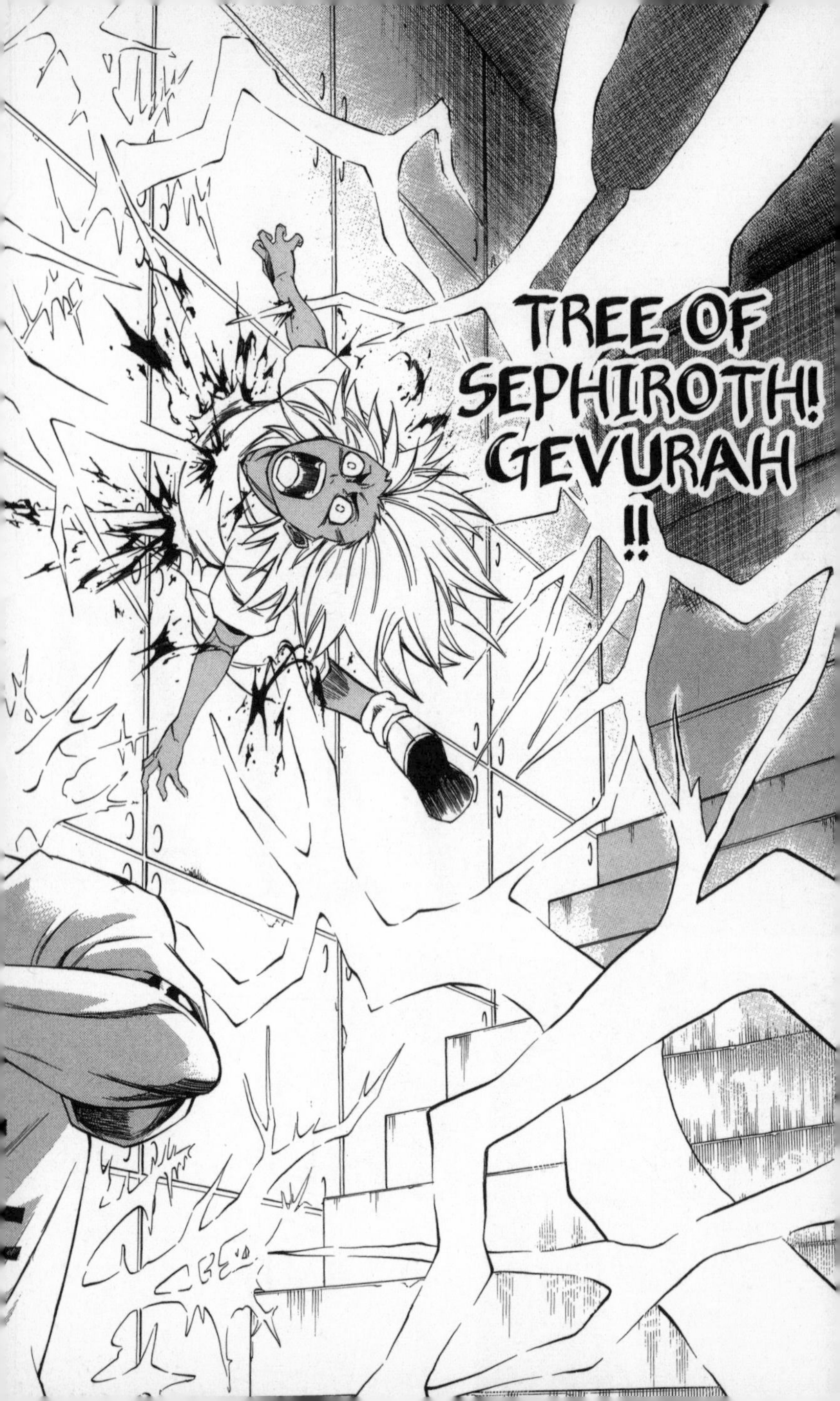
TREE OF SEPHIROTH! GEVURAH !!

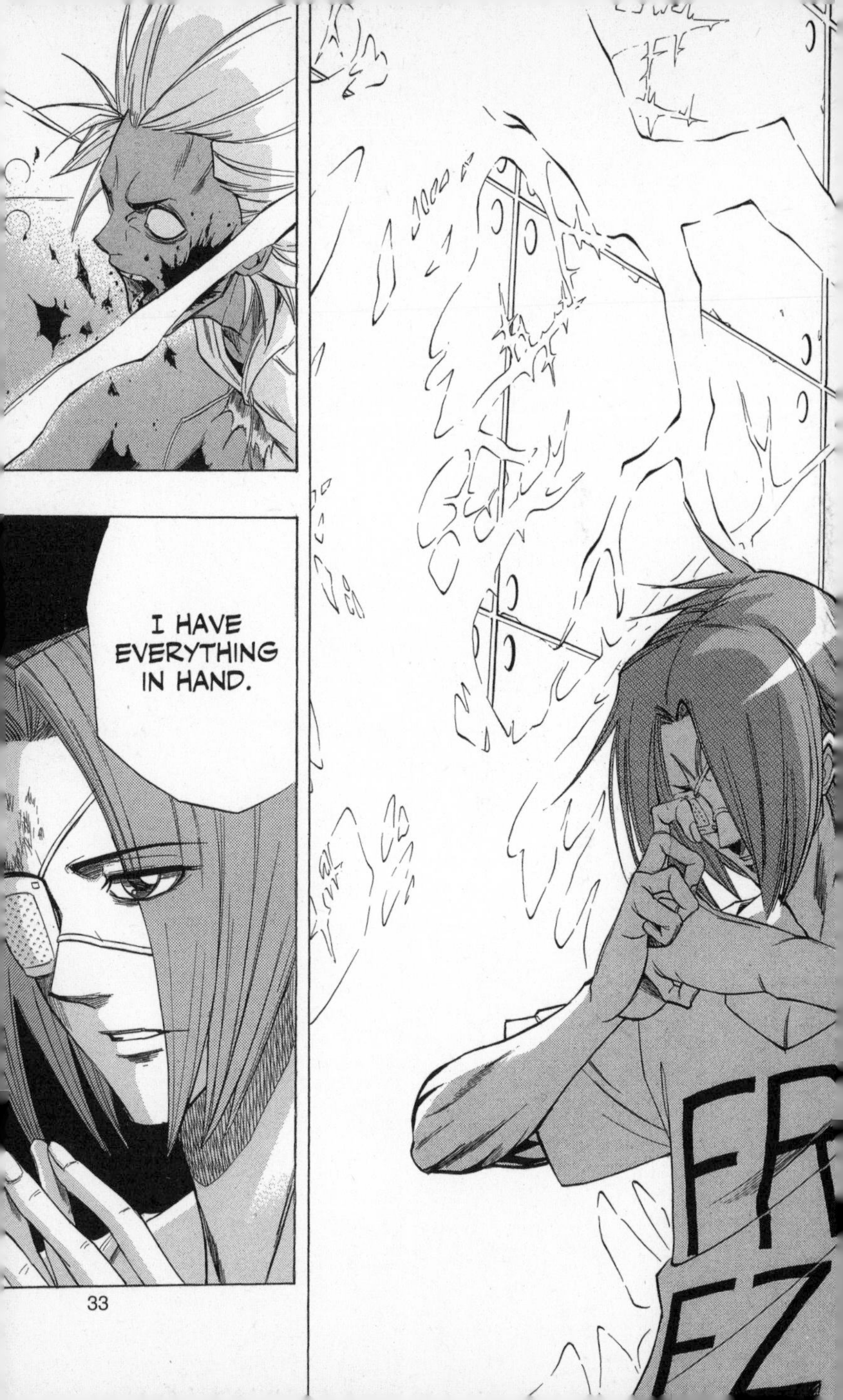
I HAVE EVERYTHING IN HAND.

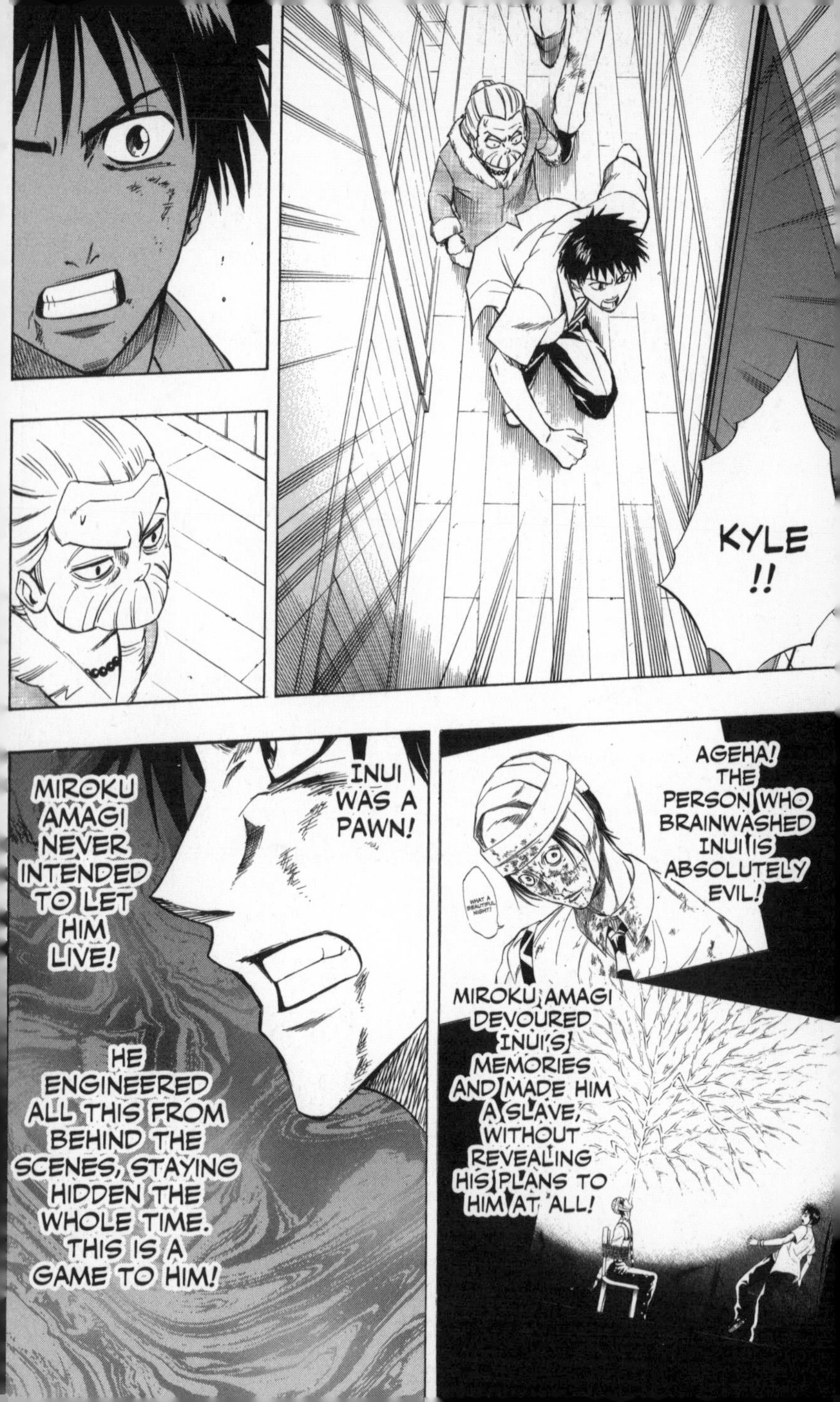
KYLE !!
AGEHA! THE PERSON WHO BRAINWASHED INUI IS ABSOLUTELY EVIL!
WHAT A BEAUTIFUL NIGHT!
MIROKU AMAGI DEVOURED INUI'S MEMORIES AND MADE HIM A SLAVE, WITHOUT REVEALING HIS PLANS TO HIM AT ALL!
INUI WAS A PAWN!
MIROKU AMAGI NEVER INTENDED TO LET HIM LIVE!
HE ENGINEERED ALL THIS FROM BEHIND THE SCENES, STAYING HIDDEN THE WHOLE TIME. THIS IS A GAME TO HIM!

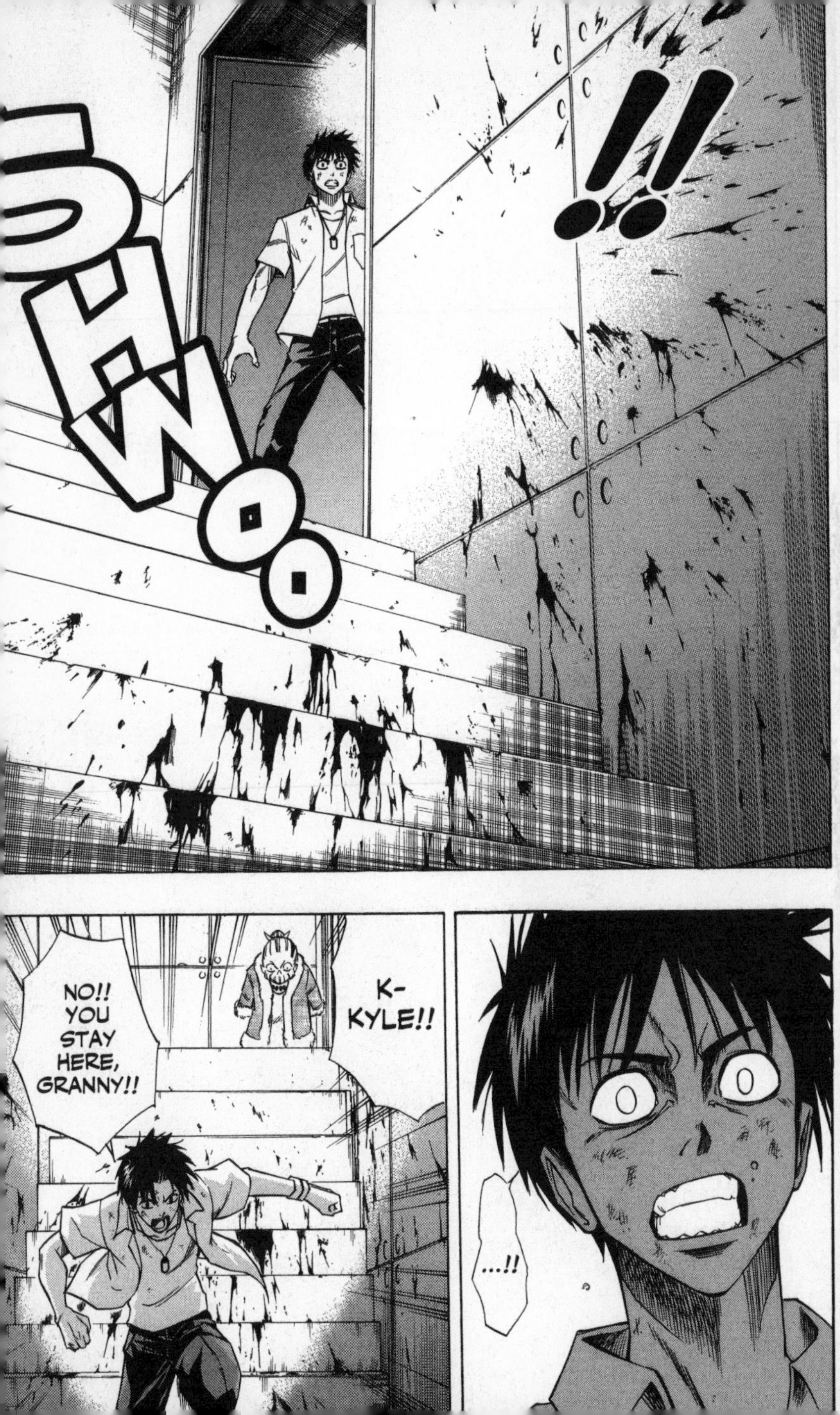

SHWOO
!!
...!!
K-KYLE!!
NO!! YOU STAY HERE, GRANNY!!

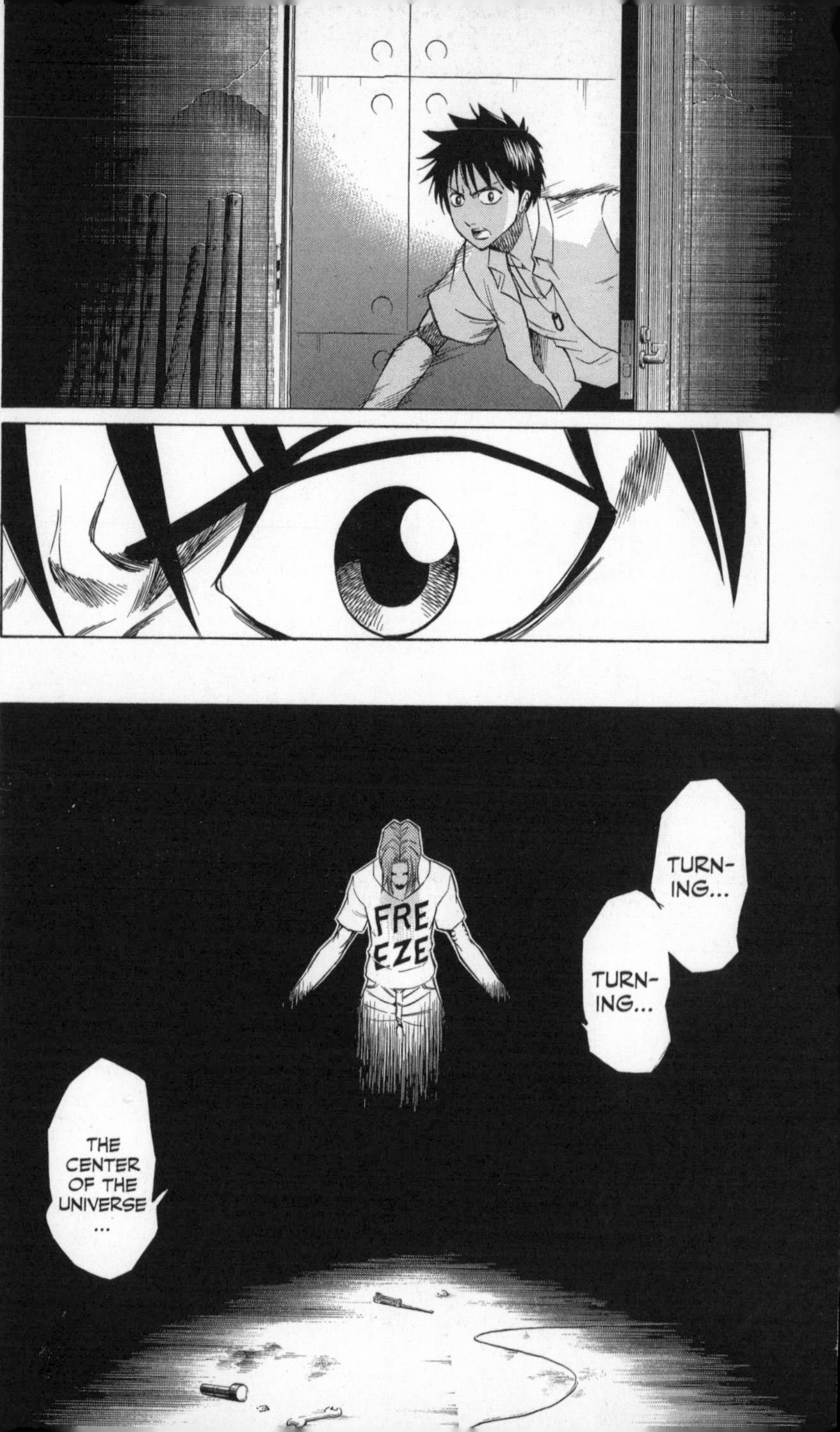
TURN-ING...
TURN-ING...
FRE EZE
THE CENTER OF THE UNIVERSE ...

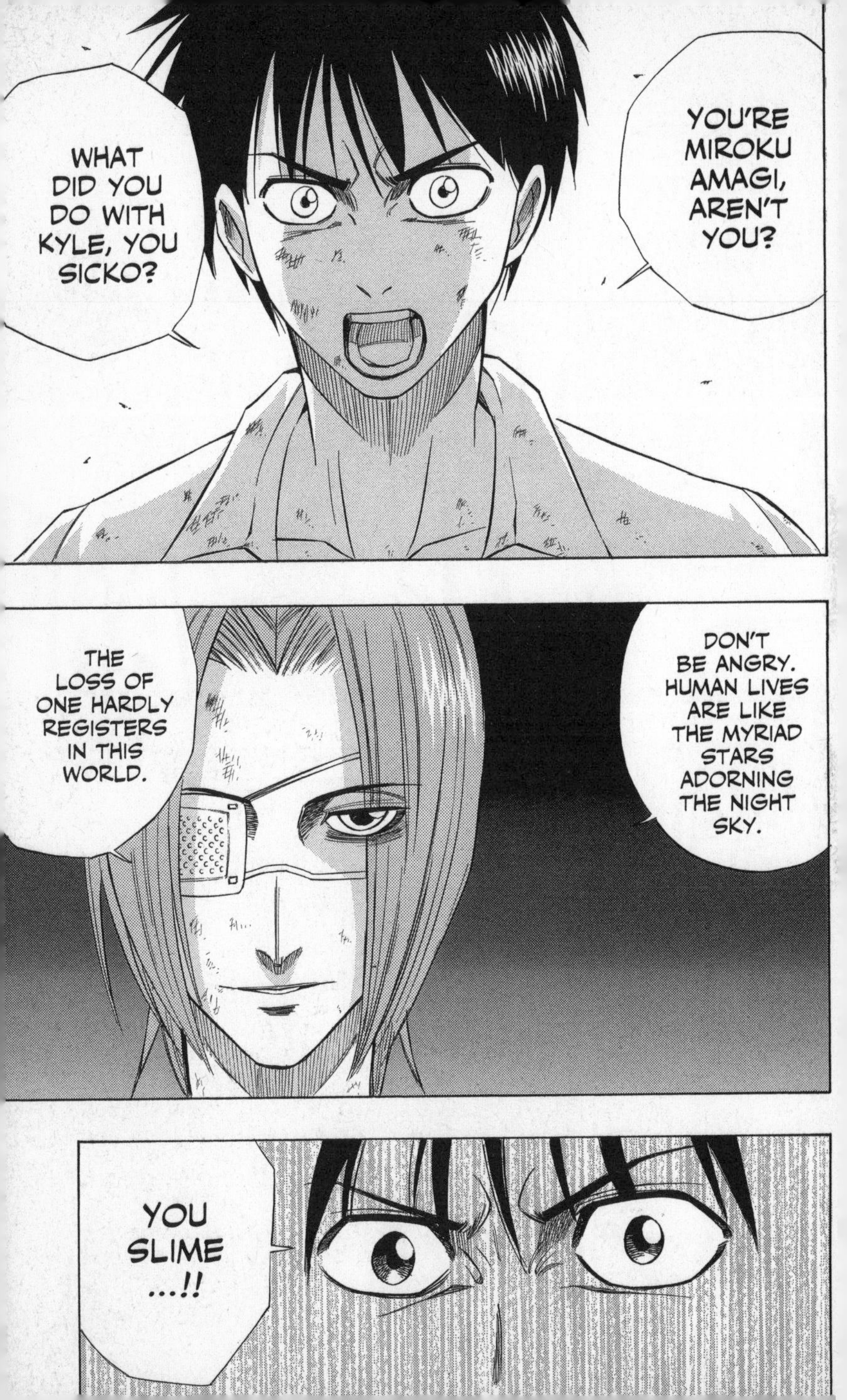
YOU'RE MIROKU AMAGI, AREN'T YOU?
WHAT DID YOU DO WITH KYLE, YOU SICKO?
DON'T BE ANGRY. HUMAN LIVES ARE LIKE THE MYRIAD STARS ADORNING THE NIGHT SKY.
THE LOSS OF ONE HARDLY REGISTERS IN THIS WORLD.
YOU SLIME ...!!

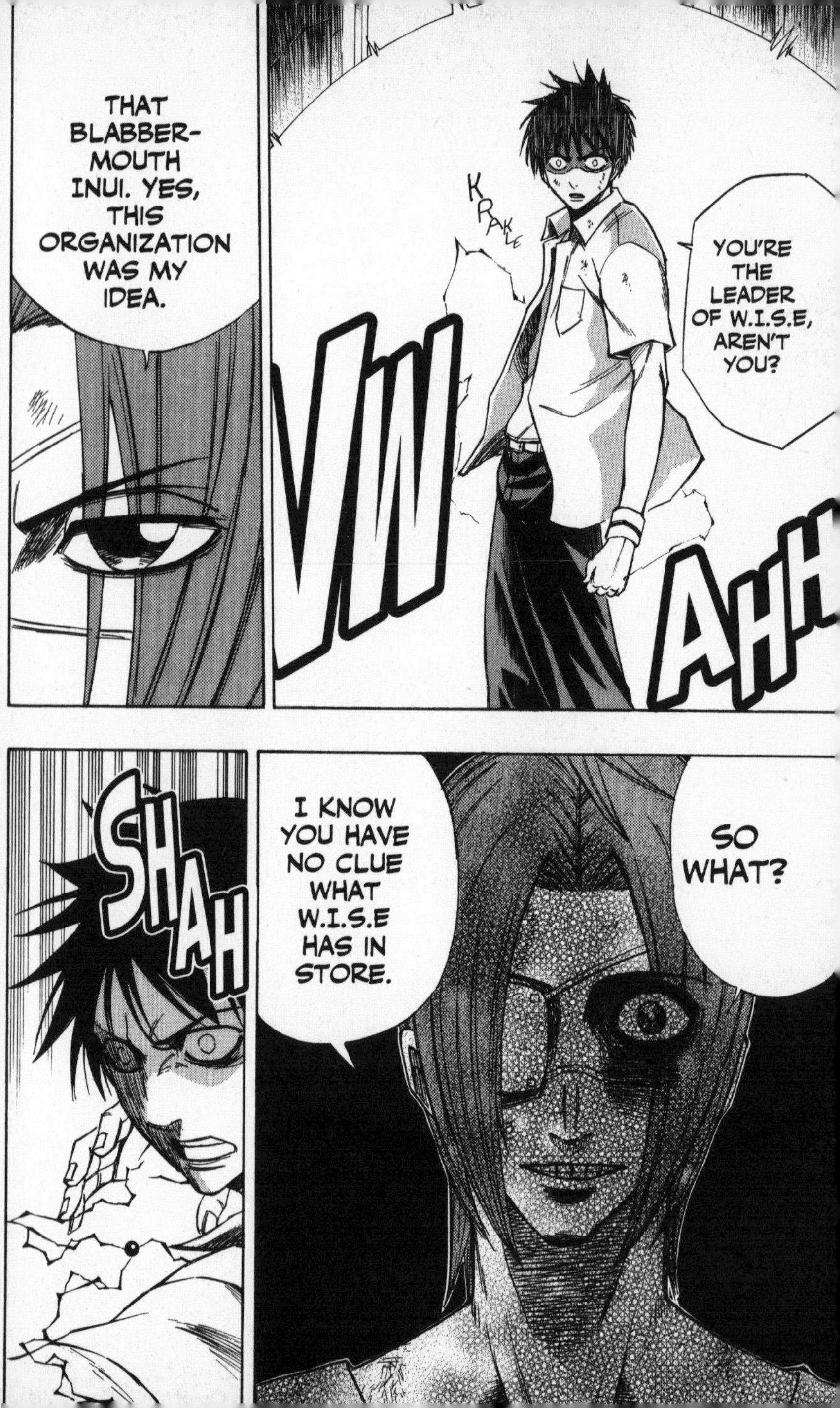
YOU'RE THE LEADER OF W.I.S.E, AREN'T YOU?
KRAKLE
VIN
AHH
THAT BLABBER-MOUTH INUI. YES, THIS ORGANIZATION WAS MY IDEA.
SO WHAT?
I KNOW YOU HAVE NO CLUE WHAT W.I.S.E HAS IN STORE.
SHAH

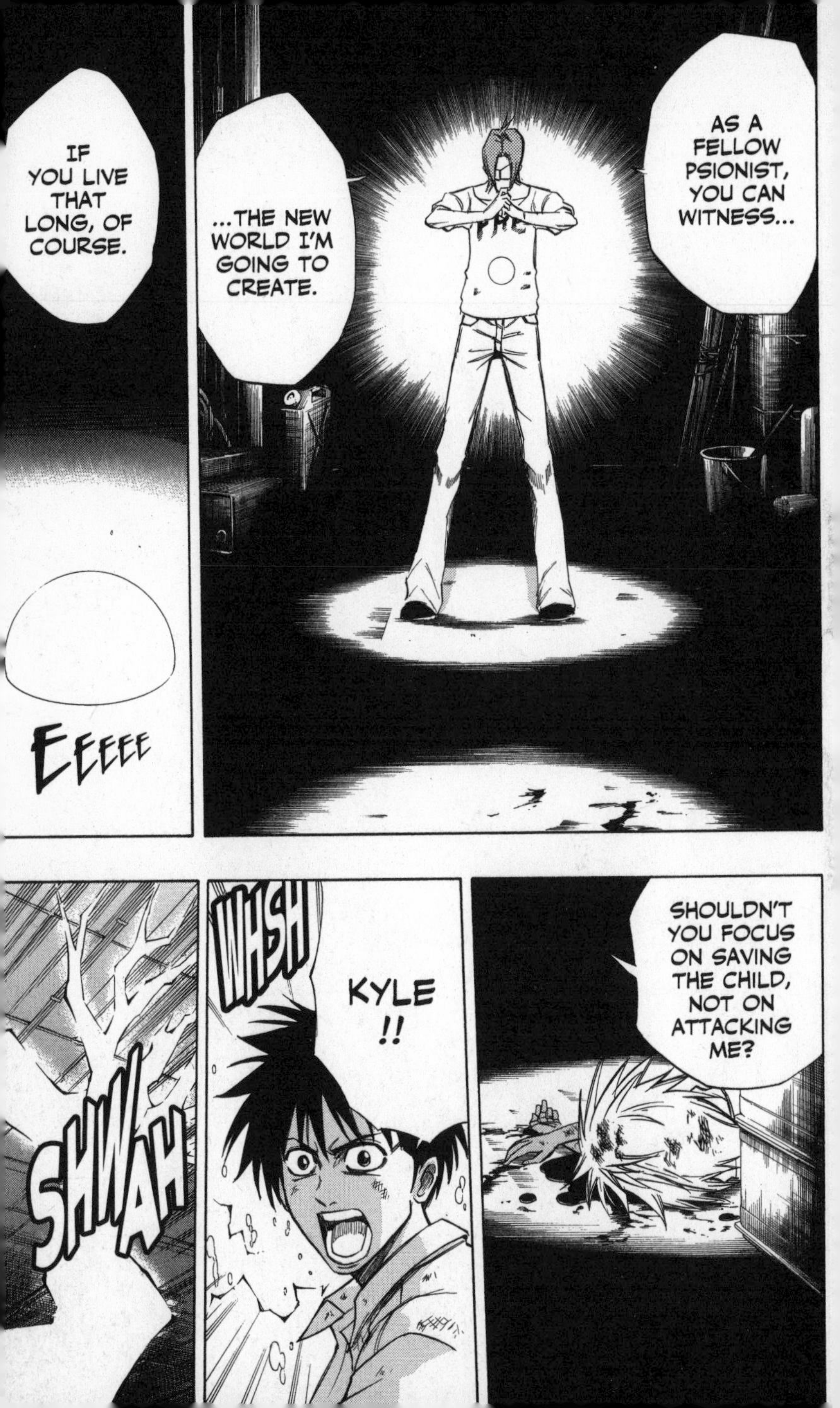

AS A FELLOW PSIONIST, YOU CAN WITNESS...
...THE NEW WORLD I'M GOING TO CREATE.
IF YOU LIVE THAT LONG, OF COURSE.
EEEEE
SHOULDN'T YOU FOCUS ON SAVING THE CHILD, NOT ON ATTACKING ME?
WHSH
KYLE !!
SHWAH

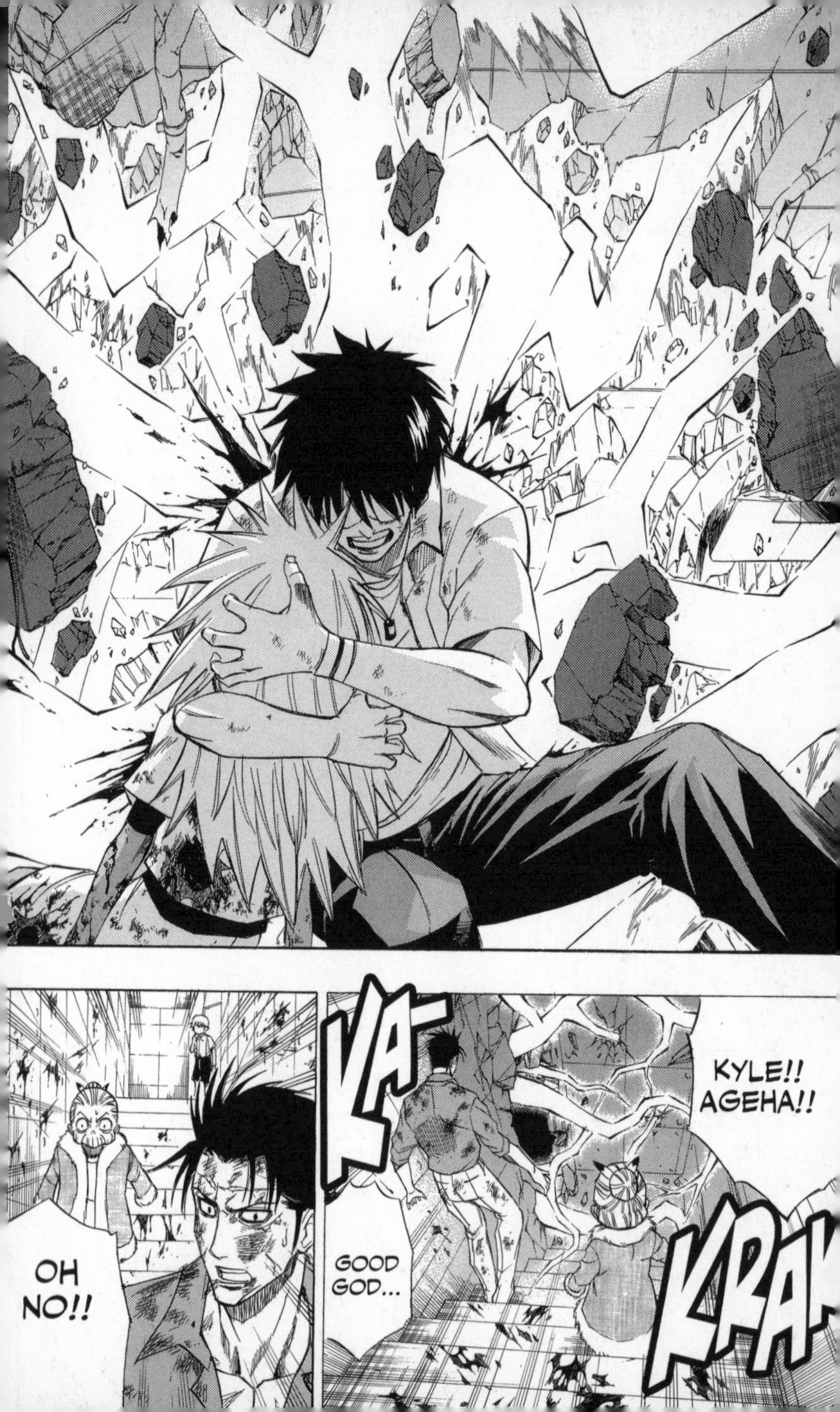
KYLE!! AGEHA!!
VA
GOOD GOD...
KRAK
OH NO!!

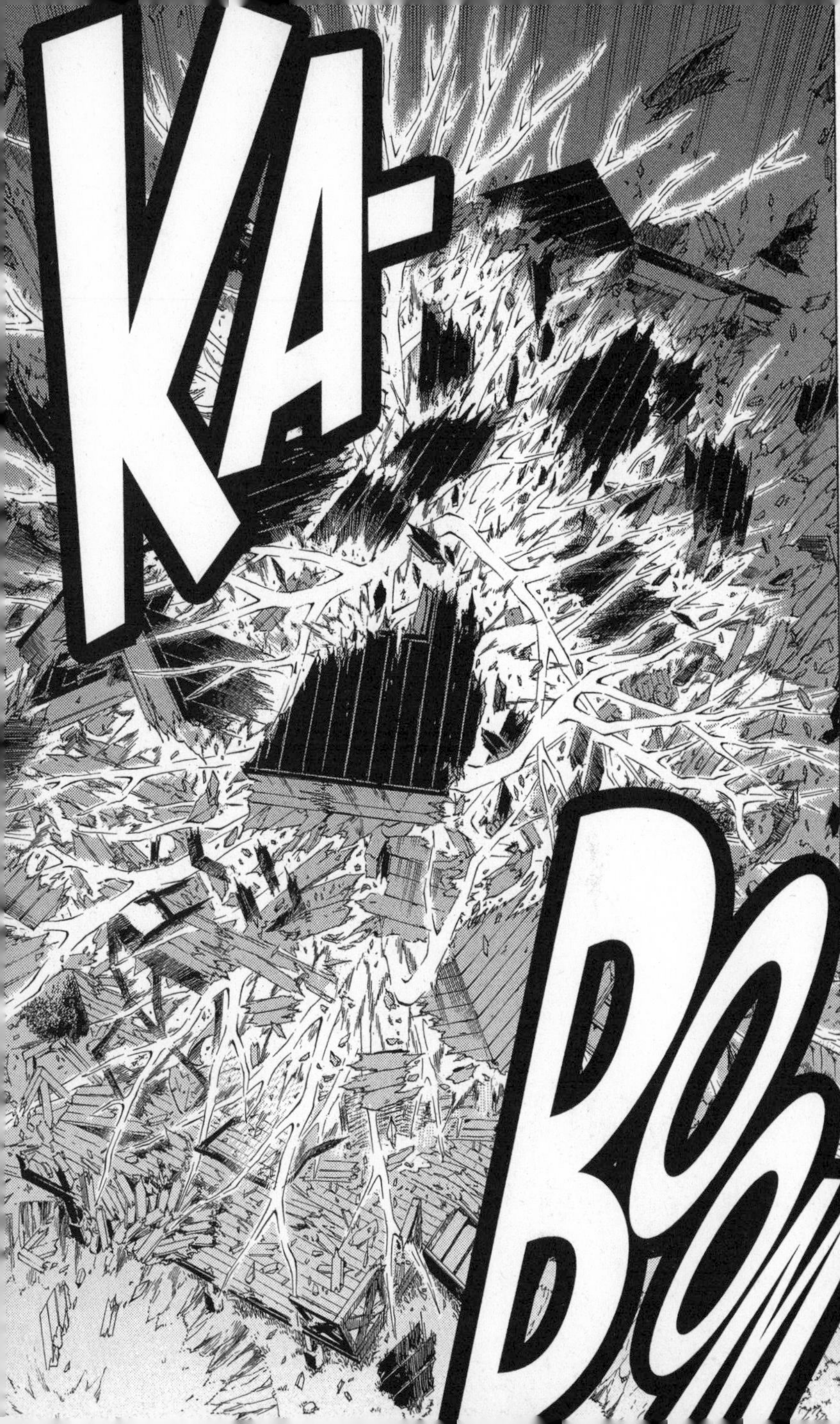
KA-
BOOM

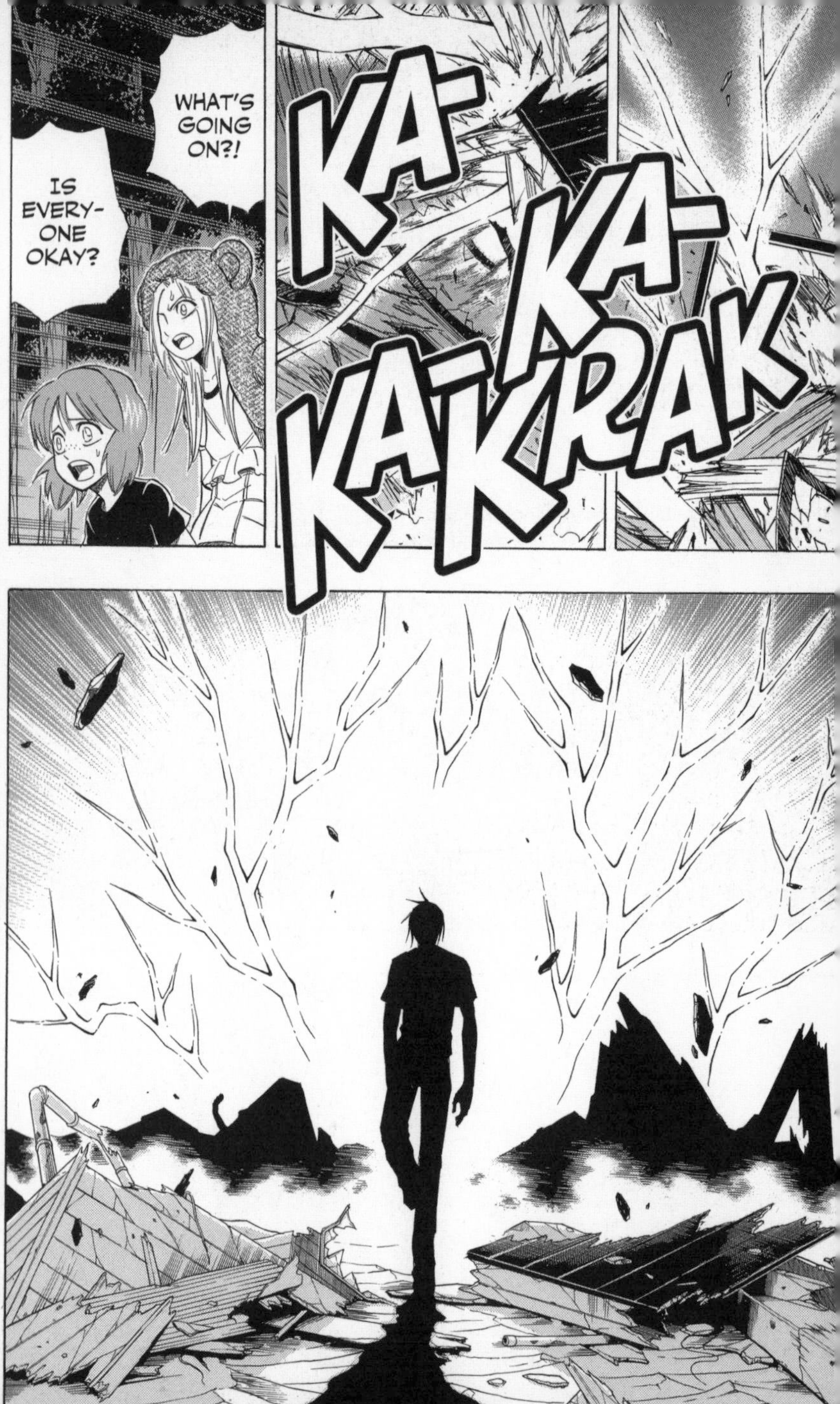
KA-KA-KA-KRAK
WHAT'S GOING ON?!
IS EVERY-ONE OKAY?

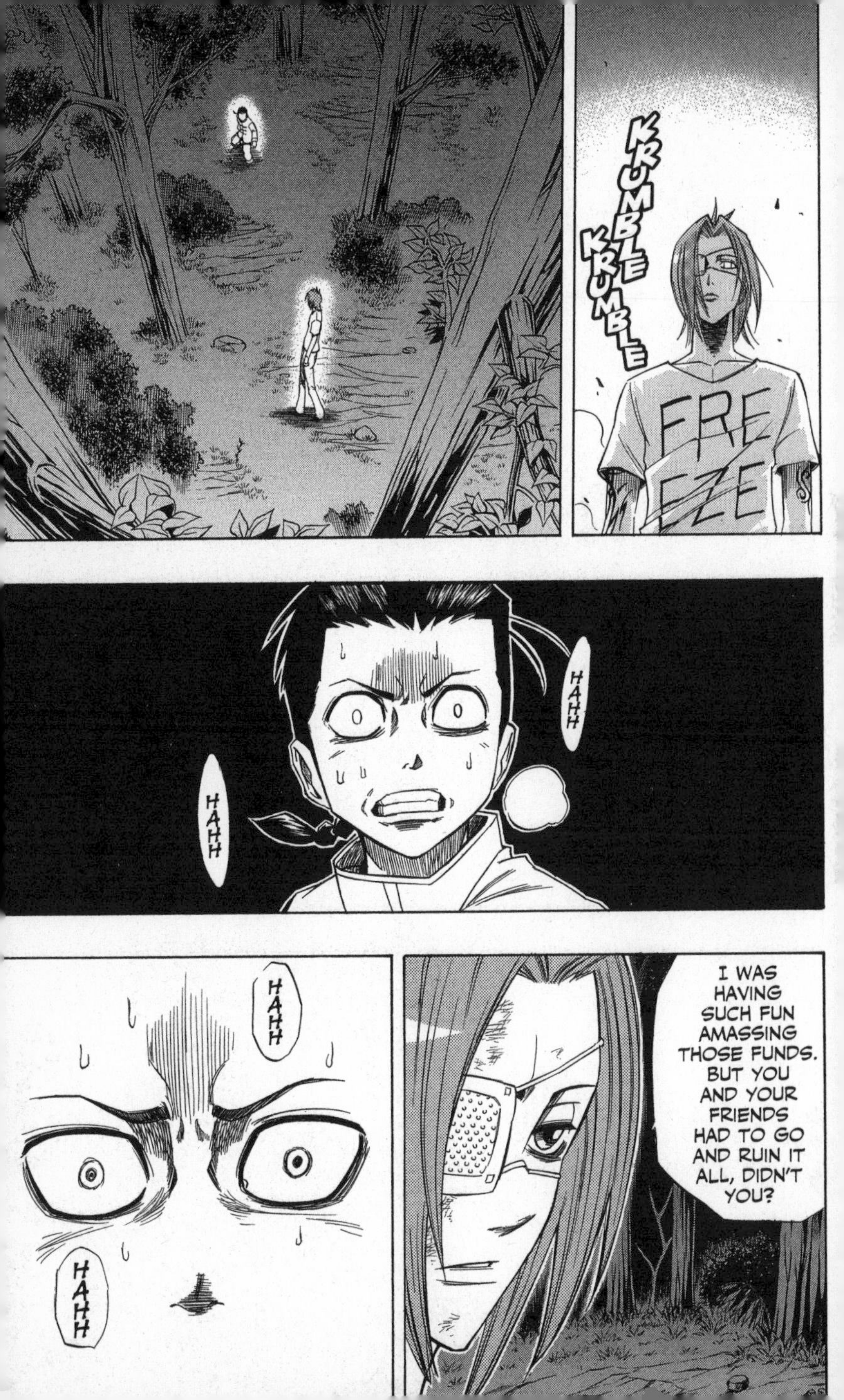
KRUMBLE
KRUMBLE
FREEZE
HAHH
HAHH
HAHH
HAHH
I WAS HAVING SUCH FUN AMASSING THOSE FUNDS. BUT YOU AND YOUR FRIENDS HAD TO GO AND RUIN IT ALL, DIDN'T YOU?

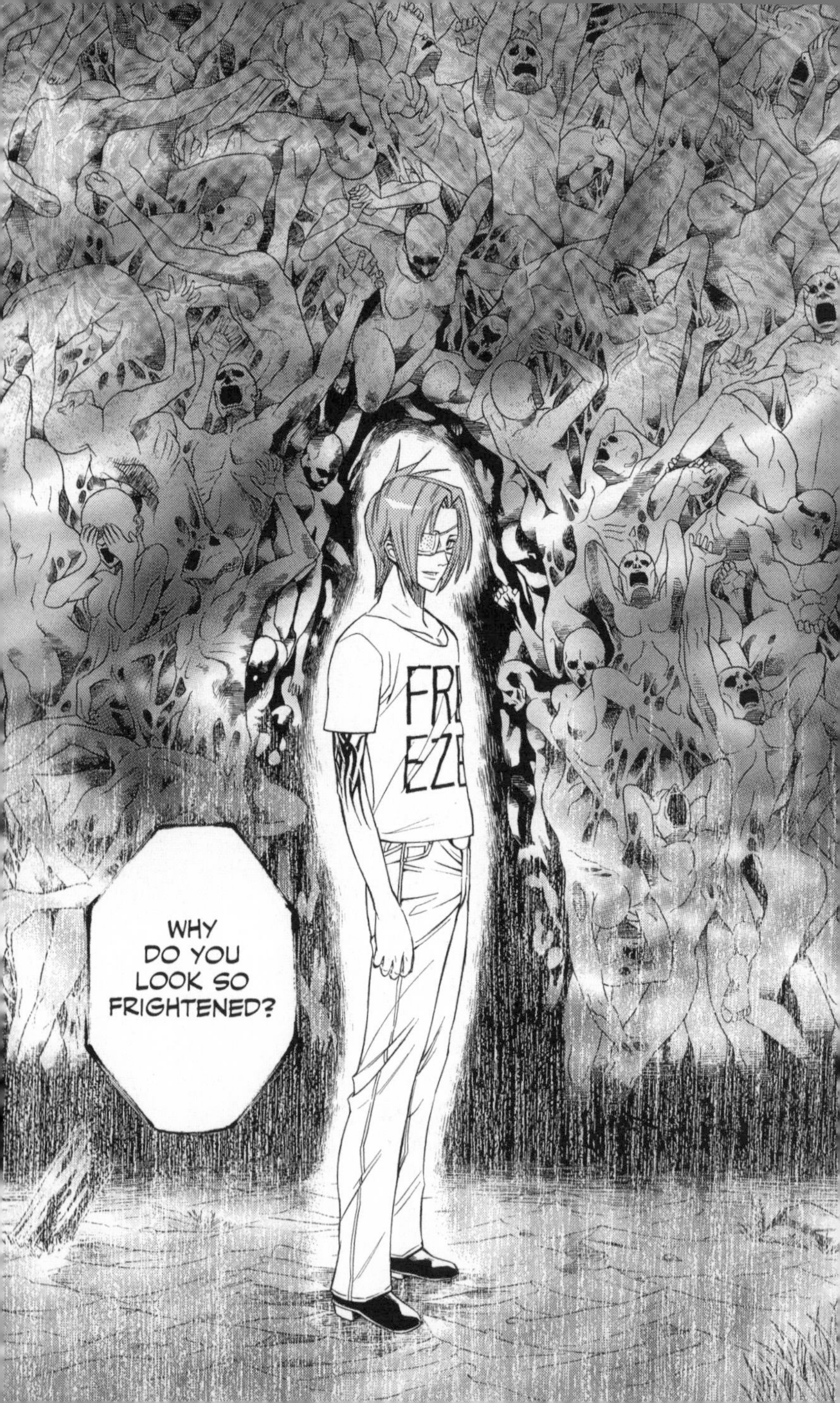
WHY DO YOU LOOK SO FRIGHTENED?

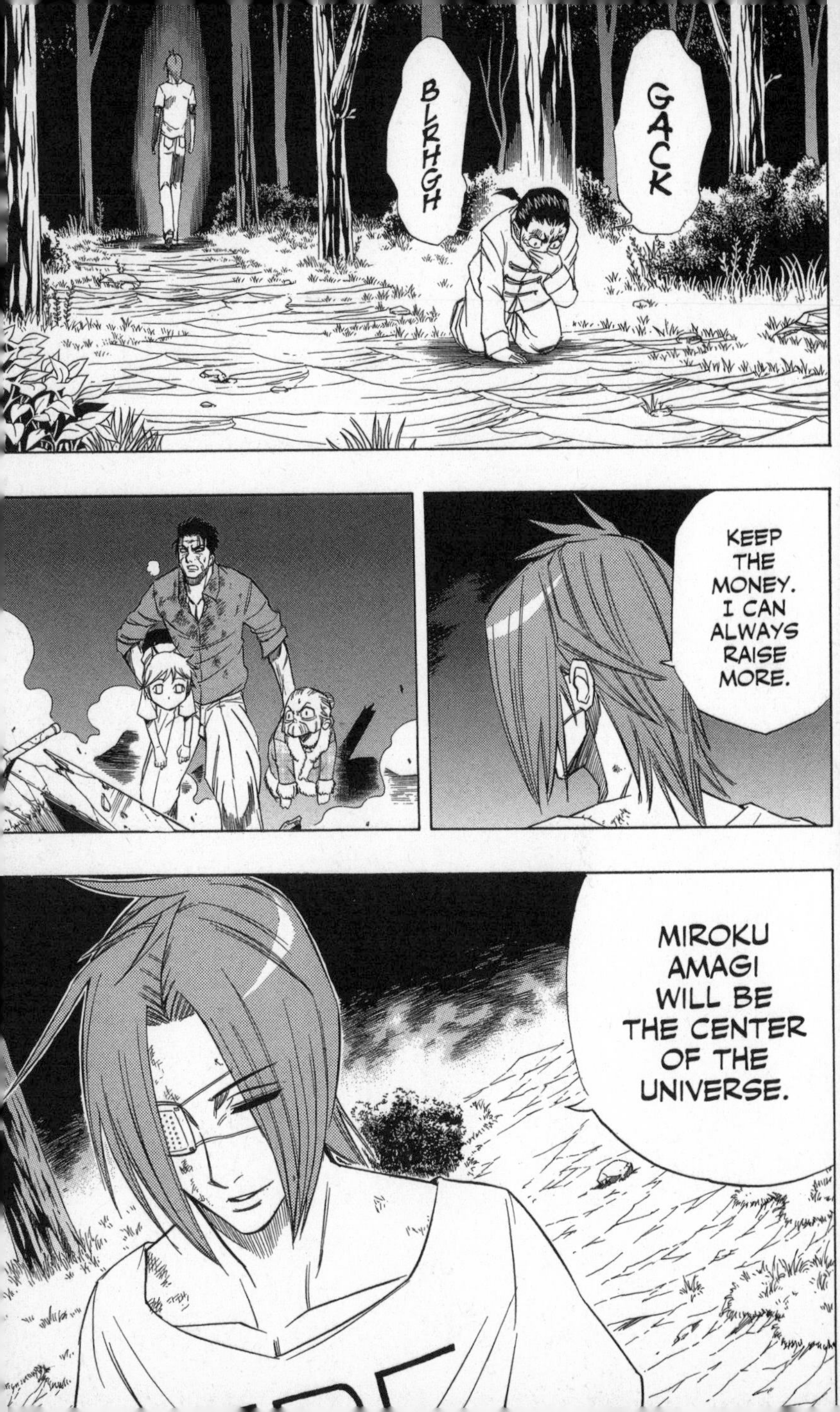
GACK
BLRHGH
KEEP THE MONEY. I CAN ALWAYS RAISE MORE.
MIROKU AMAGI WILL BE THE CENTER OF THE UNIVERSE.

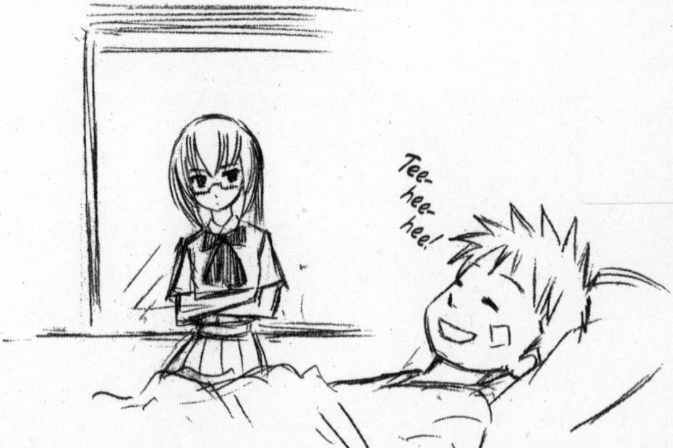
Tee-hee-hee!

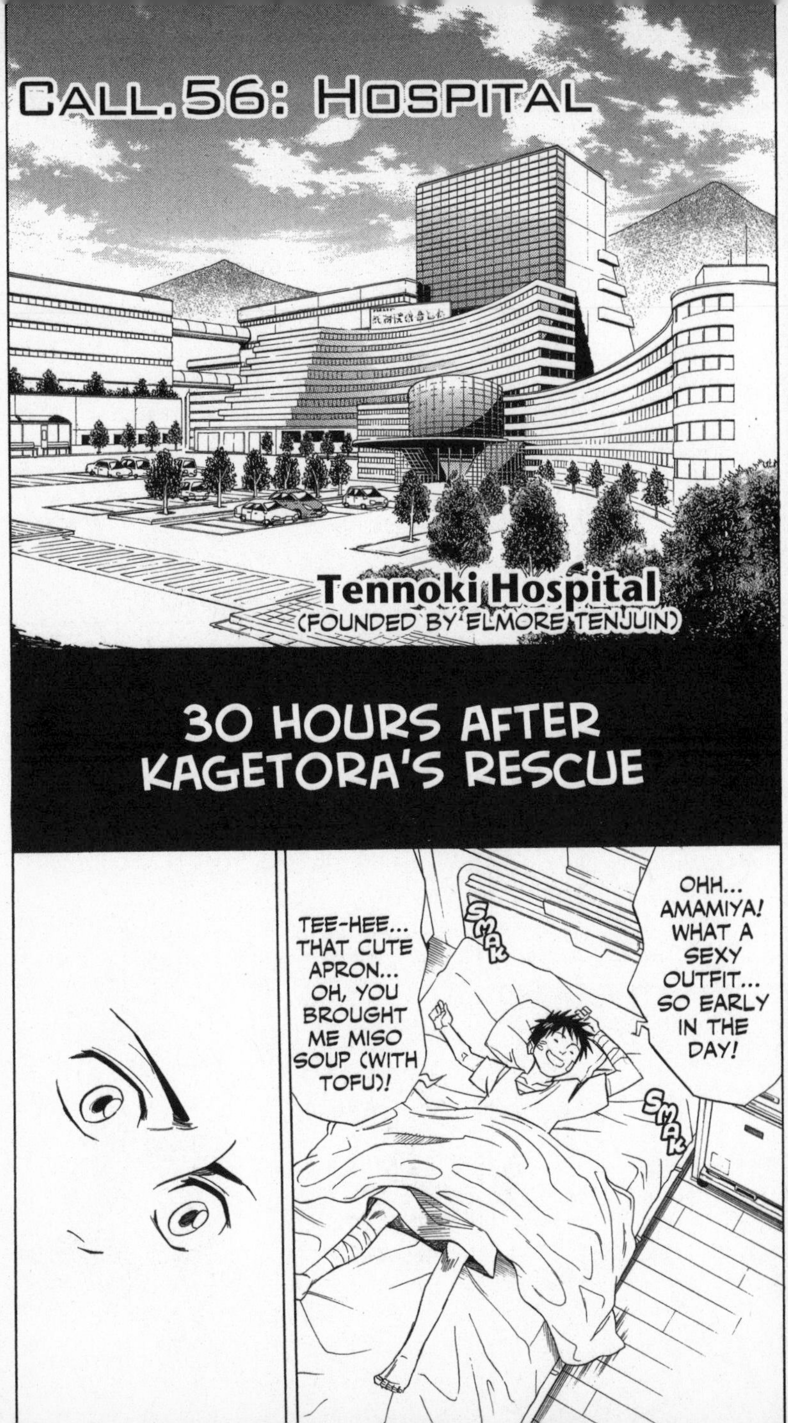
CALL.56: HOSPITAL
Tennoki Hospital
(FOUNDED BY ELMORE TENJUIN)
30 HOURS AFTER KAGETORA'S RESCUE
OHH... AMAMIYA! WHAT A SEXY OUTFIT... SO EARLY IN THE DAY!
SMAK
TEE-HEE... THAT CUTE APRON... OH, YOU BROUGHT ME MISO SOUP (WITH TOFU)!
SMAK

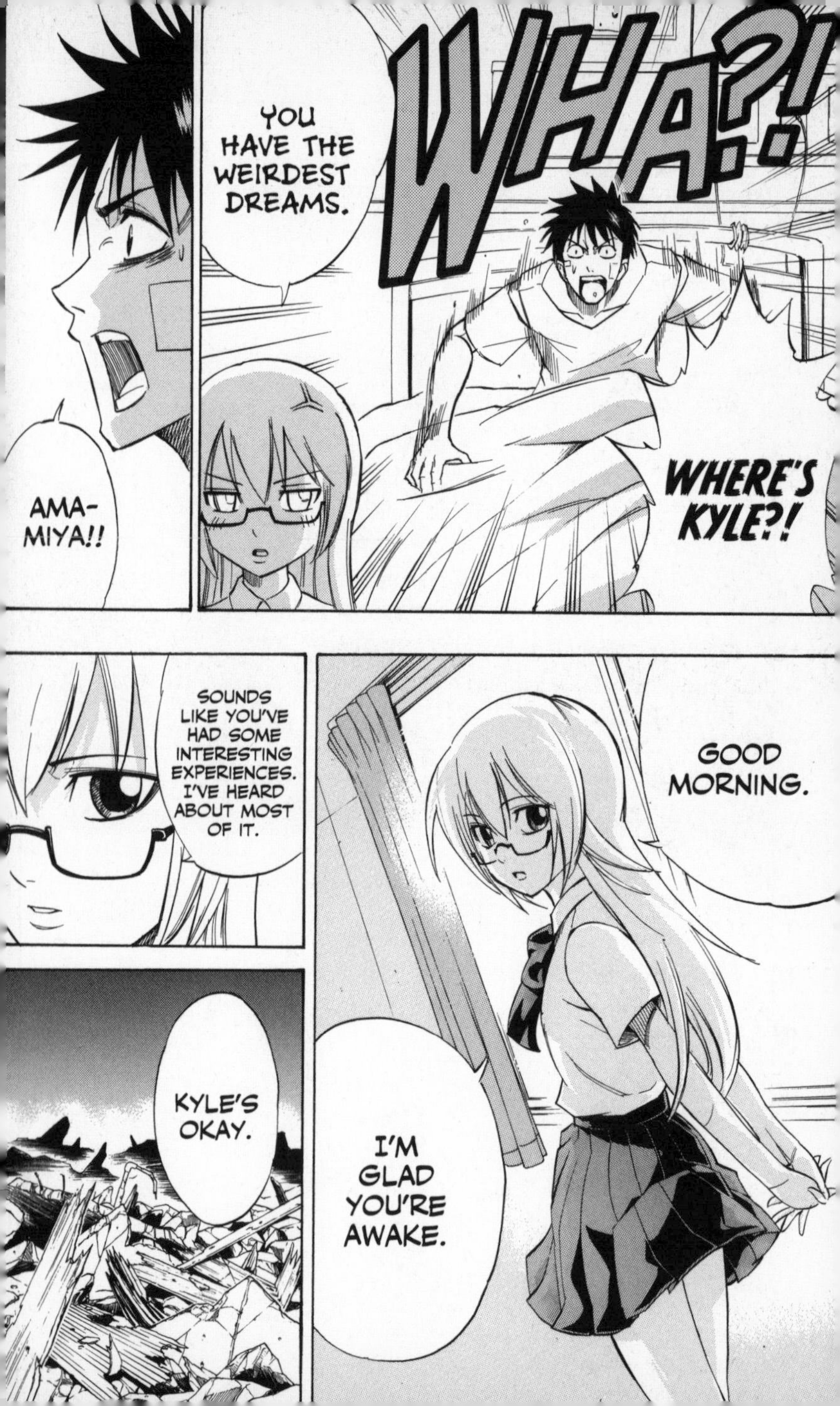
WHA?!
WHERE'S KYLE?!
YOU HAVE THE WEIRDEST DREAMS.
AMA-MIYA!!
GOOD MORNING.
I'M GLAD YOU'RE AWAKE.
SOUNDS LIKE YOU'VE HAD SOME INTERESTING EXPERIENCES. I'VE HEARD ABOUT MOST OF IT.
KYLE'S OKAY.

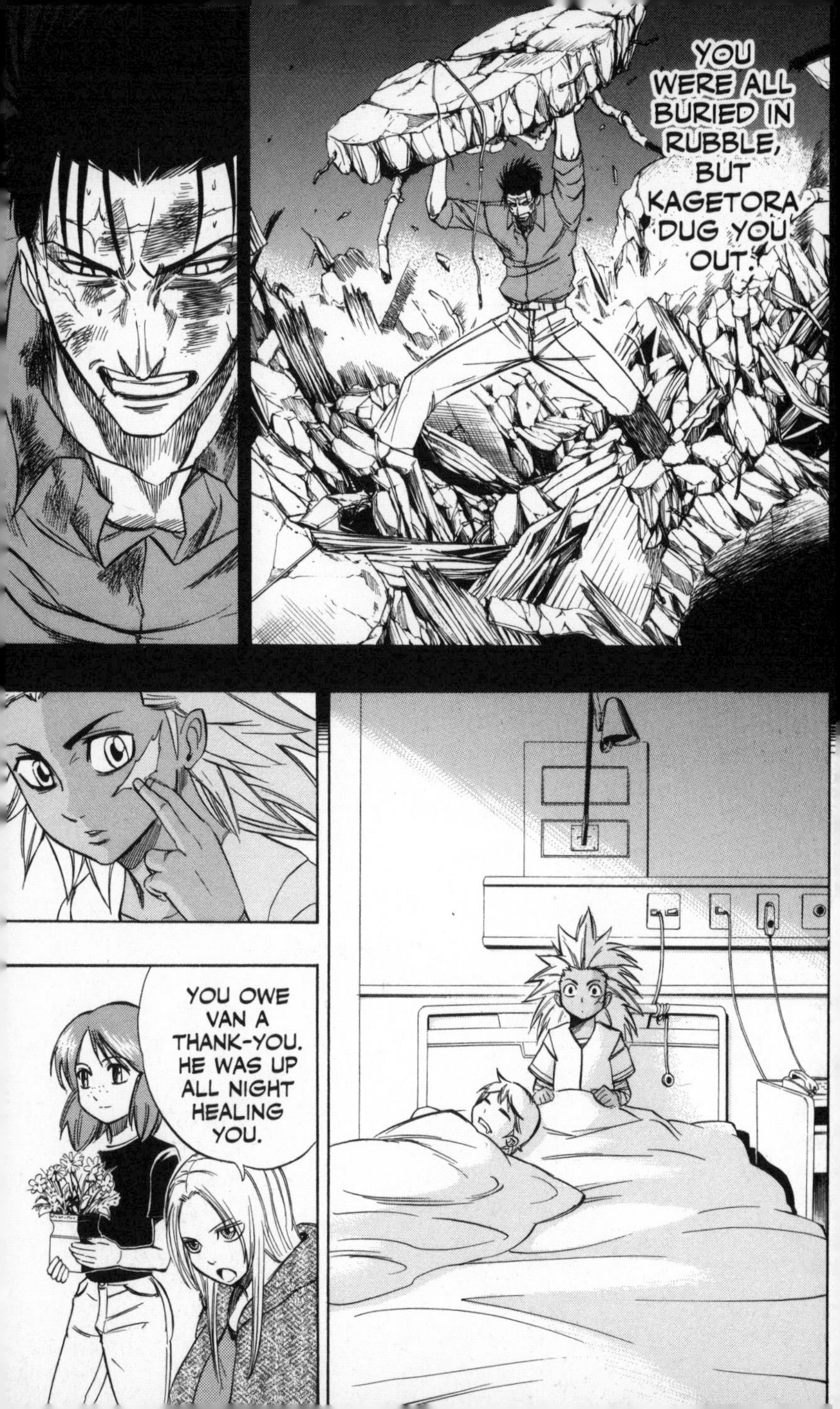
YOU WERE ALL BURIED IN RUBBLE, BUT KAGETORA DUG YOU OUT.
YOU OWE VAN A THANK-YOU. HE WAS UP ALL NIGHT HEALING YOU.

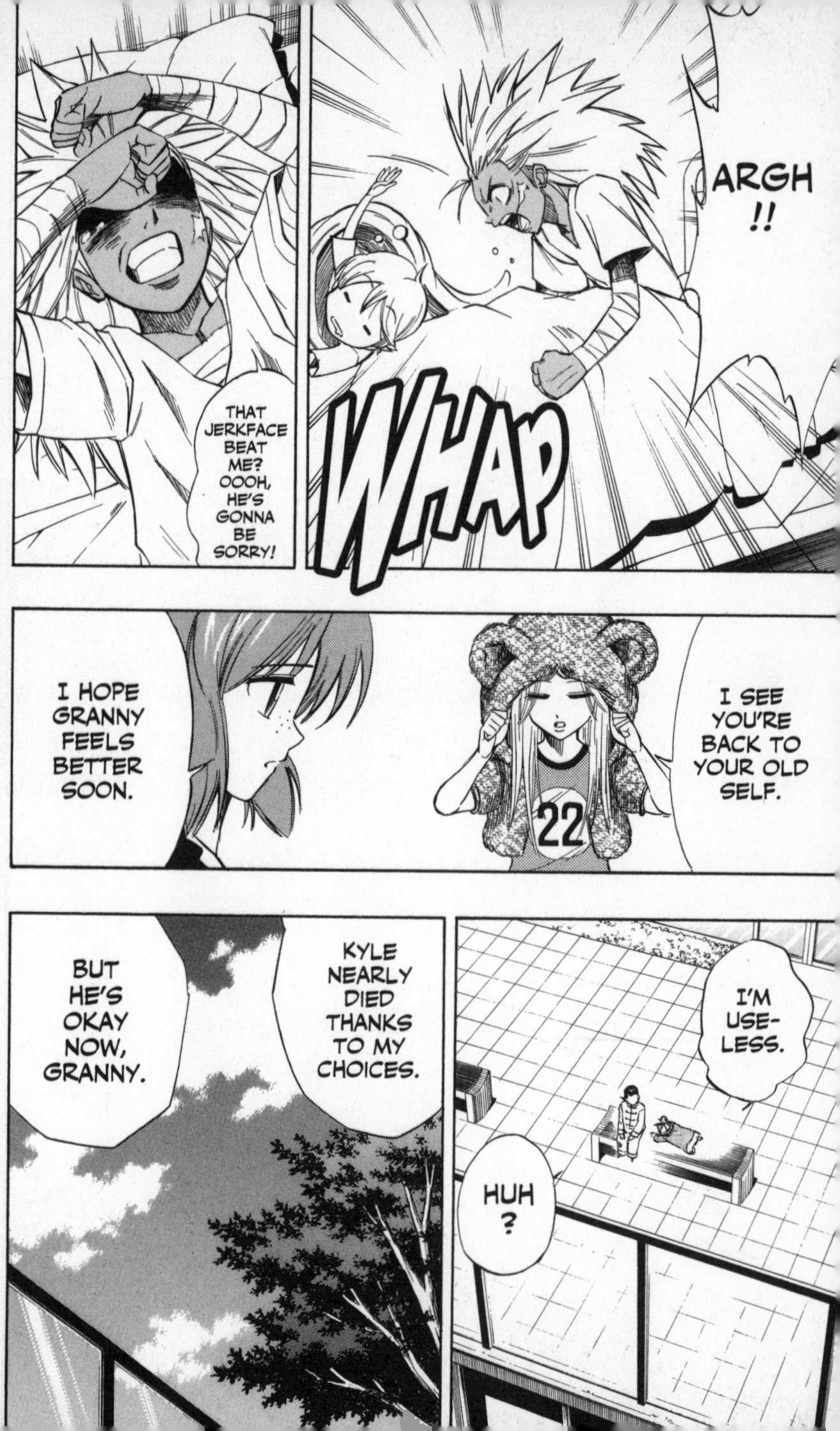
ARGH !!
WHAP
THAT JERKFACE BEAT ME? OOOH, HE'S GONNA BE SORRY!
I SEE YOU'RE BACK TO YOUR OLD SELF.
I HOPE GRANNY FEELS BETTER SOON.
I'M USE-LESS.
HUH ?
KYLE NEARLY DIED THANKS TO MY CHOICES.
BUT HE'S OKAY NOW, GRANNY.

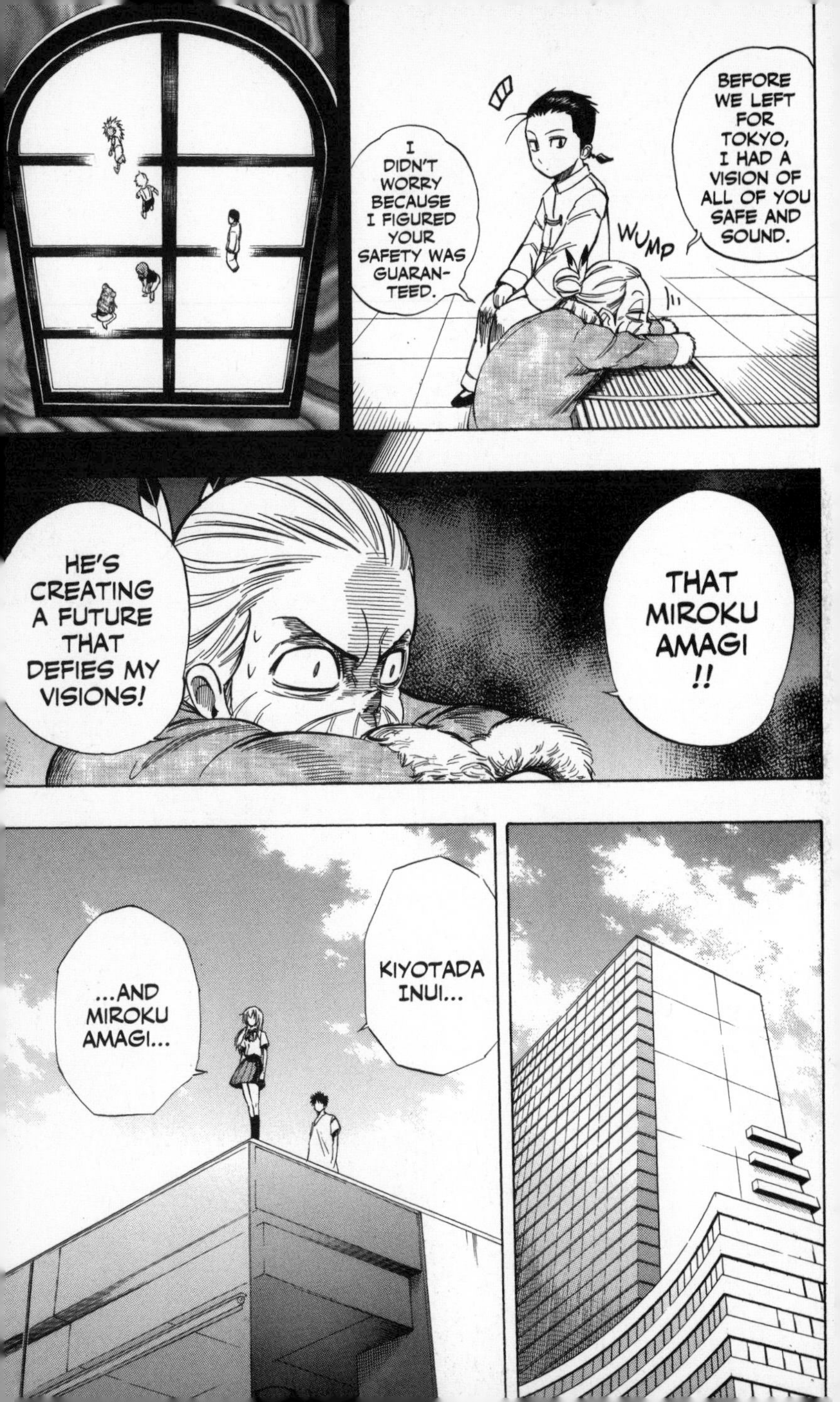
BEFORE WE LEFT FOR TOKYO, I HAD A VISION OF ALL OF YOU SAFE AND SOUND.
WUMP
I DIDN'T WORRY BECAUSE I FIGURED YOUR SAFETY WAS GUARAN-TEED.
THAT MIROKU AMAGI !!
HE'S CREATING A FUTURE THAT DEFIES MY VISIONS!
KIYOTADA INUI...
...AND MIROKU AMAGI...

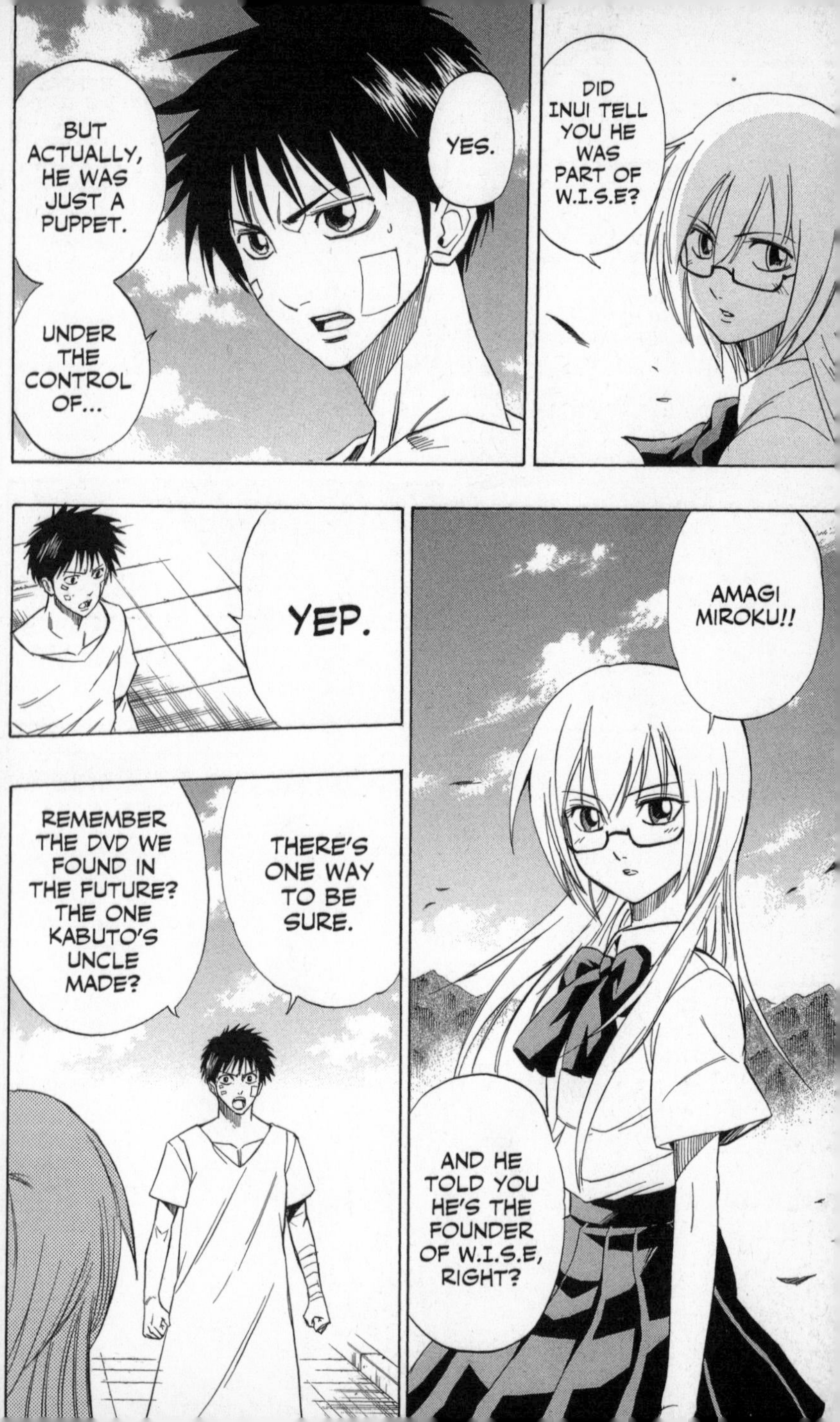
DID INUI TELL YOU HE WAS PART OF W.I.S.E?
YES.
BUT ACTUALLY, HE WAS JUST A PUPPET.
UNDER THE CONTROL OF...
AMAGI MIROKU!!
AND HE TOLD YOU HE'S THE FOUNDER OF W.I.S.E, RIGHT?
YEP.
THERE'S ONE WAY TO BE SURE.
REMEMBER THE DVD WE FOUND IN THE FUTURE? THE ONE KABUTO'S UNCLE MADE?

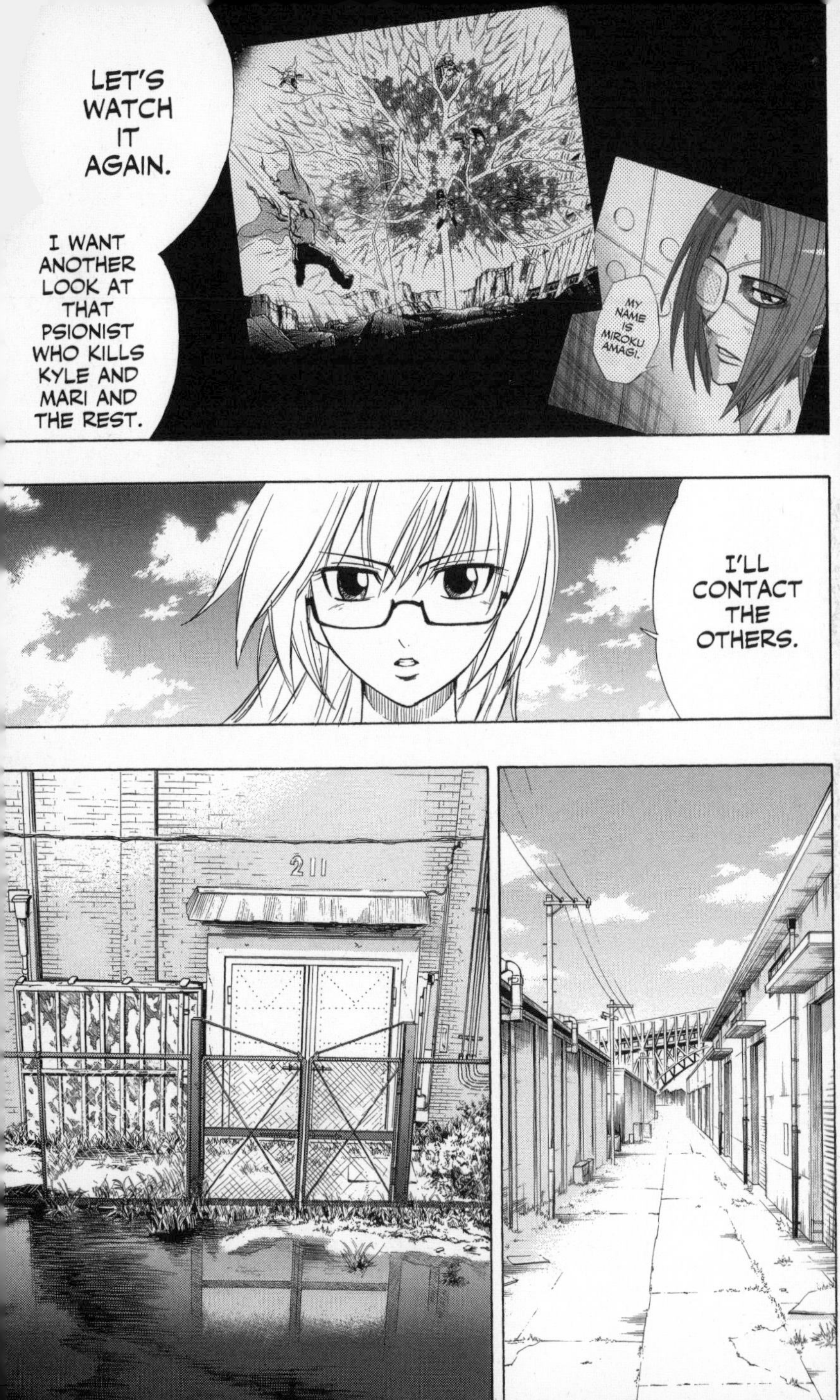
MY NAME IS MIROKU AMAGI.
LET'S WATCH IT AGAIN.
I WANT ANOTHER LOOK AT THAT PSIONIST WHO KILLS KYLE AND MARI AND THE REST.
I'LL CONTACT THE OTHERS.

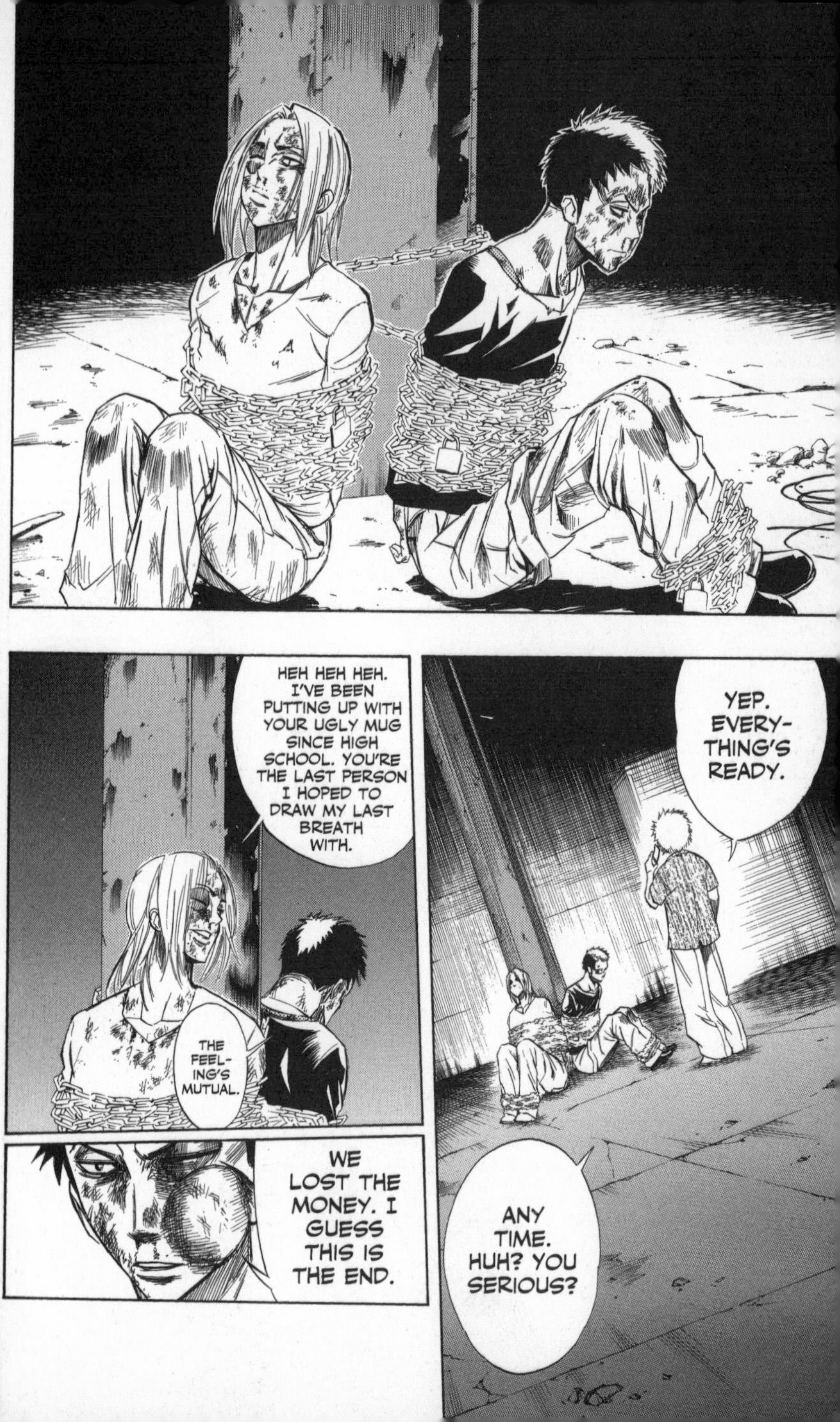
YEP. EVERYTHING'S READY.
ANY TIME. HUH? YOU SERIOUS?
HEH HEH HEH. I'VE BEEN PUTTING UP WITH YOUR UGLY MUG SINCE HIGH SCHOOL. YOU'RE THE LAST PERSON I HOPED TO DRAW MY LAST BREATH WITH.
THE FEELING'S MUTUAL.
WE LOST THE MONEY. I GUESS THIS IS THE END.

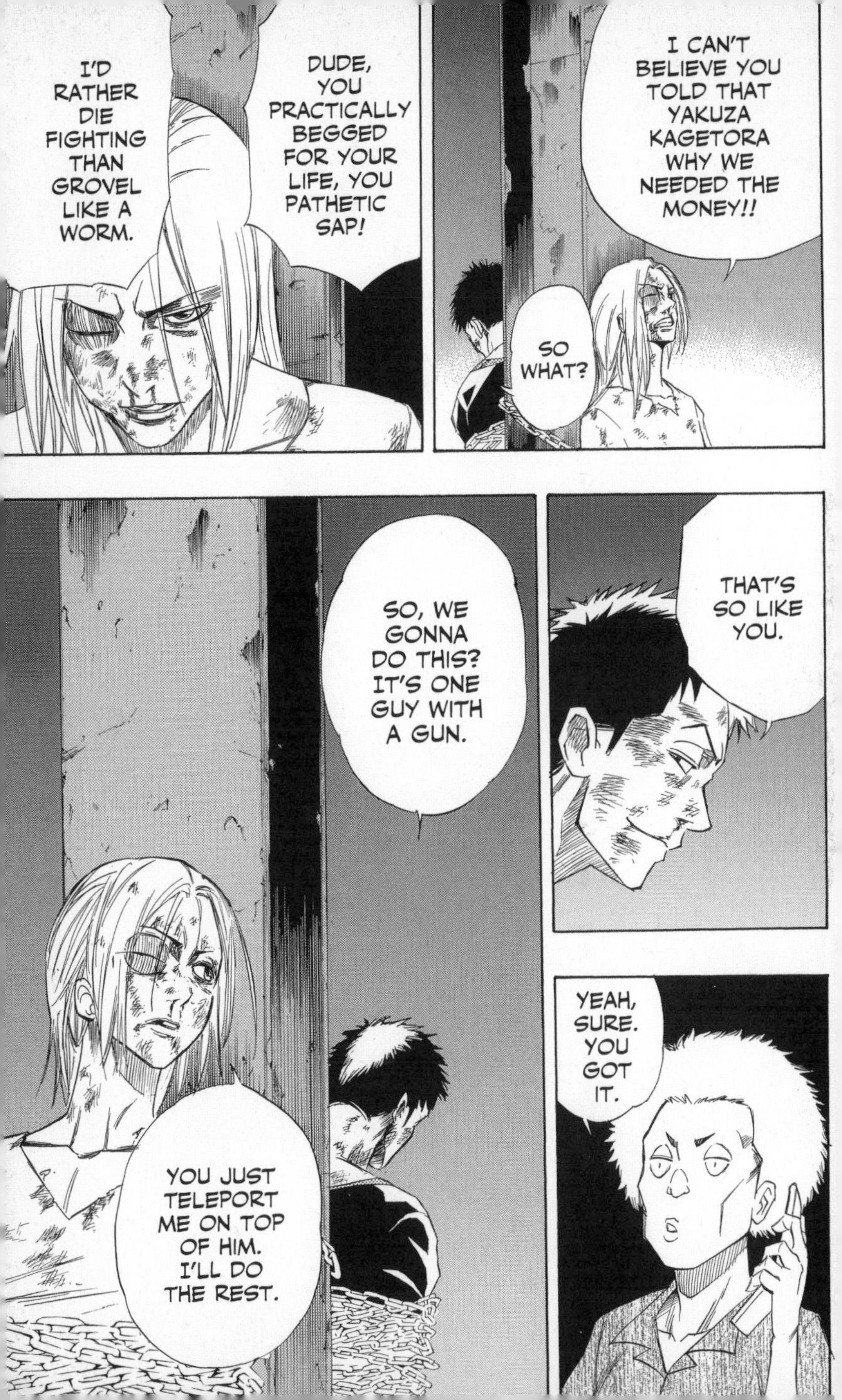
I CAN'T BELIEVE YOU TOLD THAT YAKUZA KAGETORA WHY WE NEEDED THE MONEY!!
SO WHAT?
DUDE, YOU PRACTICALLY BEGGED FOR YOUR LIFE, YOU PATHETIC SAP!
I'D RATHER DIE FIGHTING THAN GROVEL LIKE A WORM.
THAT'S SO LIKE YOU.
YEAH, SURE. YOU GOT IT.
SO, WE GONNA DO THIS? IT'S ONE GUY WITH A GUN.
YOU JUST TELEPORT ME ON TOP OF HIM. I'LL DO THE REST.

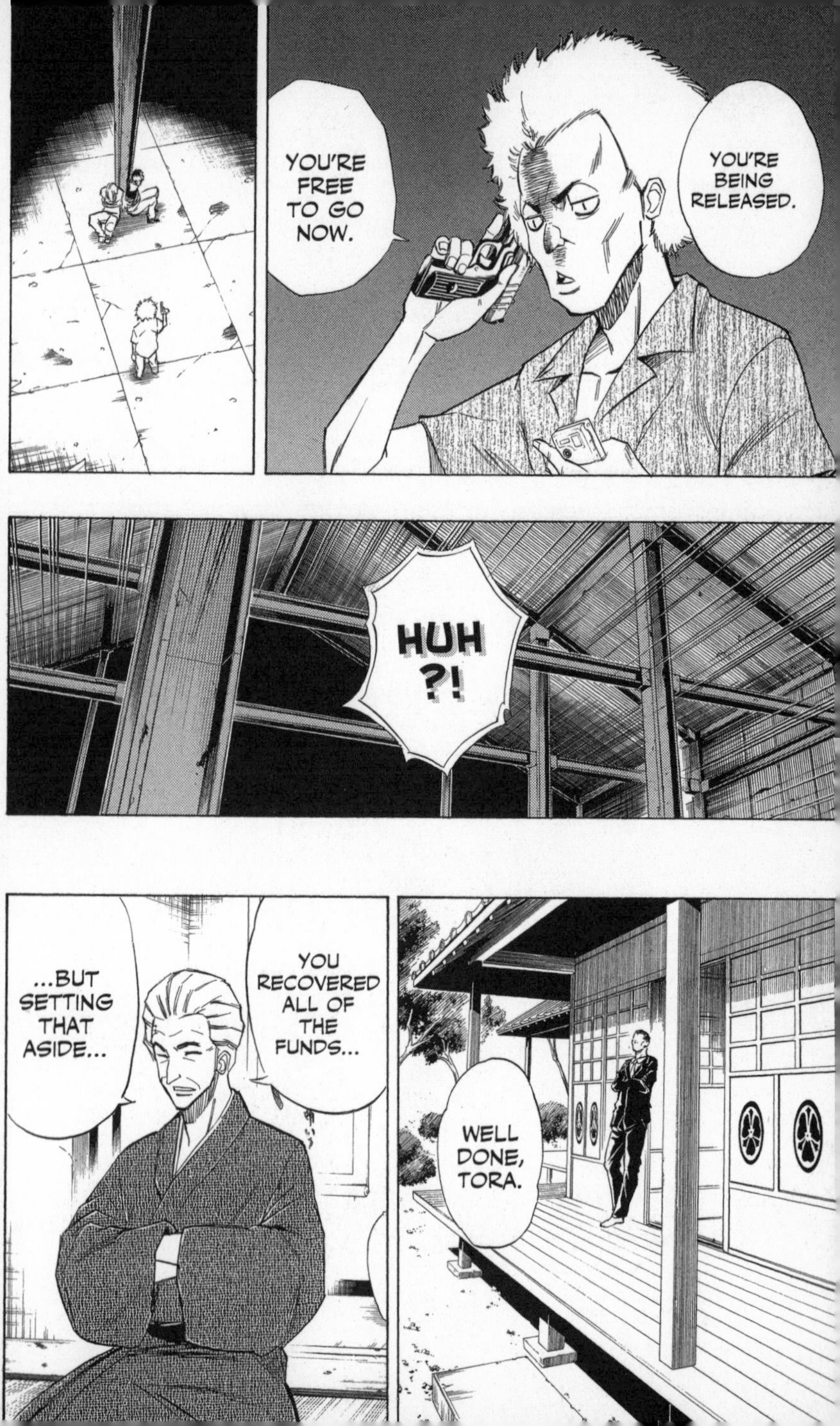
YOU'RE BEING RELEASED.
YOU'RE FREE TO GO NOW.
HUH ?!
WELL DONE, TORA.
YOU RECOVERED ALL OF THE FUNDS...
...BUT SETTING THAT ASIDE...

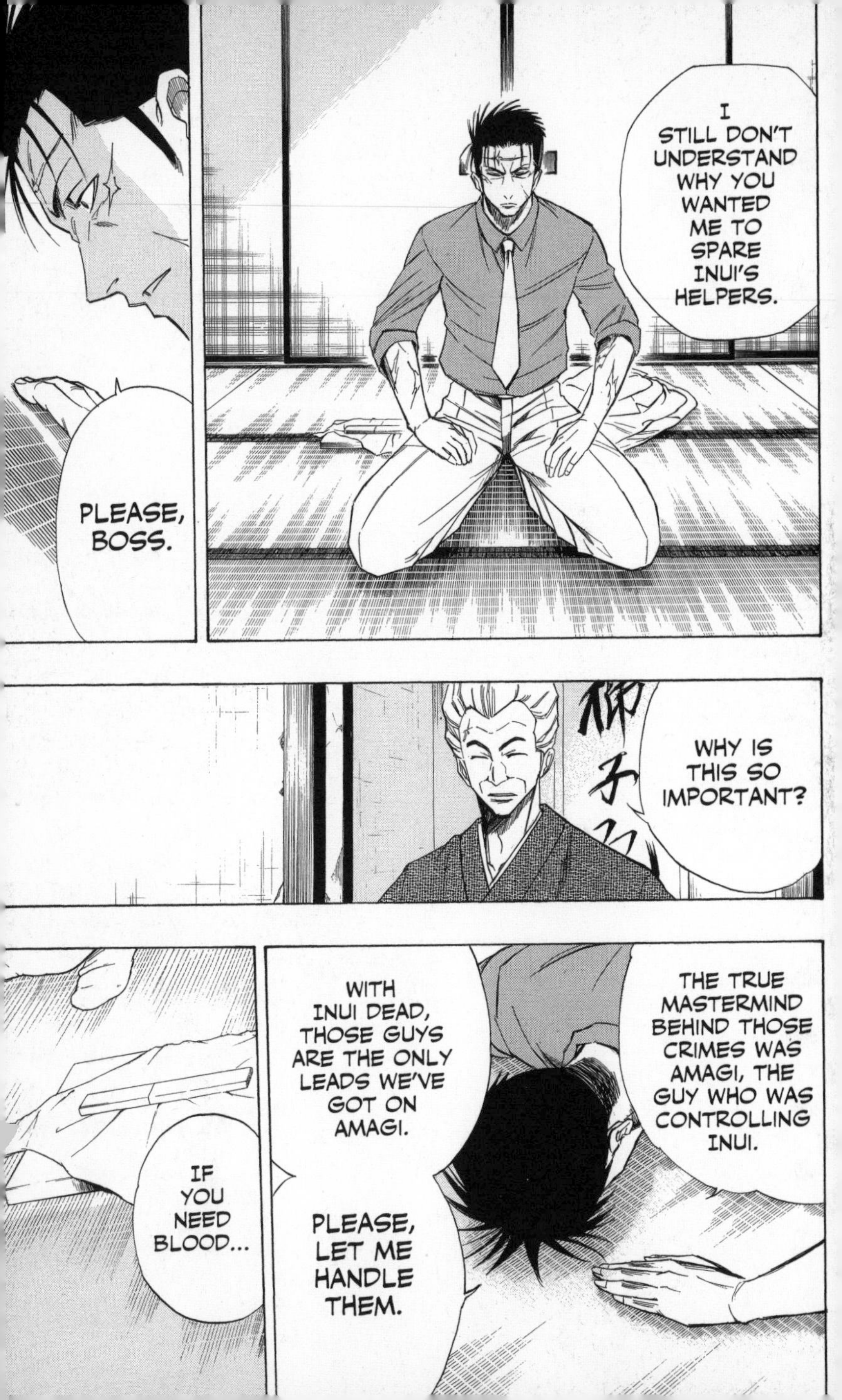
I STILL DON'T UNDERSTAND WHY YOU WANTED ME TO SPARE INUI'S HELPERS.
PLEASE, BOSS.
WHY IS THIS SO IMPORTANT?
THE TRUE MASTERMIND BEHIND THOSE CRIMES WAS AMAGI, THE GUY WHO WAS CONTROLLING INUI.
WITH INUI DEAD, THOSE GUYS ARE THE ONLY LEADS WE'VE GOT ON AMAGI.
PLEASE, LET ME HANDLE THEM.
IF YOU NEED BLOOD...

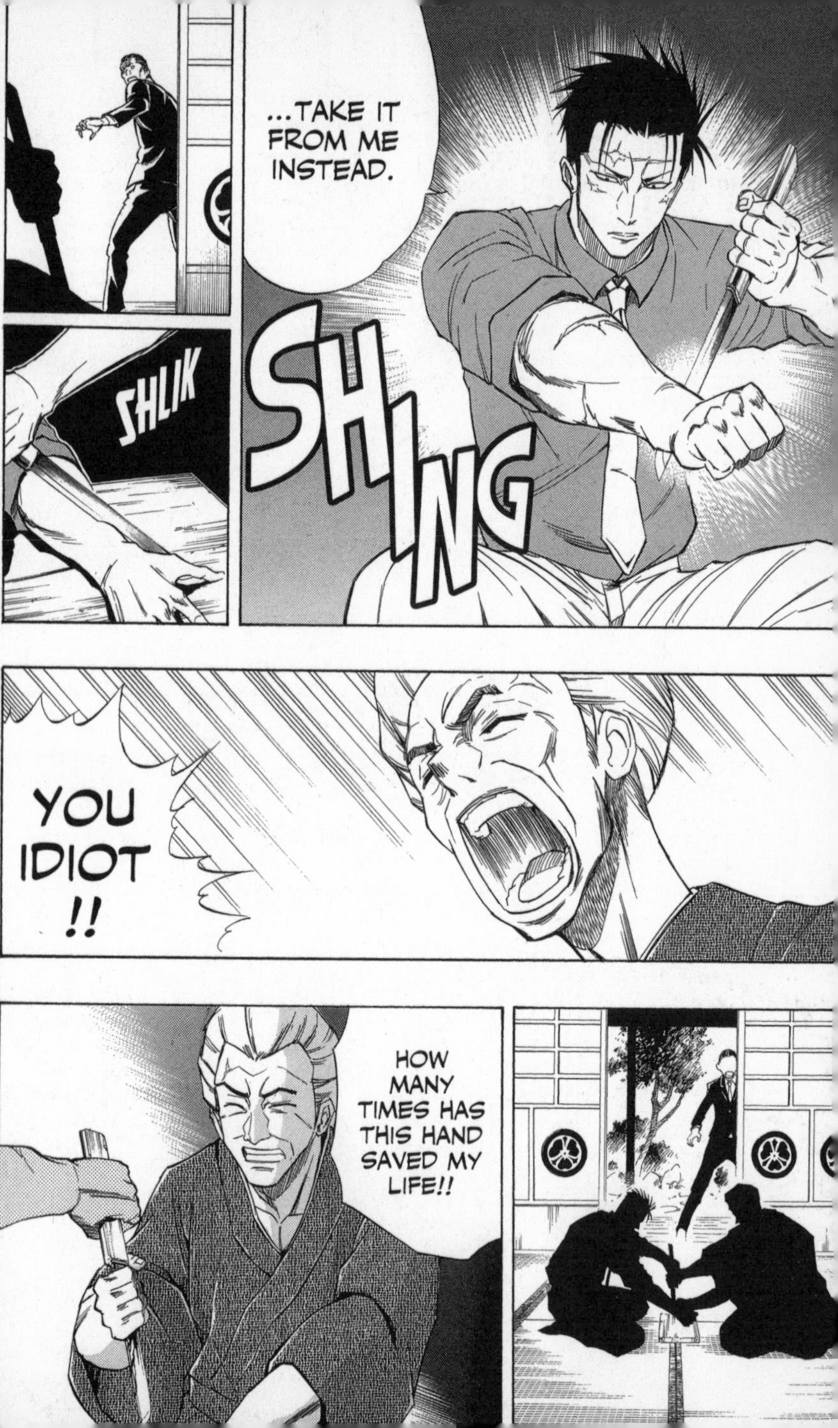
...TAKE IT FROM ME INSTEAD.
SHING
SHLIK
YOU IDIOT!!
HOW MANY TIMES HAS THIS HAND SAVED MY LIFE!!

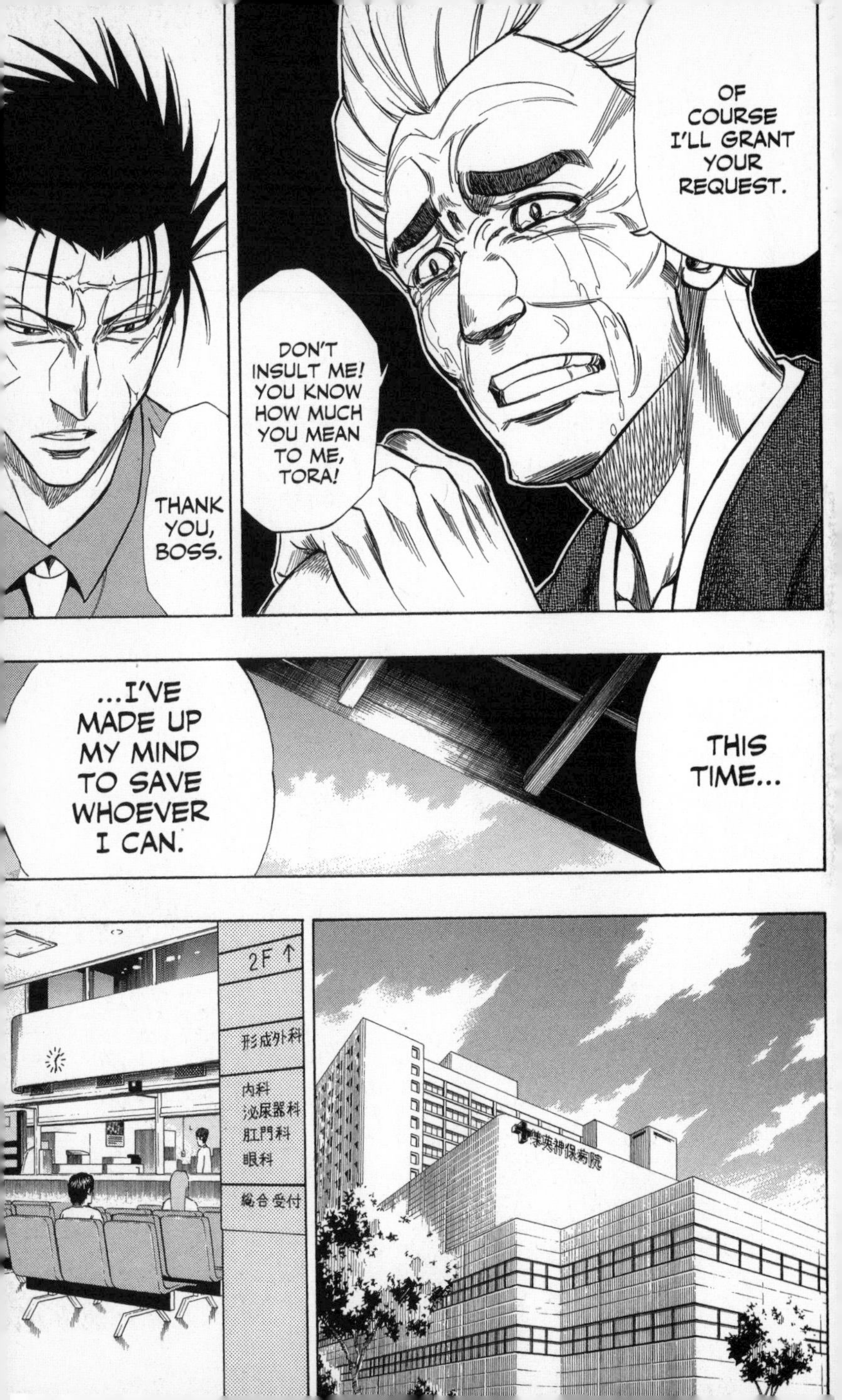
OF COURSE I'LL GRANT YOUR REQUEST.
DON'T INSULT ME! YOU KNOW HOW MUCH YOU MEAN TO ME, TORA!
THANK YOU, BOSS.
THIS TIME...
...I'VE MADE UP MY MIND TO SAVE WHOEVER I CAN.
2F ↑
形成外科
内科
泌尿器科
肛門科
眼科
総合受付

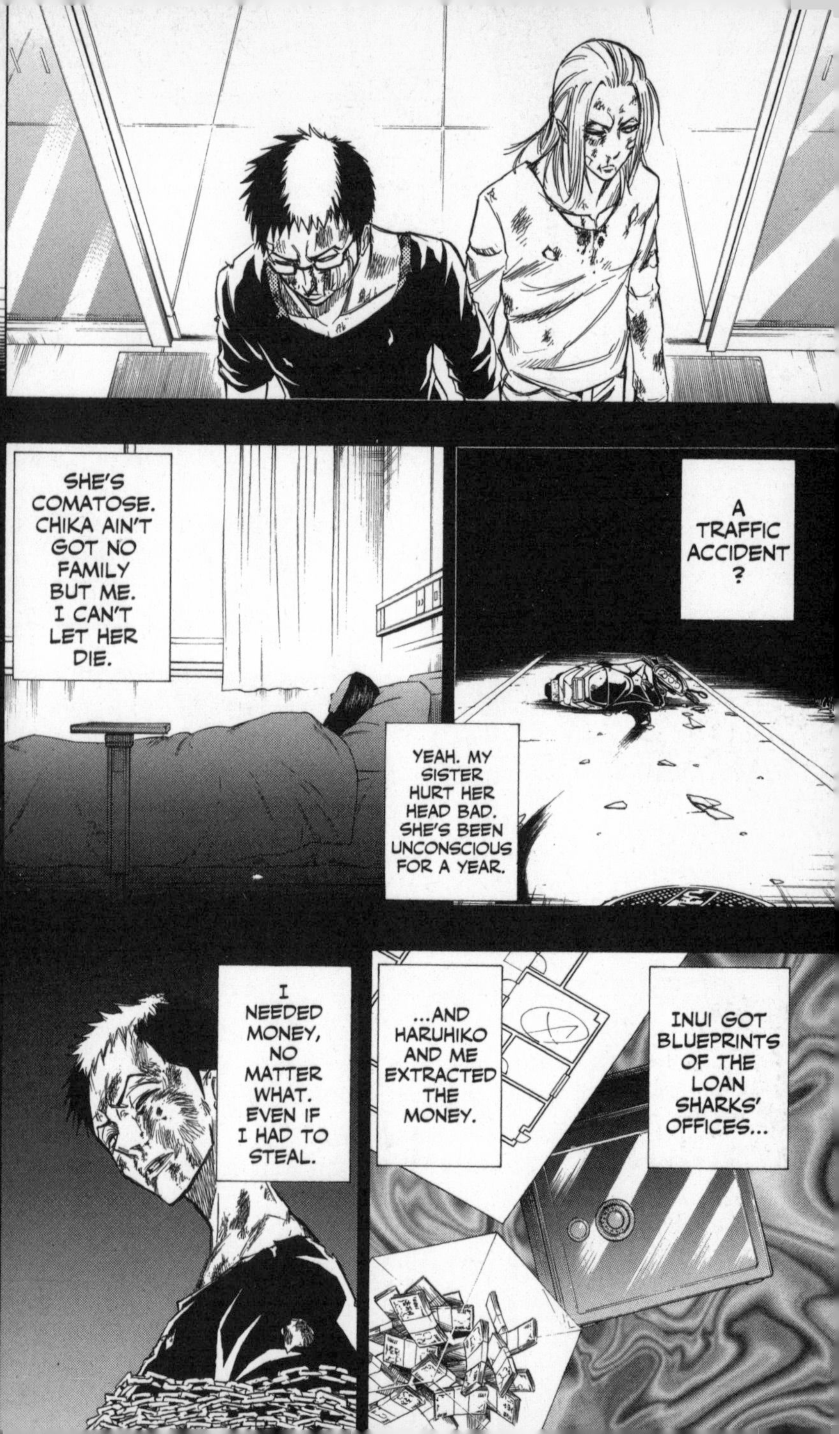
A TRAFFIC ACCIDENT?
YEAH. MY SISTER HURT HER HEAD BAD. SHE'S BEEN UNCONSCIOUS FOR A YEAR.
SHE'S COMATOSE. CHIKA AIN'T GOT NO FAMILY BUT ME. I CAN'T LET HER DIE.
INUI GOT BLUEPRINTS OF THE LOAN SHARKS' OFFICES...
...AND HARUHIKO AND ME EXTRACTED THE MONEY.
I NEEDED MONEY, NO MATTER WHAT. EVEN IF I HAD TO STEAL.

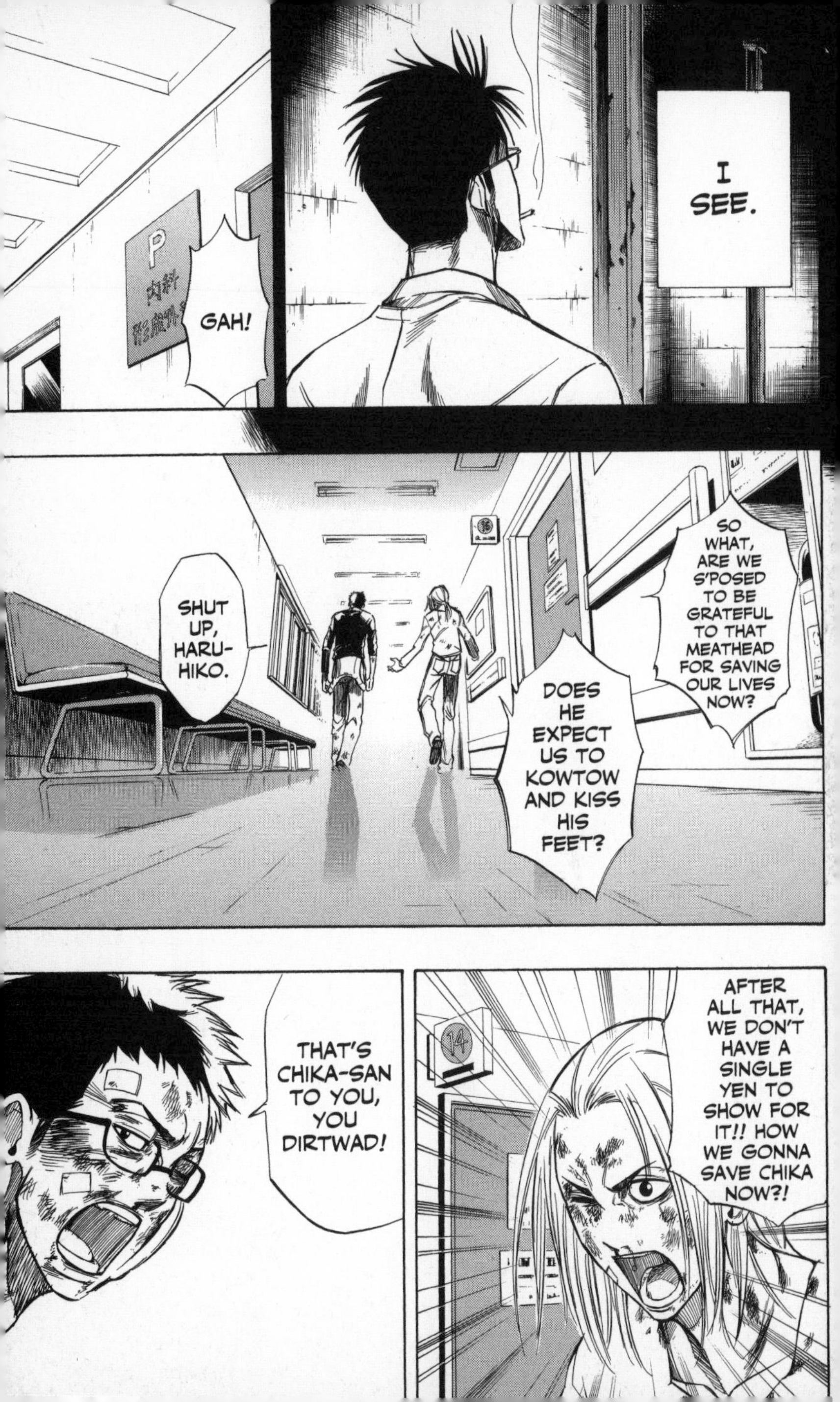
I SEE.
GAH!
SO WHAT, ARE WE S'POSED TO BE GRATEFUL TO THAT MEATHEAD FOR SAVING OUR LIVES NOW?
DOES HE EXPECT US TO KOWTOW AND KISS HIS FEET?
SHUT UP, HARU-HIKO.
AFTER ALL THAT, WE DON'T HAVE A SINGLE YEN TO SHOW FOR IT!! HOW WE GONNA SAVE CHIKA NOW?!
THAT'S CHIKA-SAN TO YOU, YOU DIRTWAD!

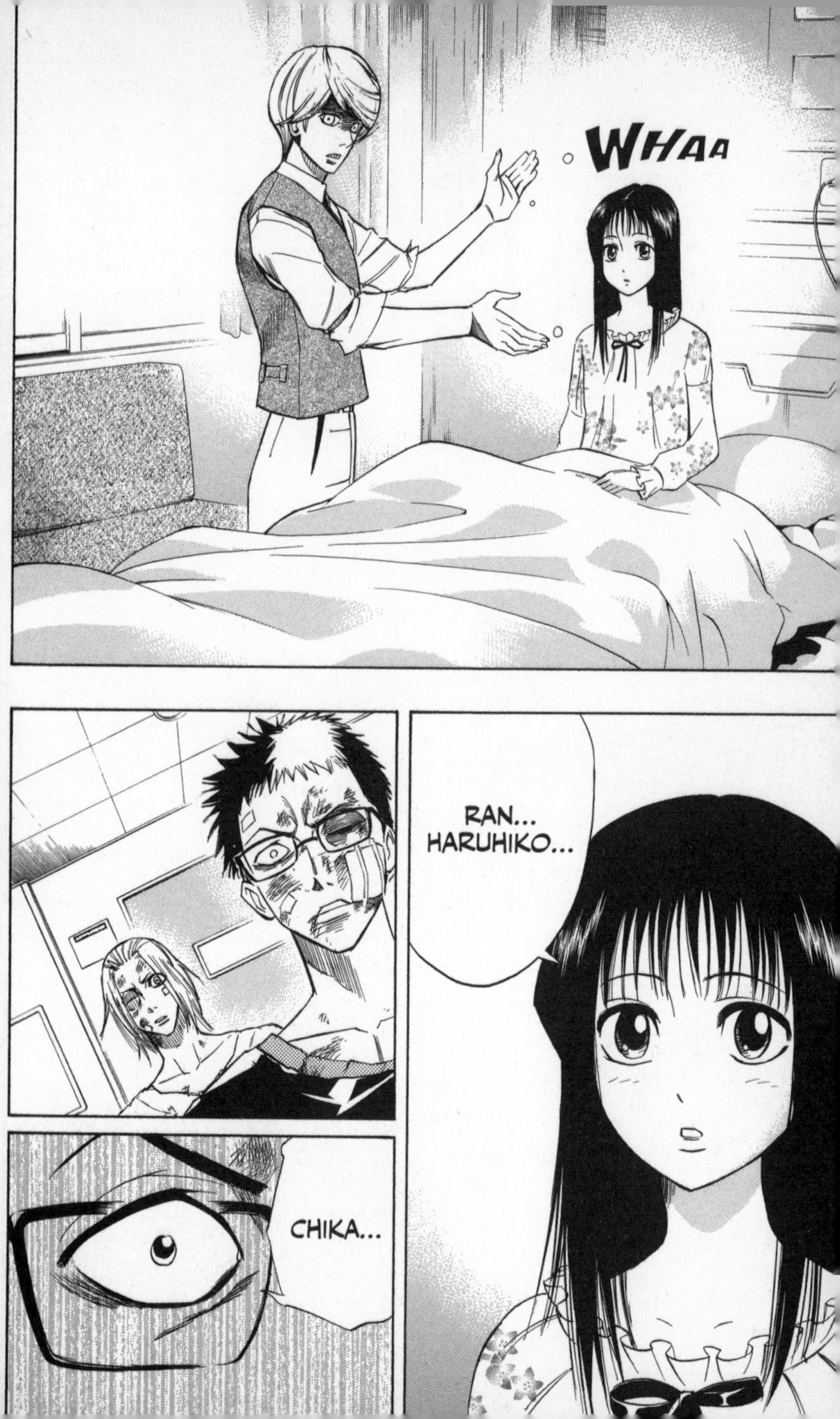
WHAA
RAN... HARUHIKO...
CHIKA...

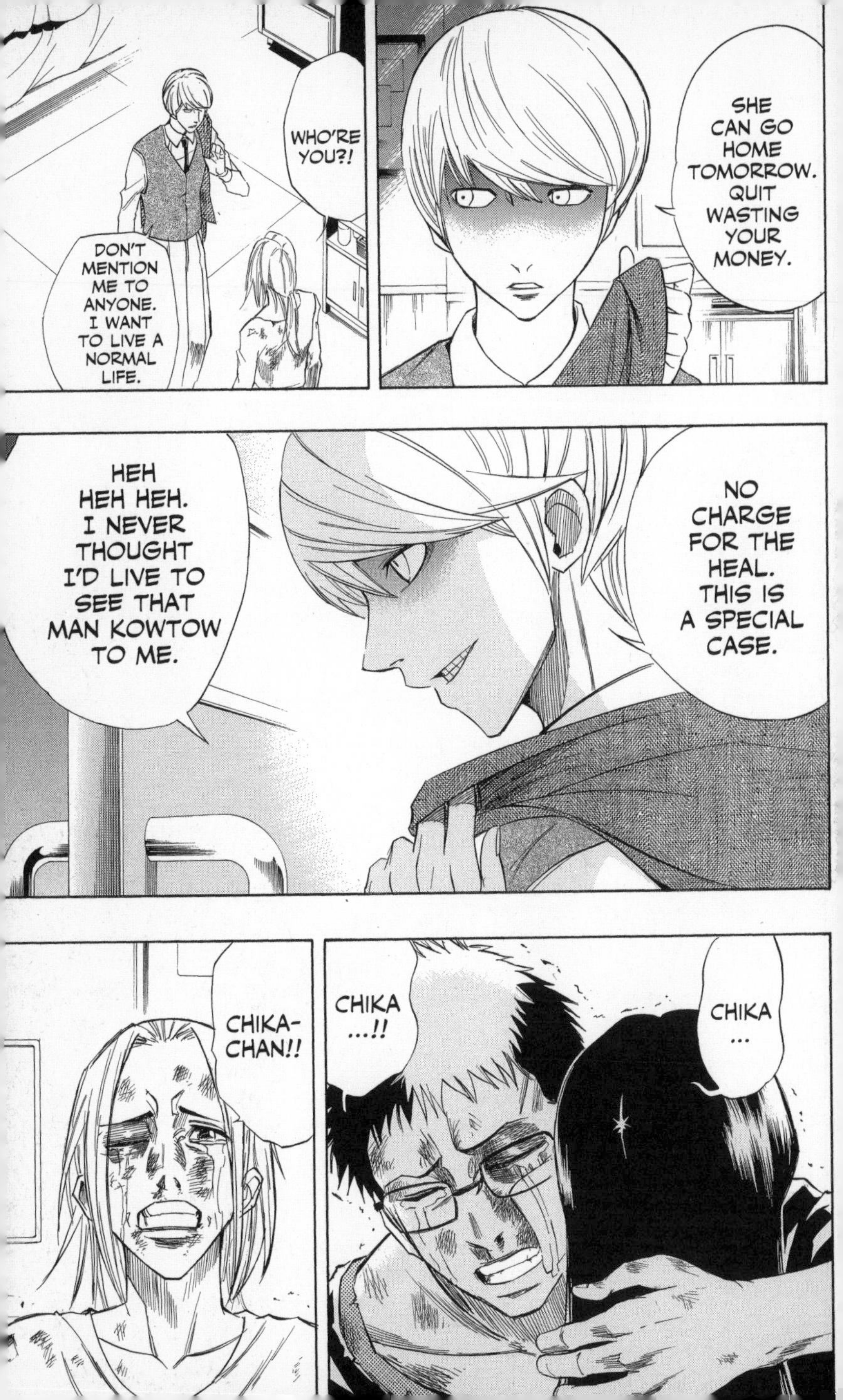
SHE CAN GO HOME TOMORROW. QUIT WASTING YOUR MONEY.
WHO'RE YOU?!
DON'T MENTION ME TO ANYONE. I WANT TO LIVE A NORMAL LIFE.
NO CHARGE FOR THE HEAL. THIS IS A SPECIAL CASE.
HEH HEH HEH. I NEVER THOUGHT I'D LIVE TO SEE THAT MAN KOWTOW TO ME.
CHIKA ...
CHIKA ...!!
CHIKA-CHAN!!

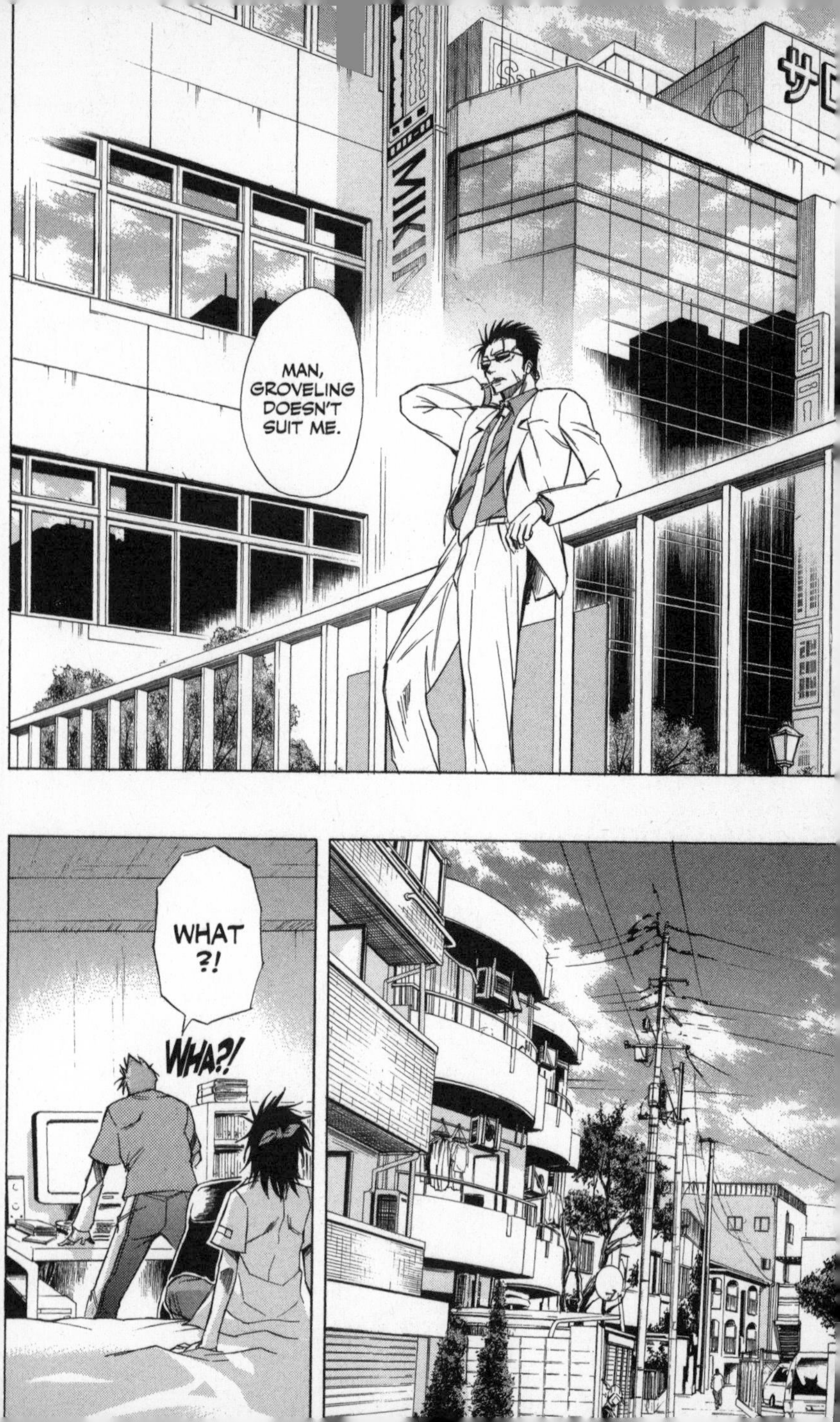
MAN, GROVELING DOESN'T SUIT ME.
WHAT ?!
WHA?!

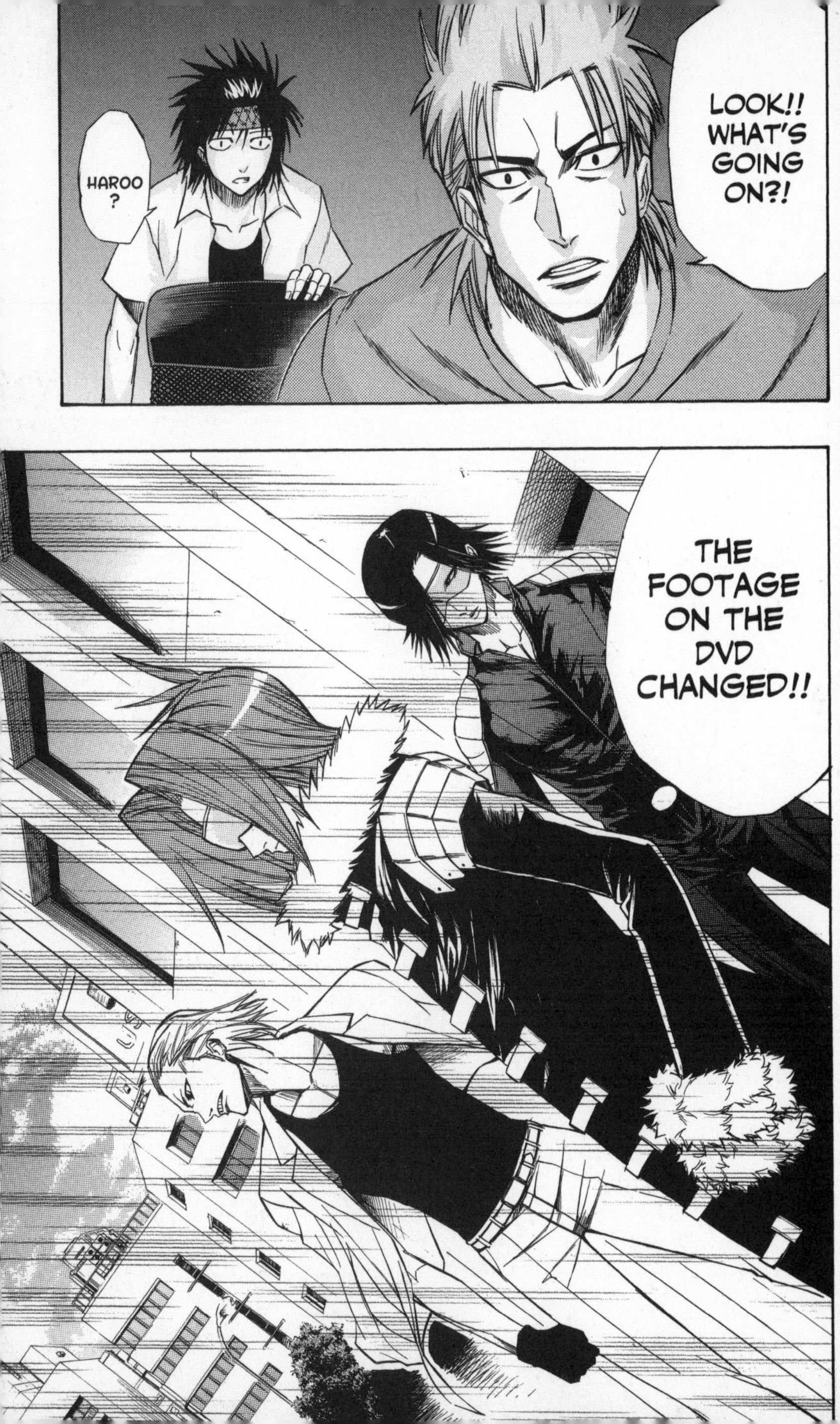
LOOK!! WHAT'S GOING ON?!
HAROO?
THE FOOTAGE ON THE DVD CHANGED!!

WE'RE AT AMAMIYA'S HOUSE...

OH, AND KAGETORA'S FINE. HE'S STRONG AS A HORSE.

HELLO... MATSURI SENSEI?

CALL.57: THE DECEMBER 2ND REVOLUTION

MID-MELBOURNE

SHMP

GIRL WHO CANCELED ALL HER PLANS AND RUSHED BACK TO JAPAN.

YOU'VE GOTTA BE KIDDING!

AW... WAS YOU WORRIED 'BOUT LIL' OL' ME?

SORRY, I FORGOT TO TELL YOU.

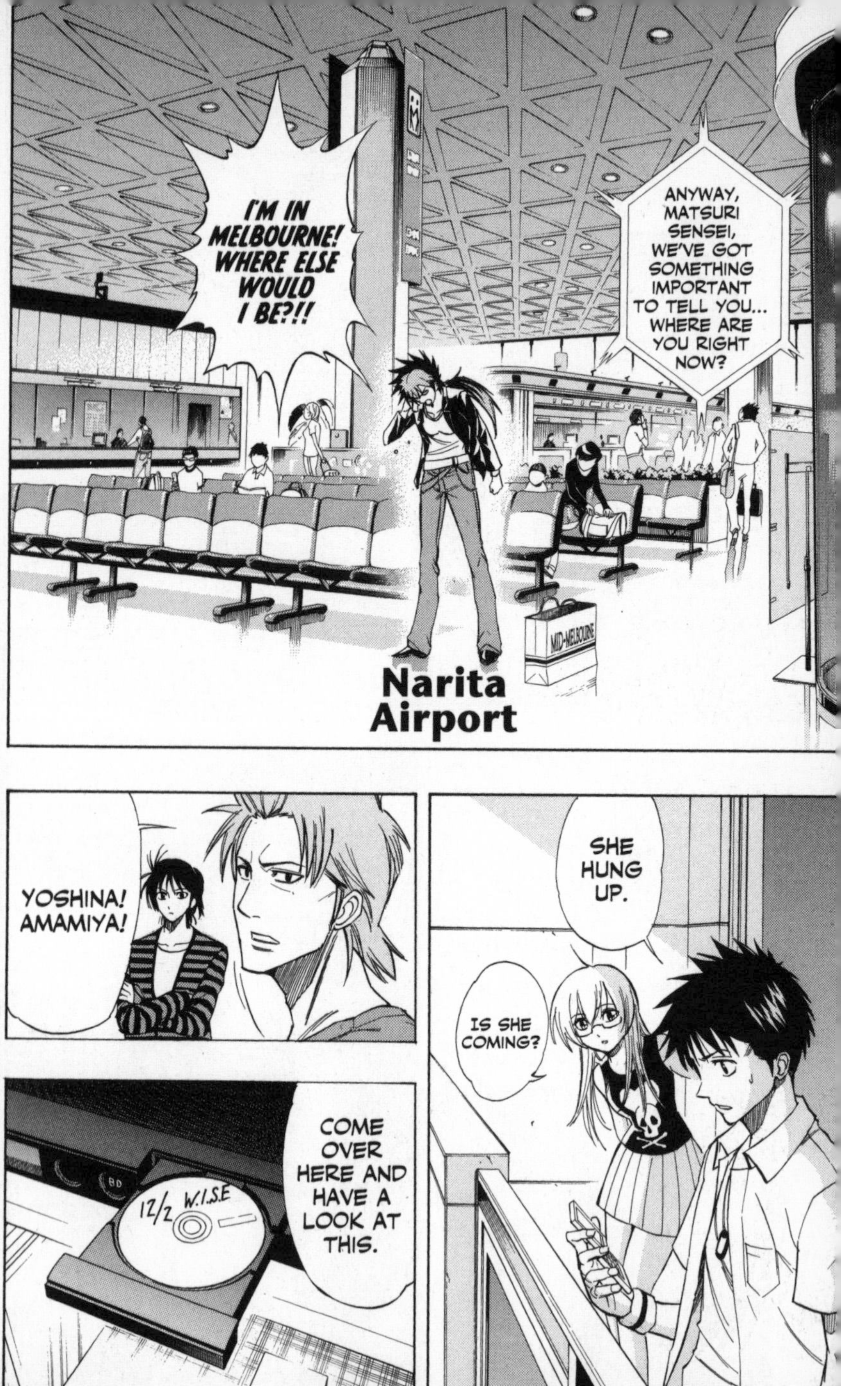
ANYWAY, MATSURI SENSEI, WE'VE GOT SOMETHING IMPORTANT TO TELL YOU... WHERE ARE YOU RIGHT NOW?
I'M IN MELBOURNE! WHERE ELSE WOULD I BE?!!
MID-MELBOURNE
Narita Airport
SHE HUNG UP.
IS SHE COMING?
YOSHINA! AMAMIYA!
COME OVER HERE AND HAVE A LOOK AT THIS.
12/2 W.I.S.E
BD

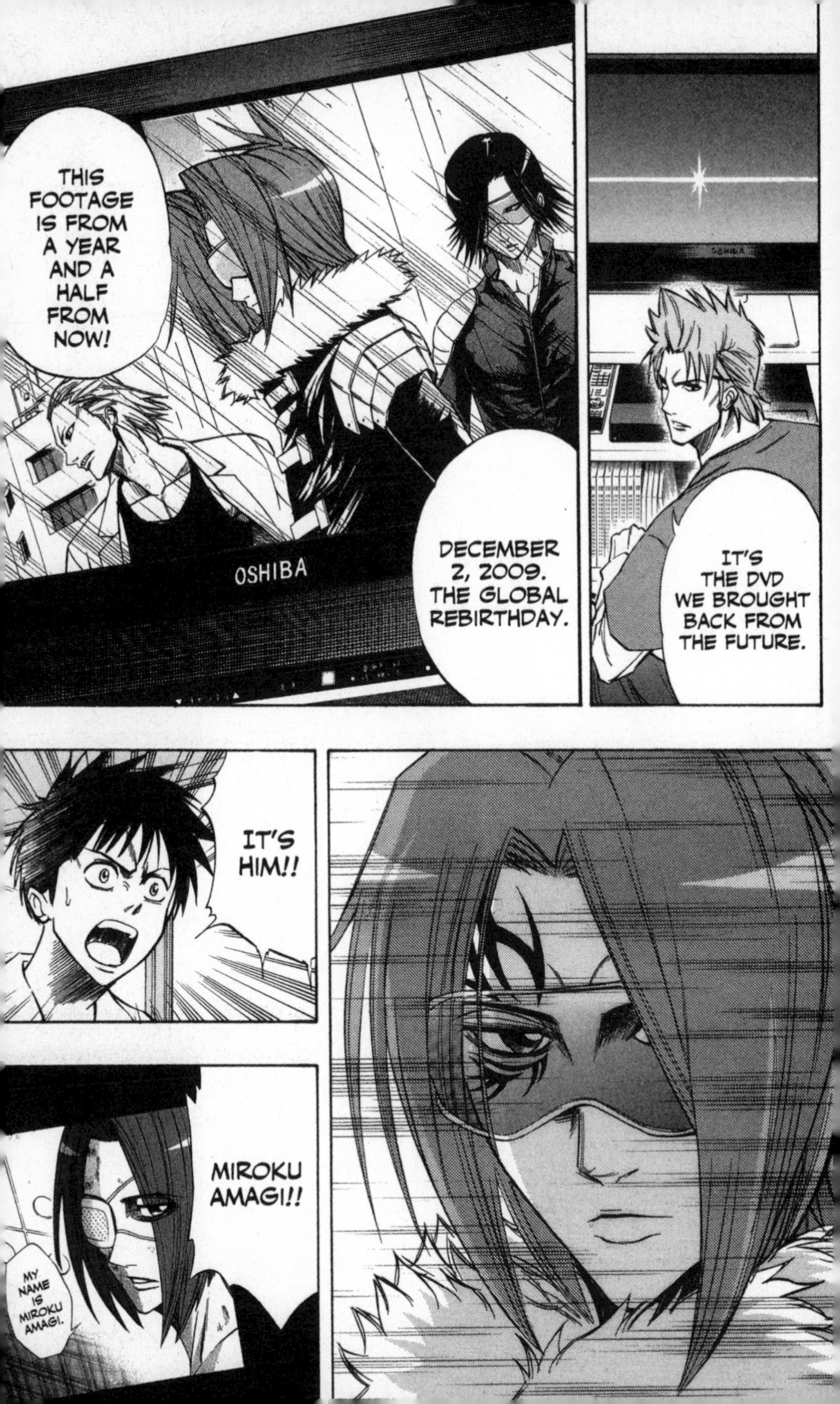
IT'S THE DVD WE BROUGHT BACK FROM THE FUTURE.
DECEMBER 2, 2009. THE GLOBAL REBIRTHDAY.
THIS FOOTAGE IS FROM A YEAR AND A HALF FROM NOW!
OSHIBA
IT'S HIM!!
MIROKU AMAGI!!
MY NAME IS MIROKU AMAGI.

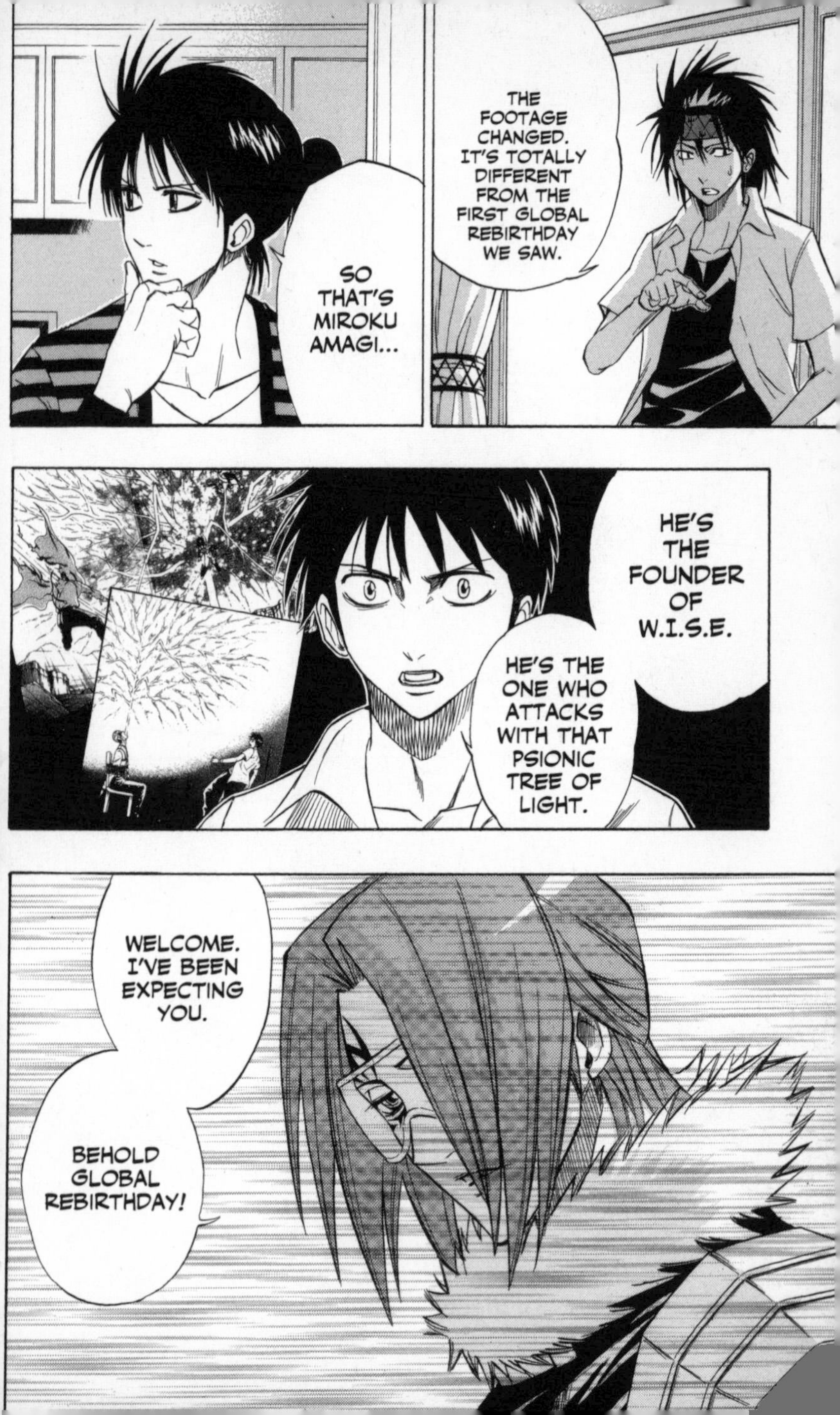
THE FOOTAGE CHANGED. IT'S TOTALLY DIFFERENT FROM THE FIRST GLOBAL REBIRTHDAY WE SAW.
SO THAT'S MIROKU AMAGI...
HE'S THE FOUNDER OF W.I.S.E.
HE'S THE ONE WHO ATTACKS WITH THAT PSIONIC TREE OF LIGHT.
WELCOME. I'VE BEEN EXPECTING YOU.
BEHOLD GLOBAL REBIRTHDAY!

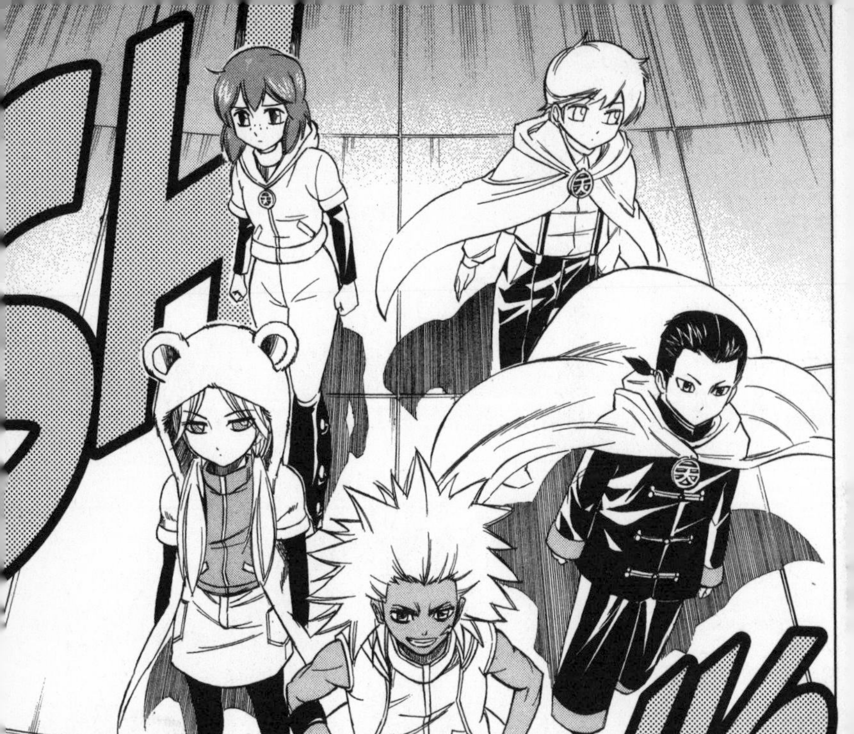

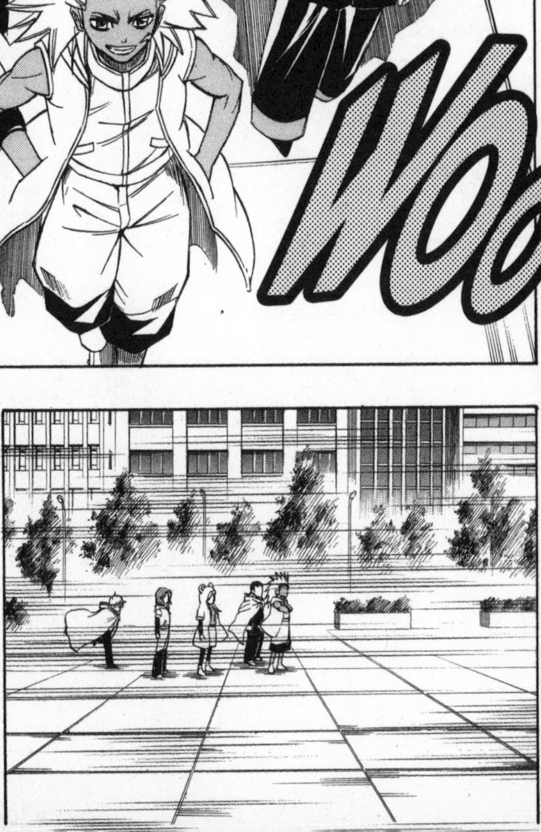

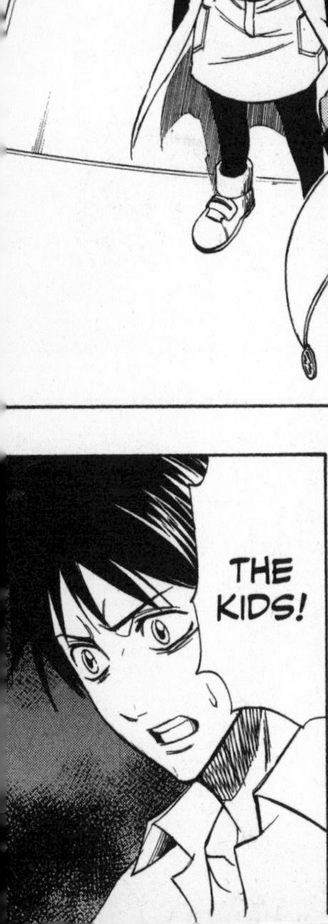
THE KIDS!

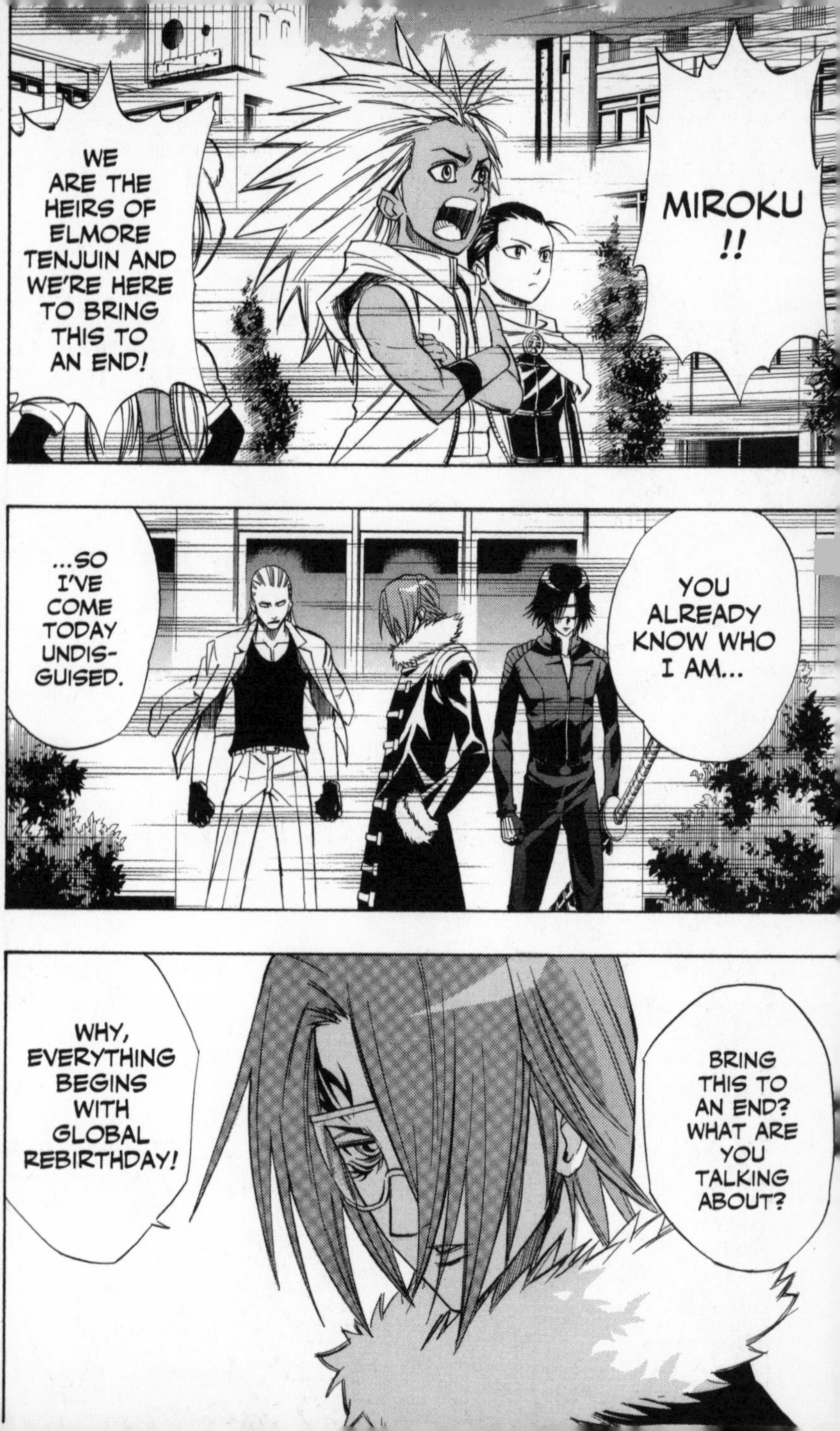
MIROKU!!
WE ARE THE HEIRS OF ELMORE TENJUIN AND WE'RE HERE TO BRING THIS TO AN END!
YOU ALREADY KNOW WHO I AM...
...SO I'VE COME TODAY UNDIS-GUISED.
BRING THIS TO AN END? WHAT ARE YOU TALKING ABOUT?
WHY, EVERYTHING BEGINS WITH GLOBAL REBIRTHDAY!

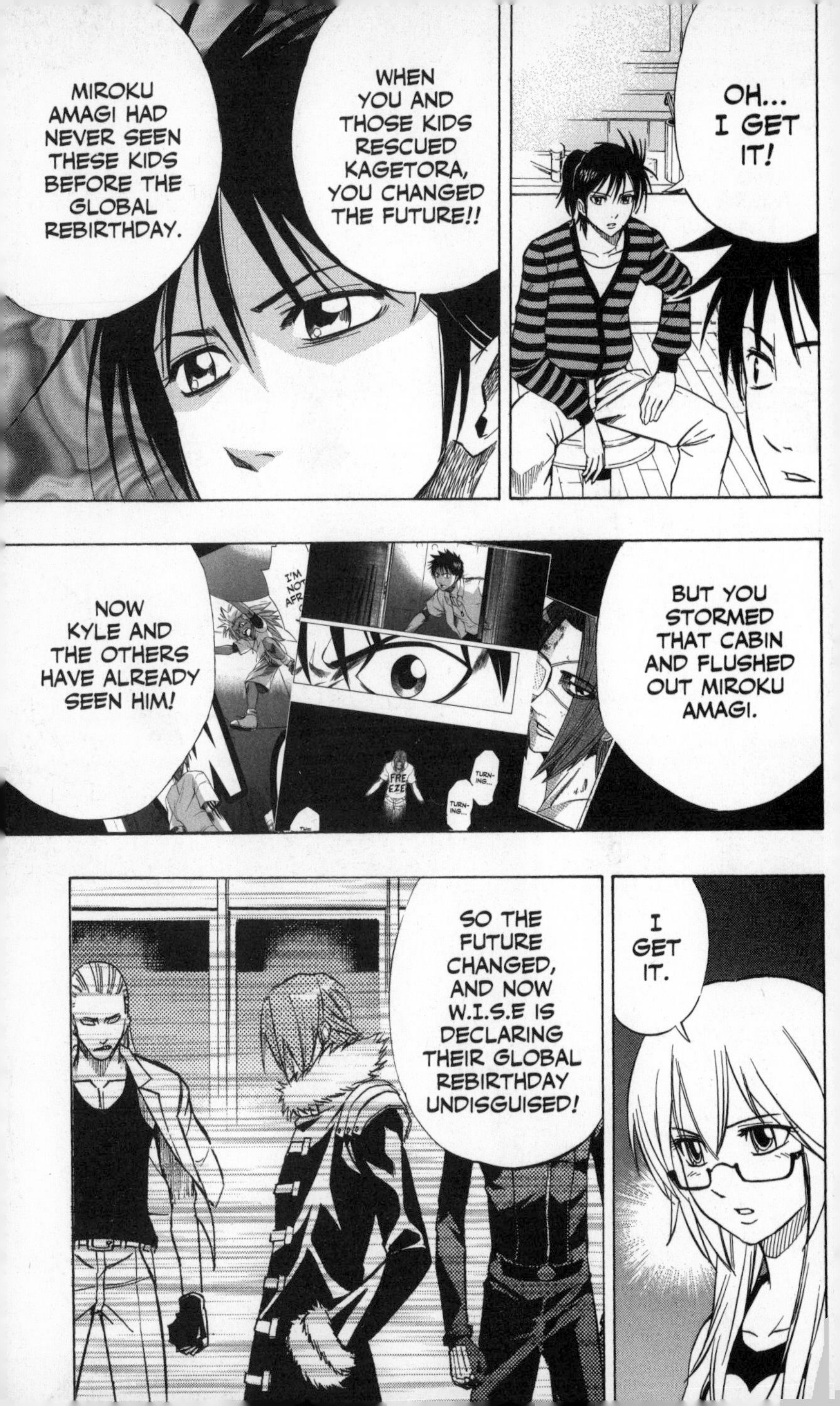

OH... I GET IT!
WHEN YOU AND THOSE KIDS RESCUED KAGETORA, YOU CHANGED THE FUTURE!!
MIROKU AMAGI HAD NEVER SEEN THESE KIDS BEFORE THE GLOBAL REBIRTHDAY.
BUT YOU STORMED THAT CABIN AND FLUSHED OUT MIROKU AMAGI.
TURNING...
TURNING...
NOW KYLE AND THE OTHERS HAVE ALREADY SEEN HIM!
I GET IT.
SO THE FUTURE CHANGED, AND NOW W.I.S.E IS DECLARING THEIR GLOBAL REBIRTHDAY UNDISGUISED!

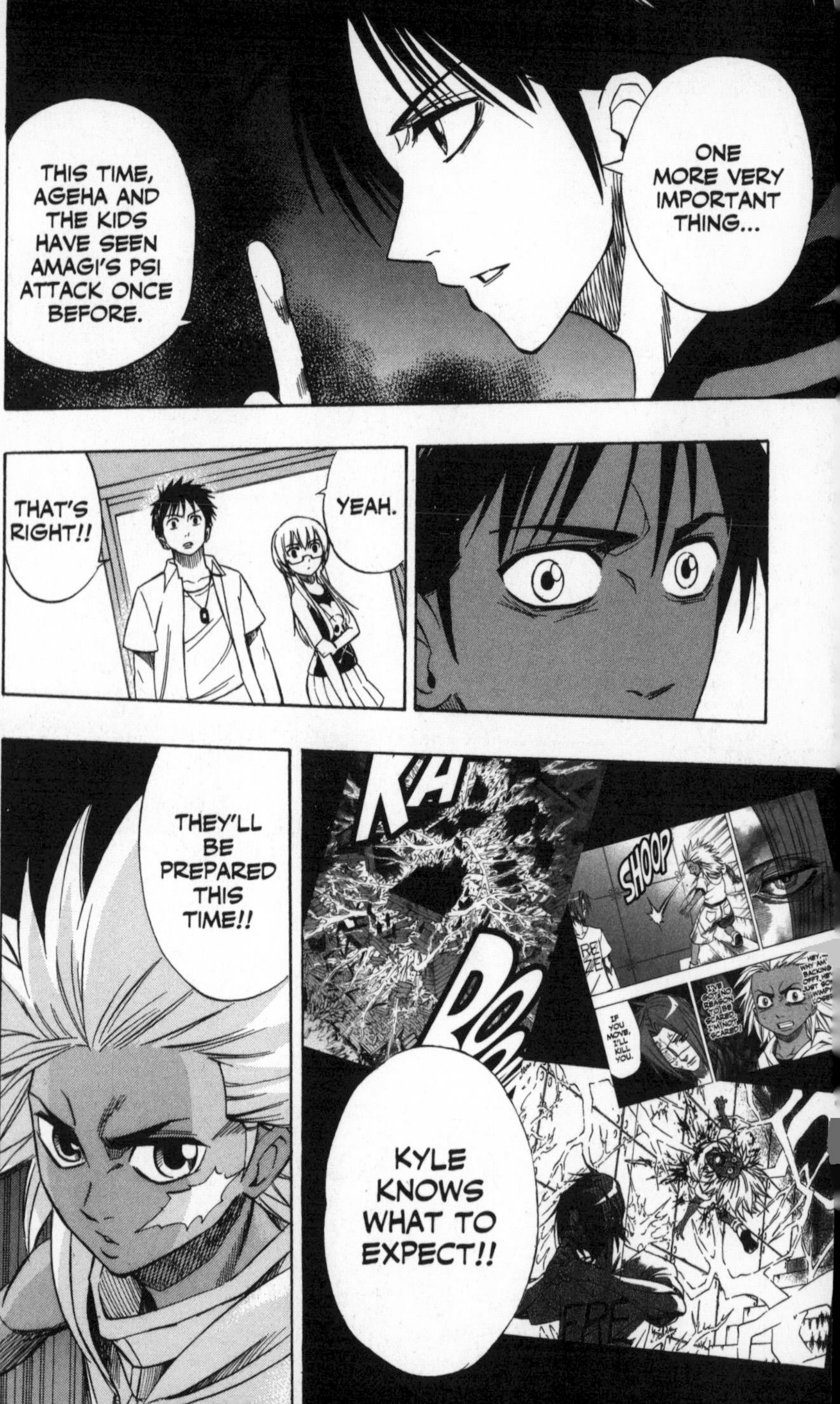
ONE MORE VERY IMPORTANT THING...
THIS TIME, AGEHA AND THE KIDS HAVE SEEN AMAGI'S PSI ATTACK ONCE BEFORE.
YEAH.
THAT'S RIGHT!!
SHOOP
I'VE GOT NO REASON TO BE SCARED. I'M NOT SCARED!
IF YOU MOVE, I'LL KILL YOU.
KYLE KNOWS WHAT TO EXPECT!!
THEY'LL BE PREPARED THIS TIME!!

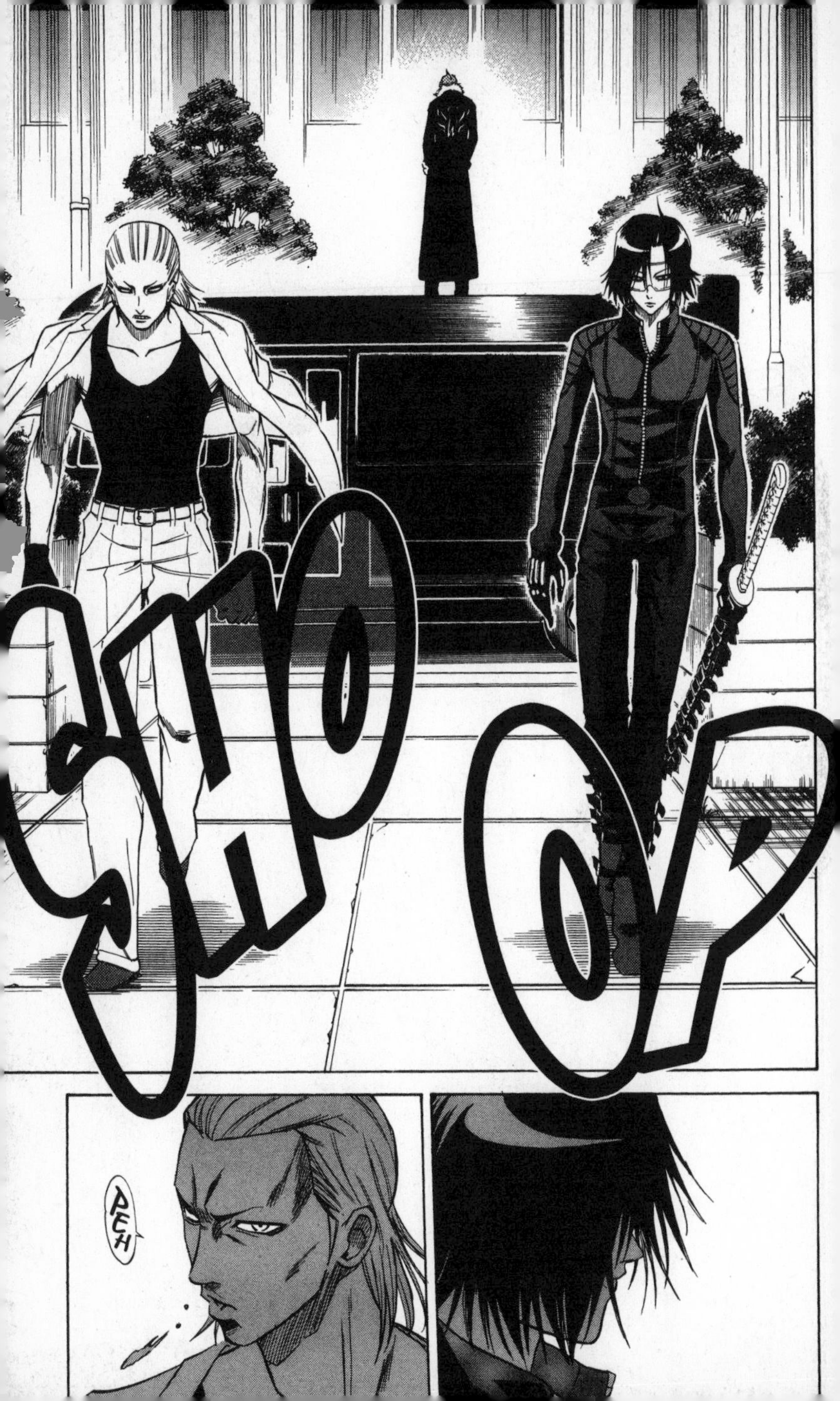
SHOOP
PECH

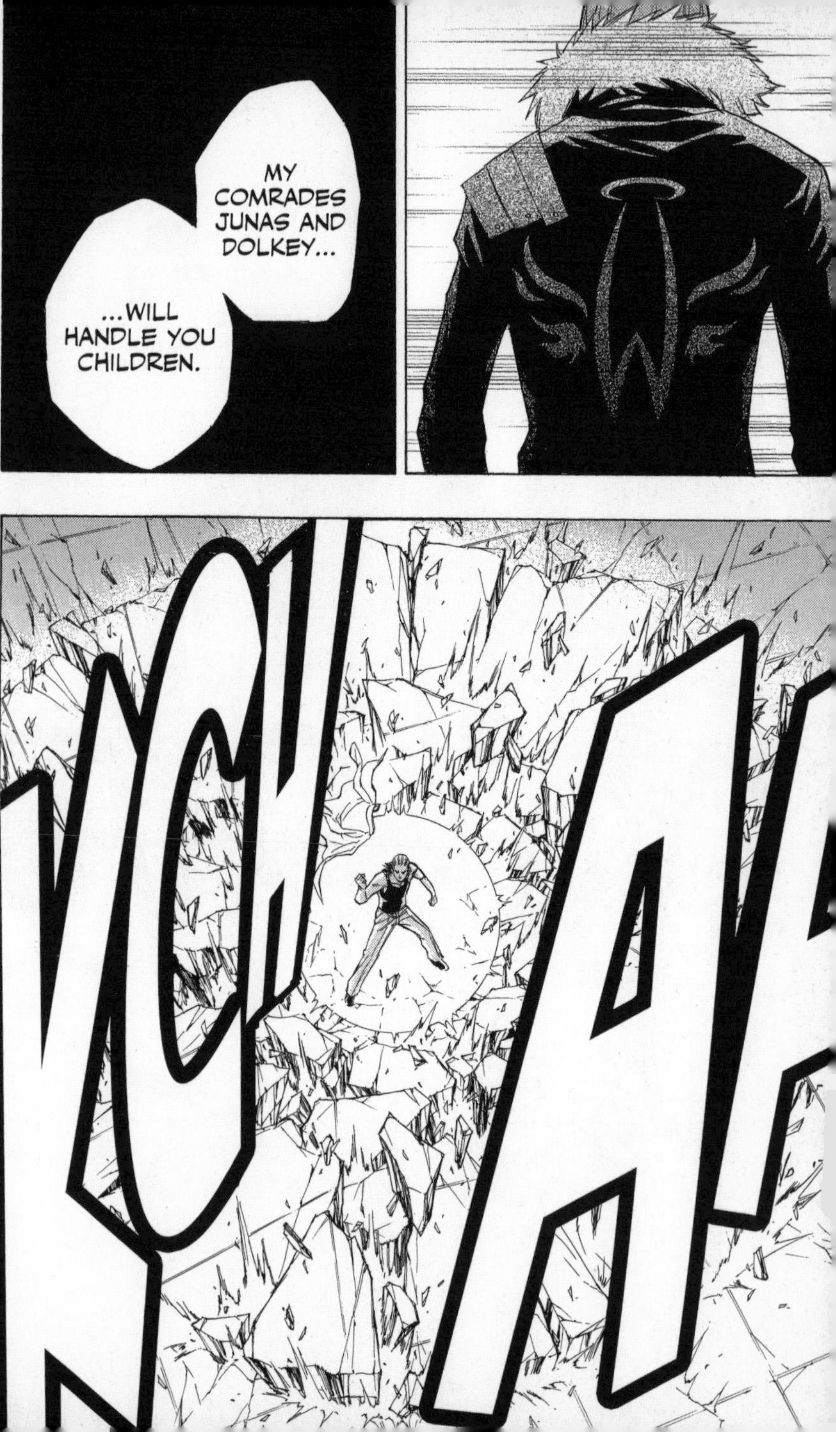
MY COMRADES JUNAS AND DOLKEY...
...WILL HANDLE YOU CHILDREN.

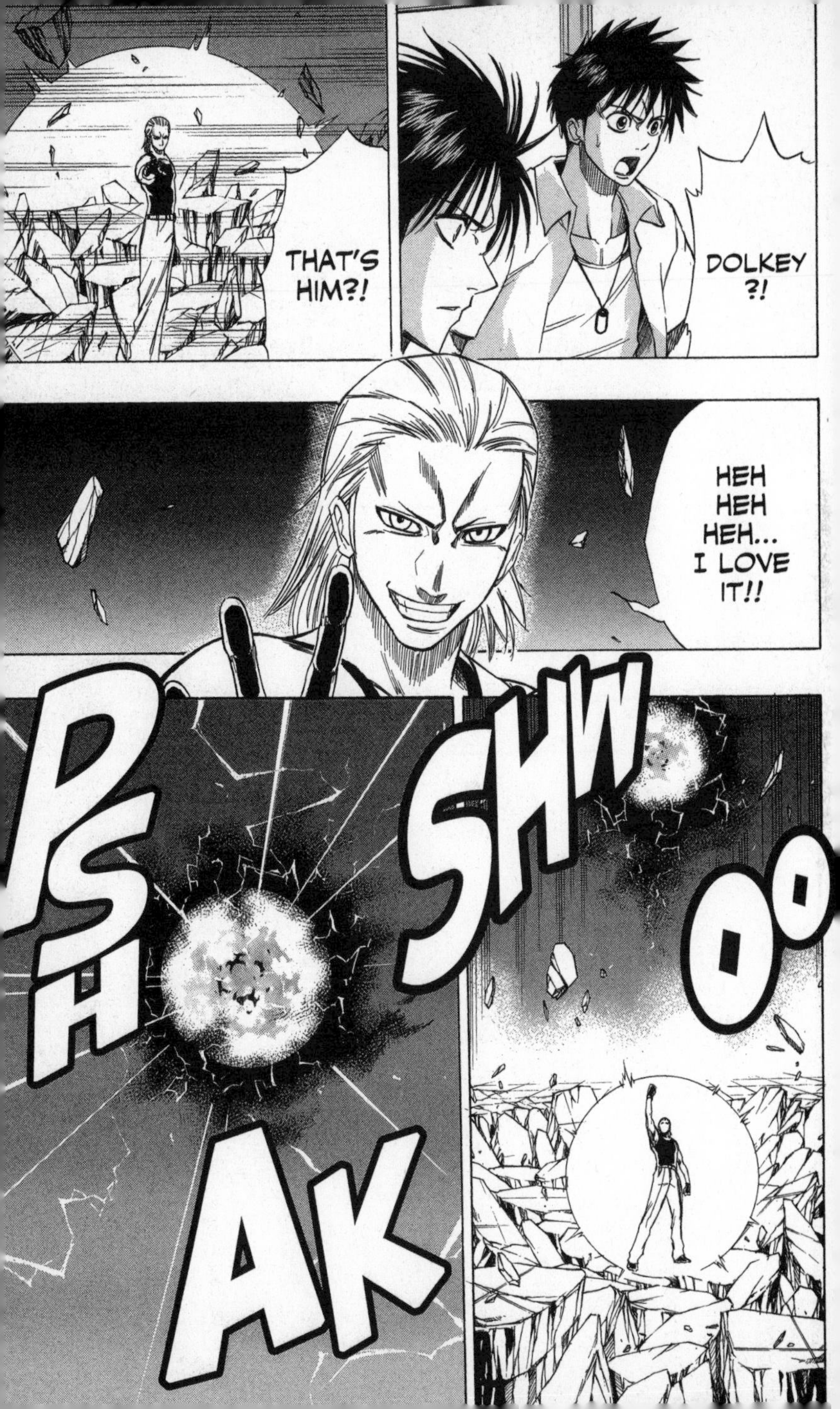
DOLKEY ?!
THAT'S HIM?!
HEH HEH HEH... I LOVE IT!!
SHWOO
PSHAK

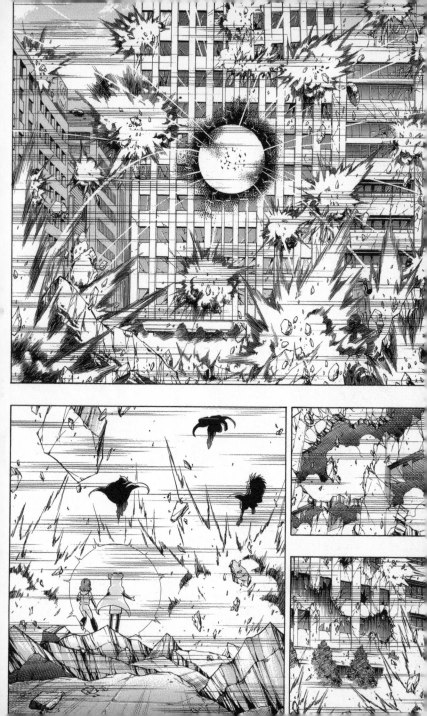

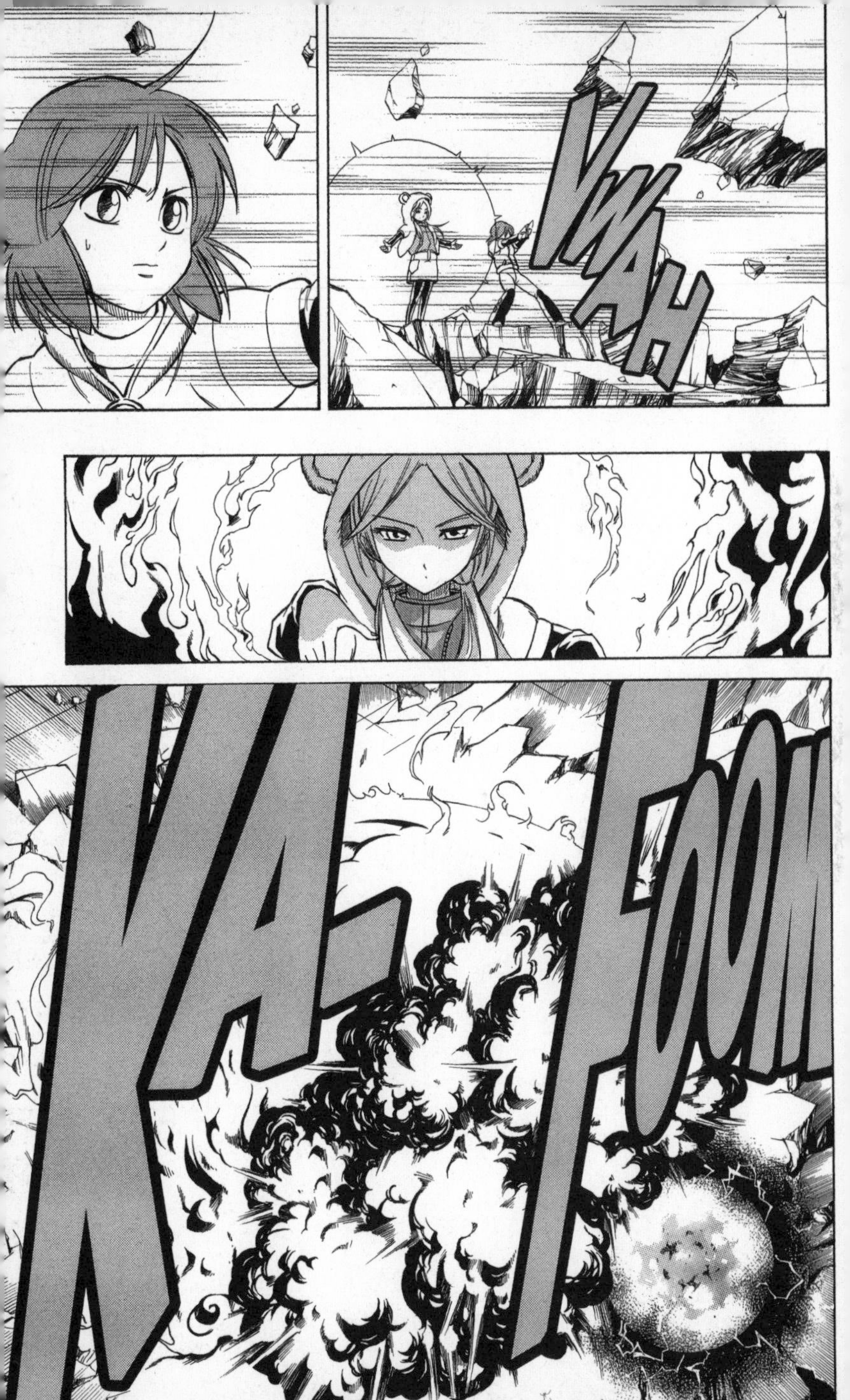

VWAH
KA-FOOM

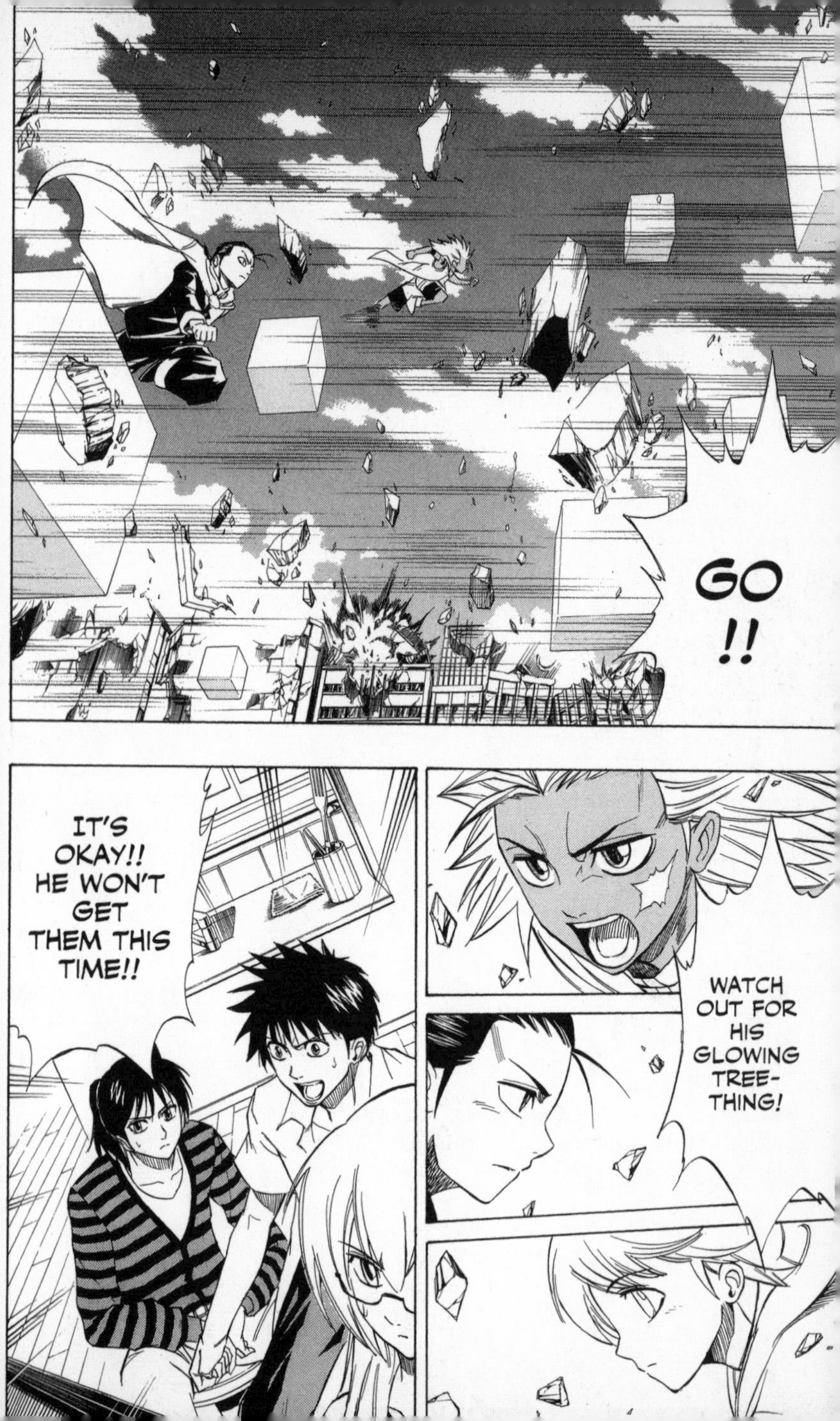
GO !!
WATCH OUT FOR HIS GLOWING TREE-THING!
IT'S OKAY!! HE WON'T GET THEM THIS TIME!!

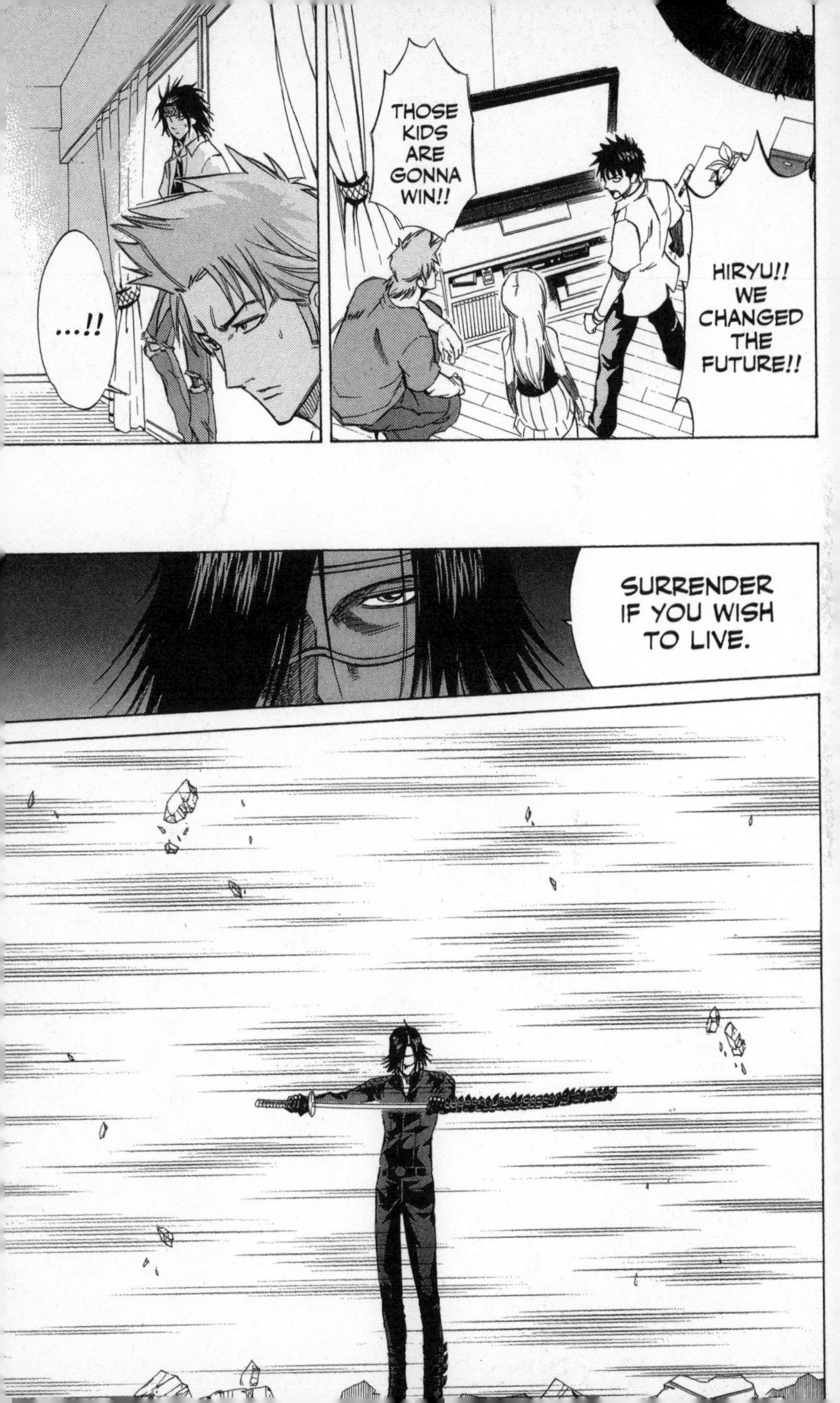
HIRYU!! WE CHANGED THE FUTURE!!
THOSE KIDS ARE GONNA WIN!!
...!!
SURRENDER IF YOU WISH TO LIVE.

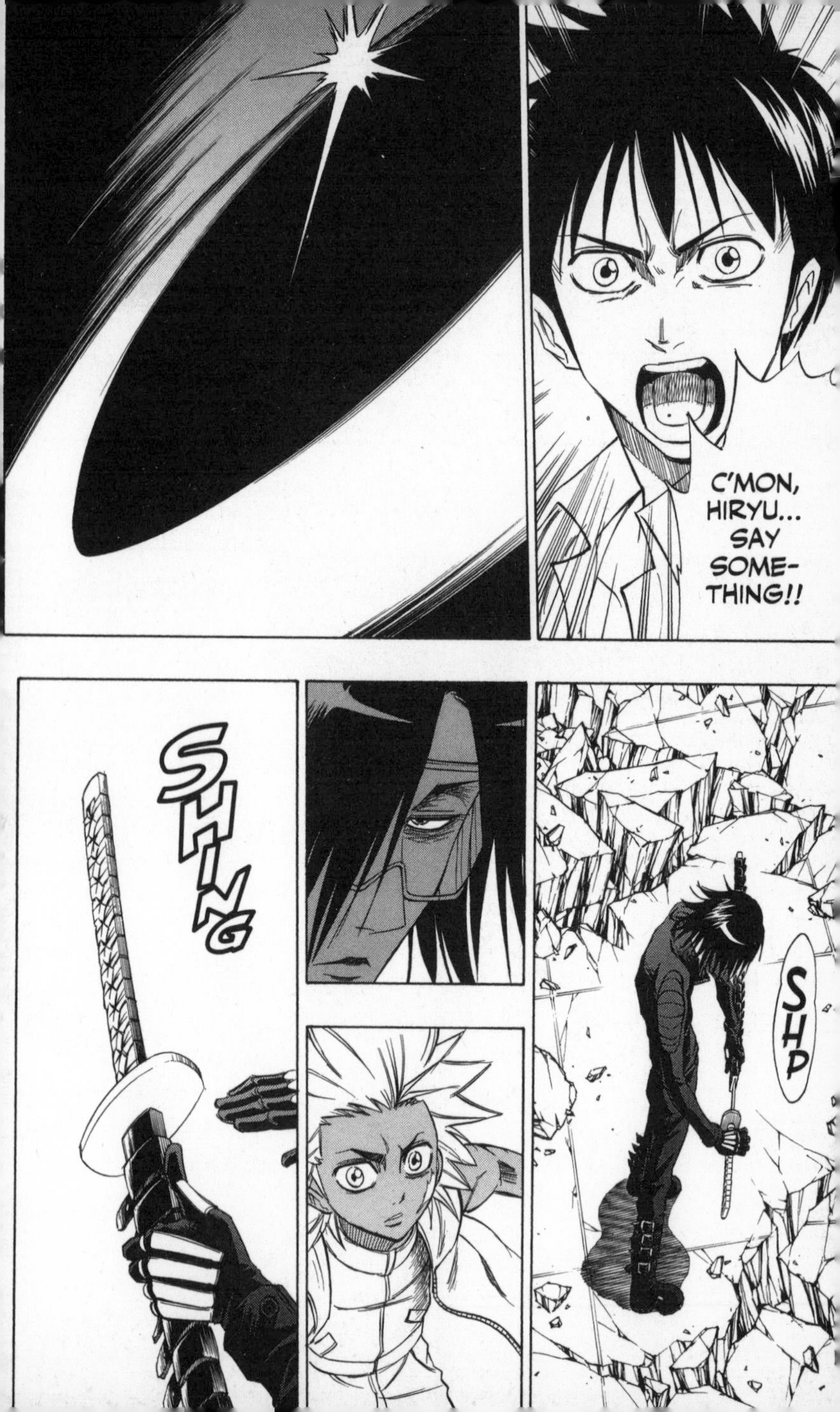
C'MON, HIRYU... SAY SOME-THING!!
SHP
SHING

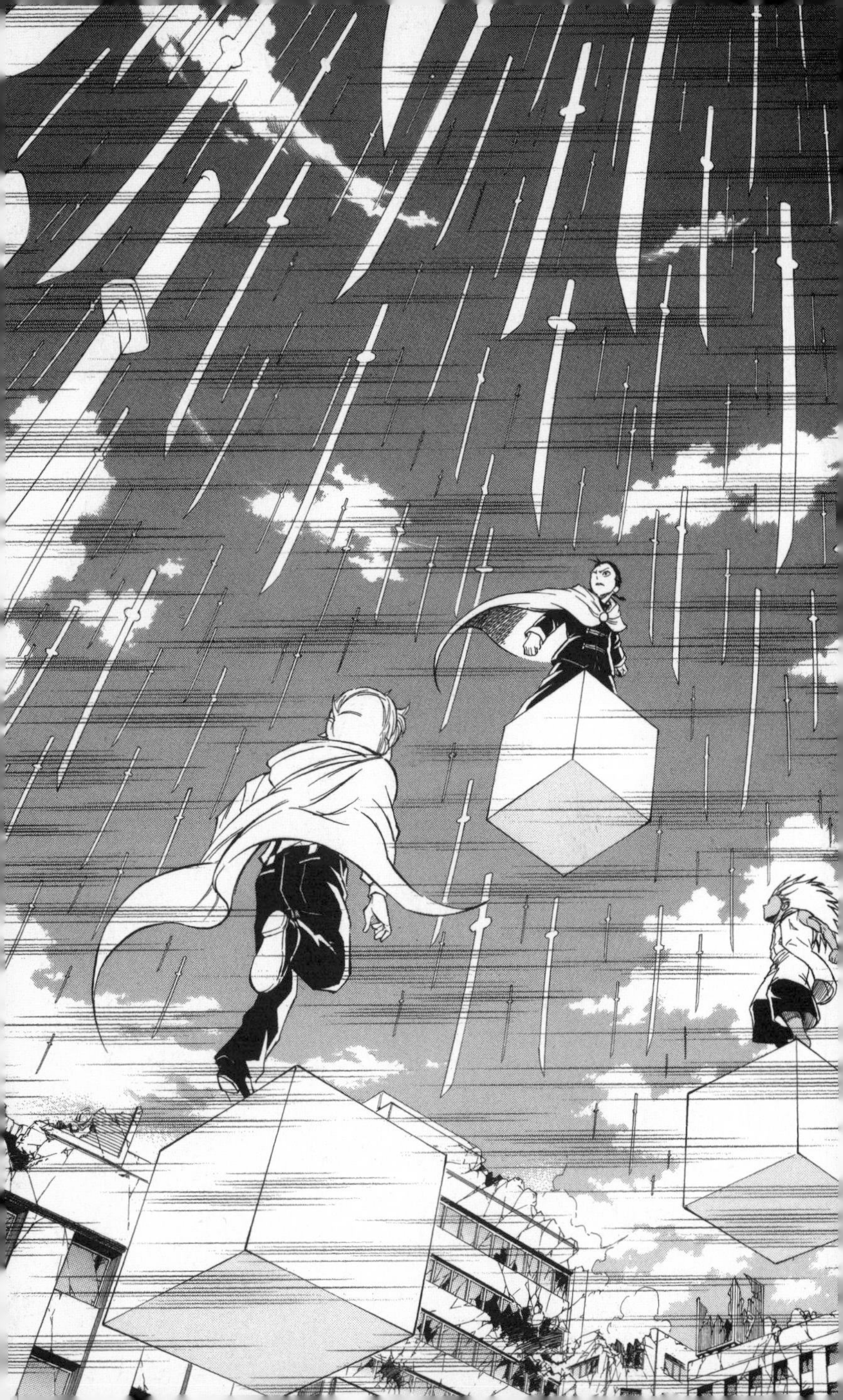

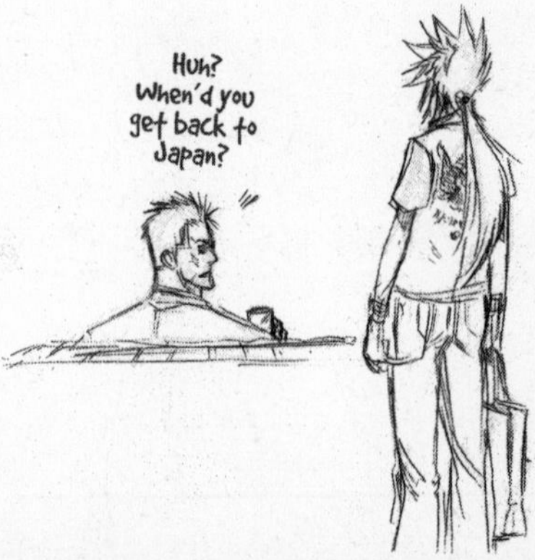
Huh? When'd you get back to Japan?

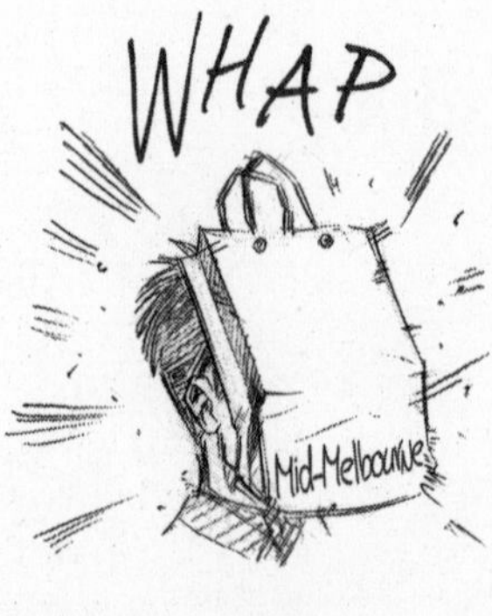
WHAP
Mid-Melbourne

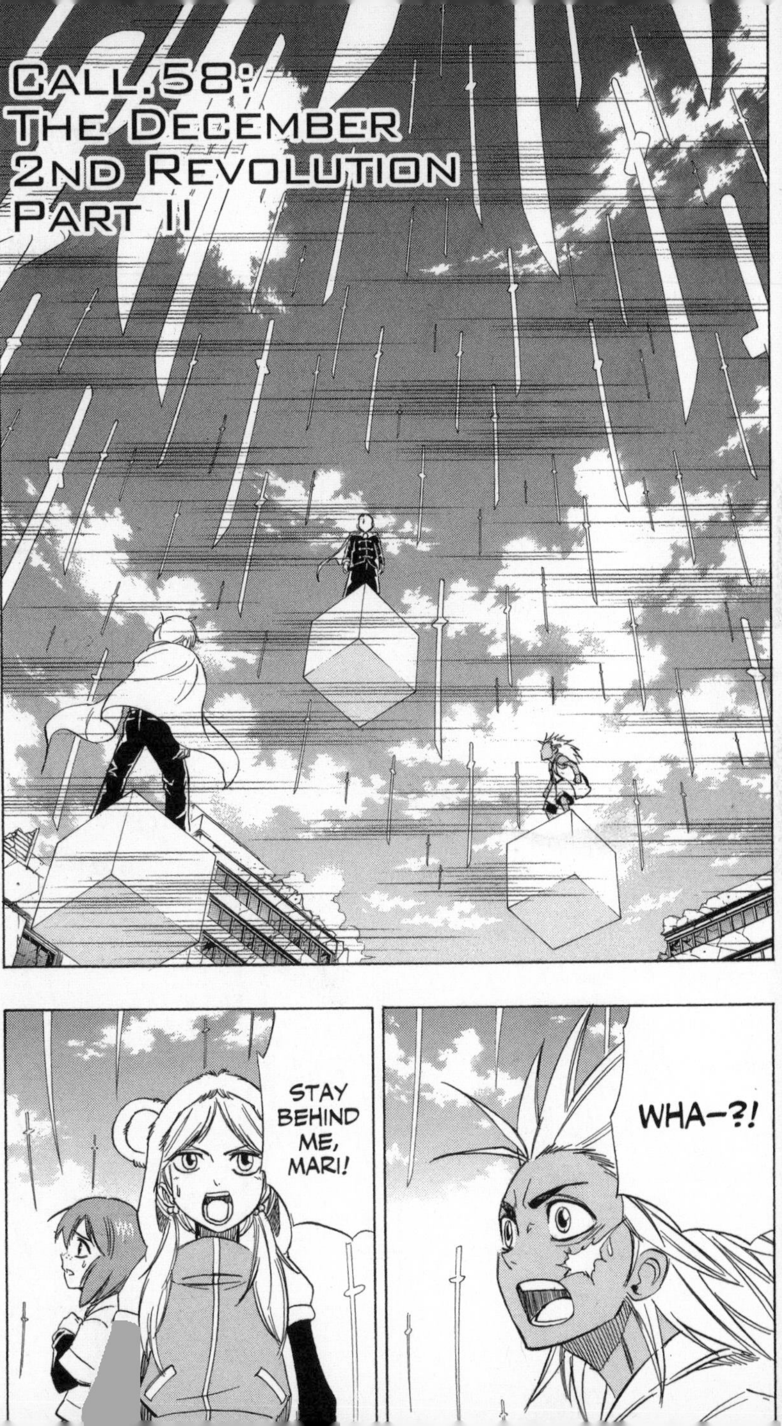
CALL.58:
THE DECEMBER 2ND REVOLUTION PART II
WHA-?!
STAY BEHIND ME, MARI!

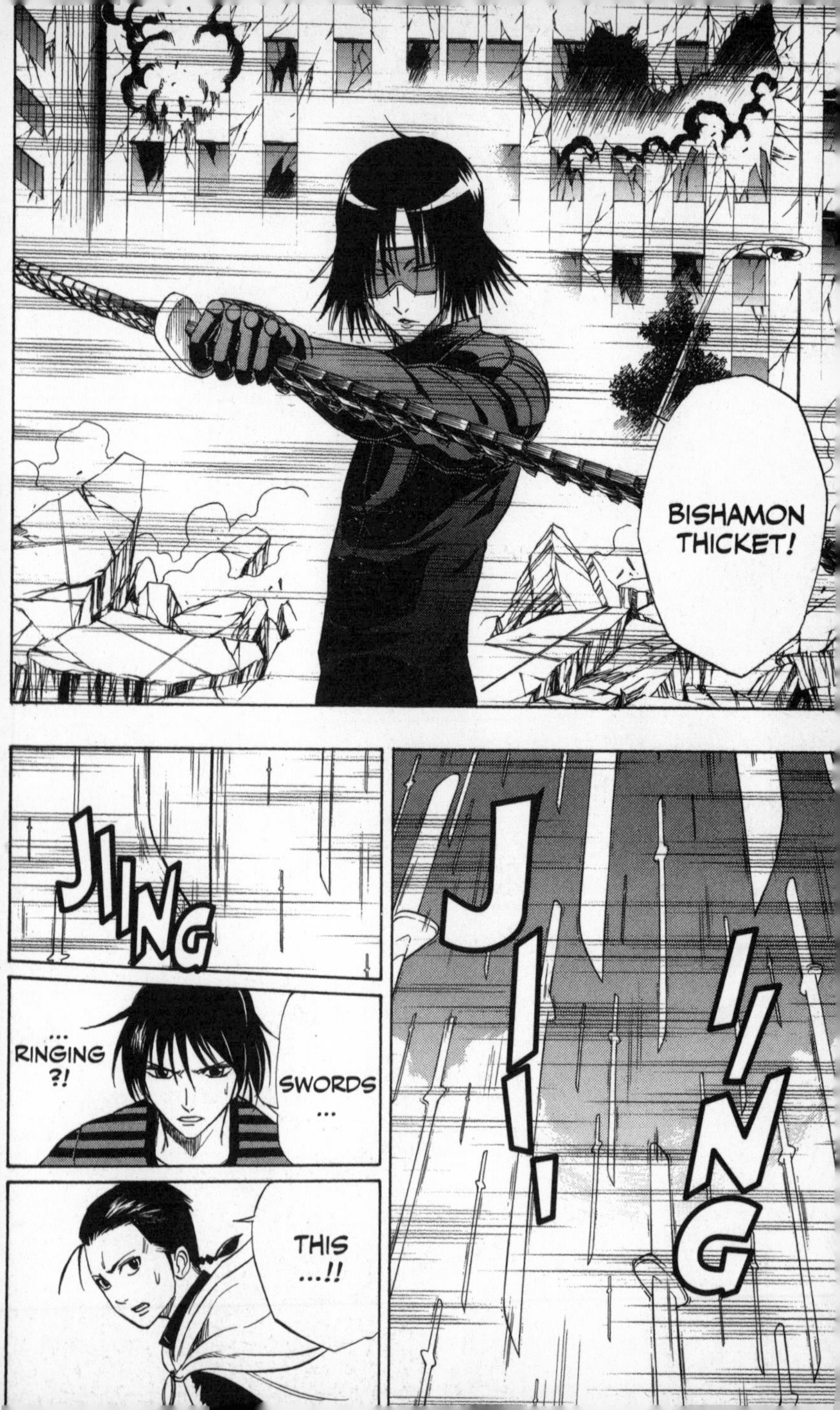
BISHAMON THICKET!
JI...IING
JING
SWORDS ...
... RINGING ?!
THIS ...!!

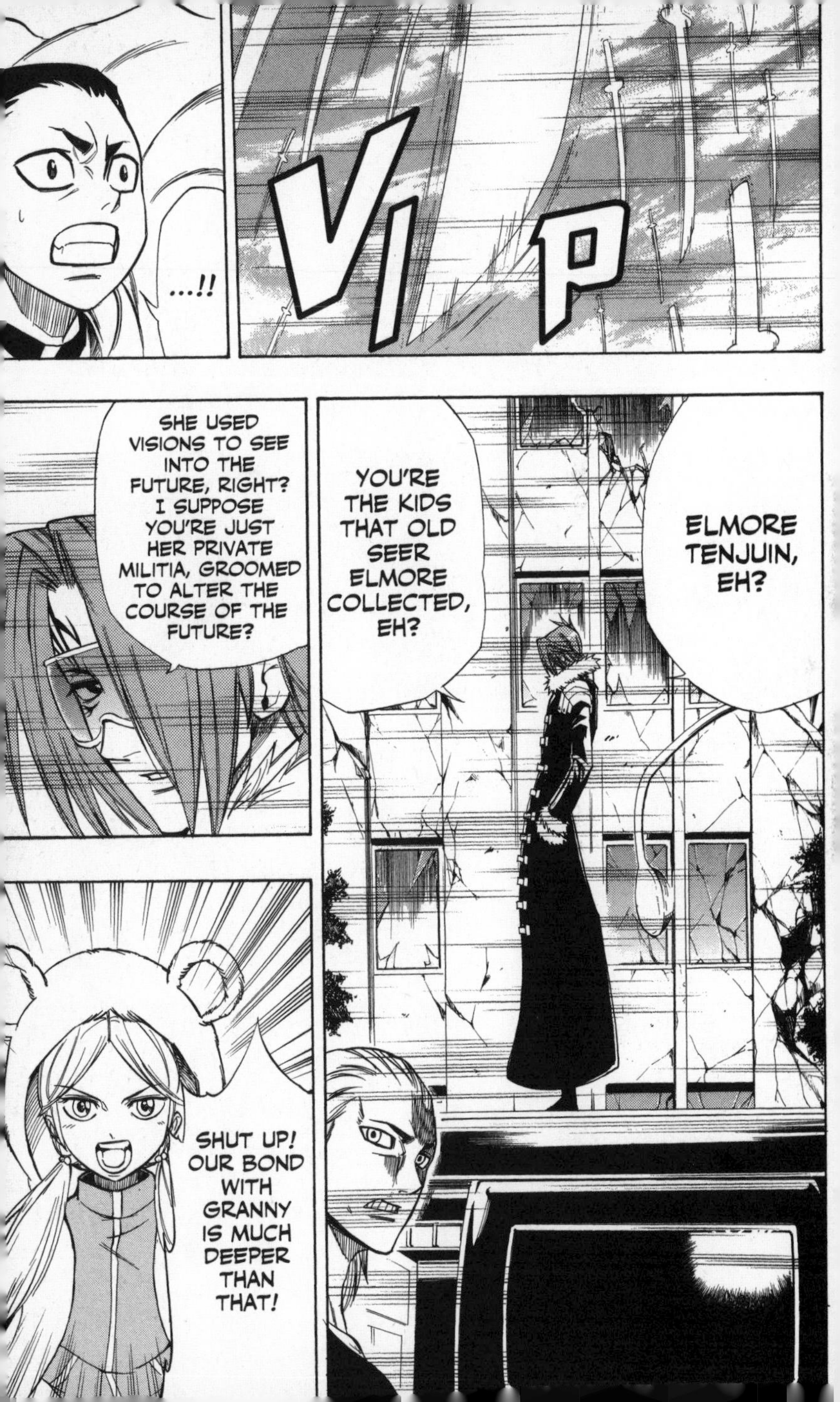
VIP
...!!
ELMORE TENJUIN, EH?
YOU'RE THE KIDS THAT OLD SEER ELMORE COLLECTED, EH?
SHE USED VISIONS TO SEE INTO THE FUTURE, RIGHT? I SUPPOSE YOU'RE JUST HER PRIVATE MILITIA, GROOMED TO ALTER THE COURSE OF THE FUTURE?
SHUT UP! OUR BOND WITH GRANNY IS MUCH DEEPER THAN THAT!

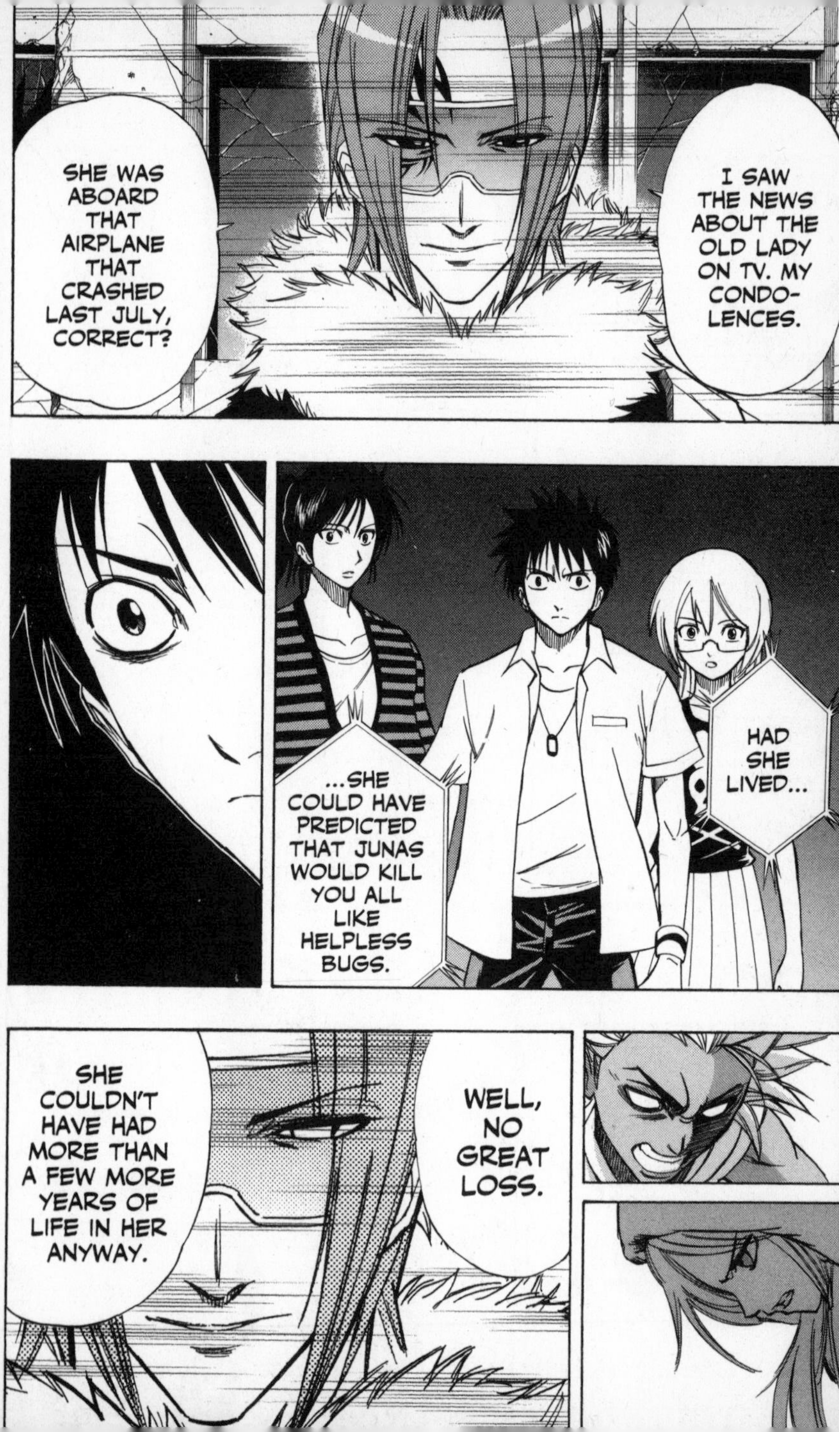

I SAW THE NEWS ABOUT THE OLD LADY ON TV. MY CONDO-LENCES.
SHE WAS ABOARD THAT AIRPLANE THAT CRASHED LAST JULY, CORRECT?
HAD SHE LIVED...
...SHE COULD HAVE PREDICTED THAT JUNAS WOULD KILL YOU ALL LIKE HELPLESS BUGS.
WELL, NO GREAT LOSS.
SHE COULDN'T HAVE HAD MORE THAN A FEW MORE YEARS OF LIFE IN HER ANYWAY.

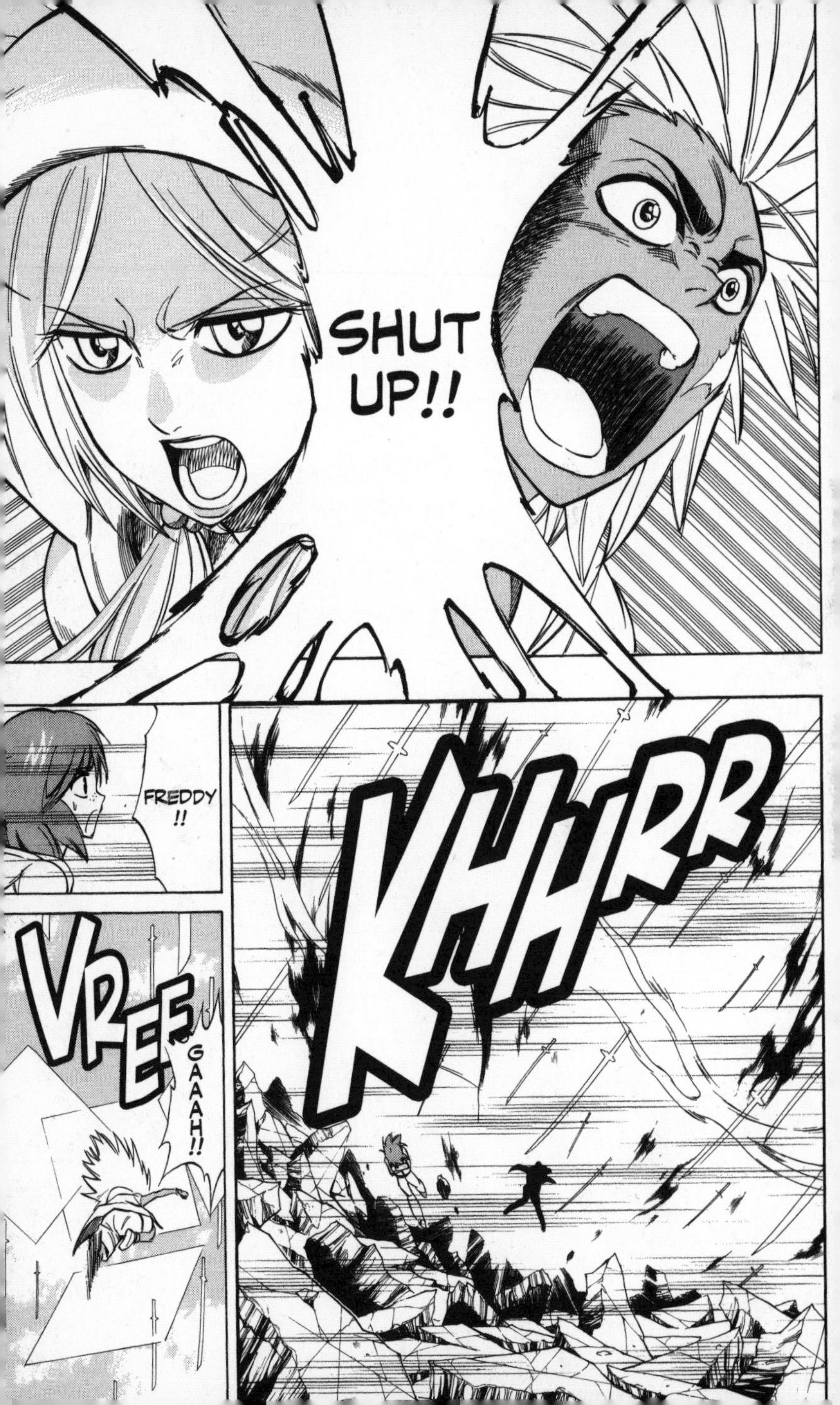
SHUT UP!!
KHHRR
FREDDY !!
VREEE
GAAAH!!

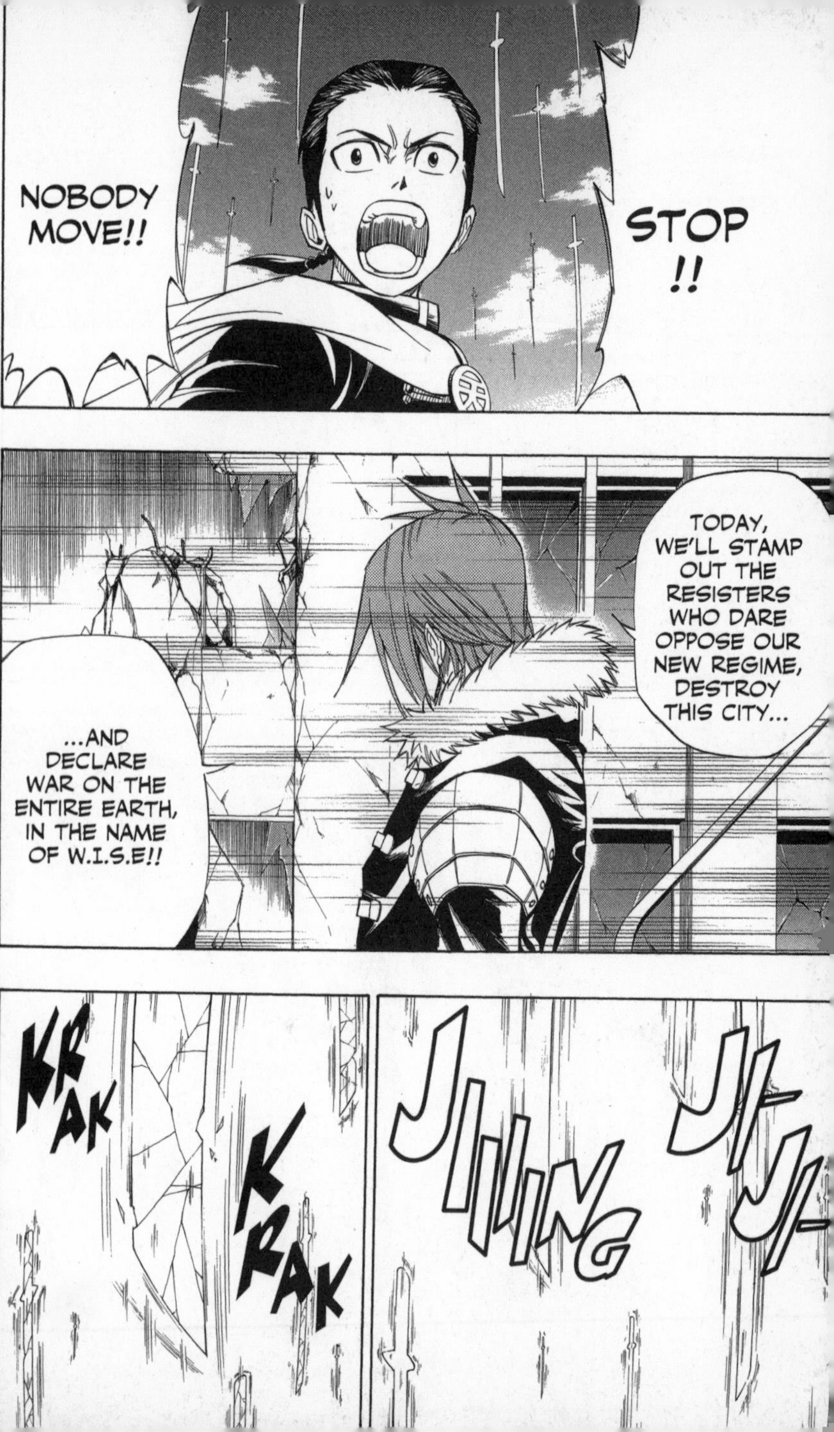
STOP !!
NOBODY MOVE!!
TODAY, WE'LL STAMP OUT THE RESISTERS WHO DARE OPPOSE OUR NEW REGIME, DESTROY THIS CITY...
...AND DECLARE WAR ON THE ENTIRE EARTH, IN THE NAME OF W.I.S.E!!
JIIIING
JI-JI-
KRAK
KRAK

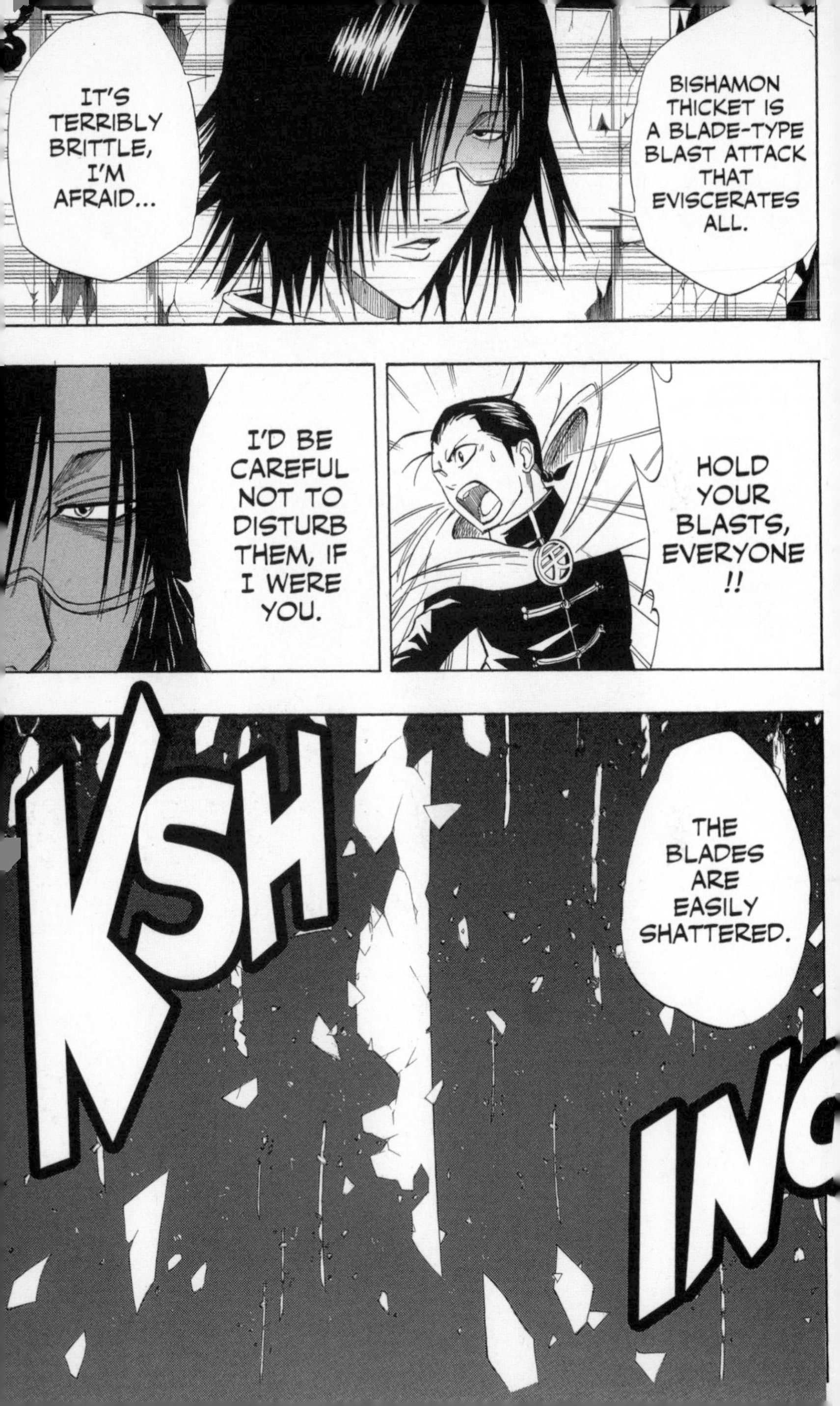
BISHAMON THICKET IS A BLADE-TYPE BLAST ATTACK THAT EVISCERATES ALL.
IT'S TERRIBLY BRITTLE, I'M AFRAID...
HOLD YOUR BLASTS, EVERYONE !!
I'D BE CAREFUL NOT TO DISTURB THEM, IF I WERE YOU.
THE BLADES ARE EASILY SHATTERED.
KSH
IN

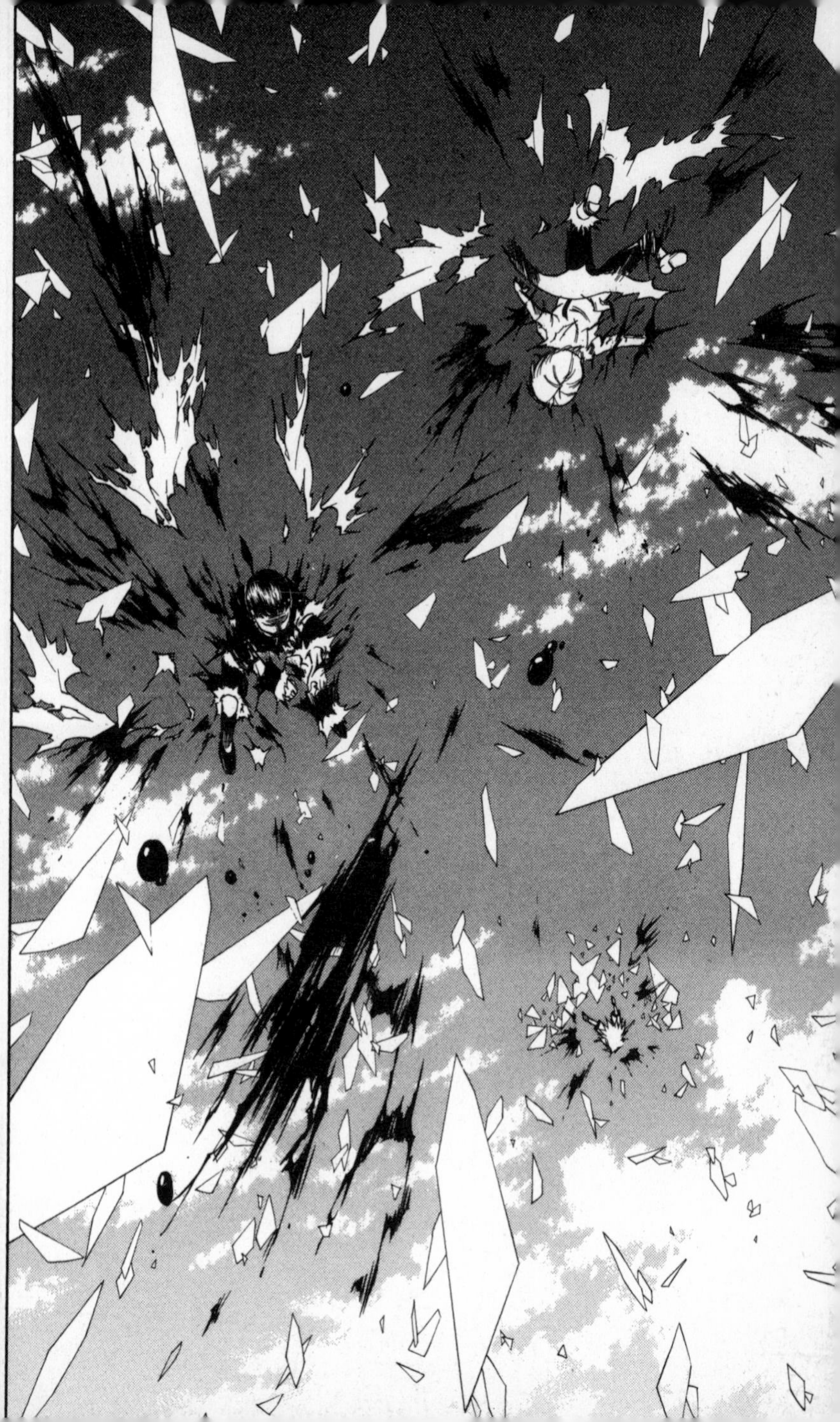

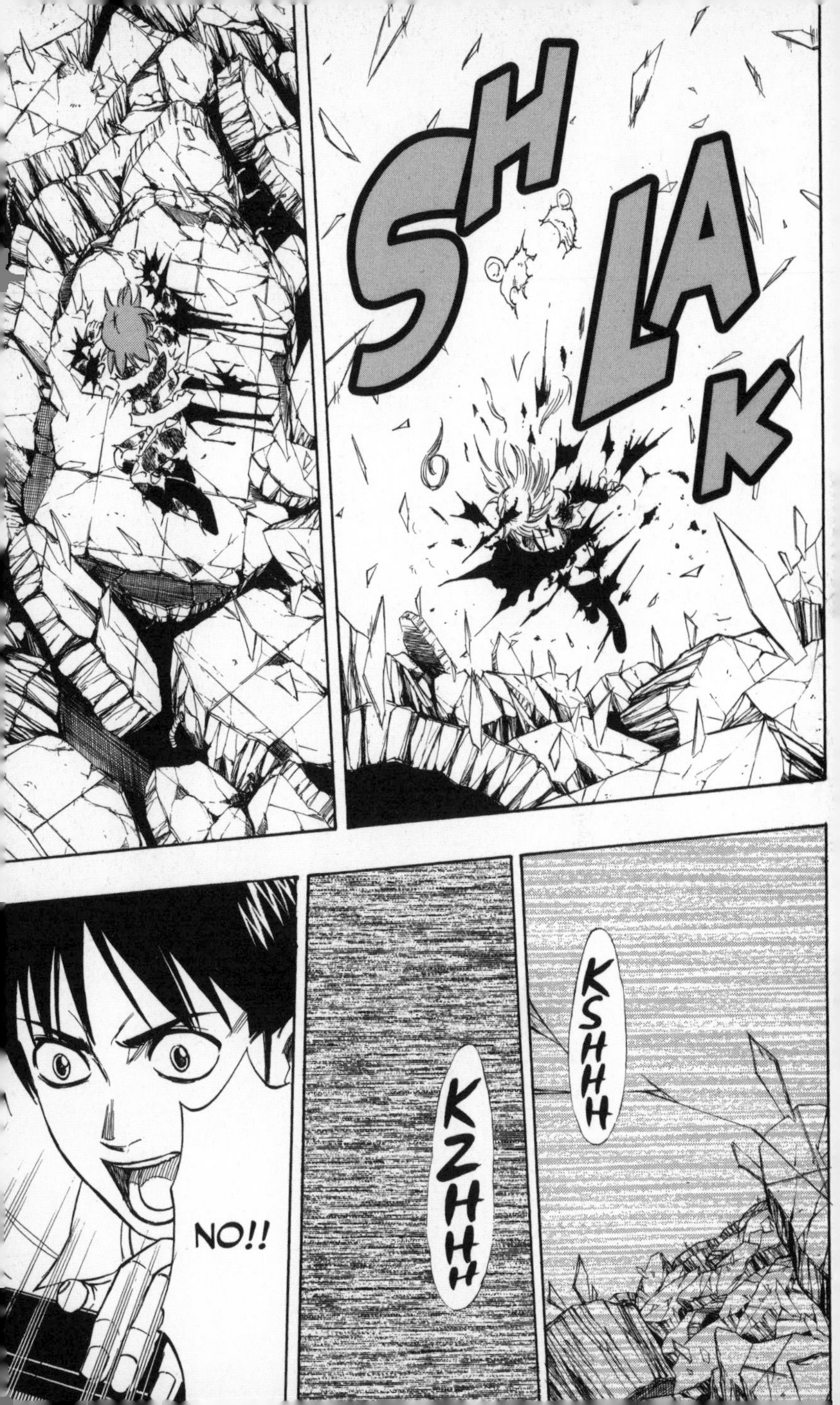
SHLAK
KSHHH
KZHHH
NO!!

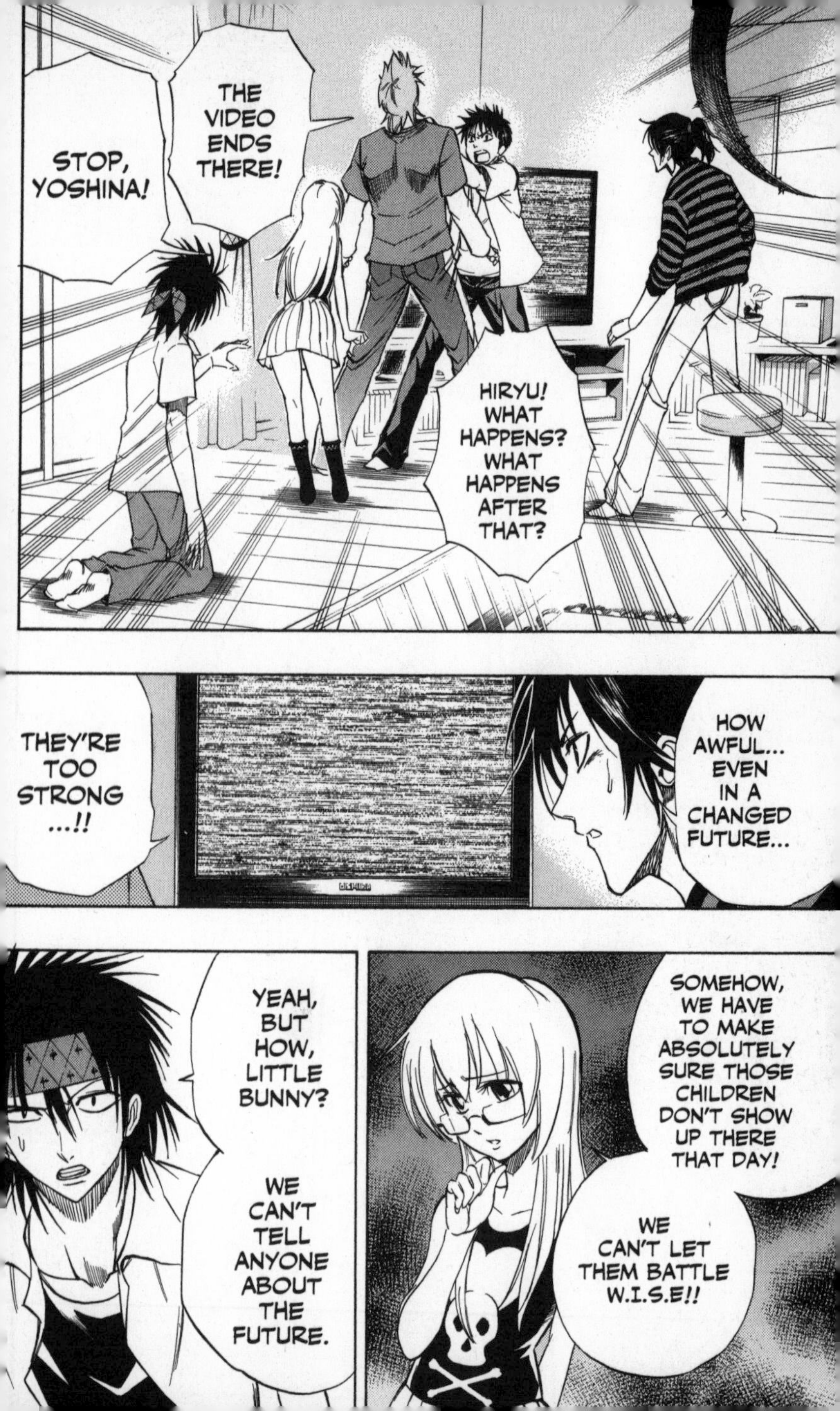
THE VIDEO ENDS THERE!
HIRYU! WHAT HAPPENS? WHAT HAPPENS AFTER THAT?
STOP, YOSHINA!
HOW AWFUL... EVEN IN A CHANGED FUTURE...
THEY'RE TOO STRONG ...!!
SOMEHOW, WE HAVE TO MAKE ABSOLUTELY SURE THOSE CHILDREN DON'T SHOW UP THERE THAT DAY!
WE CAN'T LET THEM BATTLE W.I.S.E!!
YEAH, BUT HOW, LITTLE BUNNY?
WE CAN'T TELL ANYONE ABOUT THE FUTURE.

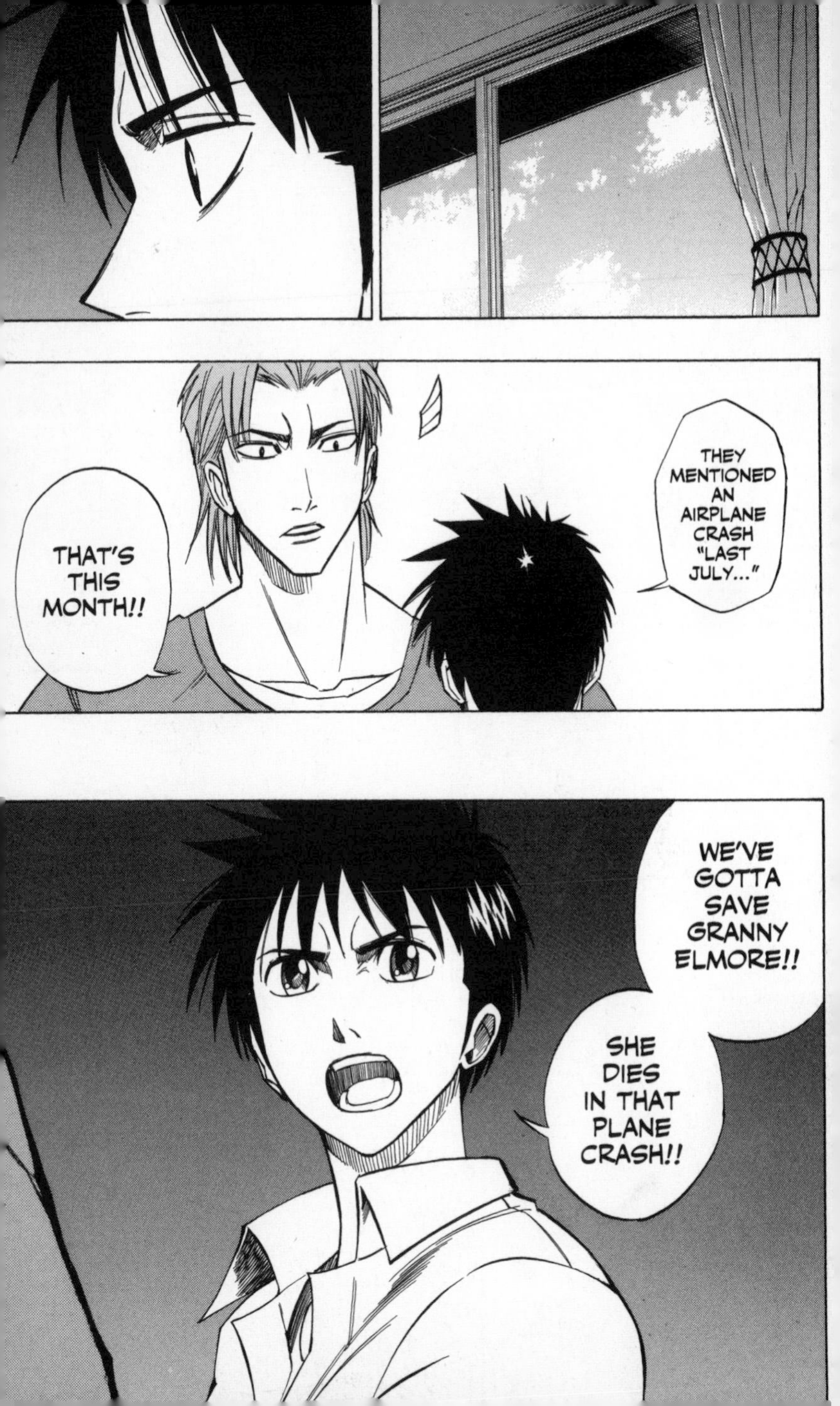
THEY MENTIONED AN AIRPLANE CRASH "LAST JULY..."
THAT'S THIS MONTH!!
WE'VE GOTTA SAVE GRANNY ELMORE!!
SHE DIES IN THAT PLANE CRASH!!

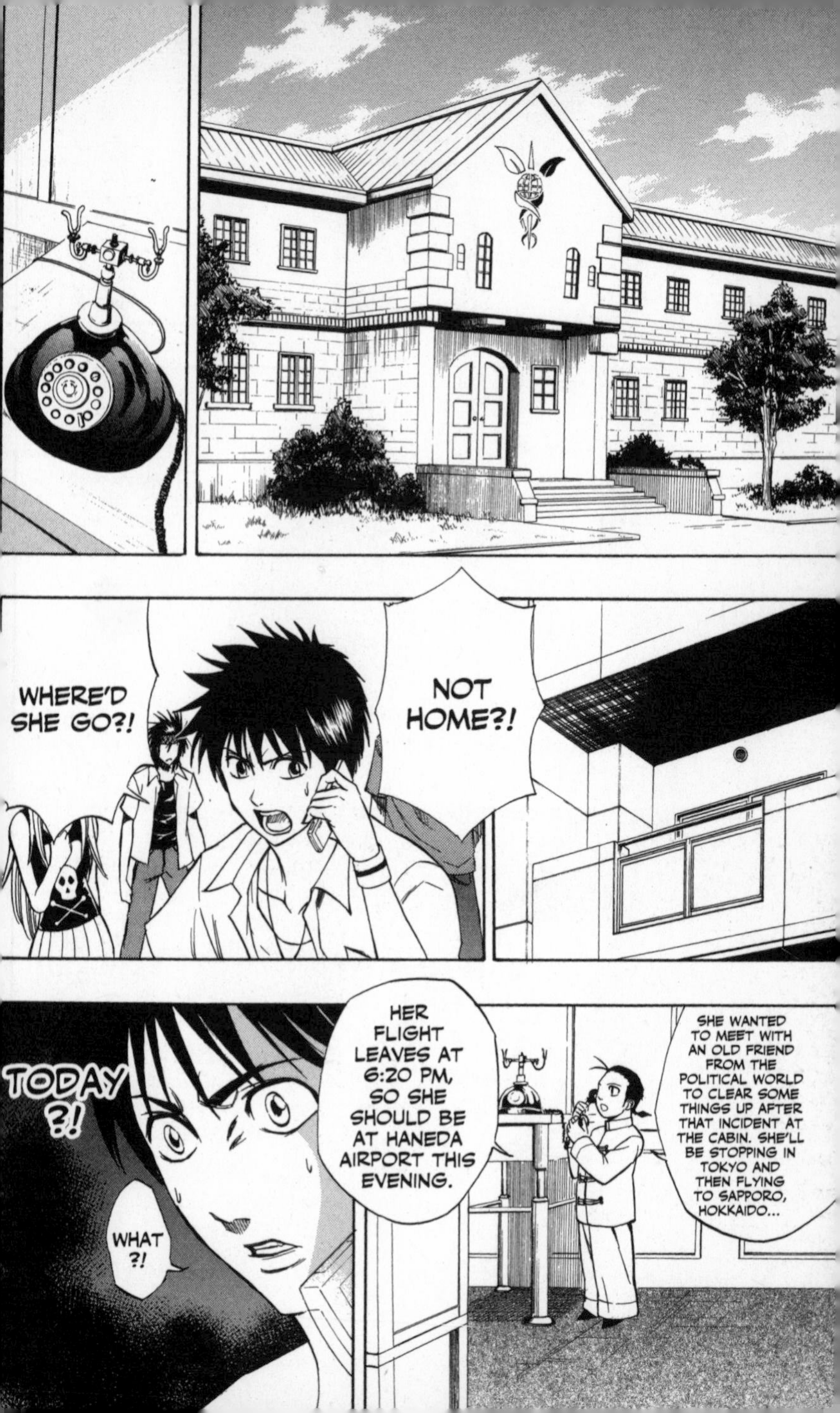
NOT HOME?!
WHERE'D SHE GO?!
SHE WANTED TO MEET WITH AN OLD FRIEND FROM THE POLITICAL WORLD TO CLEAR SOME THINGS UP AFTER THAT INCIDENT AT THE CABIN. SHE'LL BE STOPPING IN TOKYO AND THEN FLYING TO SAPPORO, HOKKAIDO...
HER FLIGHT LEAVES AT 6:20 PM, SO SHE SHOULD BE AT HANEDA AIRPORT THIS EVENING.
TODAY?!
WHAT?!

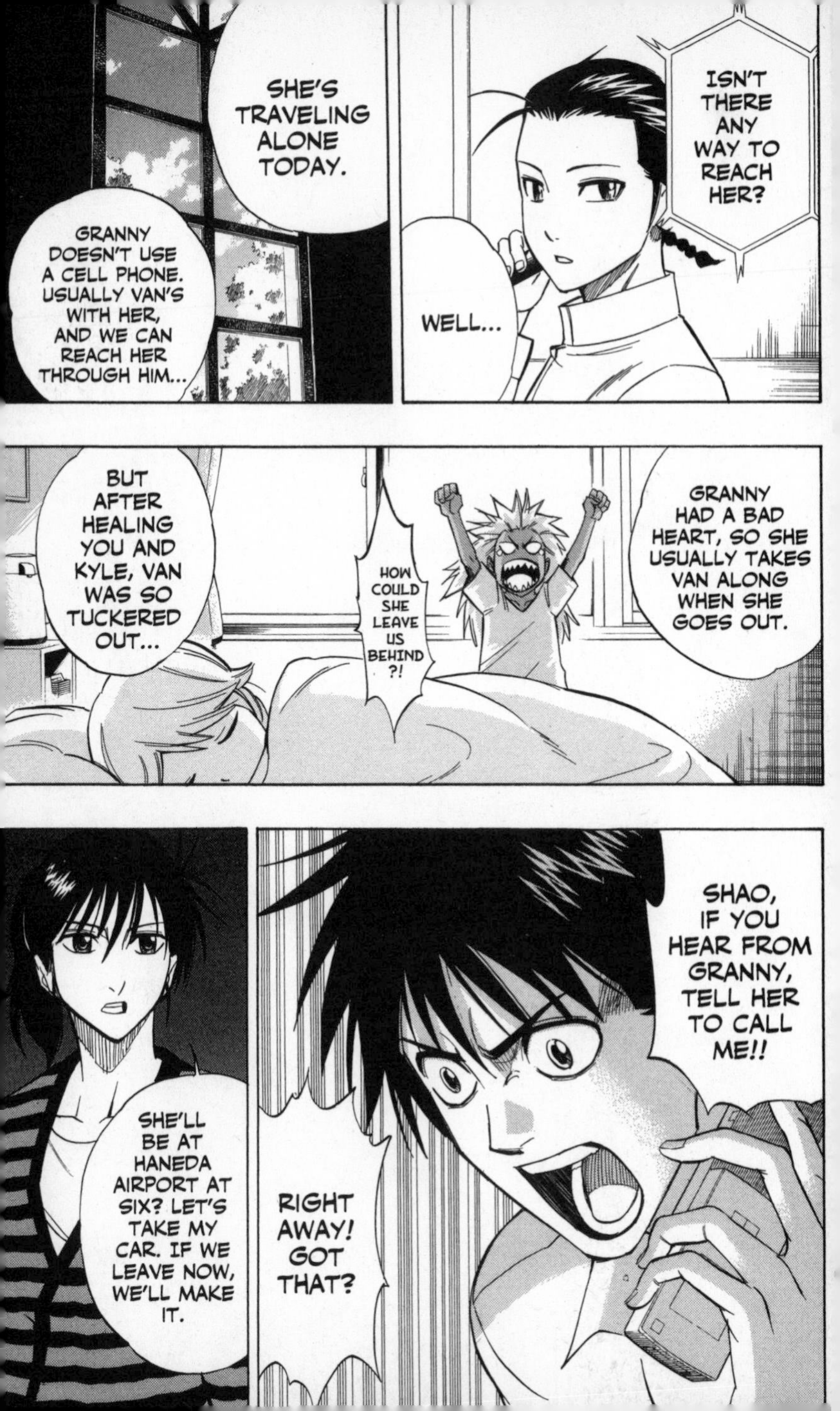
ISN'T THERE ANY WAY TO REACH HER?
WELL...
SHE'S TRAVELING ALONE TODAY.
GRANNY DOESN'T USE A CELL PHONE. USUALLY VAN'S WITH HER, AND WE CAN REACH HER THROUGH HIM...
GRANNY HAD A BAD HEART, SO SHE USUALLY TAKES VAN ALONG WHEN SHE GOES OUT.
HOW COULD SHE LEAVE US BEHIND?!
BUT AFTER HEALING YOU AND KYLE, VAN WAS SO TUCKERED OUT...
SHAO, IF YOU HEAR FROM GRANNY, TELL HER TO CALL ME!!
RIGHT AWAY! GOT THAT?
SHE'LL BE AT HANEDA AIRPORT AT SIX? LET'S TAKE MY CAR. IF WE LEAVE NOW, WE'LL MAKE IT.

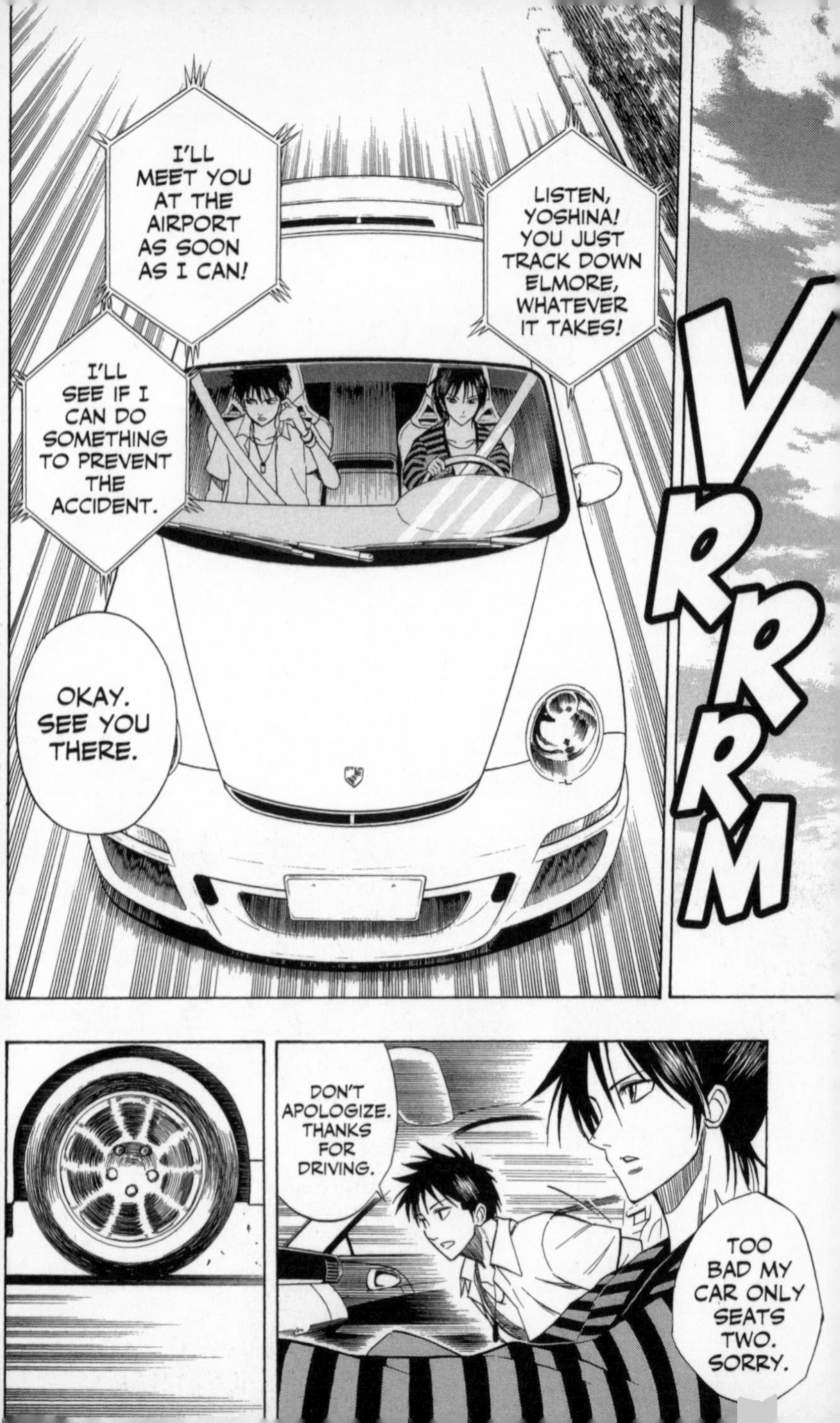
VRRRM
LISTEN, YOSHINA! YOU JUST TRACK DOWN ELMORE, WHATEVER IT TAKES!
I'LL MEET YOU AT THE AIRPORT AS SOON AS I CAN!
I'LL SEE IF I CAN DO SOMETHING TO PREVENT THE ACCIDENT.
OKAY. SEE YOU THERE.
TOO BAD MY CAR ONLY SEATS TWO. SORRY.
DON'T APOLOGIZE. THANKS FOR DRIVING.

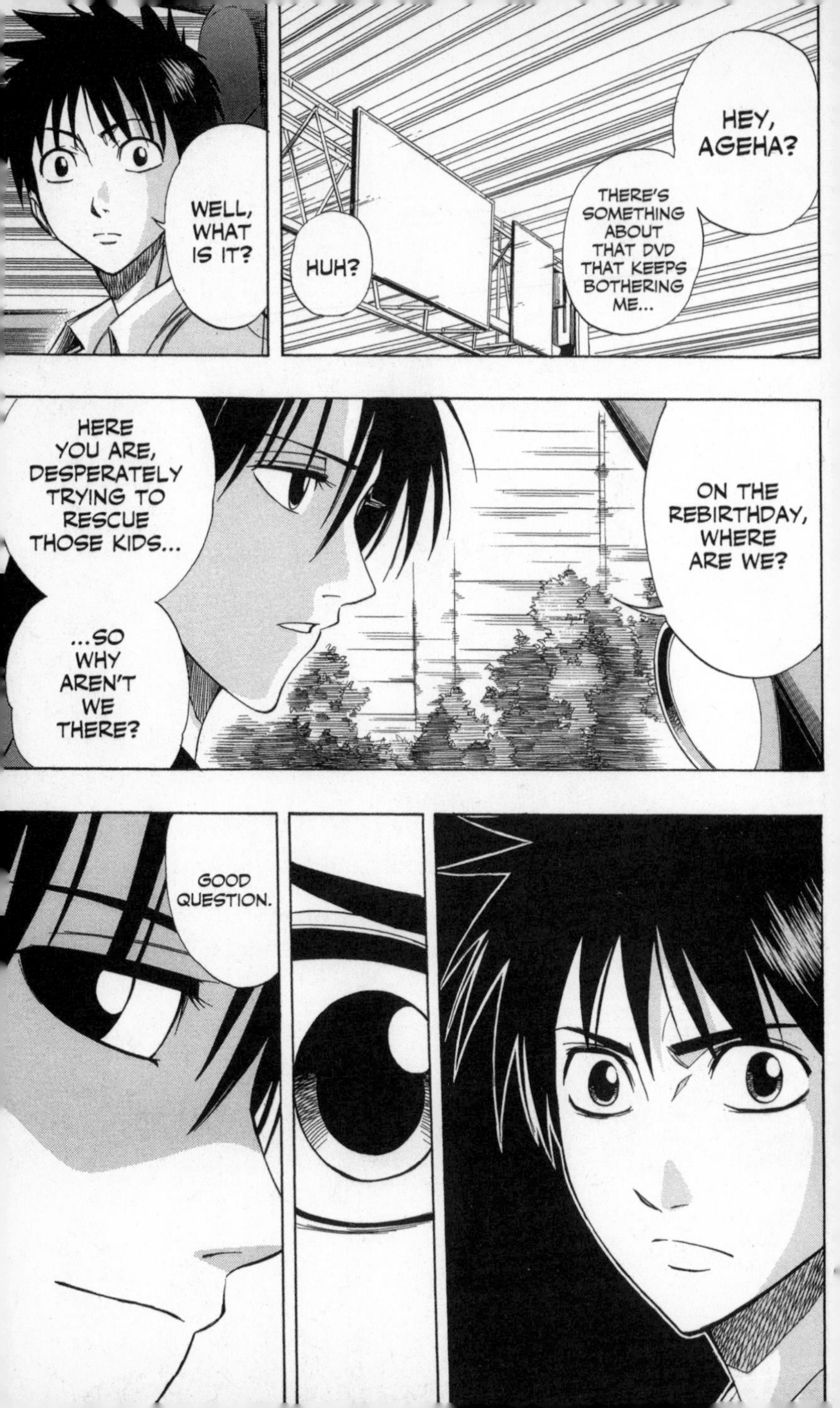
HEY, AGEHA?
THERE'S SOMETHING ABOUT THAT DVD THAT KEEPS BOTHERING ME...
HUH?
WELL, WHAT IS IT?
ON THE REBIRTHDAY, WHERE ARE WE?
HERE YOU ARE, DESPERATELY TRYING TO RESCUE THOSE KIDS...
...SO WHY AREN'T WE THERE?
GOOD QUESTION.

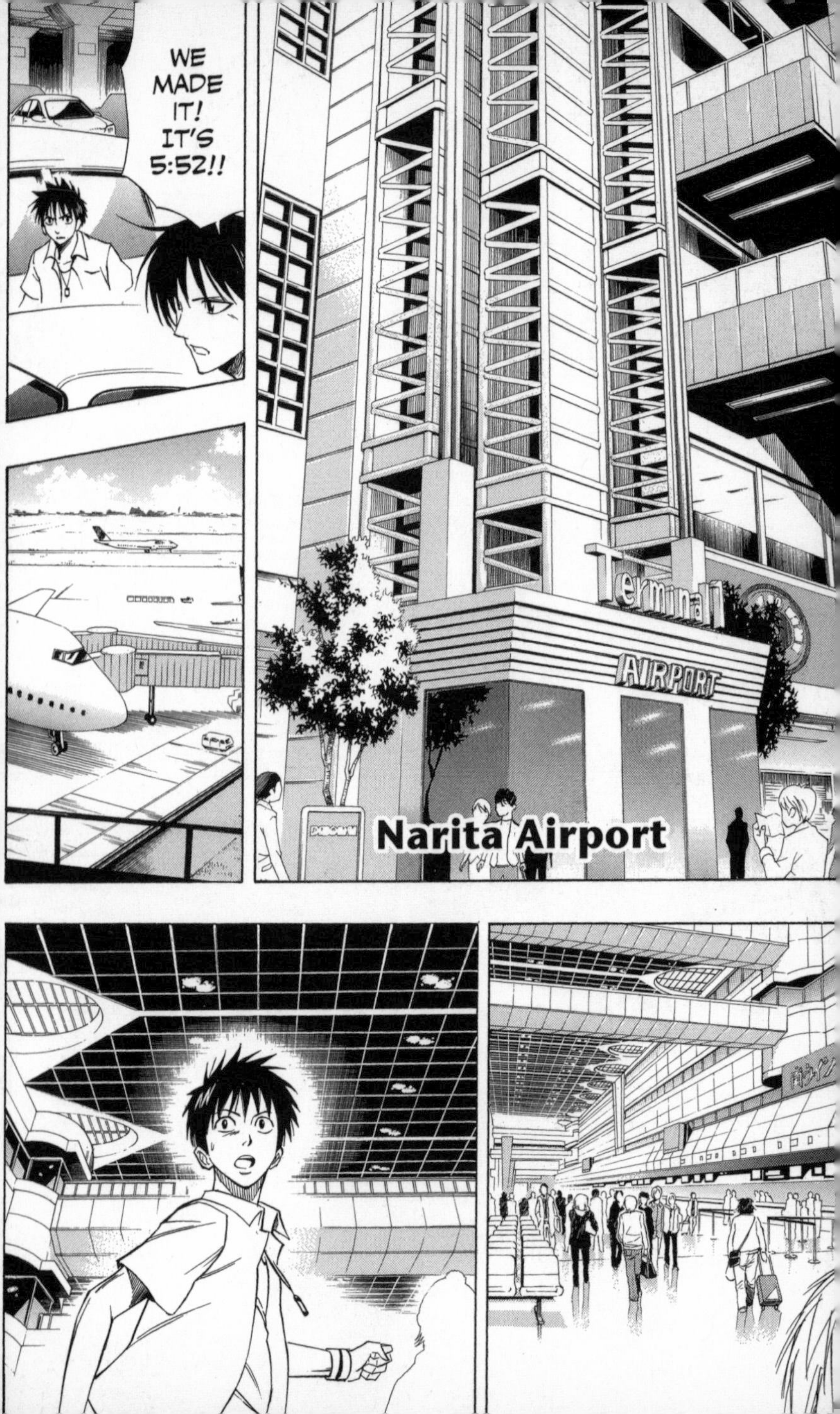
Terminal 1
AIRPORT
Narita Airport
WE MADE IT! IT'S 5:52!!

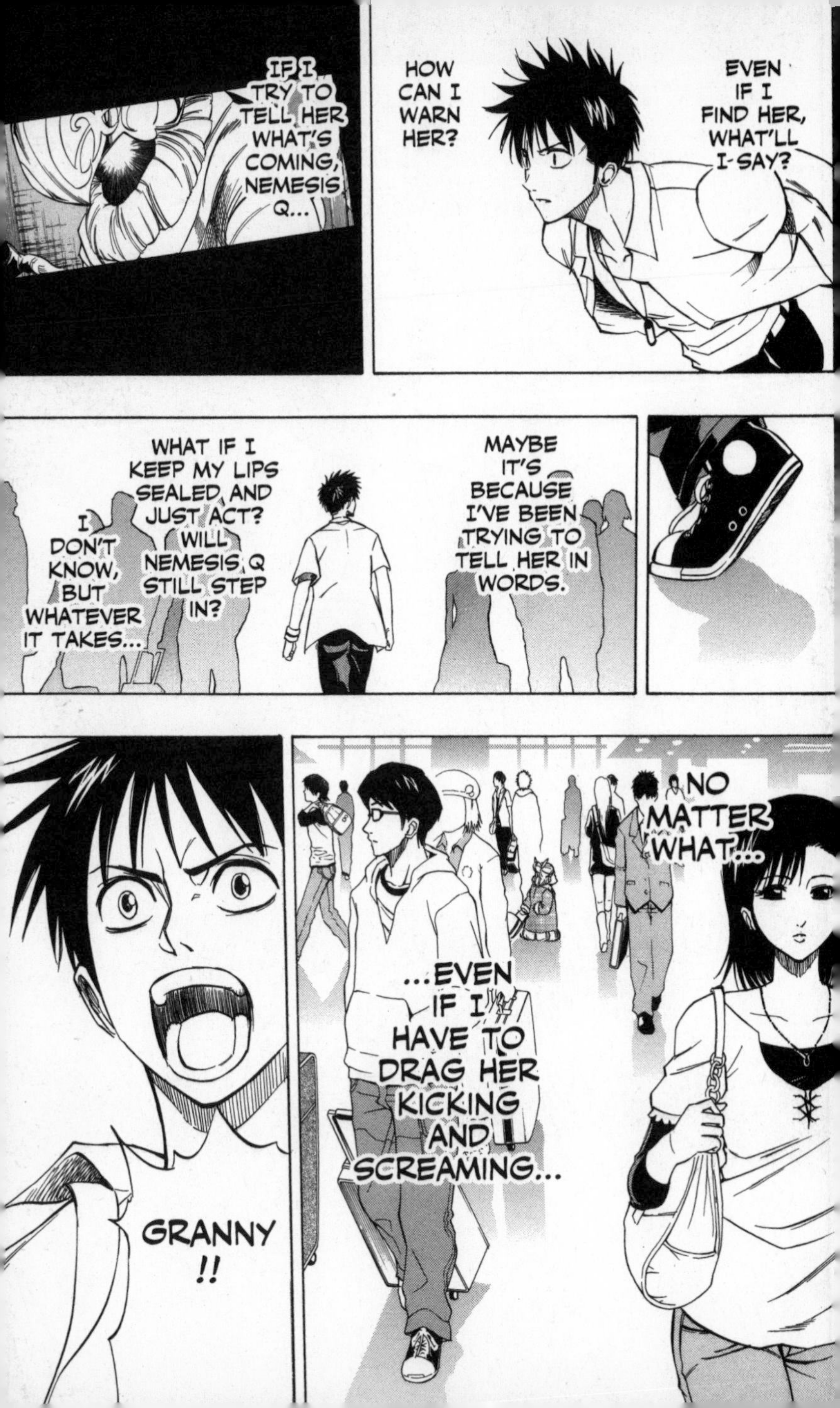
EVEN IF I FIND HER, WHAT'LL I SAY?
HOW CAN I WARN HER?
IF I TRY TO TELL HER WHAT'S COMING, NEMESIS Q...
MAYBE IT'S BECAUSE I'VE BEEN TRYING TO TELL HER IN WORDS.
WHAT IF I KEEP MY LIPS SEALED AND JUST ACT? WILL NEMESIS Q STILL STEP IN?
I DON'T KNOW, BUT WHATEVER IT TAKES...
NO MATTER WHAT...
...EVEN IF I HAVE TO DRAG HER KICKING AND SCREAMING...
GRANNY!!

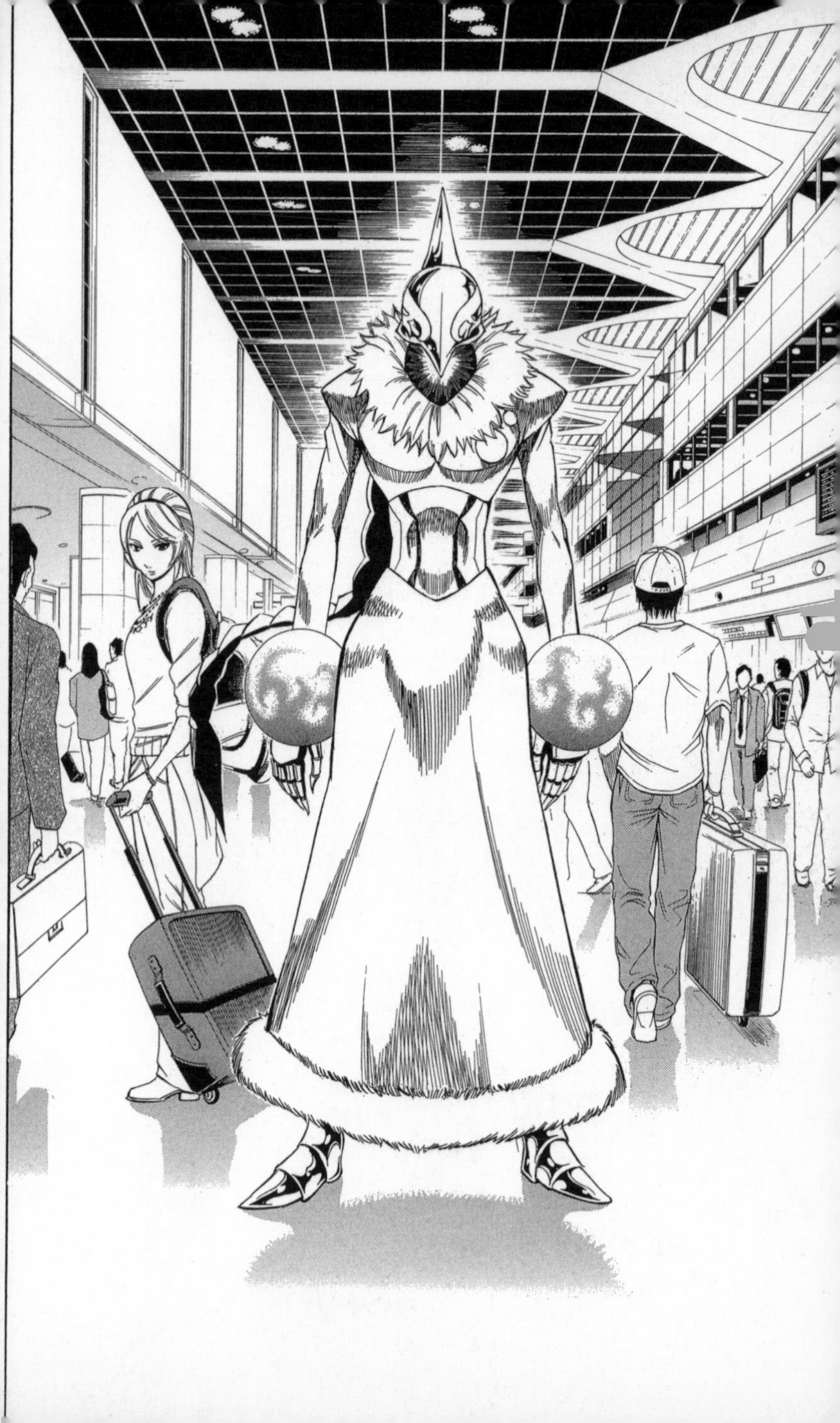

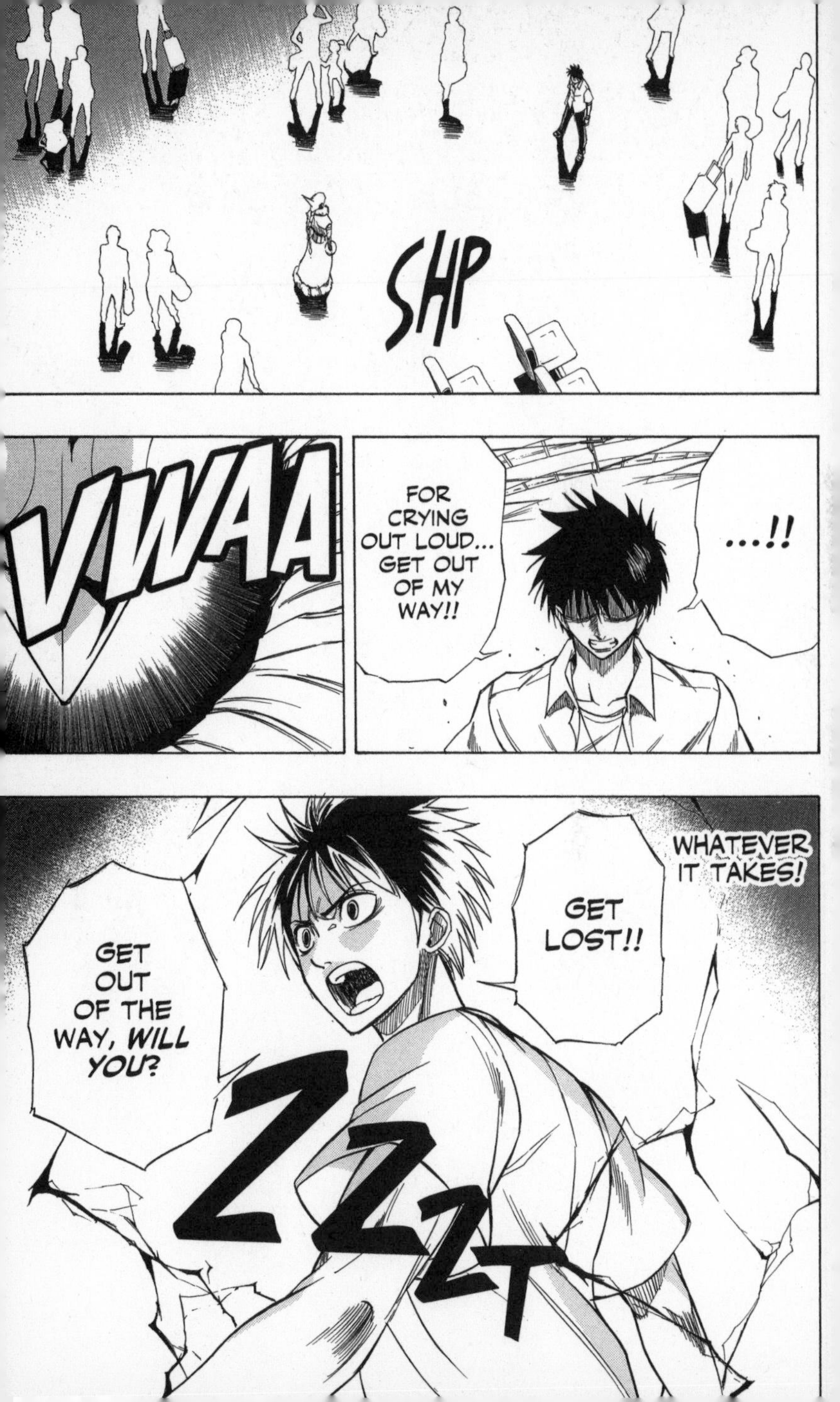
SHP
...!!
FOR CRYING OUT LOUD... GET OUT OF MY WAY!!
VWAA
WHATEVER IT TAKES!
GET LOST!!
GET OUT OF THE WAY, WILL YOU?
ZZZT

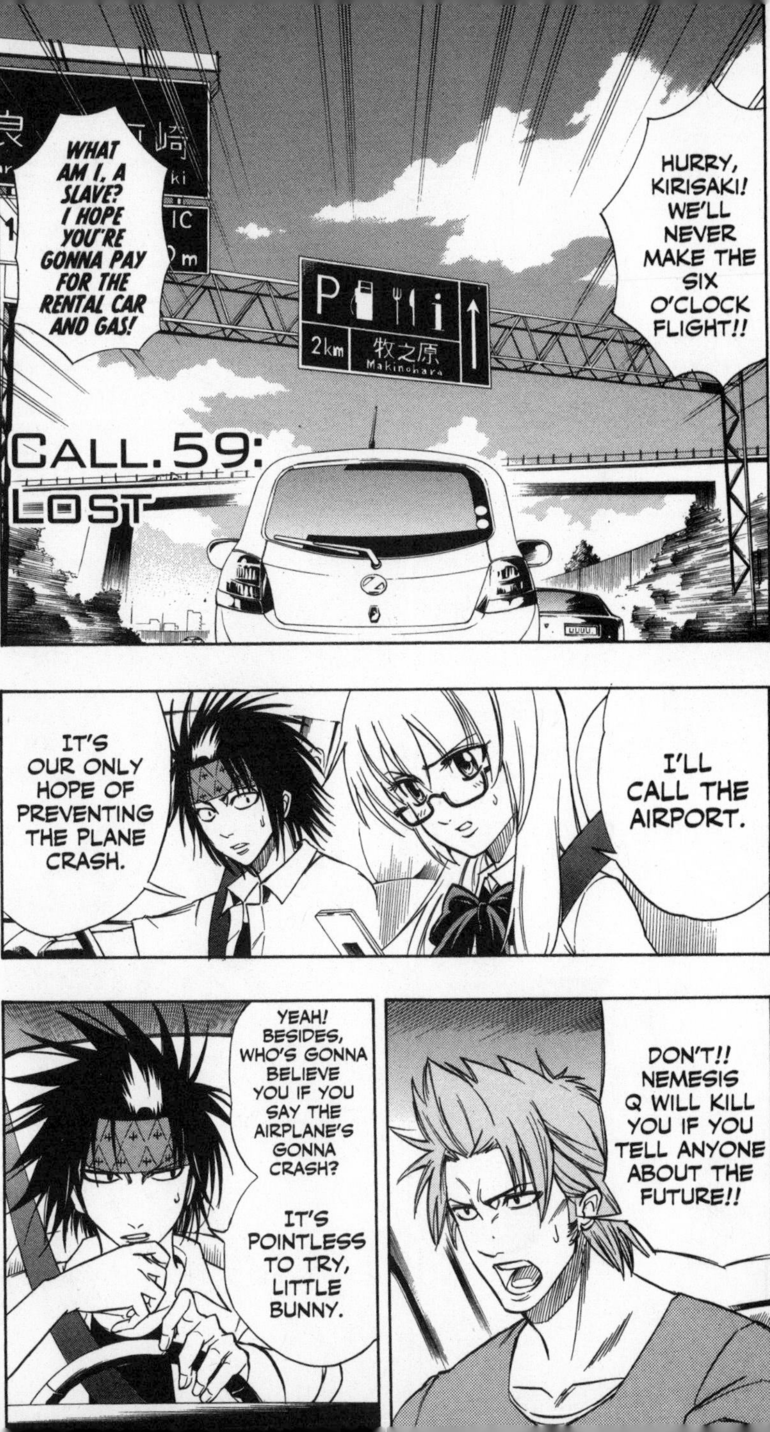
HURRY, KIRISAKI! WE'LL NEVER MAKE THE SIX O'CLOCK FLIGHT!!
WHAT AM I, A SLAVE? I HOPE YOU'RE GONNA PAY FOR THE RENTAL CAR AND GAS!
2km 牧之原 Makinohara
CALL. 59: LOST
I'LL CALL THE AIRPORT.
IT'S OUR ONLY HOPE OF PREVENTING THE PLANE CRASH.
DON'T!! NEMESIS Q WILL KILL YOU IF YOU TELL ANYONE ABOUT THE FUTURE!!
YEAH! BESIDES, WHO'S GONNA BELIEVE YOU IF YOU SAY THE AIRPLANE'S GONNA CRASH?
IT'S POINTLESS TO TRY, LITTLE BUNNY.

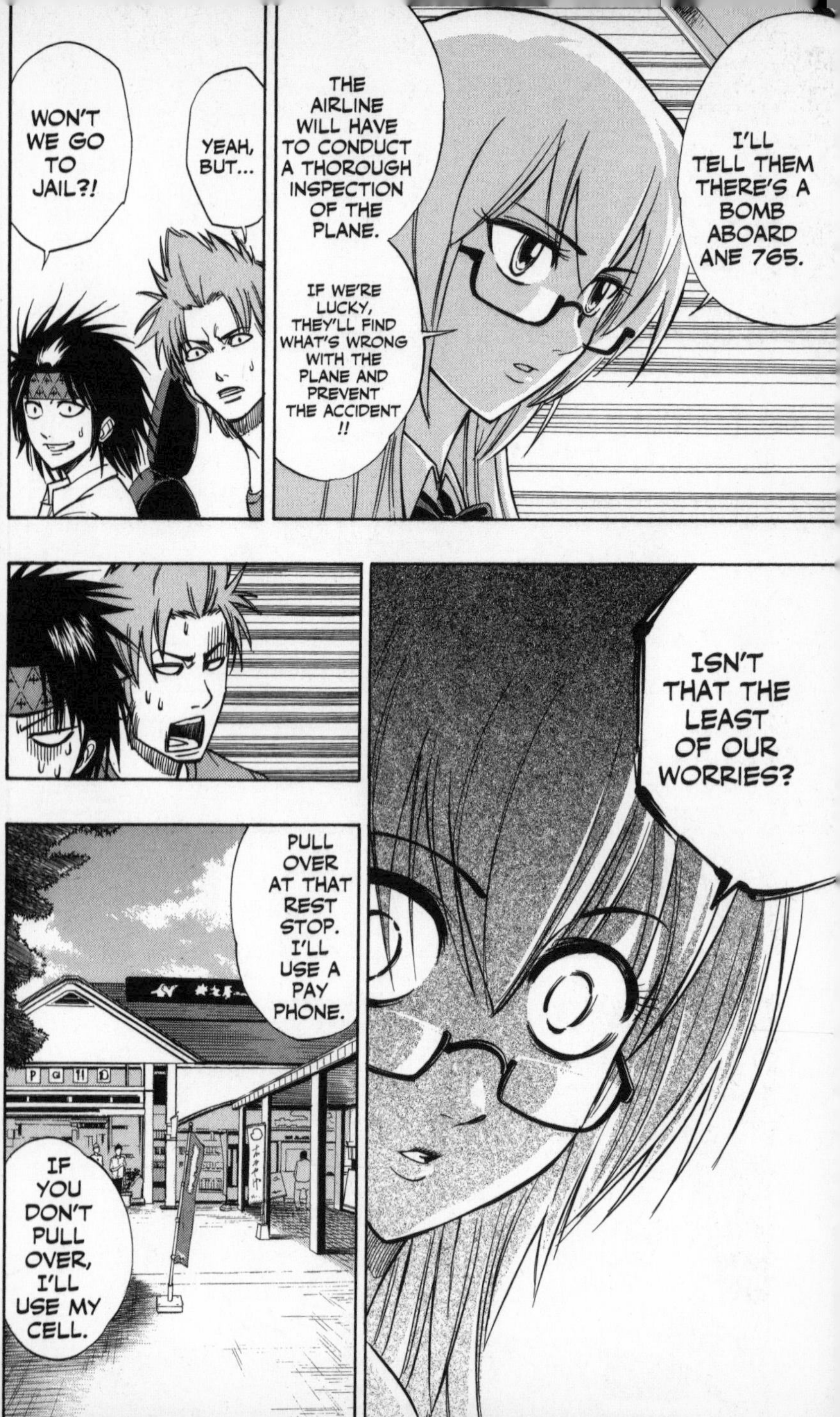
I'LL TELL THEM THERE'S A BOMB ABOARD ANE 765.
THE AIRLINE WILL HAVE TO CONDUCT A THOROUGH INSPECTION OF THE PLANE.
IF WE'RE LUCKY, THEY'LL FIND WHAT'S WRONG WITH THE PLANE AND PREVENT THE ACCIDENT!!
YEAH, BUT...
WON'T WE GO TO JAIL?!
ISN'T THAT THE LEAST OF OUR WORRIES?
PULL OVER AT THAT REST STOP. I'LL USE A PAY PHONE.
IF YOU DON'T PULL OVER, I'LL USE MY CELL.

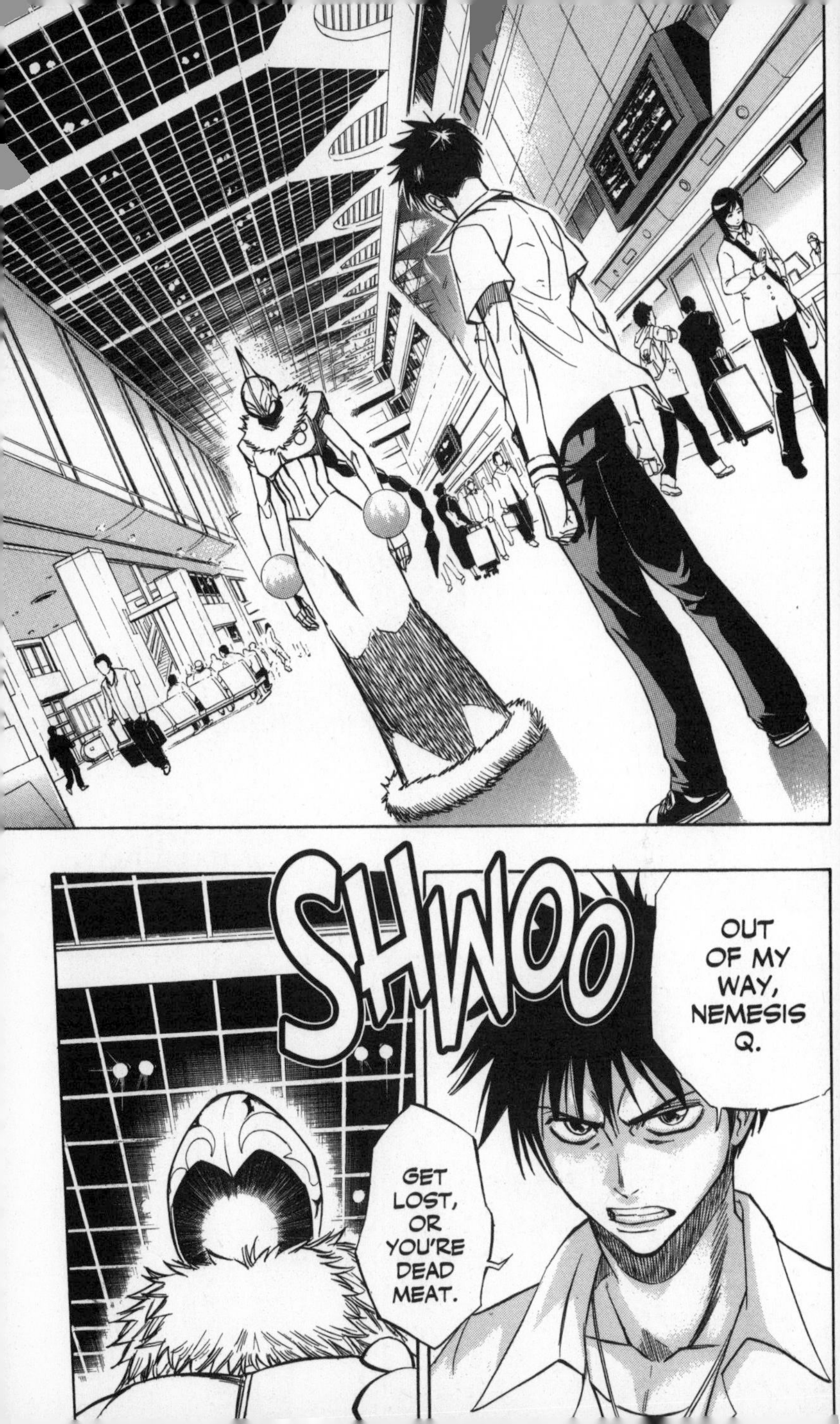
SHWOO
OUT OF MY WAY, NEMESIS Q.
GET LOST, OR YOU'RE DEAD MEAT.

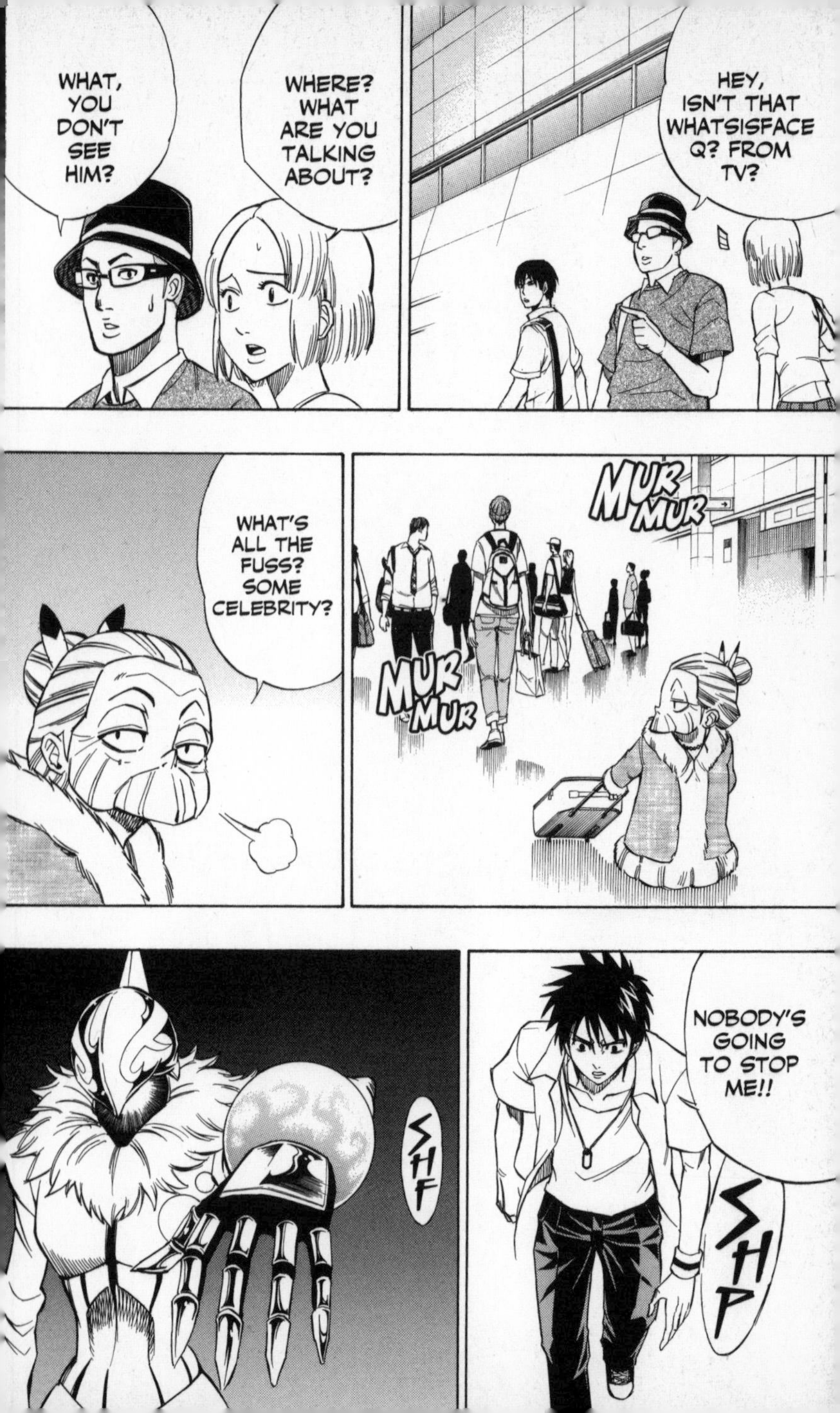
HEY, ISN'T THAT WHATSISFACE Q? FROM TV?
WHERE? WHAT ARE YOU TALKING ABOUT?
WHAT, YOU DON'T SEE HIM?
MUR MUR
MUR MUR
WHAT'S ALL THE FUSS? SOME CELEBRITY?
NOBODY'S GOING TO STOP ME!!
SHP
SHF

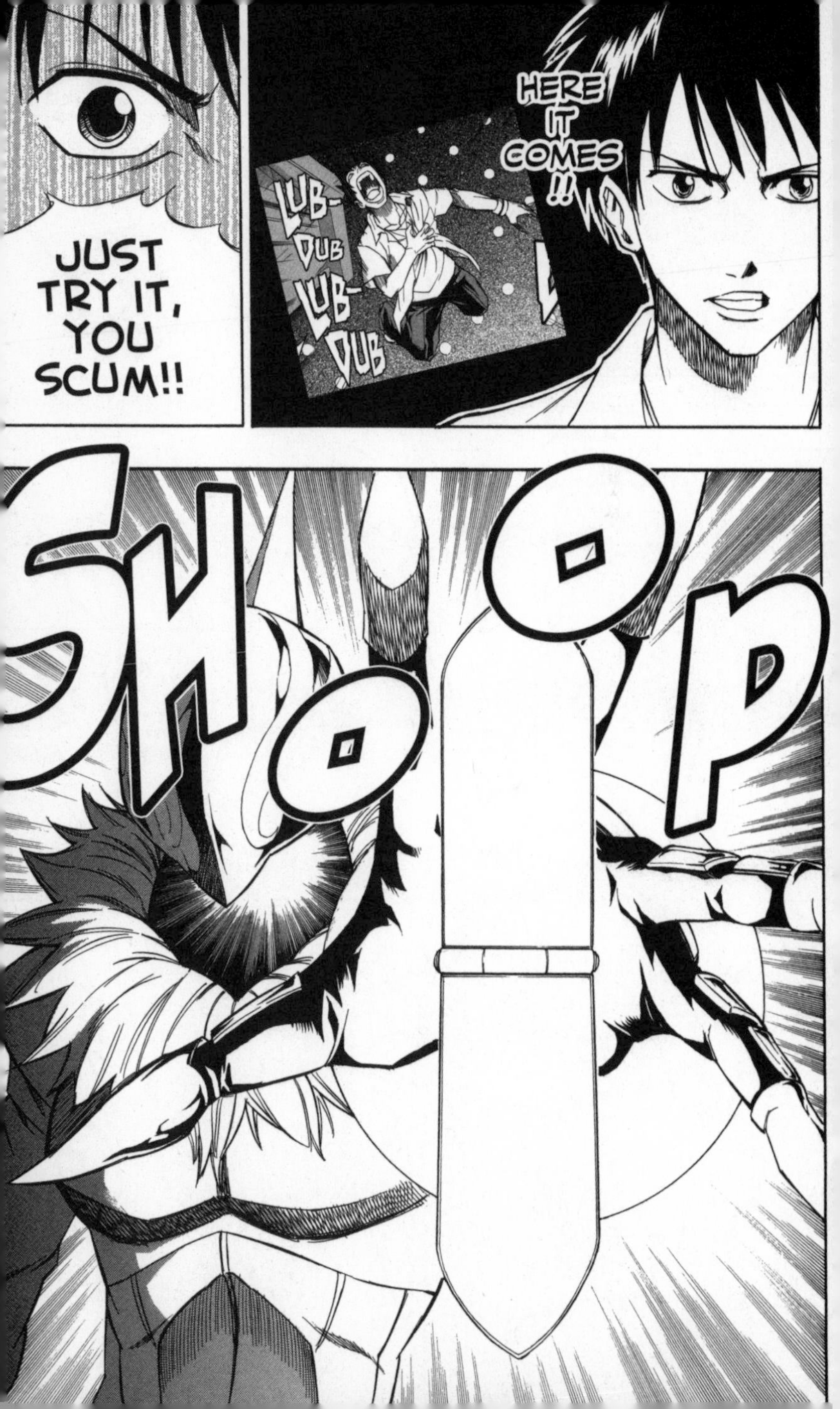

HERE IT COMES!!
LUB-DUB LUB-DUB
JUST TRY IT, YOU SCUM!!
SHOOOP

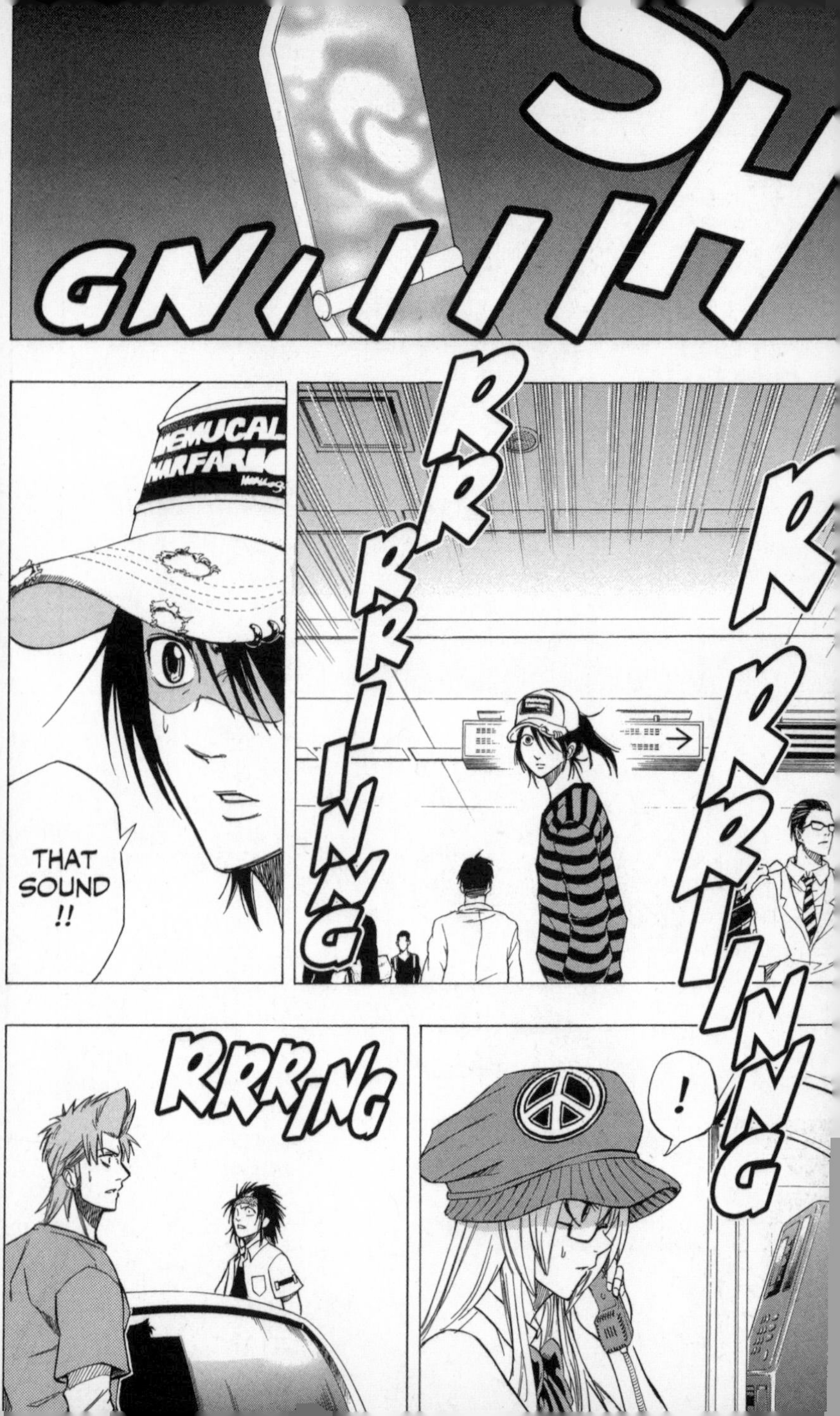
THAT SOUND !!
RRRING
!

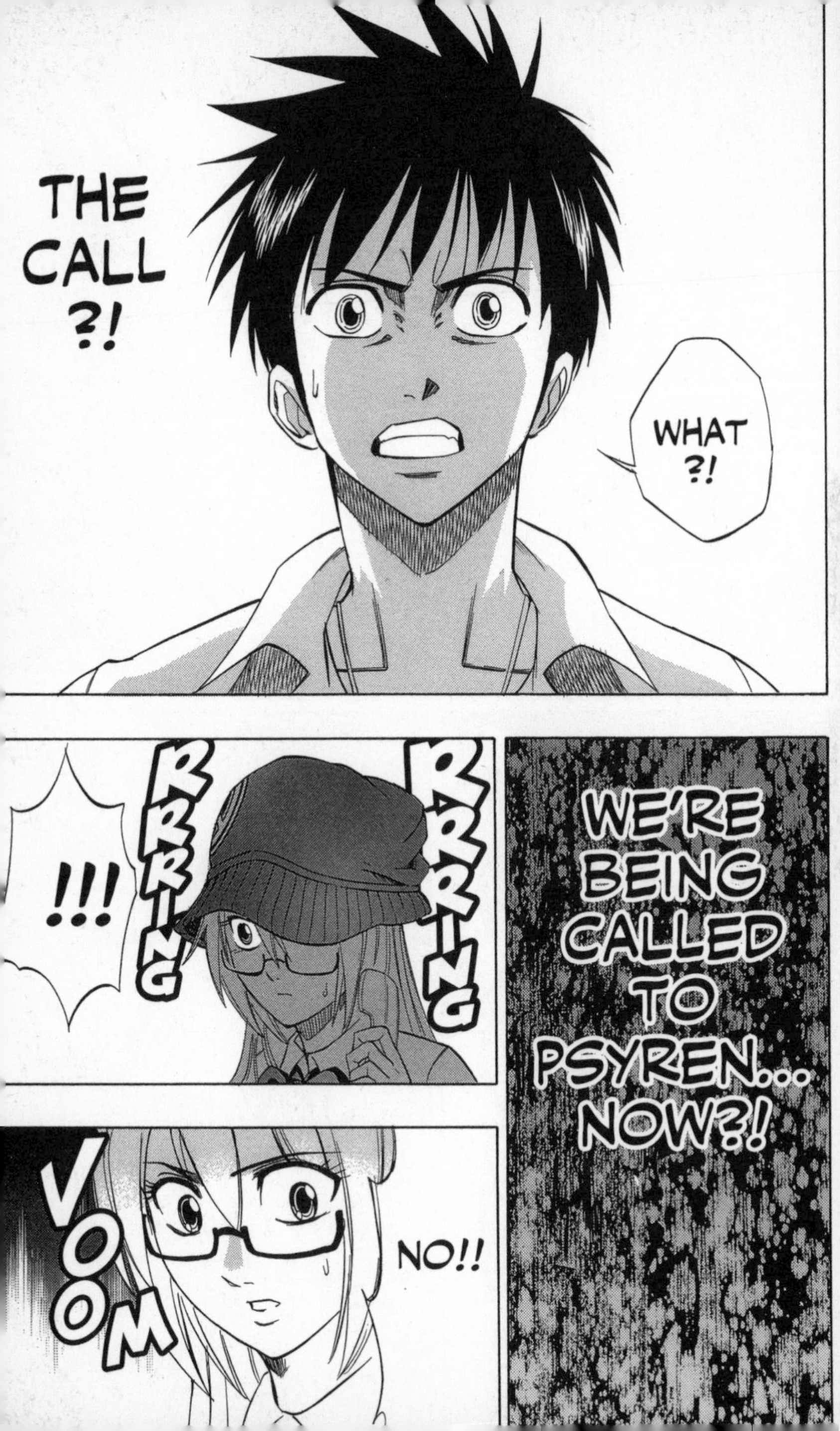
WHAT ?!
THE CALL ?!
WE'RE BEING CALLED TO PSYREN... NOW?!
RRRING
RRRING
!!!
VOOM
NO!!

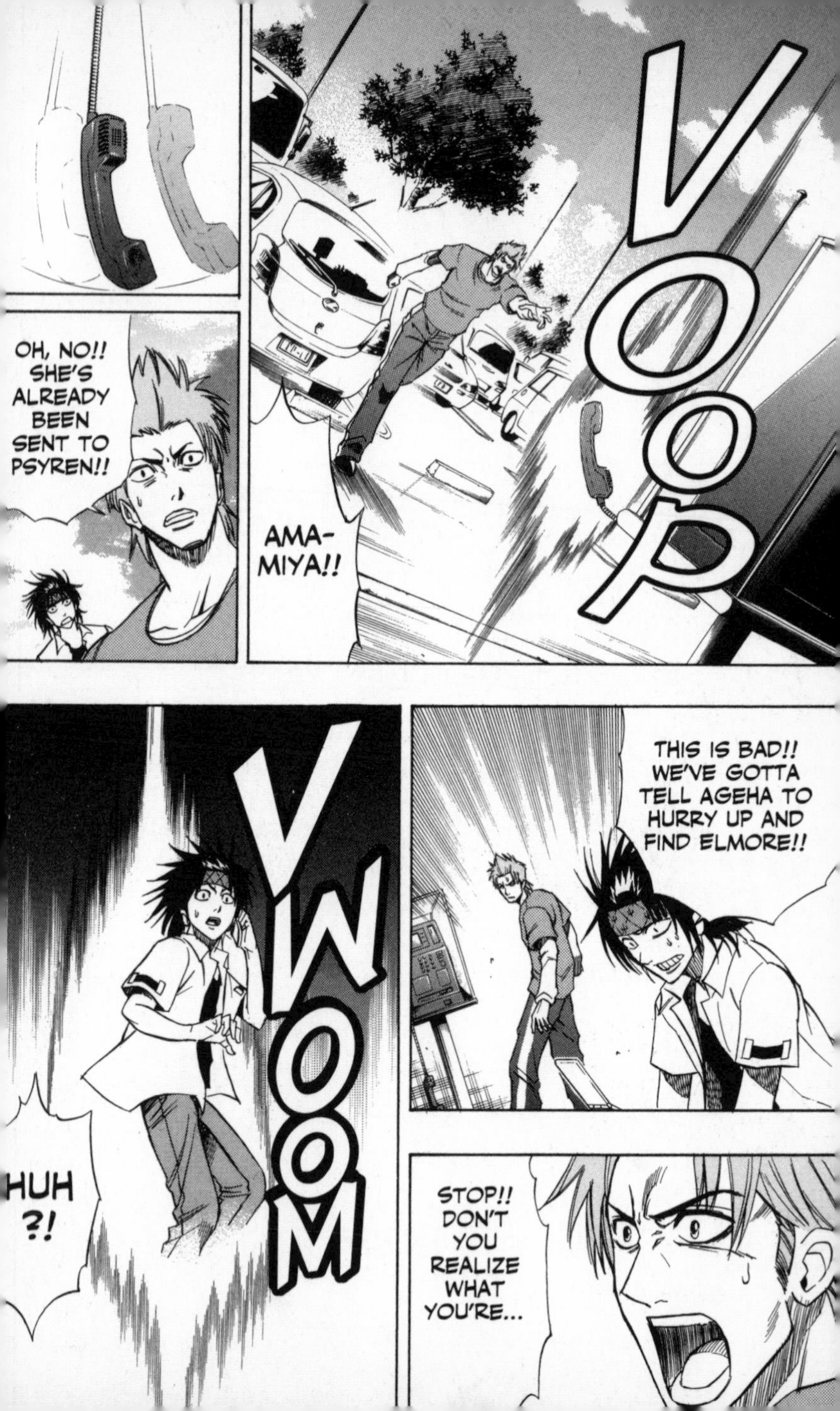
VOOP
AMA-
MIYA!!
OH, NO!!
SHE'S
ALREADY
BEEN
SENT TO
PSYREN!!
THIS IS BAD!!
WE'VE GOTTA
TELL AGEHA TO
HURRY UP AND
FIND ELMORE!!
VWOOM
HUH
?!
STOP!!
DON'T
YOU
REALIZE
WHAT
YOU'RE...

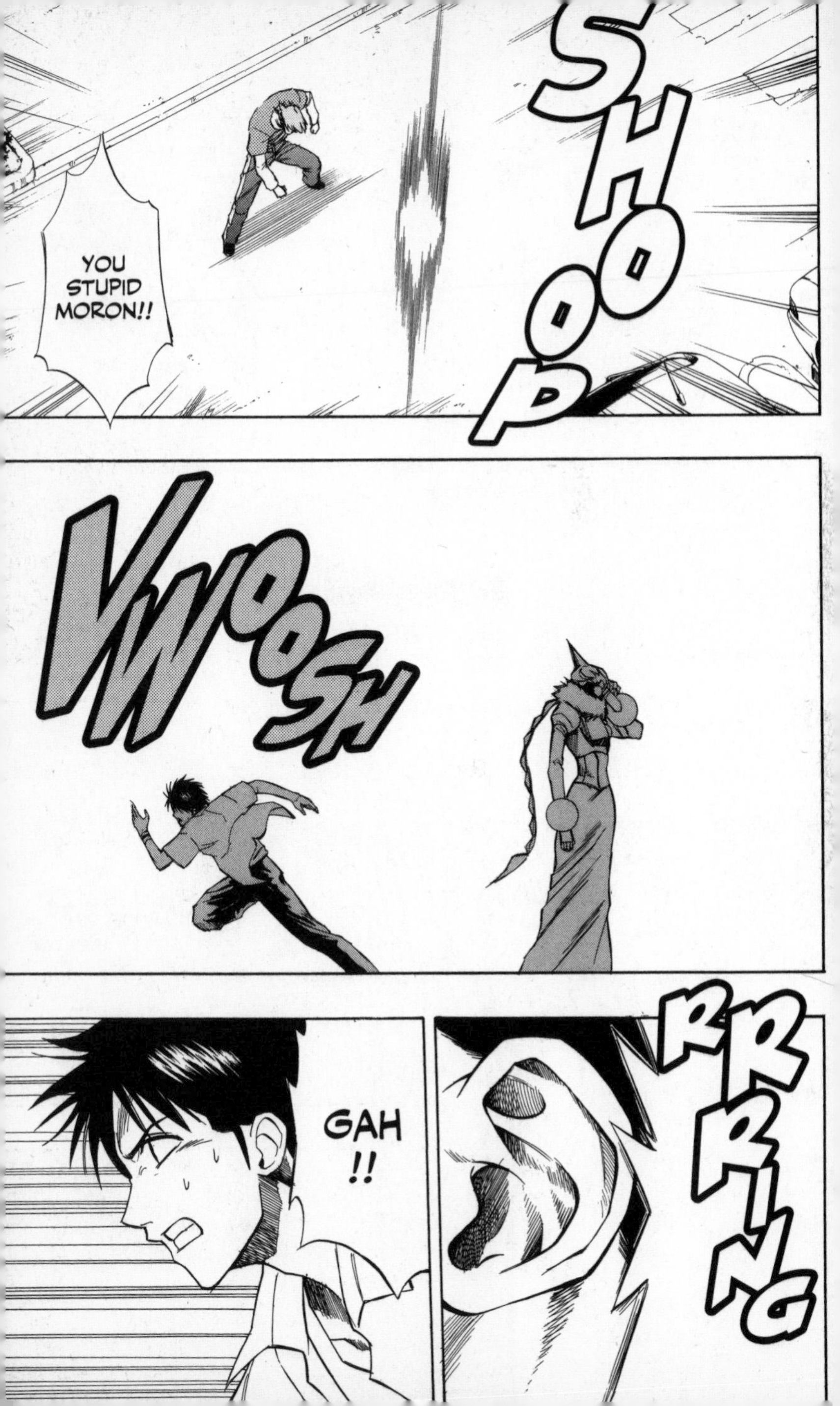
SHOOOP
YOU STUPID MORON!!
VWOOSH
RRRRING
GAH !!

SNATCH

IF I TRY TO TELL HER, NEMESIS Q'LL STOP ME. BESIDES, THERE'S NO TIME...

SORRY, GRANNY...

MY BAG!! COME BACK!!

STOP, THIEF! MY BAG! I'VE BEEN ROBBED!!

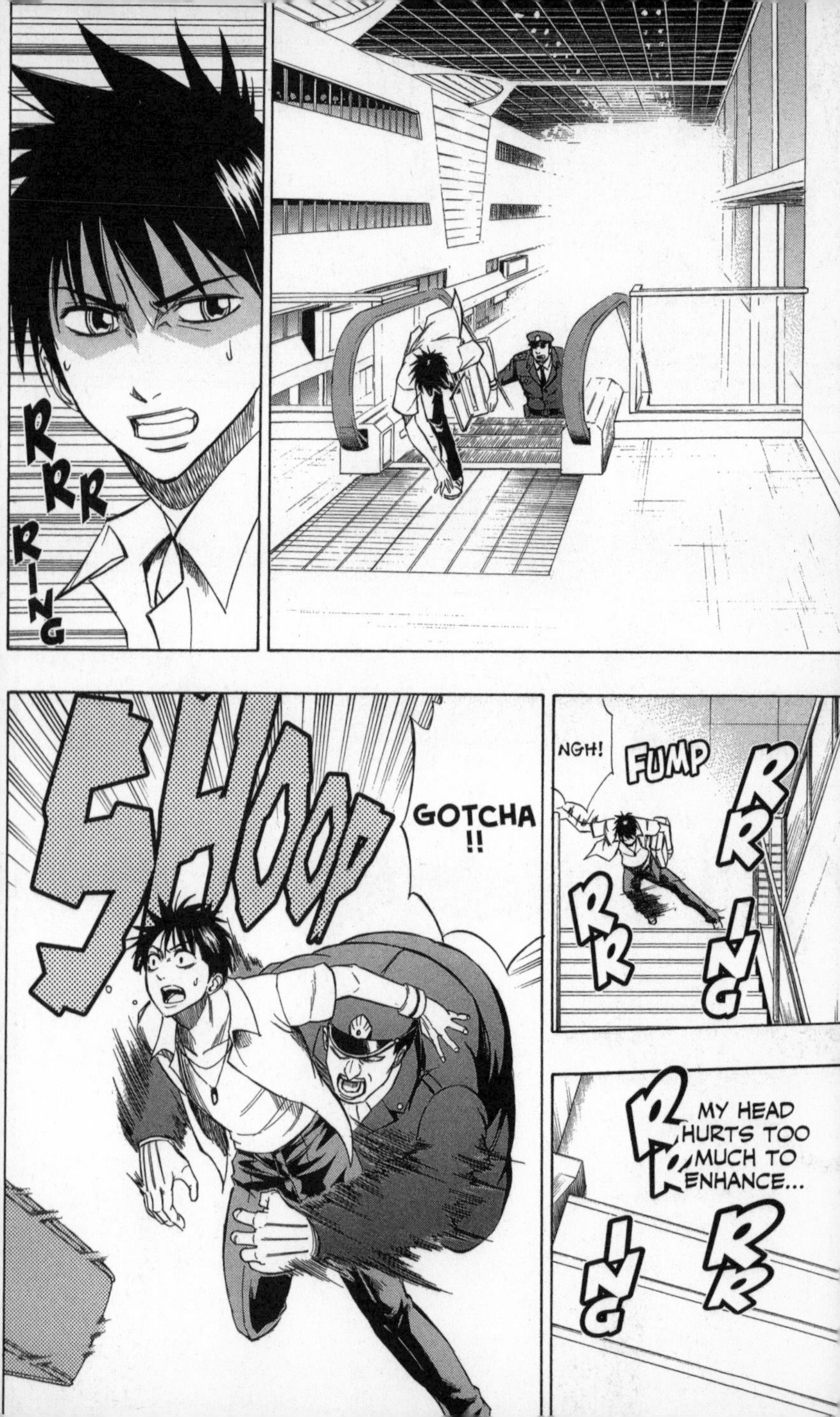
RRRRING
NGH!
FUMP
RRRRING
MY HEAD HURTS TOO MUCH TO ENHANCE...
RRRRING
SHOOP
GOTCHA !!

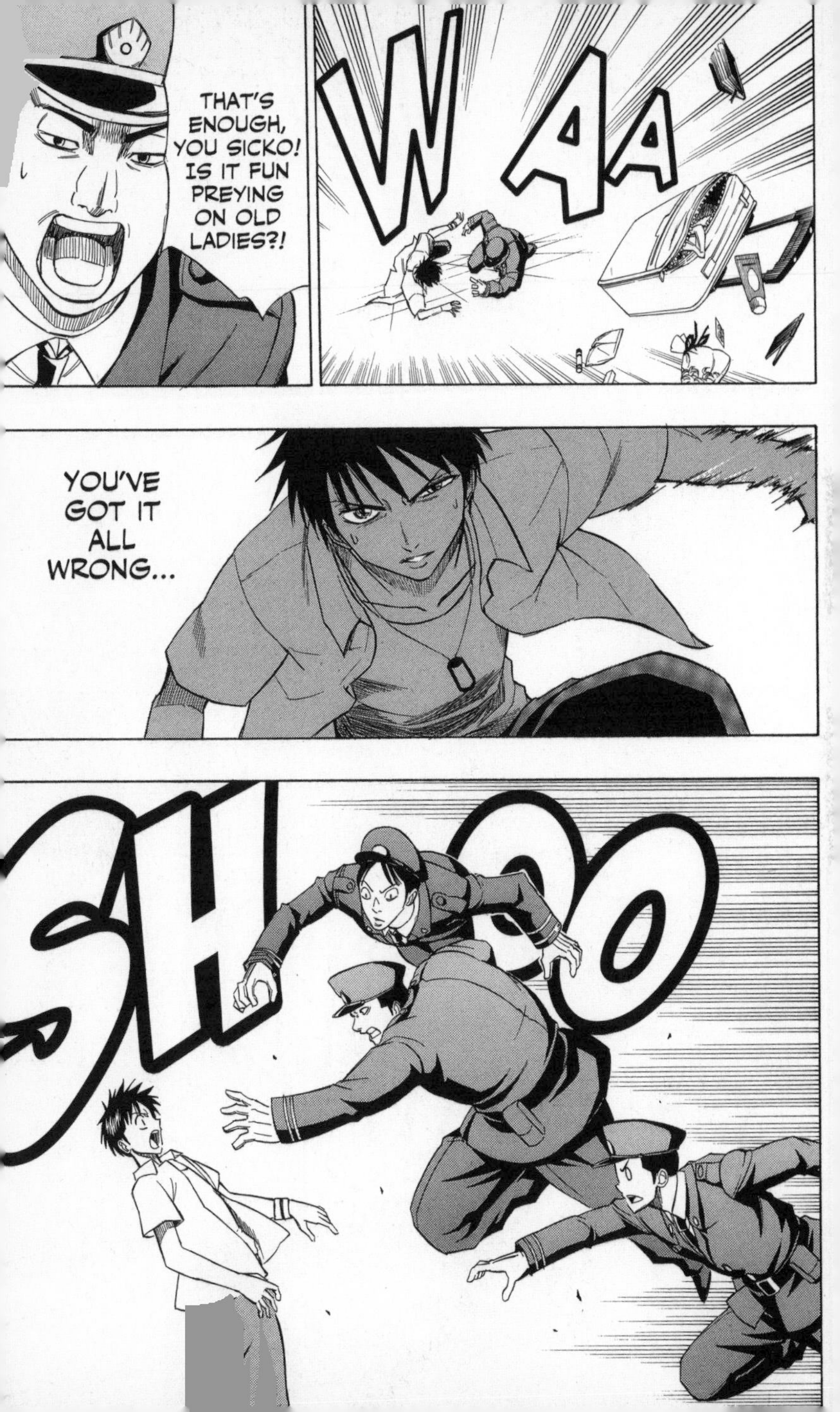
WAA
THAT'S ENOUGH, YOU SICKO! IS IT FUN PREYING ON OLD LADIES?!
YOU'VE GOT IT ALL WRONG...
SHOO

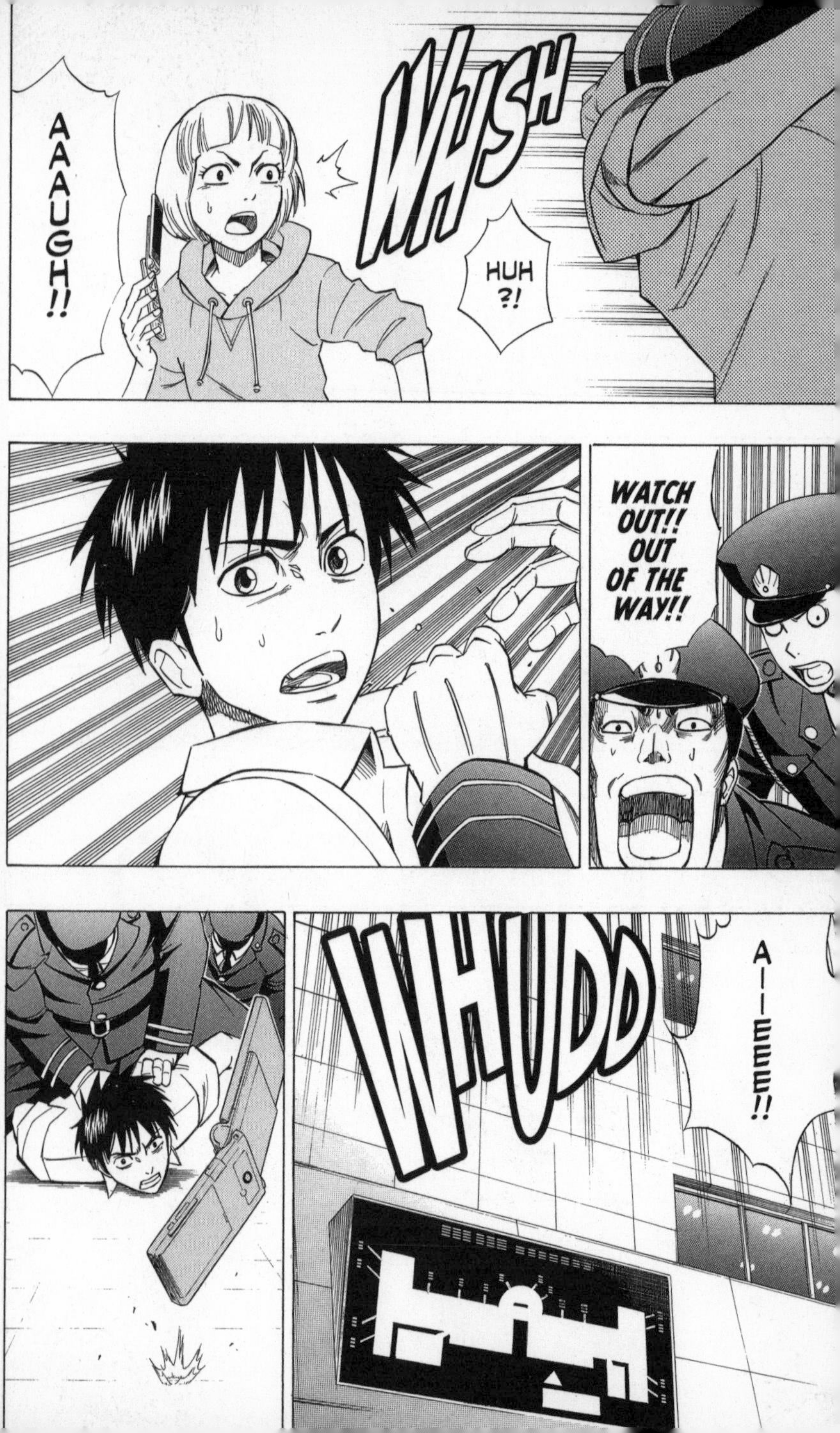
WHISH
HUH ?!
AAAUGH!!
WATCH OUT!! OUT OF THE WAY!!
AIIEEE!!
WHUDD

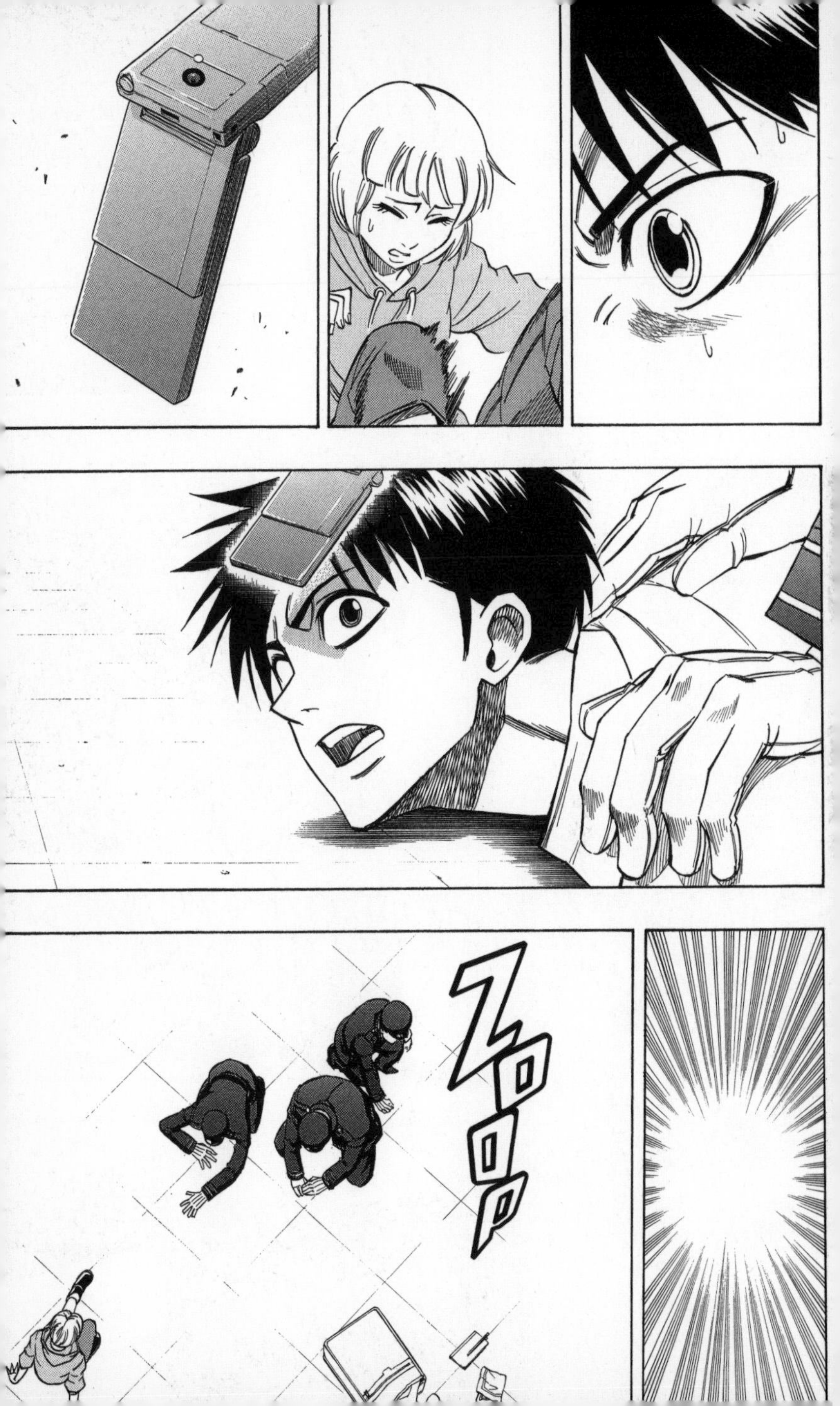
ZOOP

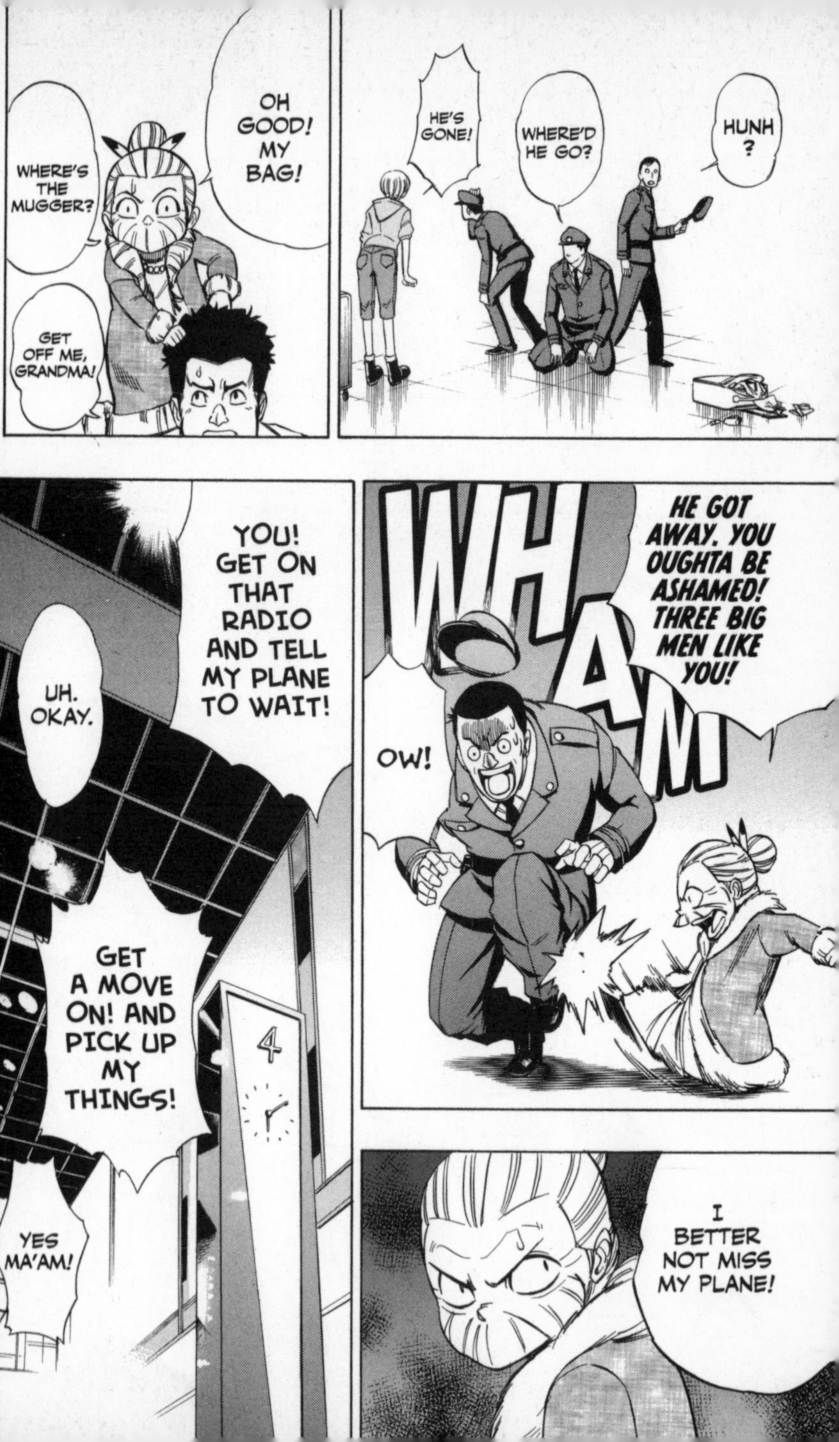
HUNH?
WHERE'D HE GO?
HE'S GONE!
OH GOOD! MY BAG!
WHERE'S THE MUGGER?
GET OFF ME, GRANDMA!
HE GOT AWAY. YOU OUGHTA BE ASHAMED! THREE BIG MEN LIKE YOU!
WHAM
OW!
I BETTER NOT MISS MY PLANE!
YOU! GET ON THAT RADIO AND TELL MY PLANE TO WAIT!
UH. OKAY.
GET A MOVE ON! AND PICK UP MY THINGS!
YES MA'AM!
4

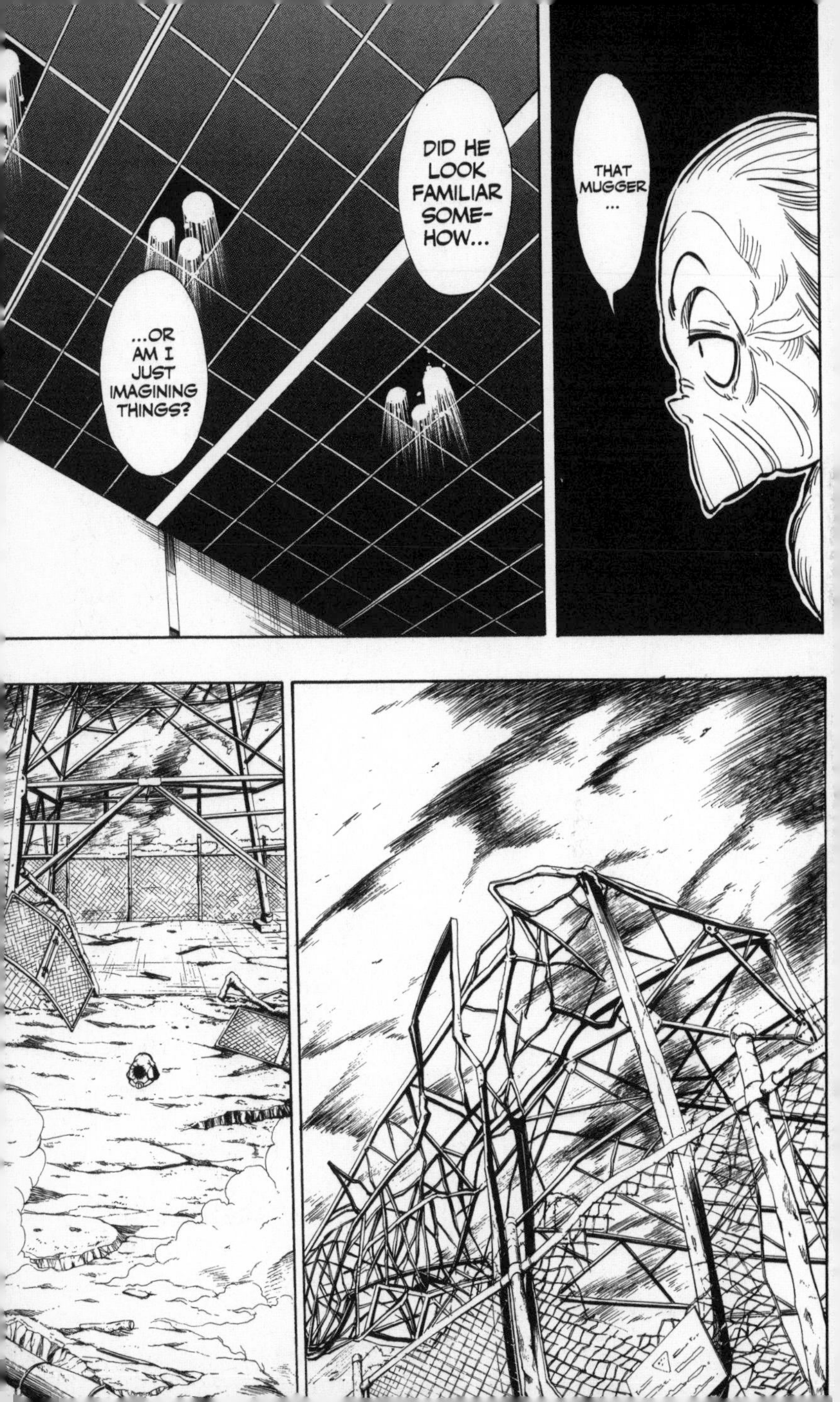
THAT MUGGER ...
DID HE LOOK FAMILIAR SOME-HOW...
...OR AM I JUST IMAGINING THINGS?

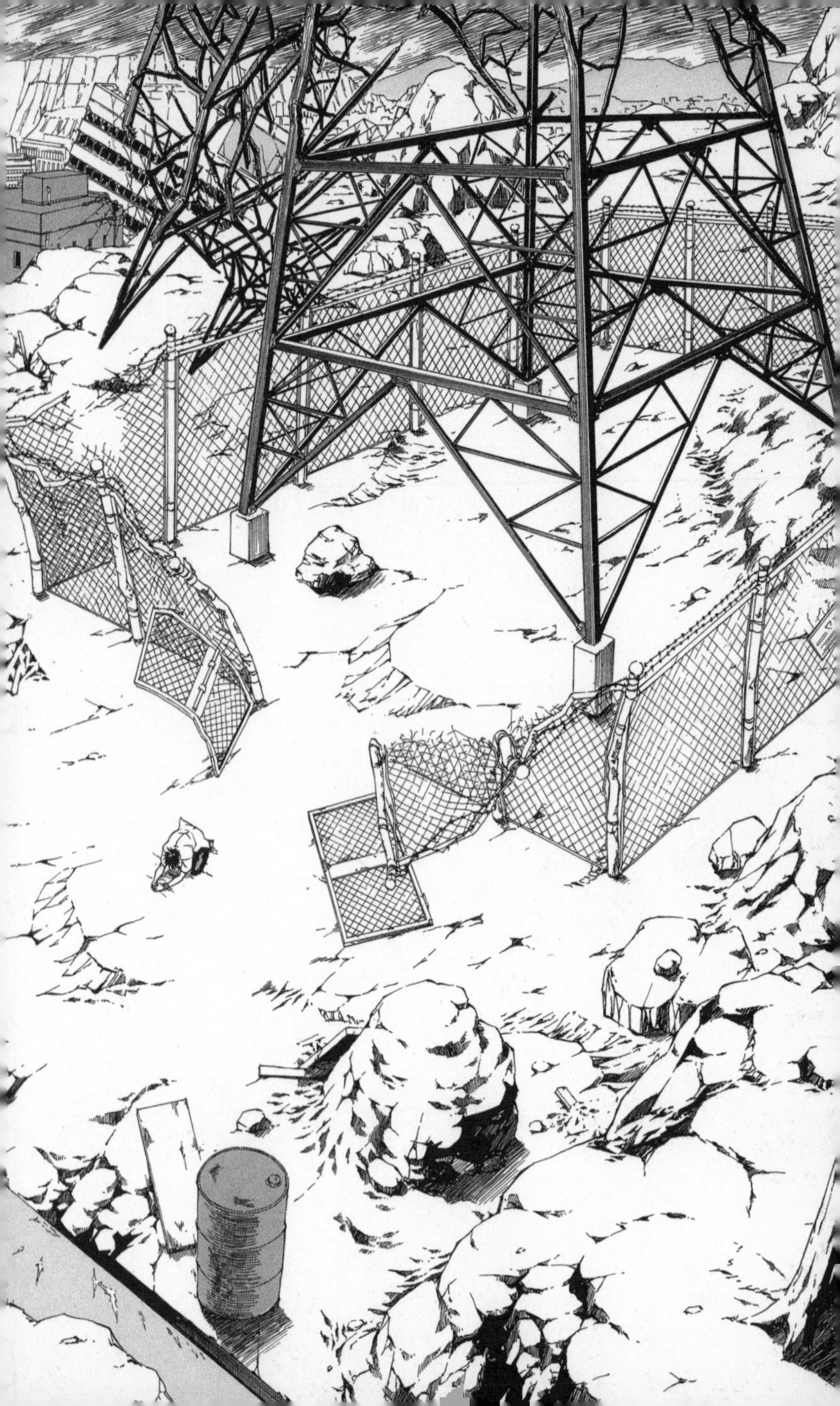

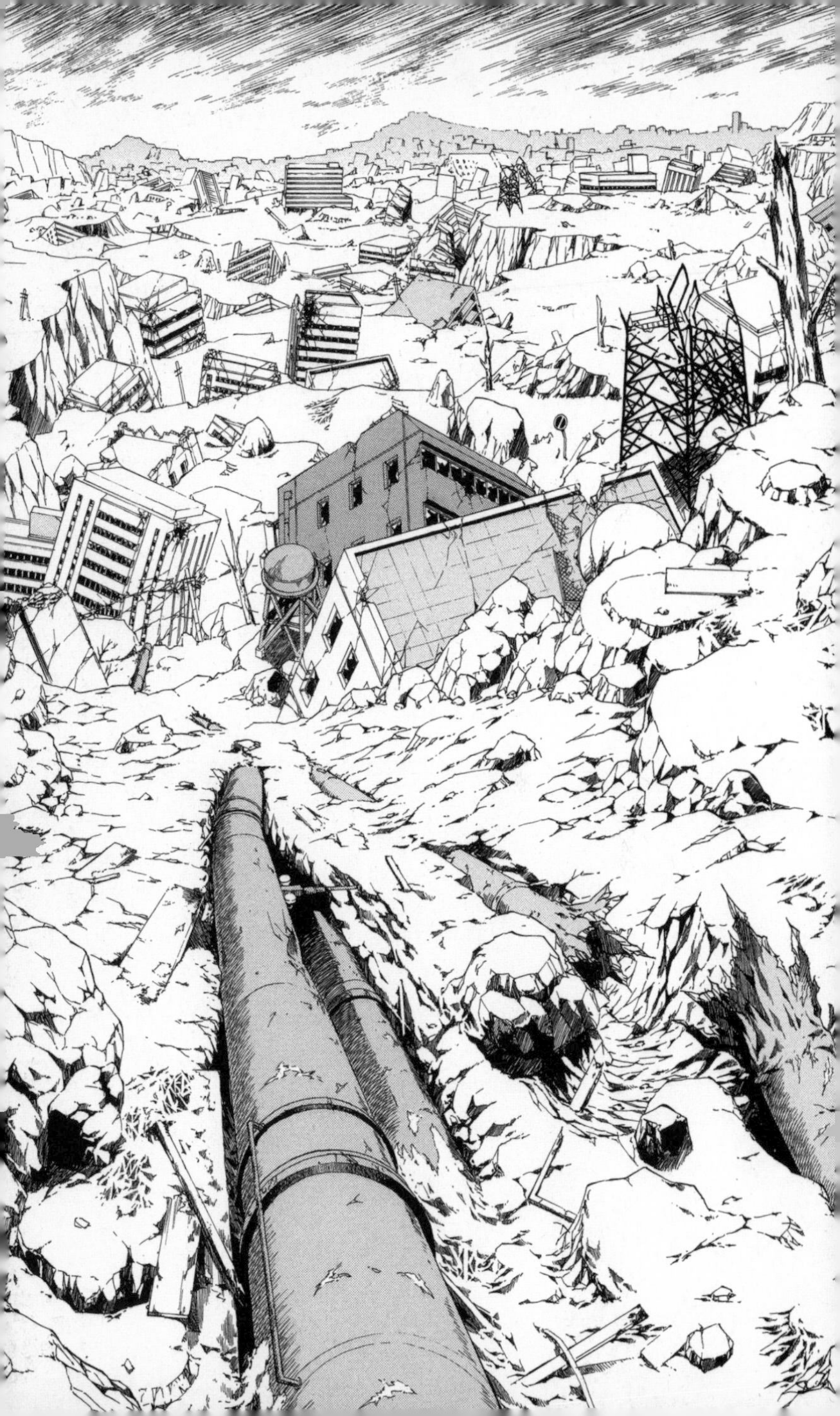

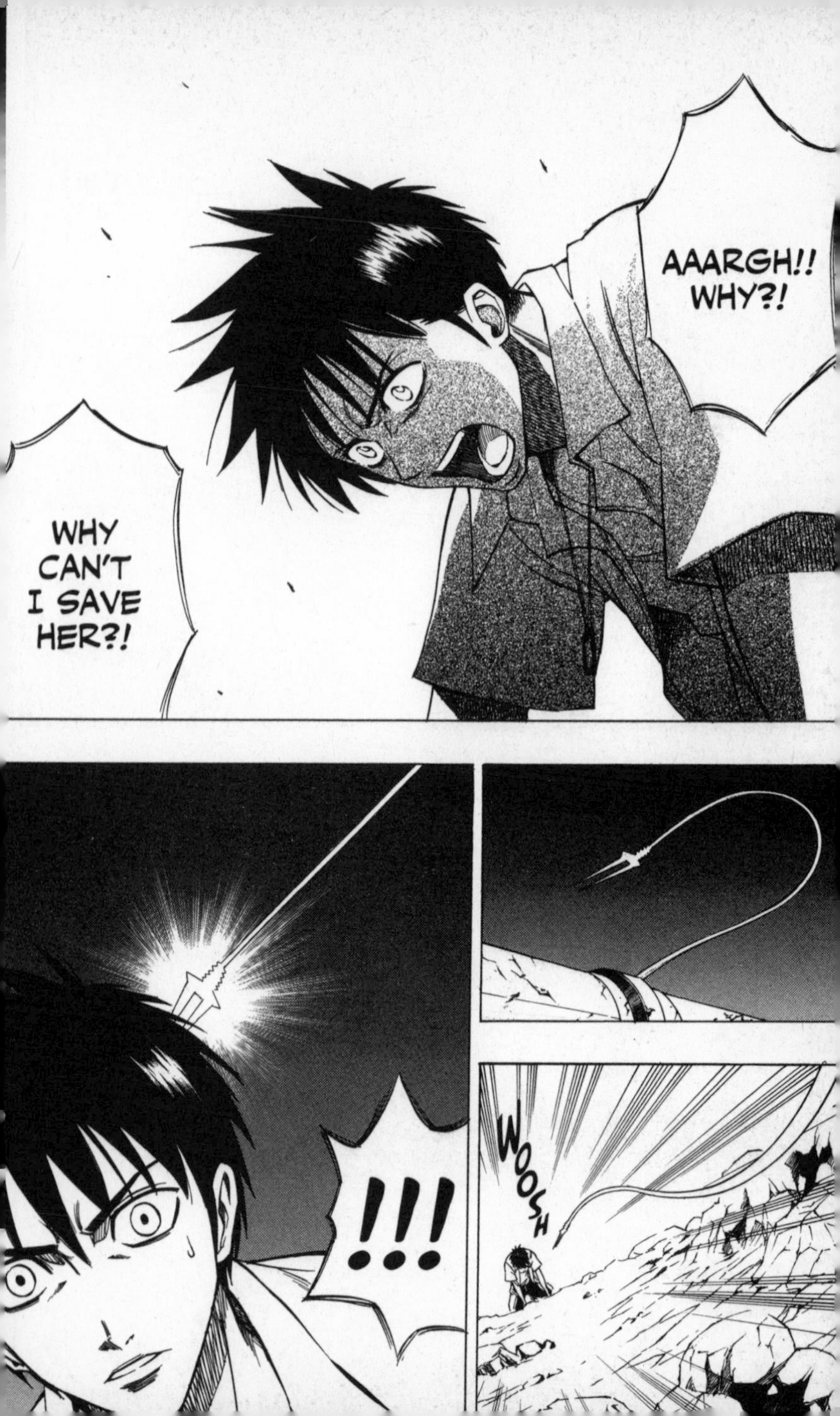
AAARGH!! WHY?!
WHY CAN'T I SAVE HER?!
!!!
WOOSH

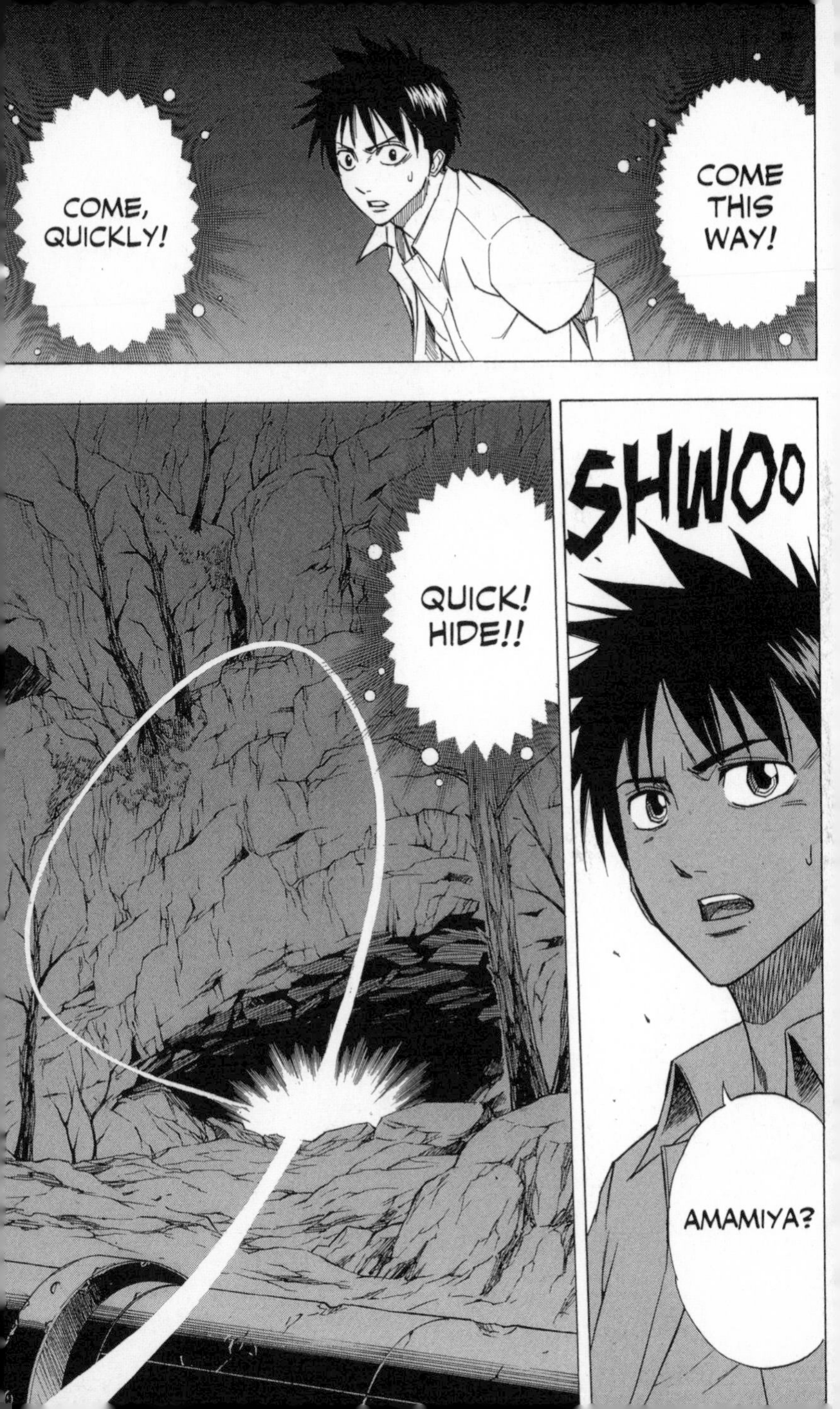
COME THIS WAY!
COME, QUICKLY!
SHWOO
AMAMIYA?
QUICK! HIDE!!

Background modified since
version published in JUMP

CALL.60: HEART OF STONE

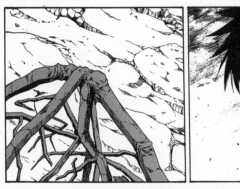

AMA-MIYA!!

CHAK

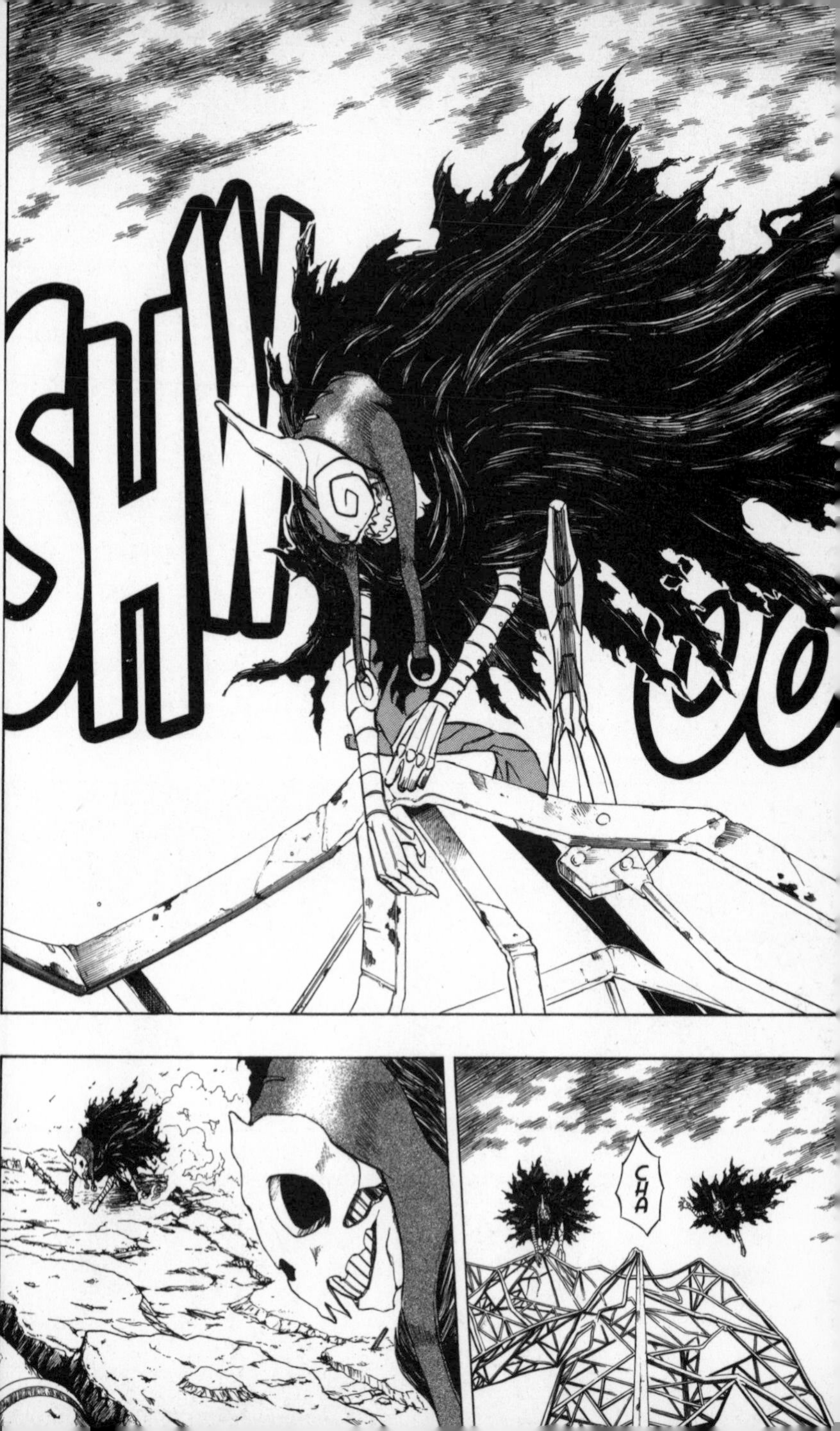
SHWOO
CHA

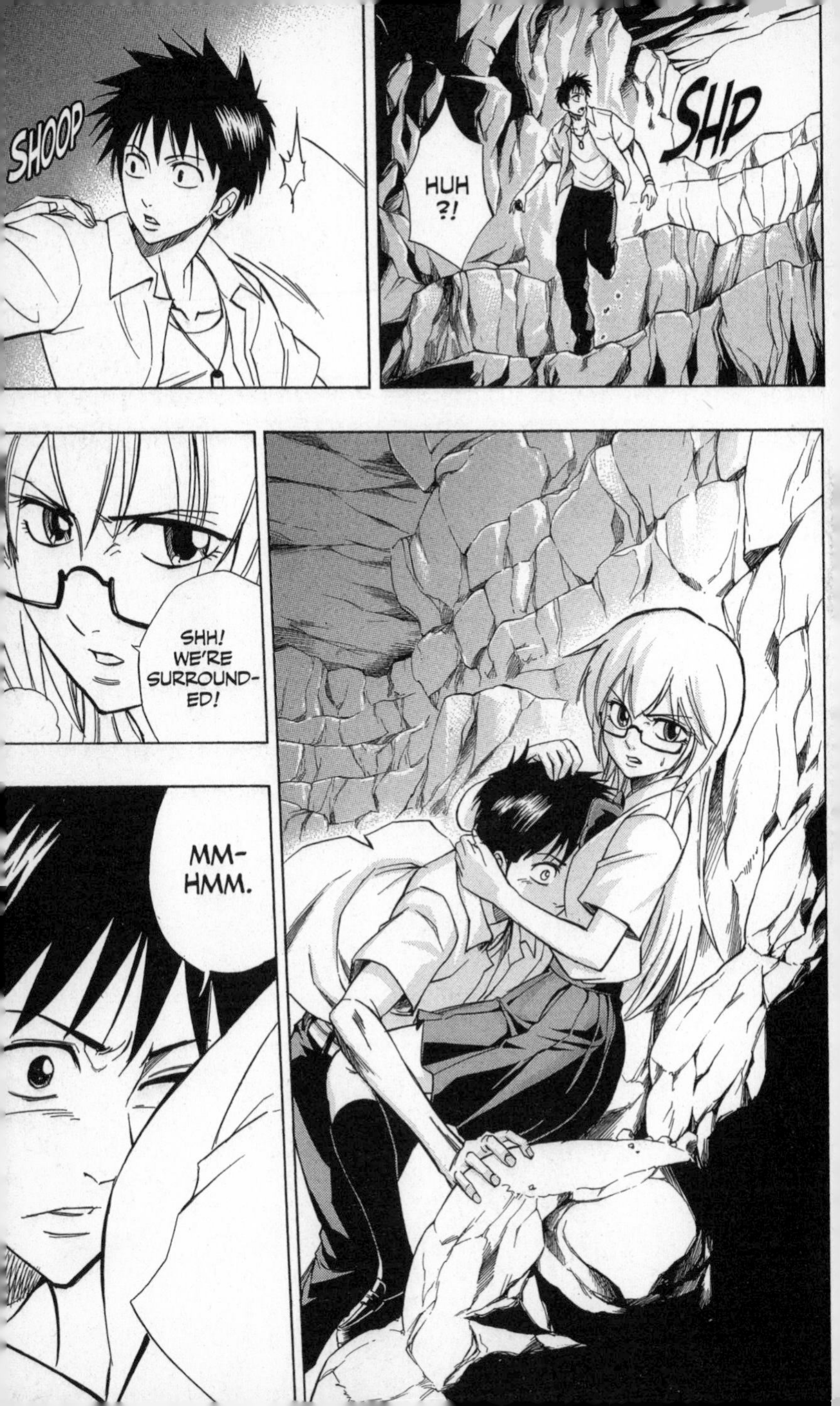
SHP
HUH ?!
SHOOP
SHH! WE'RE SURROUNDED!
MM-HMM.

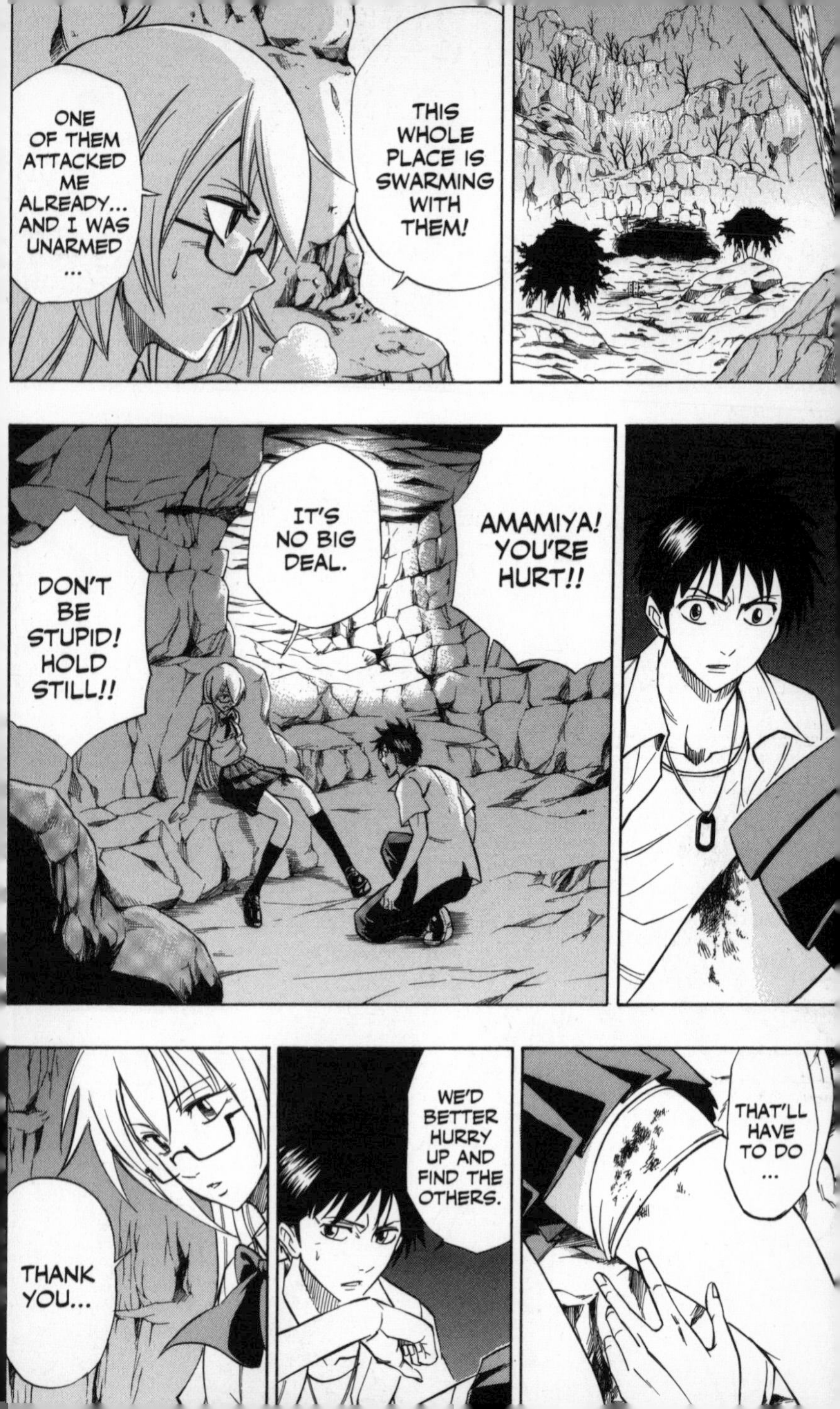
THIS WHOLE PLACE IS SWARMING WITH THEM!
ONE OF THEM ATTACKED ME ALREADY... AND I WAS UNARMED ...
AMAMIYA! YOU'RE HURT!!
IT'S NO BIG DEAL.
DON'T BE STUPID! HOLD STILL!!
THAT'LL HAVE TO DO ...
WE'D BETTER HURRY UP AND FIND THE OTHERS.
THANK YOU...

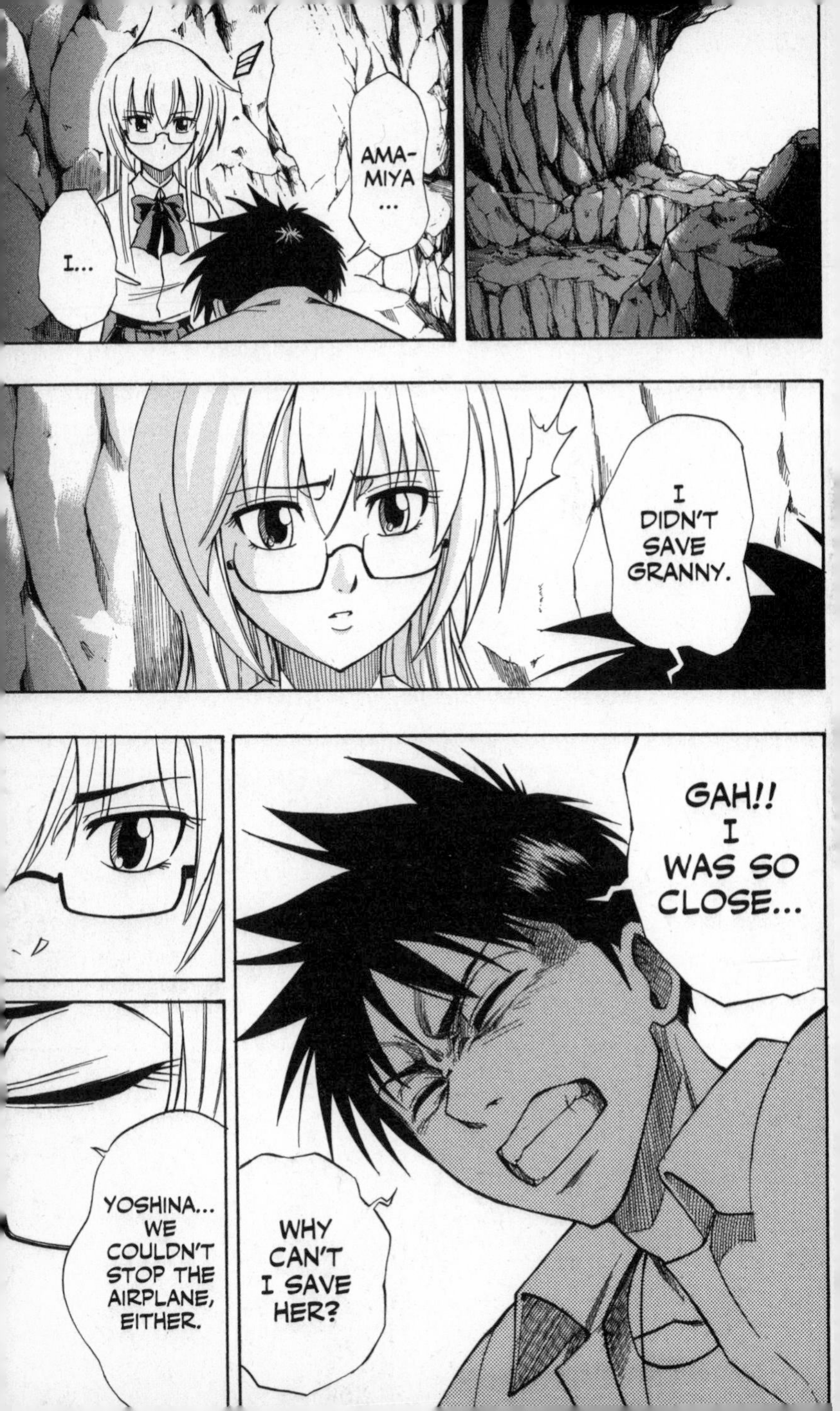
AMA-MIYA ...
I...
I DIDN'T SAVE GRANNY.
GAH!! I WAS SO CLOSE...
WHY CAN'T I SAVE HER?
YOSHINA... WE COULDN'T STOP THE AIRPLANE, EITHER.

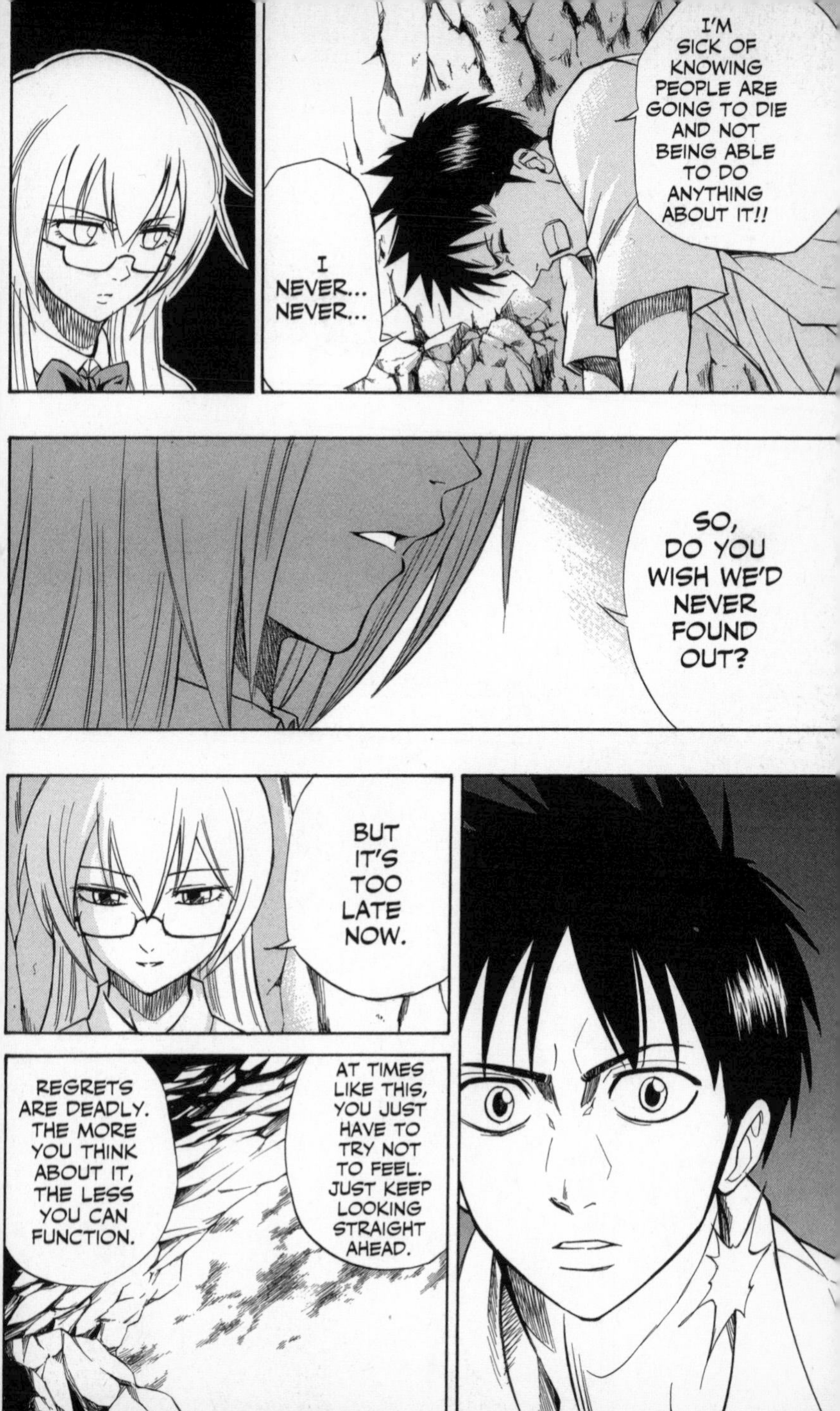
I'M SICK OF KNOWING PEOPLE ARE GOING TO DIE AND NOT BEING ABLE TO DO ANYTHING ABOUT IT!!
I NEVER... NEVER...
SO, DO YOU WISH WE'D NEVER FOUND OUT?
BUT IT'S TOO LATE NOW.
AT TIMES LIKE THIS, YOU JUST HAVE TO TRY NOT TO FEEL. JUST KEEP LOOKING STRAIGHT AHEAD.
REGRETS ARE DEADLY. THE MORE YOU THINK ABOUT IT, THE LESS YOU CAN FUNCTION.

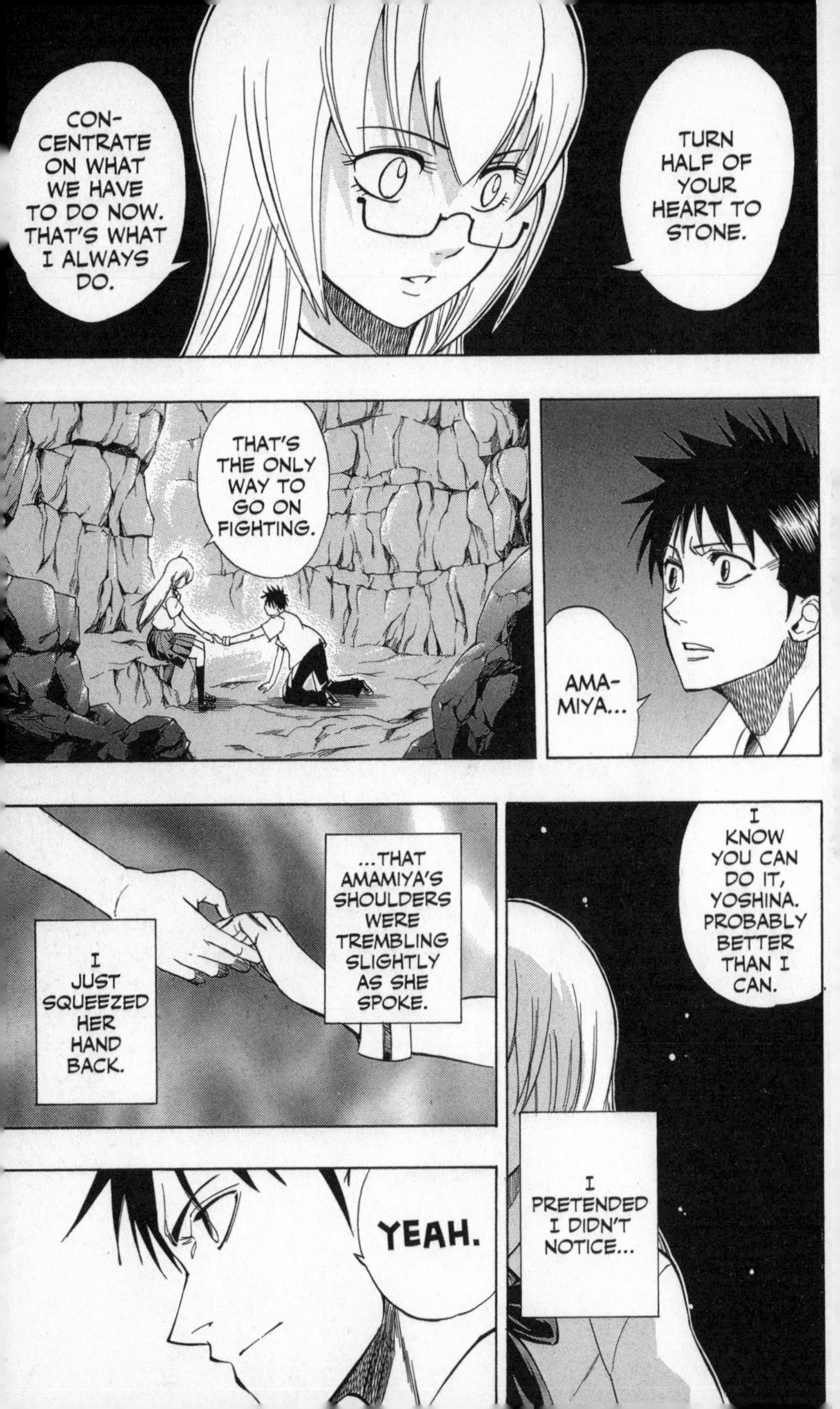
TURN HALF OF YOUR HEART TO STONE.
CON-CENTRATE ON WHAT WE HAVE TO DO NOW. THAT'S WHAT I ALWAYS DO.
AMA-MIYA...
THAT'S THE ONLY WAY TO GO ON FIGHTING.
I KNOW YOU CAN DO IT, YOSHINA. PROBABLY BETTER THAN I CAN.
I PRETENDED I DIDN'T NOTICE...
...THAT AMAMIYA'S SHOULDERS WERE TREMBLING SLIGHTLY AS SHE SPOKE.
I JUST SQUEEZED HER HAND BACK.
YEAH.

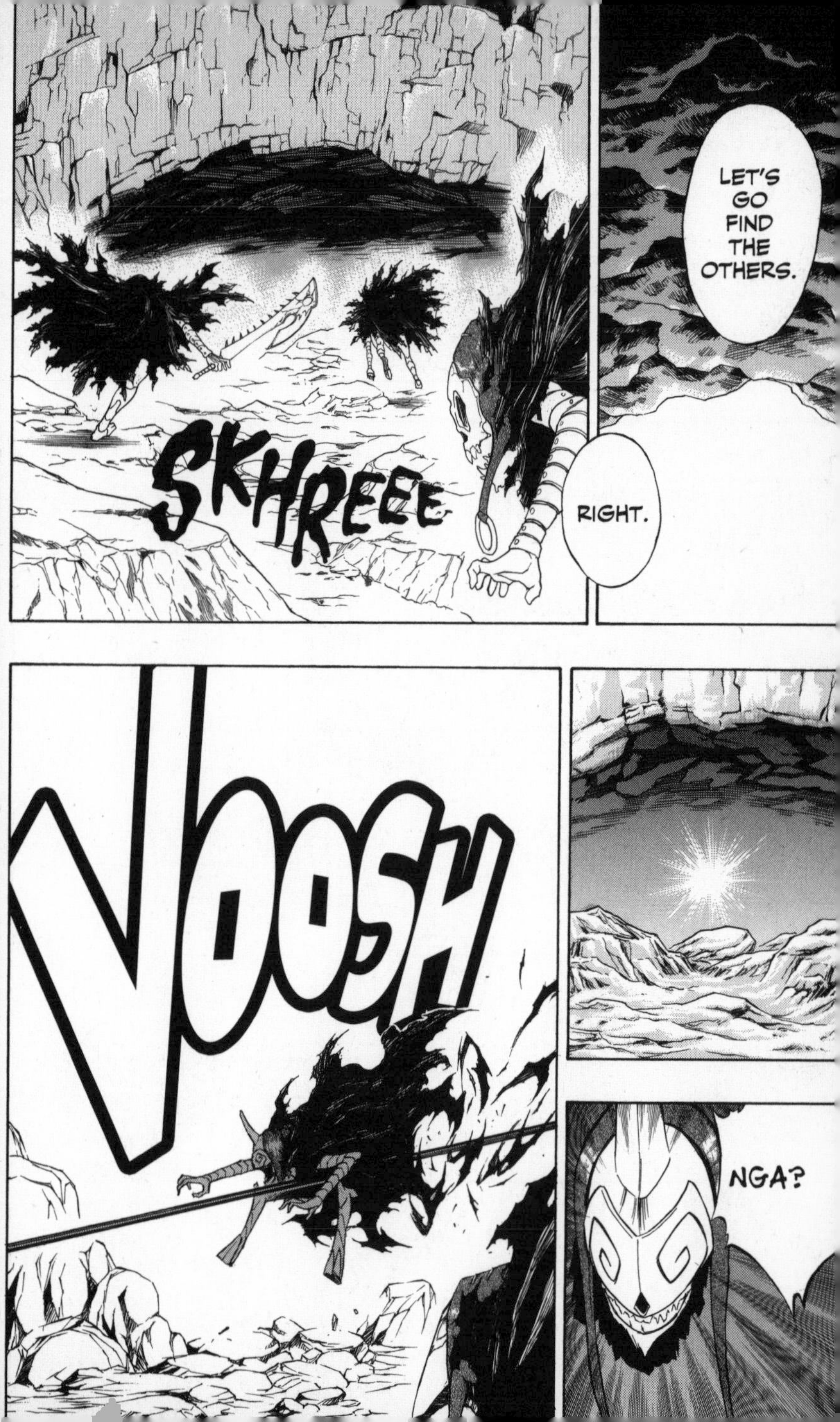
LET'S GO FIND THE OTHERS.
RIGHT.
SKHREEE
NGA?
VOOSH

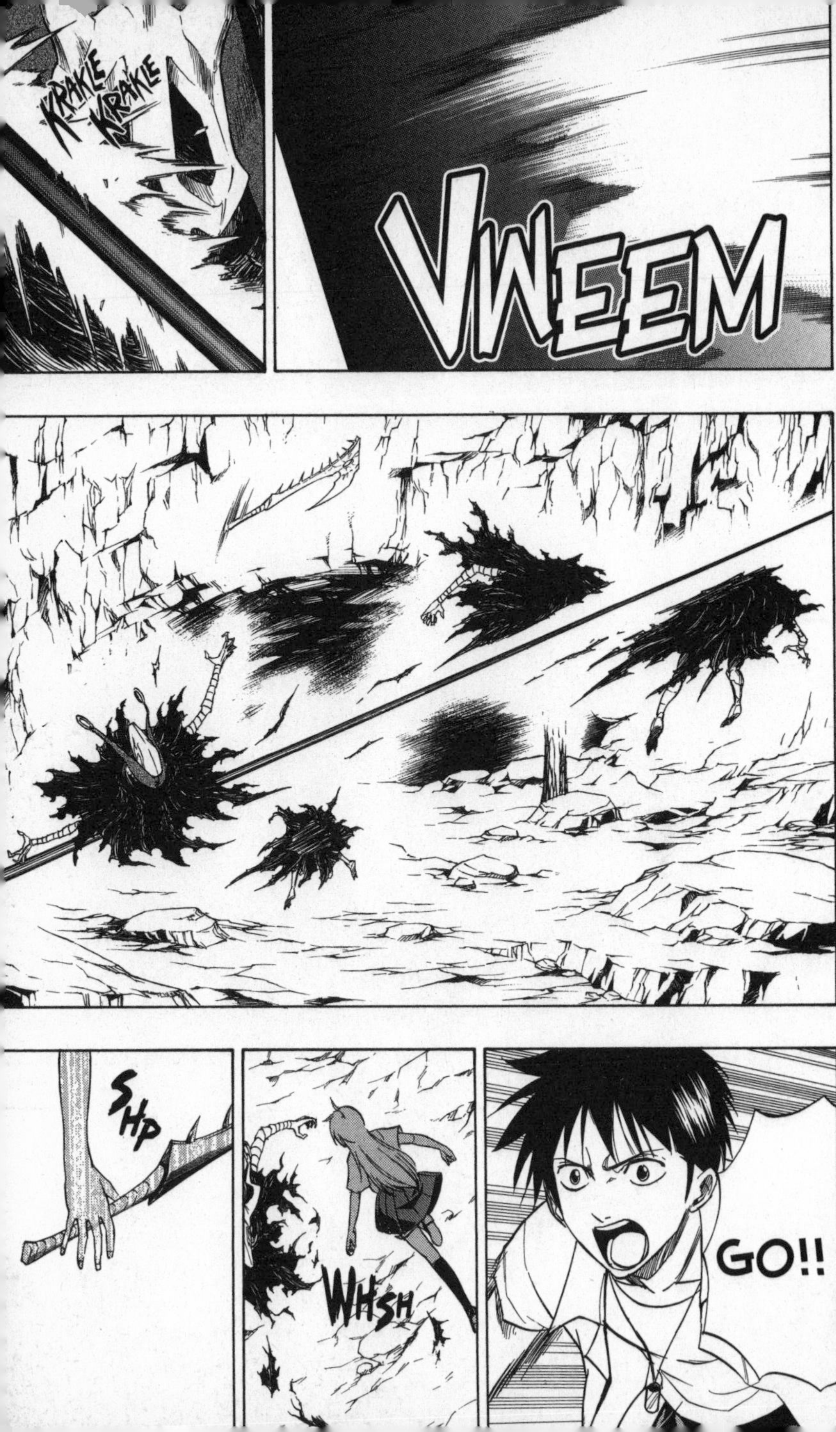
VWEEM
KRAKLE KRAKLE
GO!!
WHSH
SHP

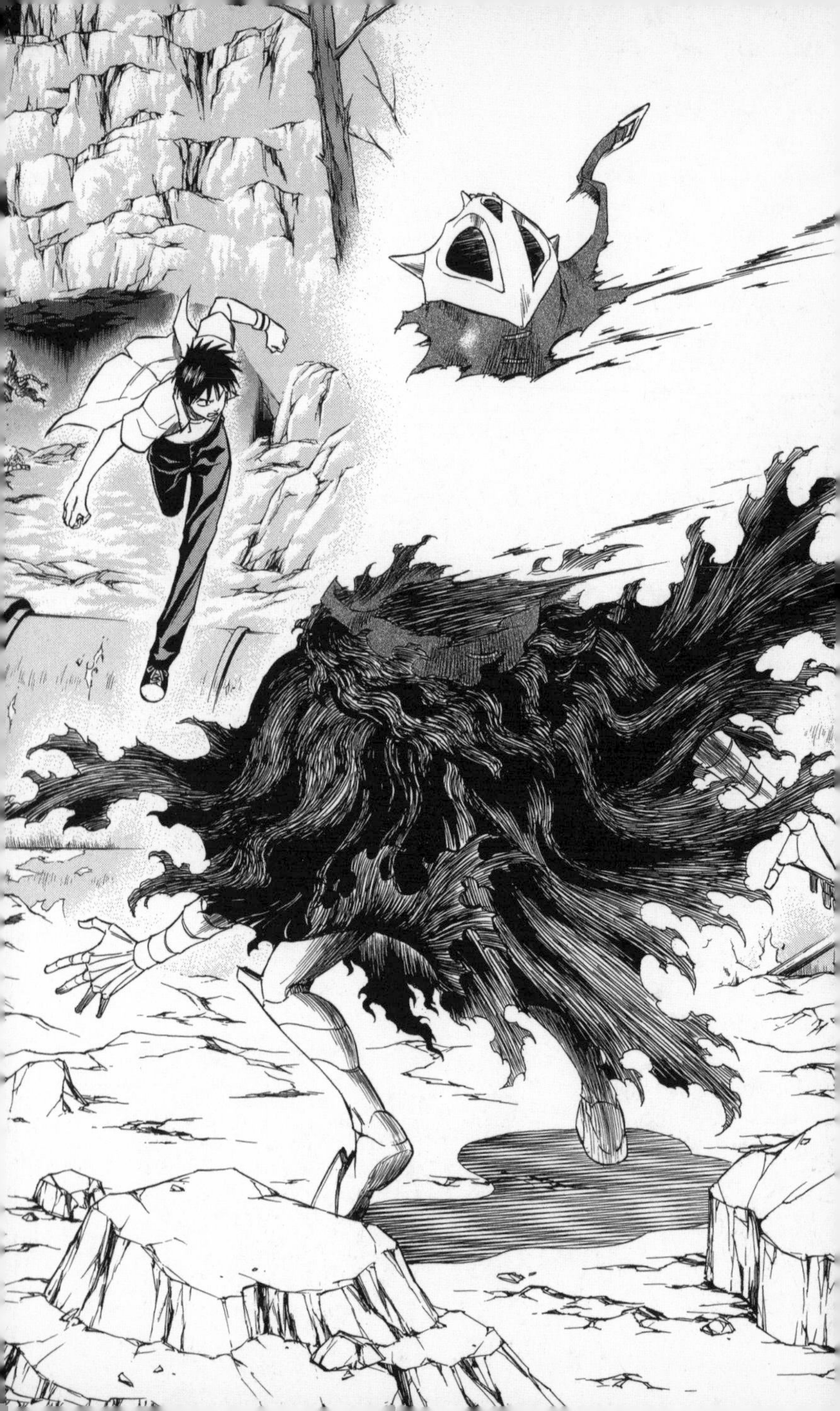

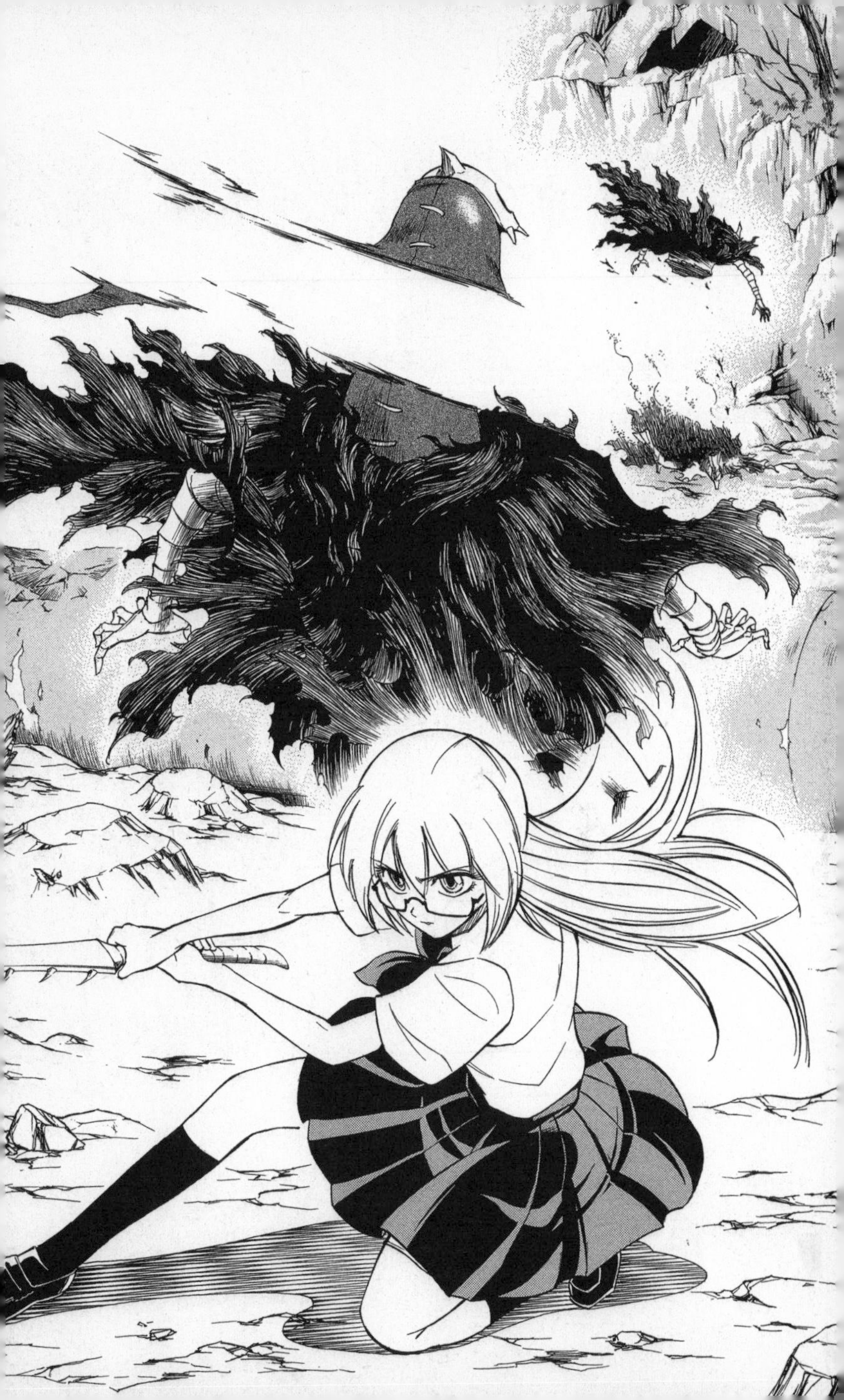

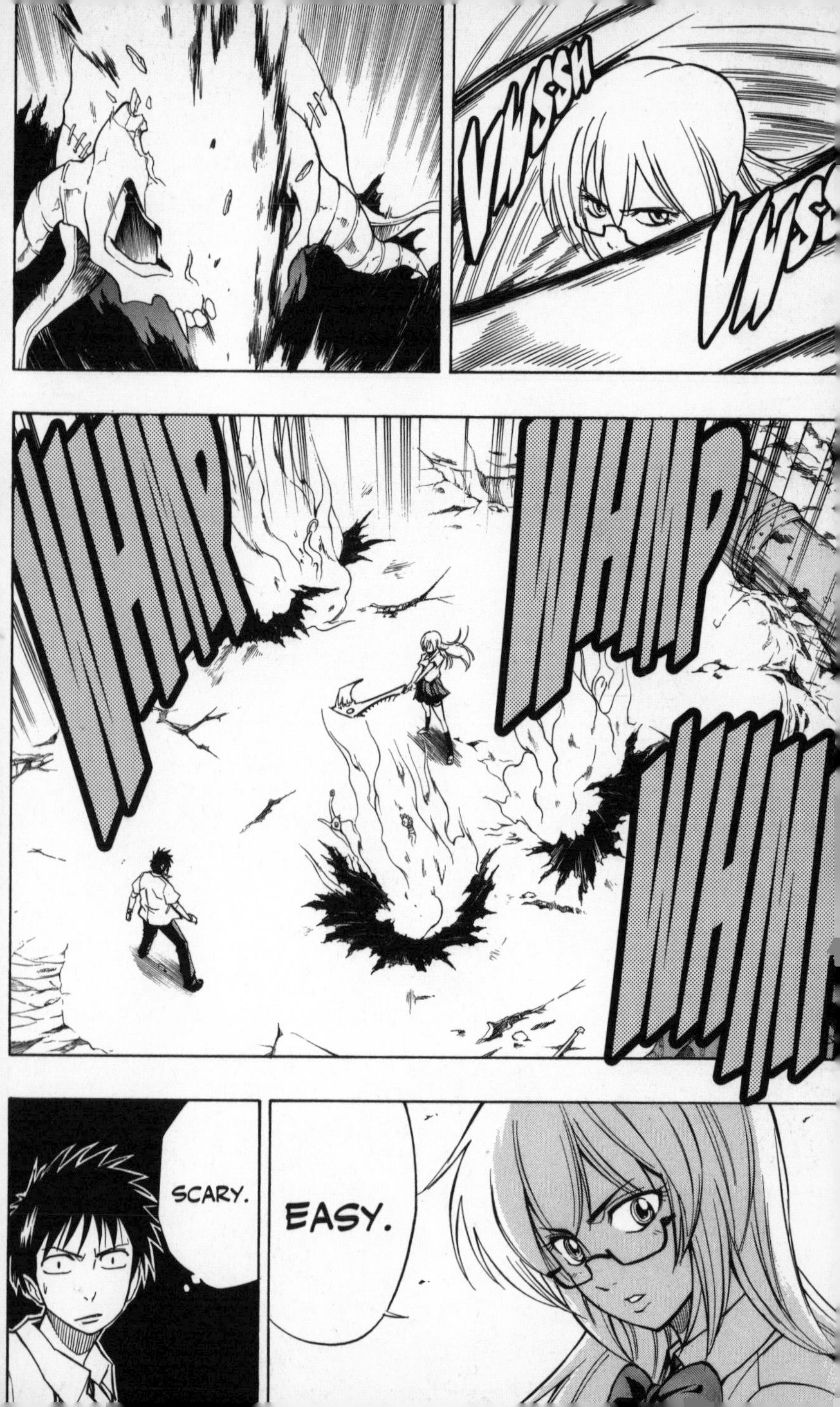
VWSSH
VWS
WHIP
WHI
WHIP
EASY.
SCARY.

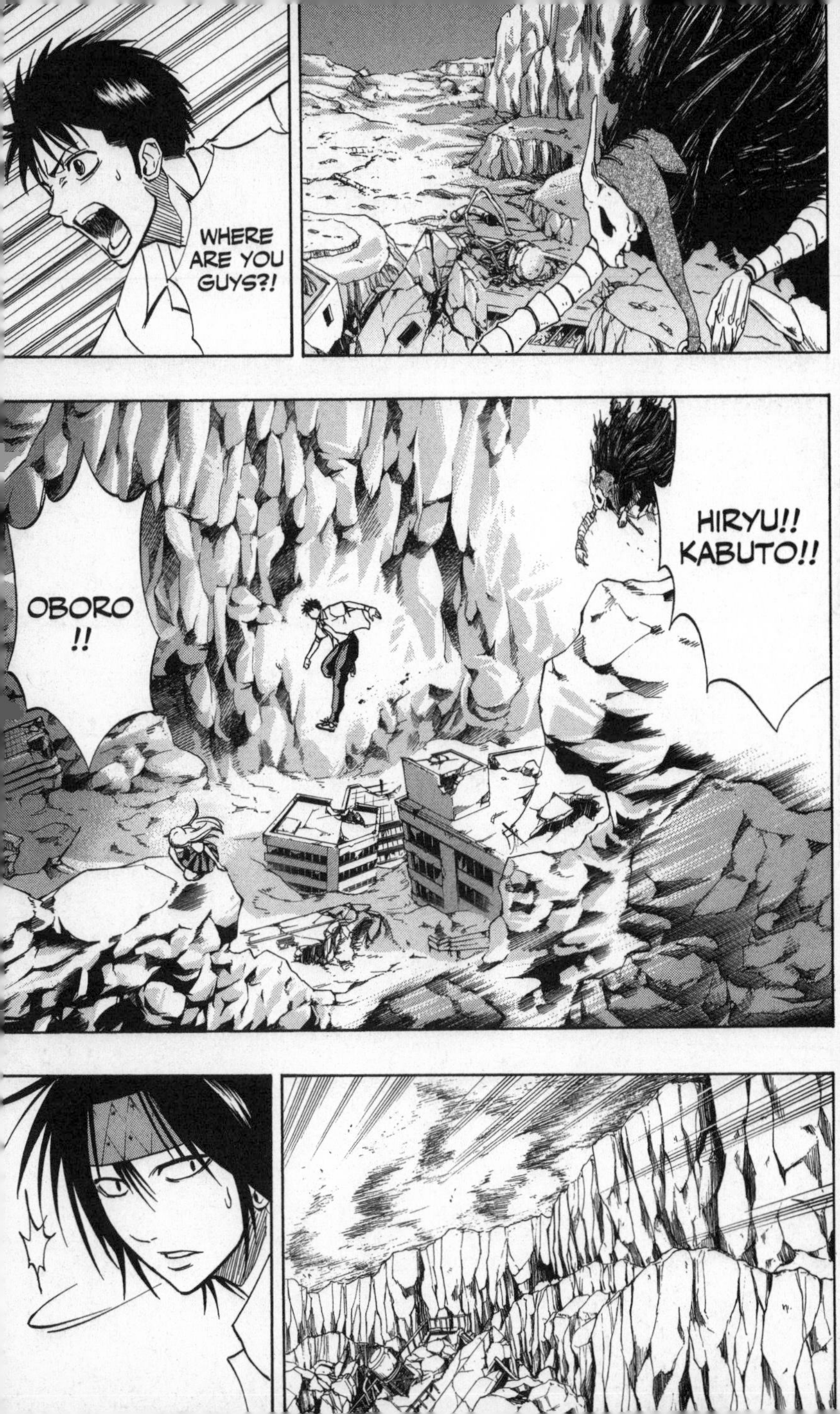
WHERE ARE YOU GUYS?!
HIRYU!! KABUTO!!
OBORO !!

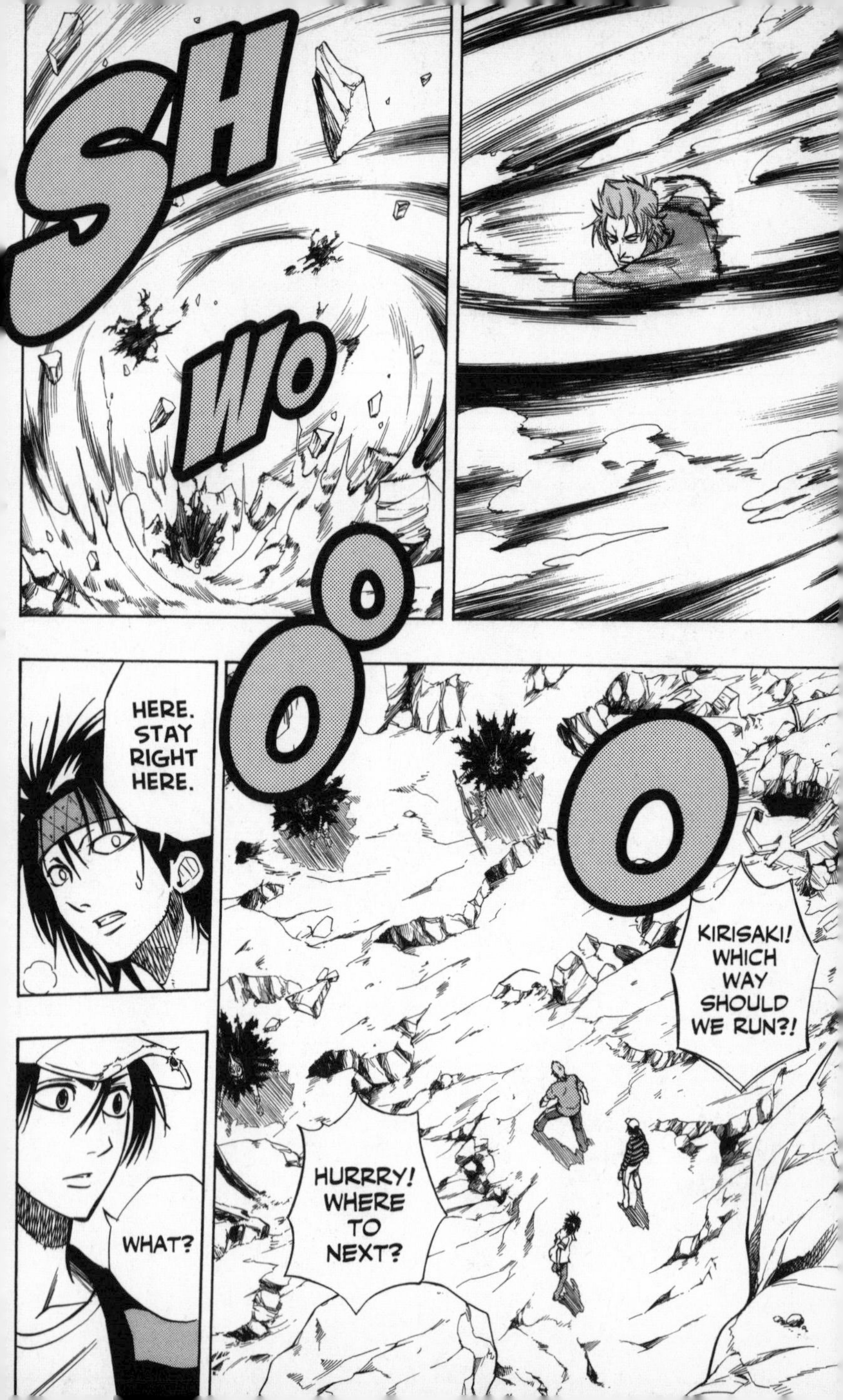
SHWOOOO
KIRISAKI! WHICH WAY SHOULD WE RUN?!
HURRRY! WHERE TO NEXT?
HERE. STAY RIGHT HERE.
WHAT?

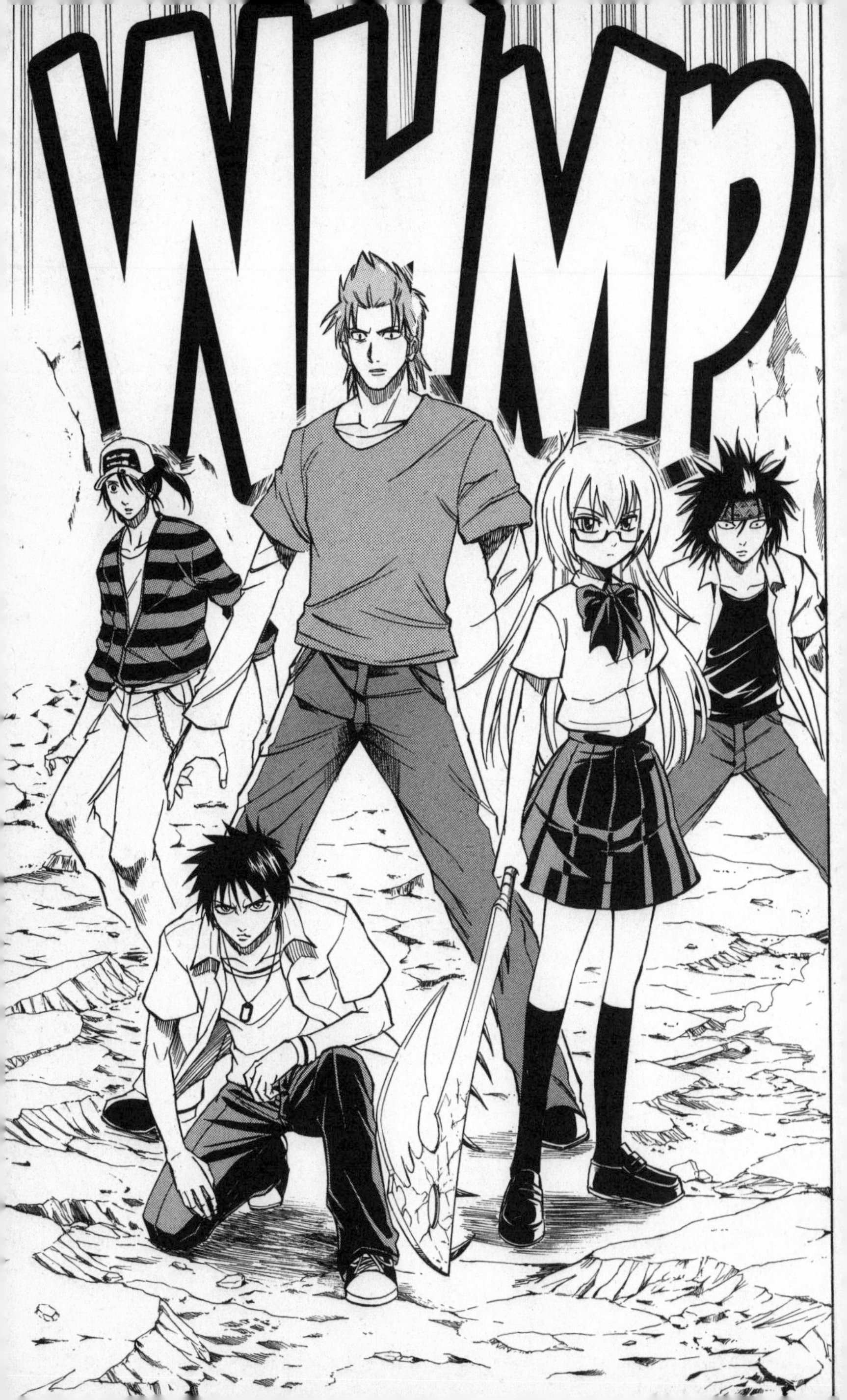
WUMP

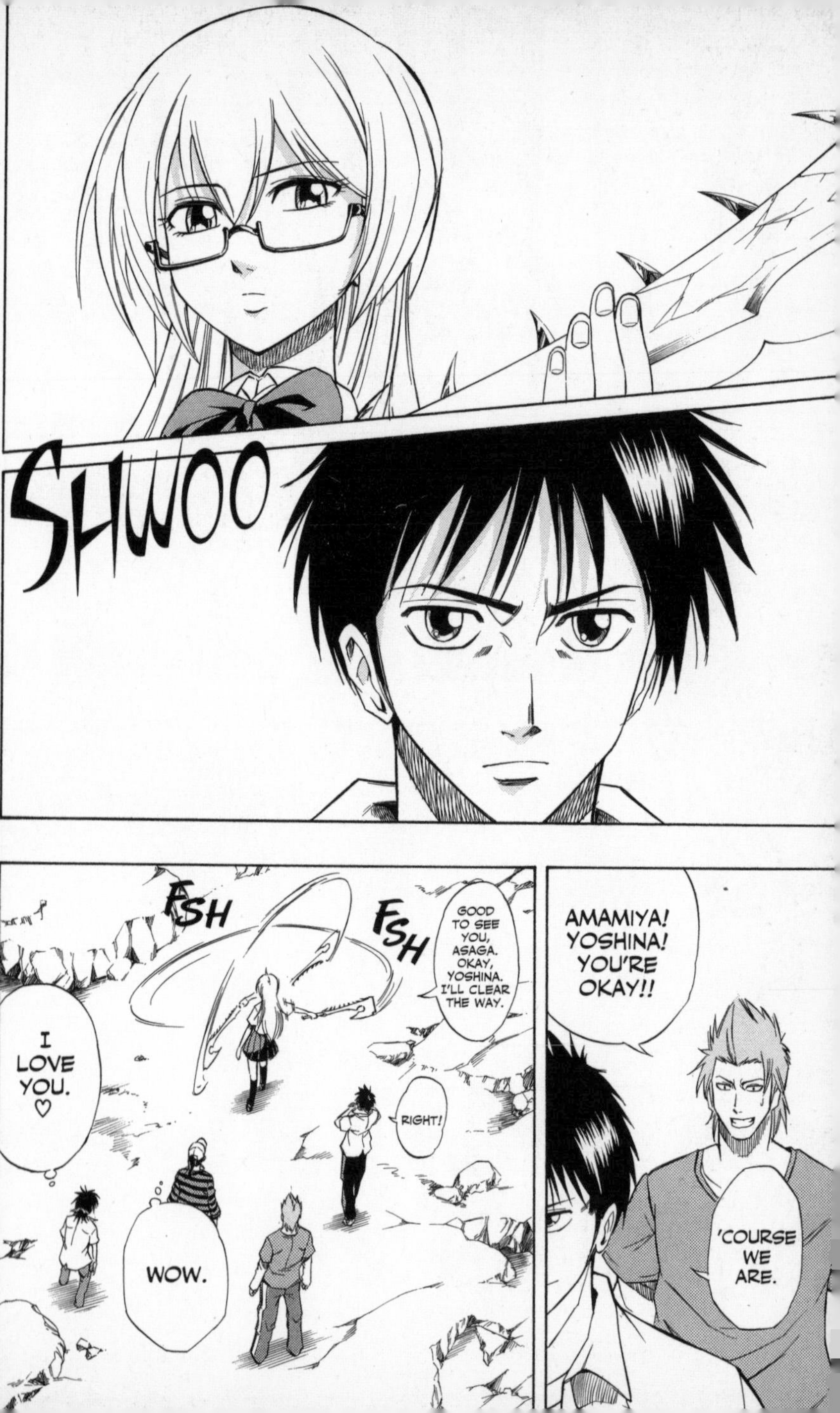
SHWOO
AMAMIYA! YOSHINA! YOU'RE OKAY!!
'COURSE WE ARE.
FSH
FSH
GOOD TO SEE YOU, ASAGA. OKAY, YOSHINA. I'LL CLEAR THE WAY.
RIGHT!
WOW.
I LOVE YOU. ♡

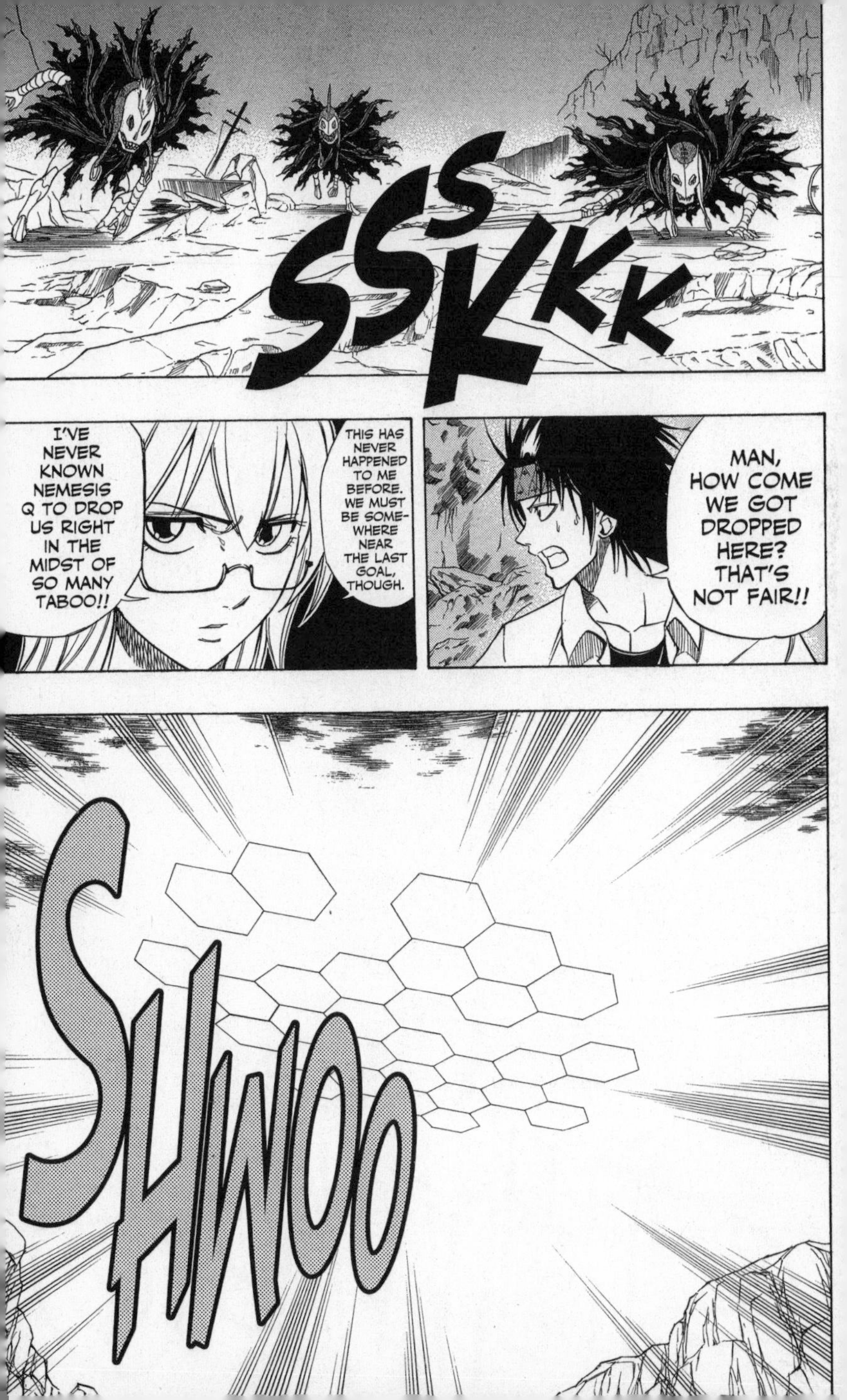
SSSKKK
MAN, HOW COME WE GOT DROPPED HERE? THAT'S NOT FAIR!!
THIS HAS NEVER HAPPENED TO ME BEFORE. WE MUST BE SOME-WHERE NEAR THE LAST GOAL, THOUGH.
I'VE NEVER KNOWN NEMESIS Q TO DROP US RIGHT IN THE MIDST OF SO MANY TABOO!!
SHWOO

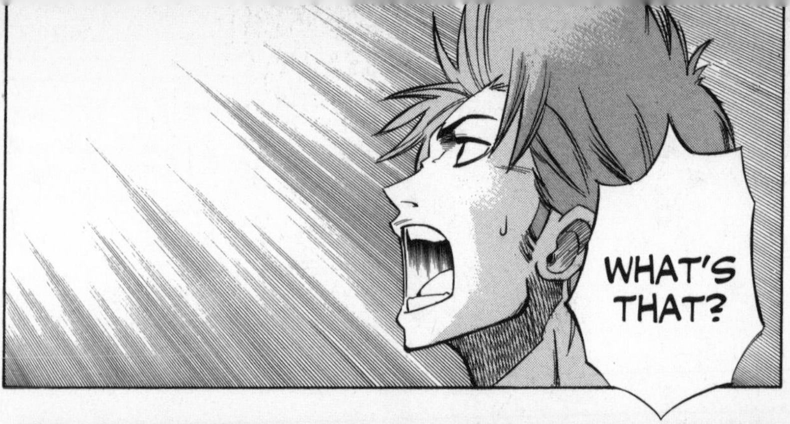
WHAT'S THAT?

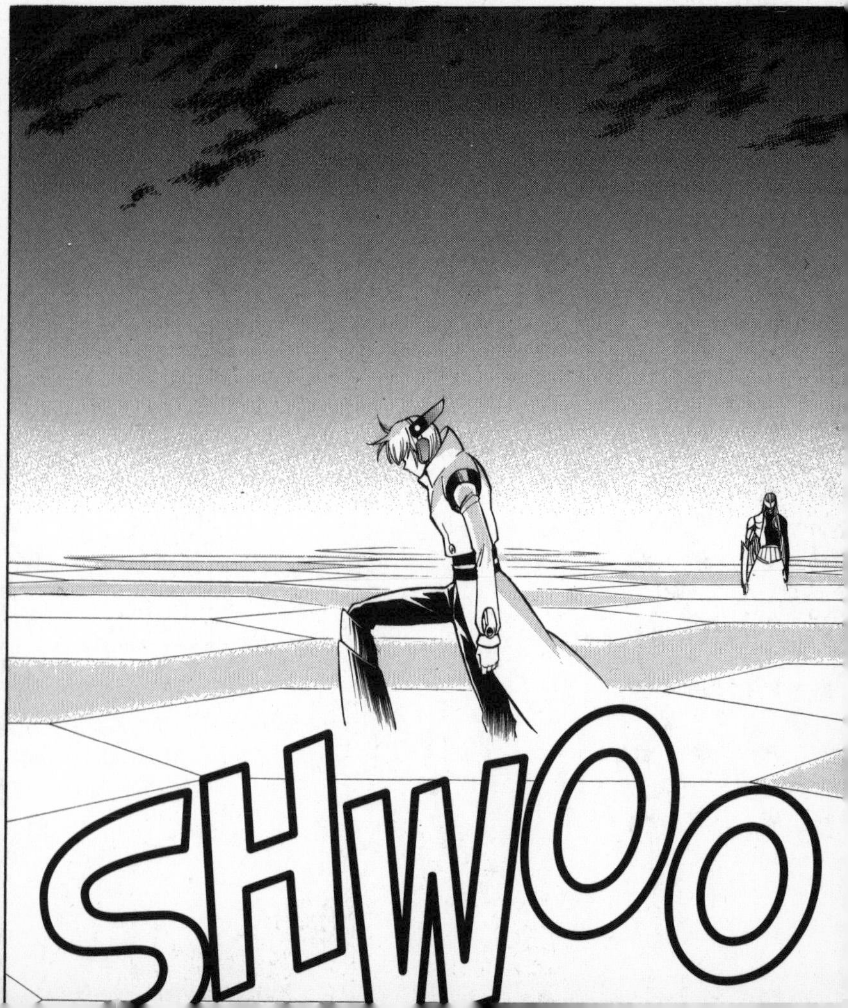
SHWOO

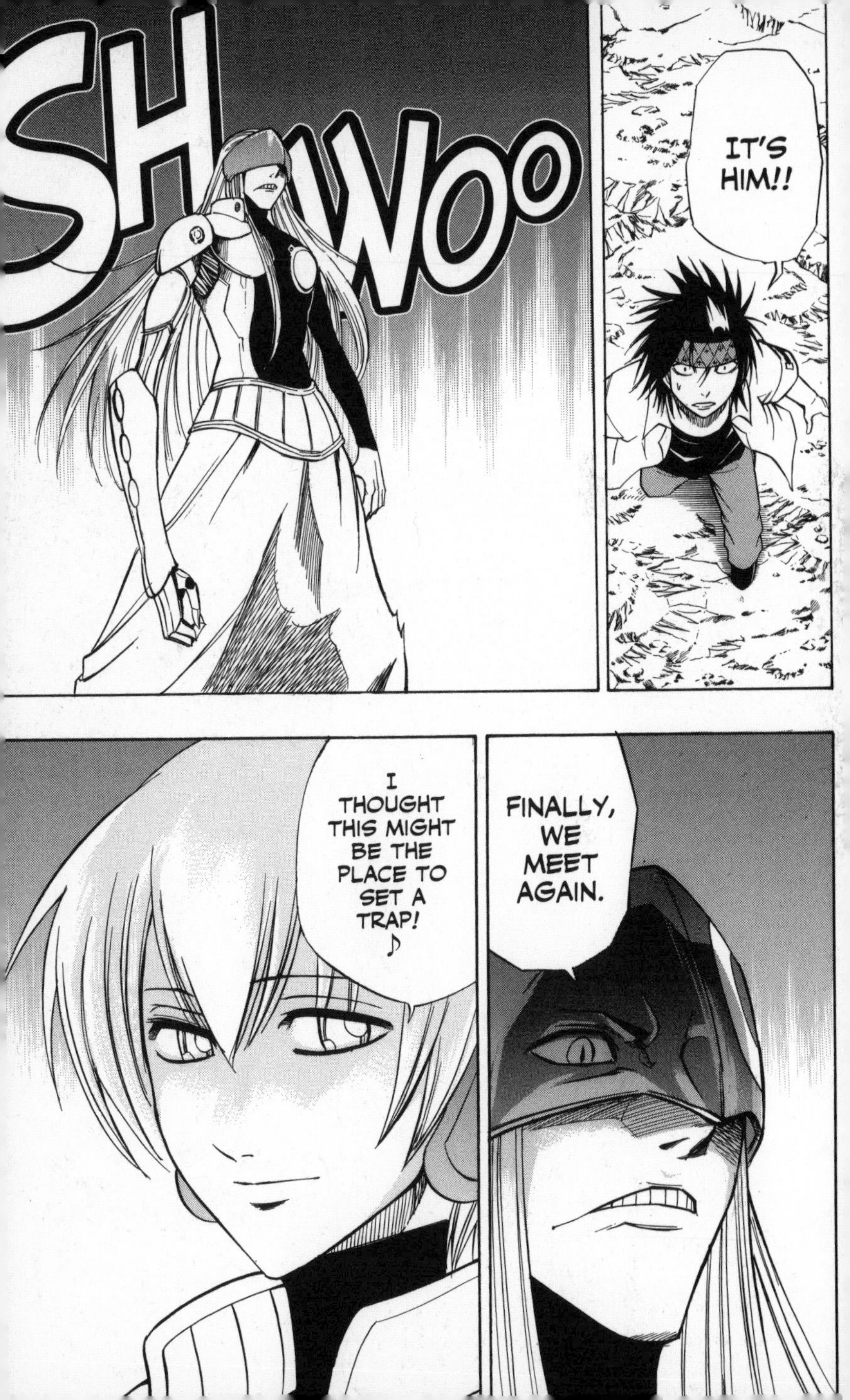
IT'S HIM!!
SHWOO
FINALLY, WE MEET AGAIN.
I THOUGHT THIS MIGHT BE THE PLACE TO SET A TRAP! ♪

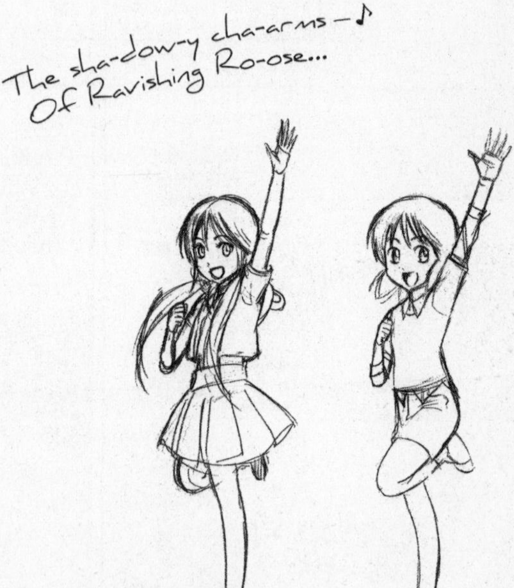
The sha-dow-y cha-arms-♪
Of Ravishing Ro-ose...

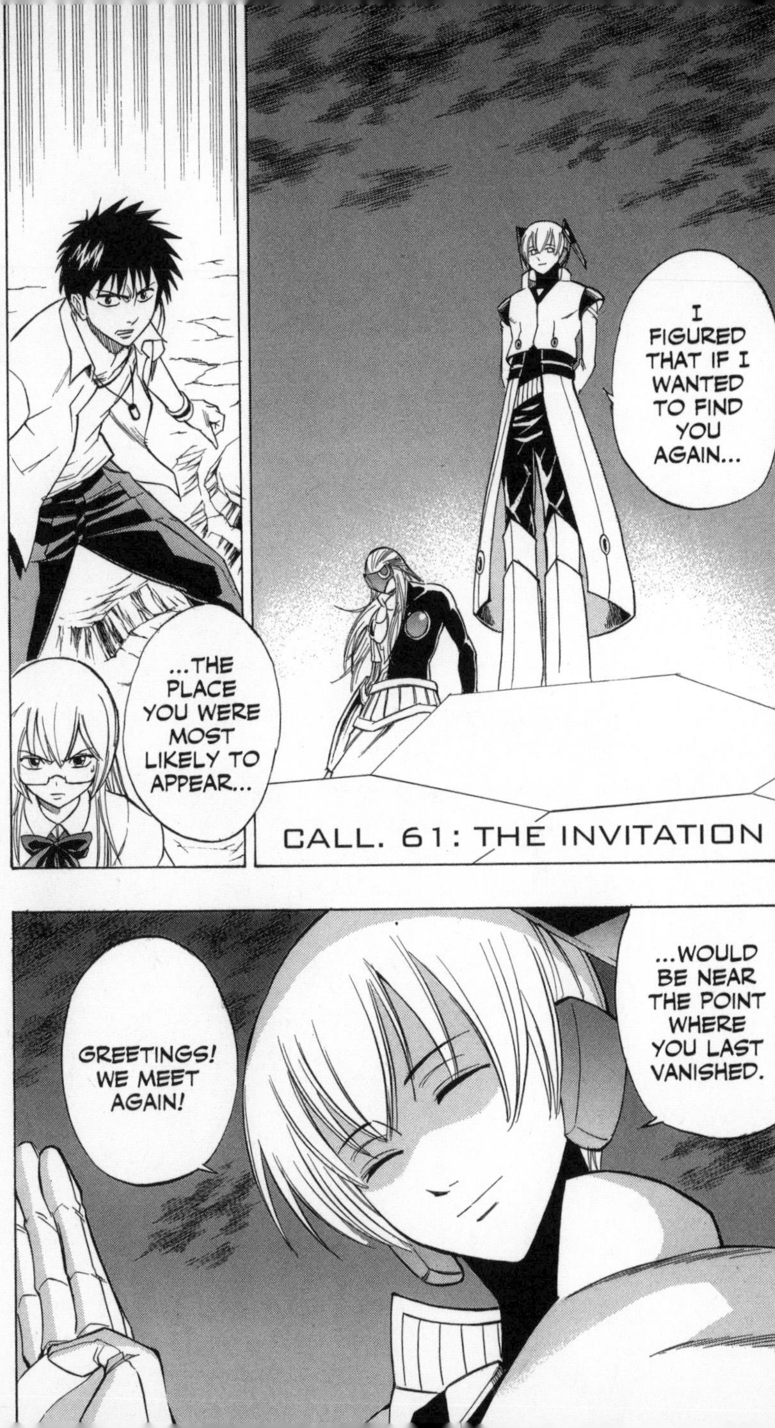
I FIGURED THAT IF I WANTED TO FIND YOU AGAIN...
CALL. 61: THE INVITATION
...THE PLACE YOU WERE MOST LIKELY TO APPEAR...
...WOULD BE NEAR THE POINT WHERE YOU LAST VANISHED.
GREETINGS! WE MEET AGAIN!

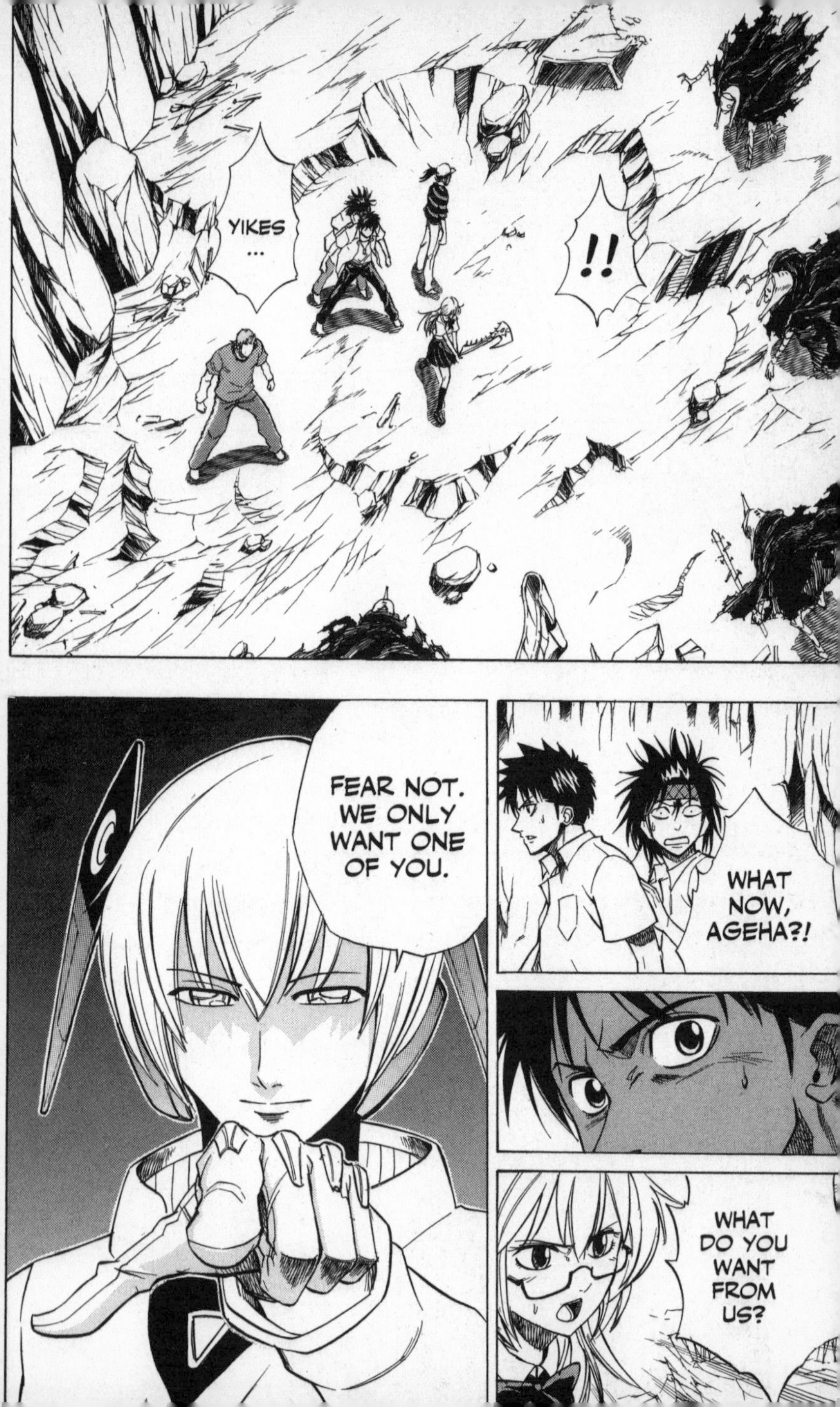
!!
YIKES ...
WHAT NOW, AGEHA?!
WHAT DO YOU WANT FROM US?
FEAR NOT. WE ONLY WANT ONE OF YOU.

YOU! THE ONE WITH THE BLACK BLAST ATTACK! BY THE ORDERS OF FIRST STAR COMMANDER GRANAR...

...I WILL NOW ESCORT YOU TO ASTRAL NAVA, W.I.S.E HEADQUARTERS!

SHWOO

REFUSAL IS NOT AN OPTION.

WHAT ?!

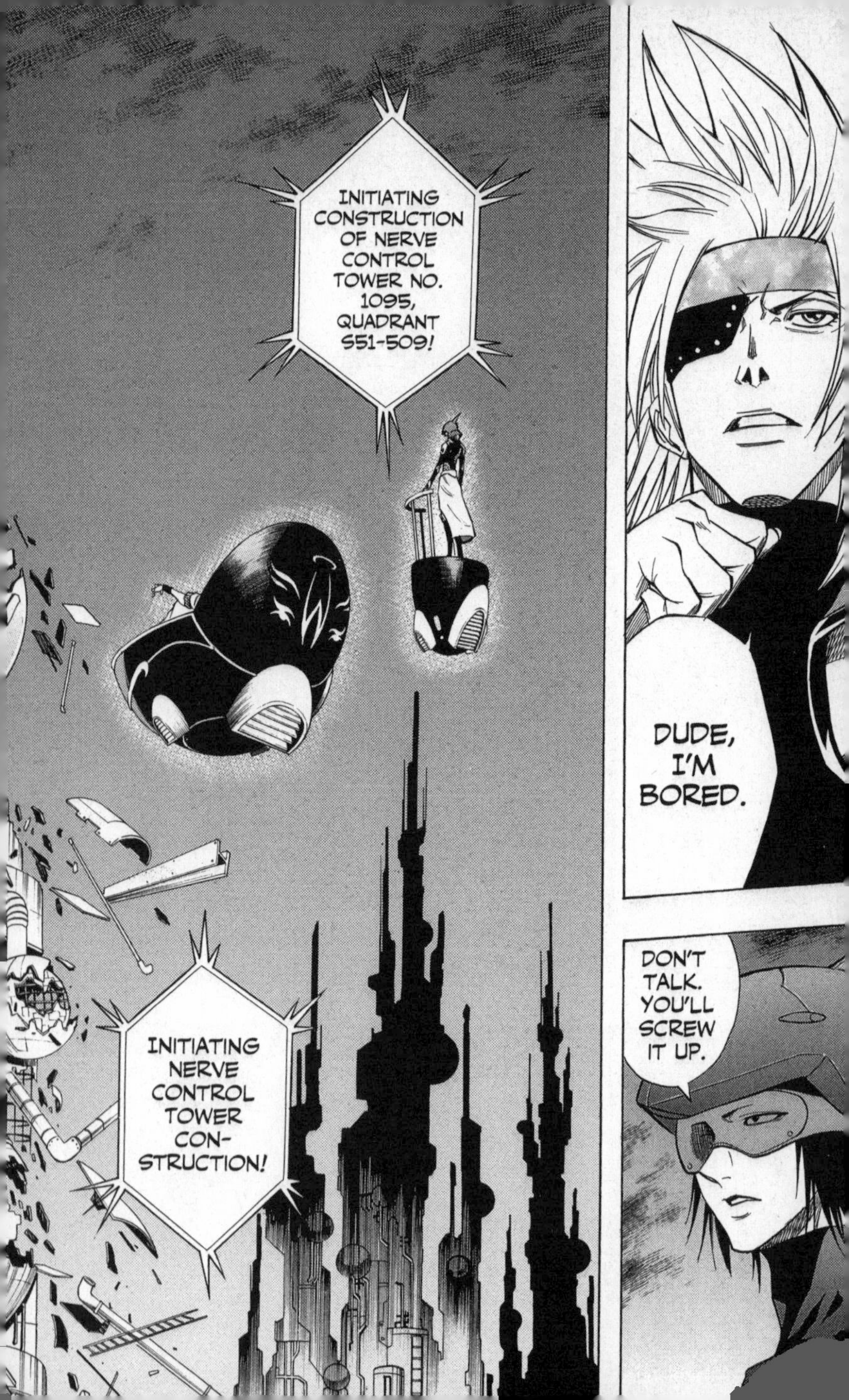
DUDE, I'M BORED.
DON'T TALK. YOU'LL SCREW IT UP.
INITIATING CONSTRUCTION OF NERVE CONTROL TOWER NO. 1095, QUADRANT S51-509!
INITIATING NERVE CONTROL TOWER CON-STRUCTION!

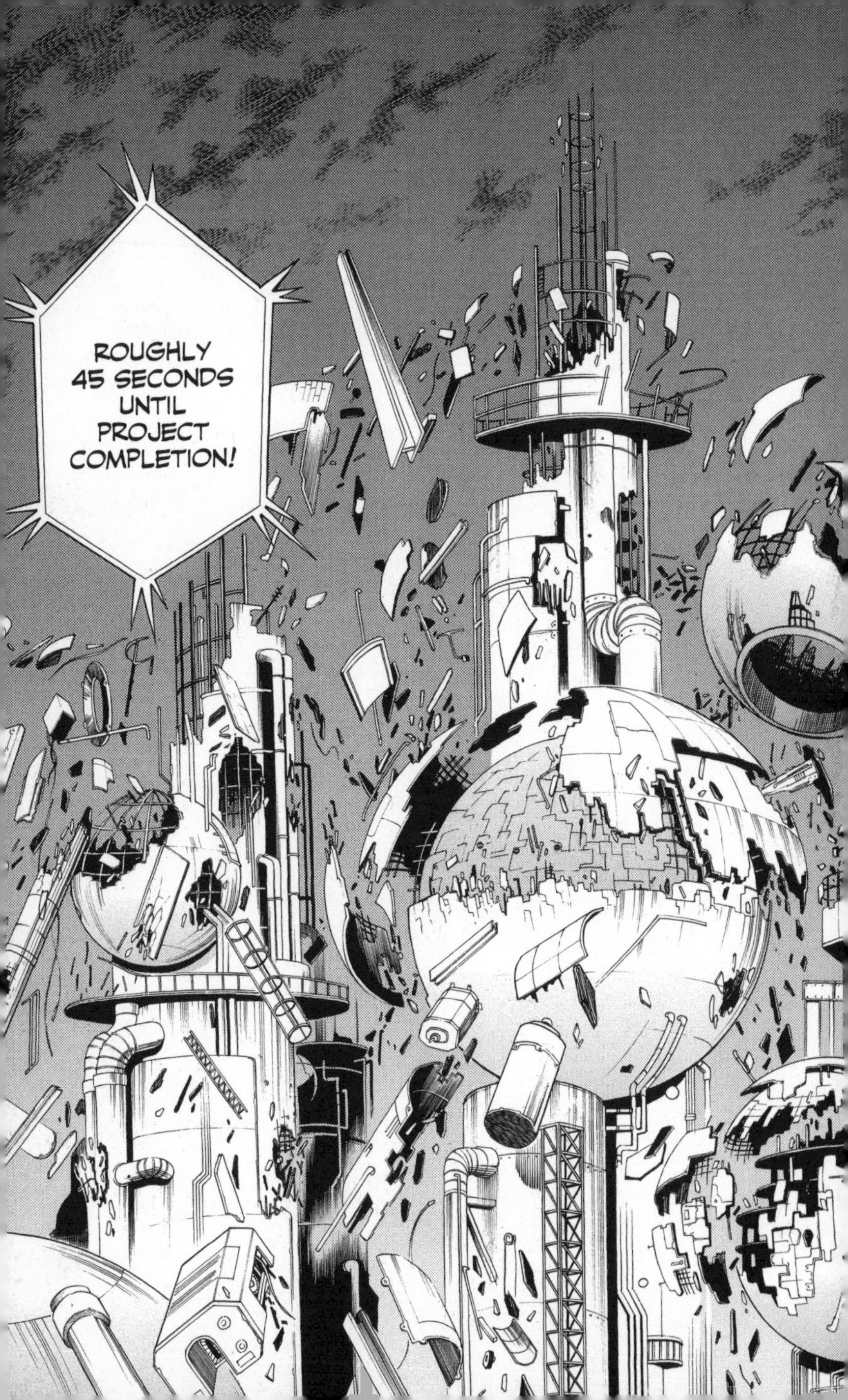
ROUGHLY 45 SECONDS UNTIL PROJECT COMPLETION!

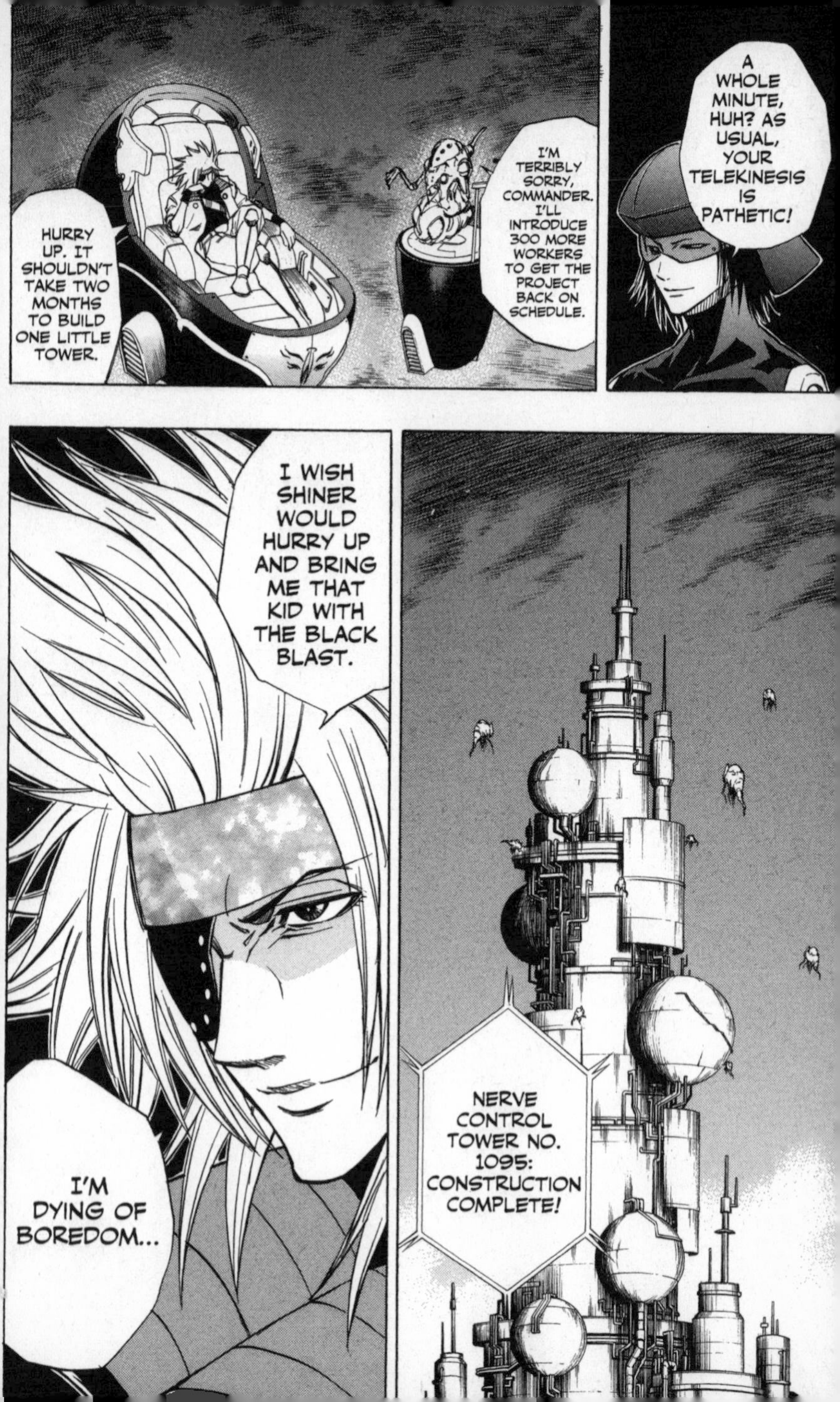
A WHOLE MINUTE, HUH? AS USUAL, YOUR TELEKINESIS IS PATHETIC!
I'M TERRIBLY SORRY, COMMANDER. I'LL INTRODUCE 300 MORE WORKERS TO GET THE PROJECT BACK ON SCHEDULE.
HURRY UP. IT SHOULDN'T TAKE TWO MONTHS TO BUILD ONE LITTLE TOWER.
NERVE CONTROL TOWER NO. 1095: CONSTRUCTION COMPLETE!
I WISH SHINER WOULD HURRY UP AND BRING ME THAT KID WITH THE BLACK BLAST.
I'M DYING OF BOREDOM...

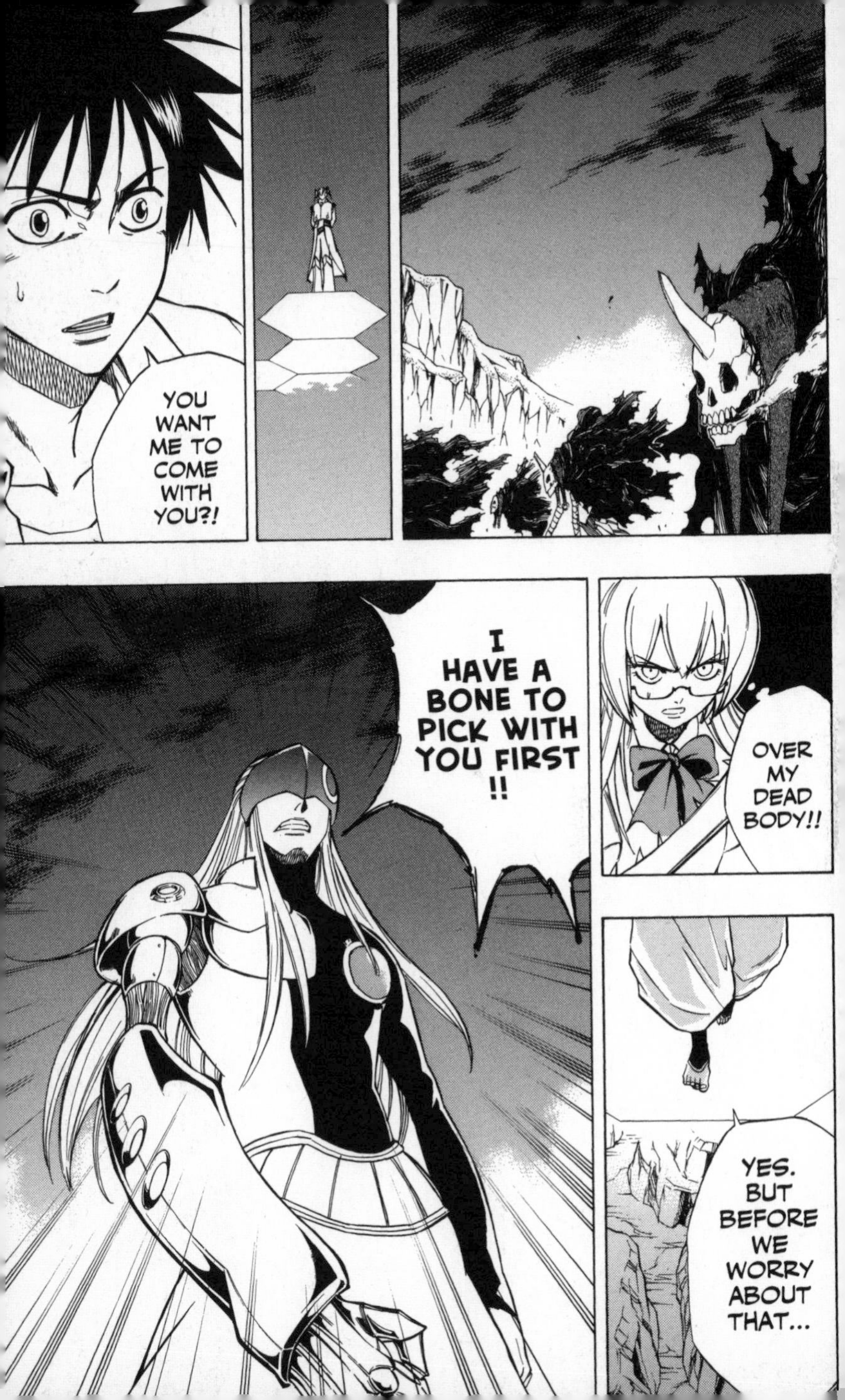
YOU WANT ME TO COME WITH YOU?!
OVER MY DEAD BODY!!
YES. BUT BEFORE WE WORRY ABOUT THAT...
I HAVE A BONE TO PICK WITH YOU FIRST!!

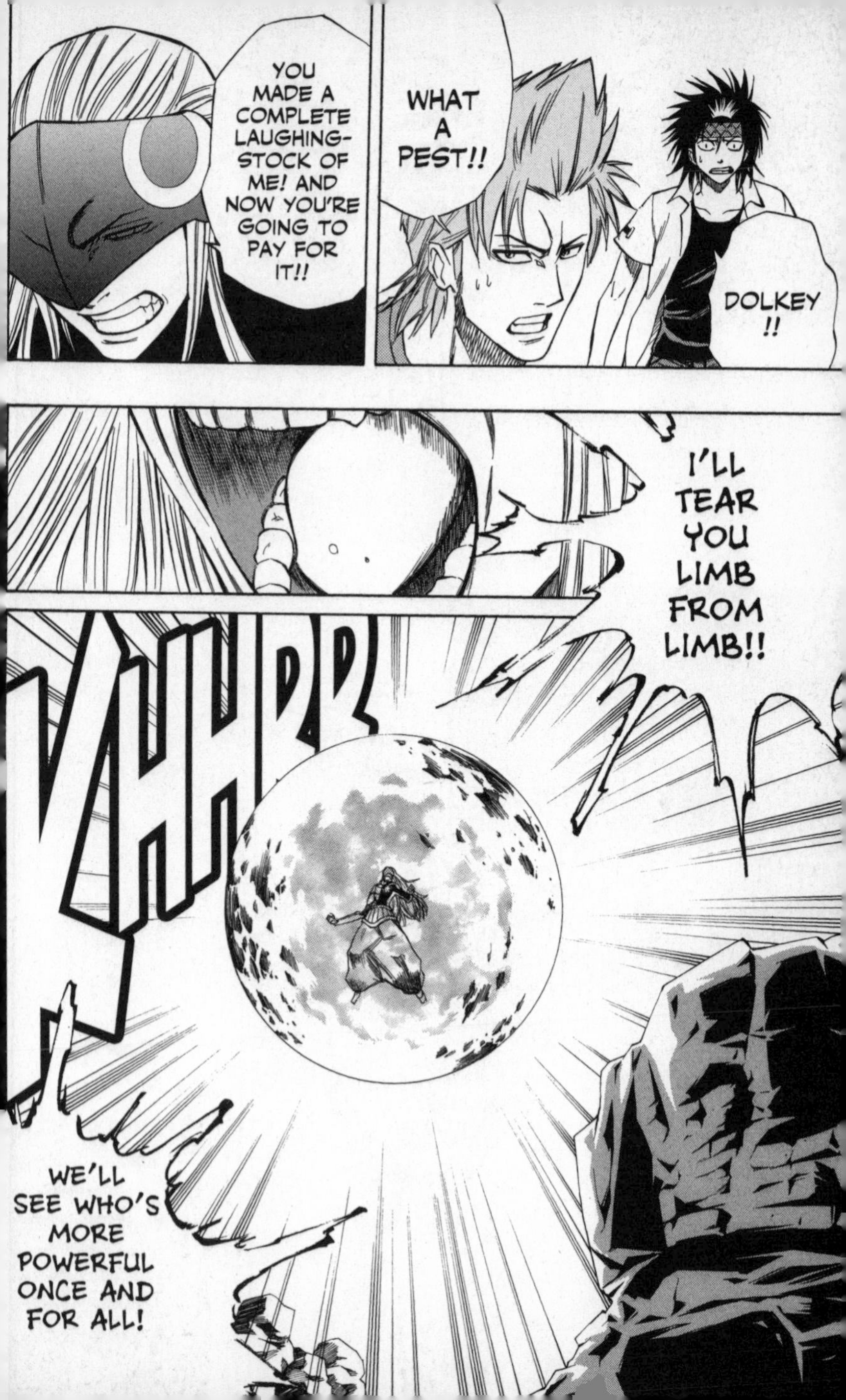
WHAT A PEST!!
DOLKEY!!
YOU MADE A COMPLETE LAUGHING-STOCK OF ME! AND NOW YOU'RE GOING TO PAY FOR IT!!
I'LL TEAR YOU LIMB FROM LIMB!!
VHRR
WE'LL SEE WHO'S MORE POWERFUL ONCE AND FOR ALL!

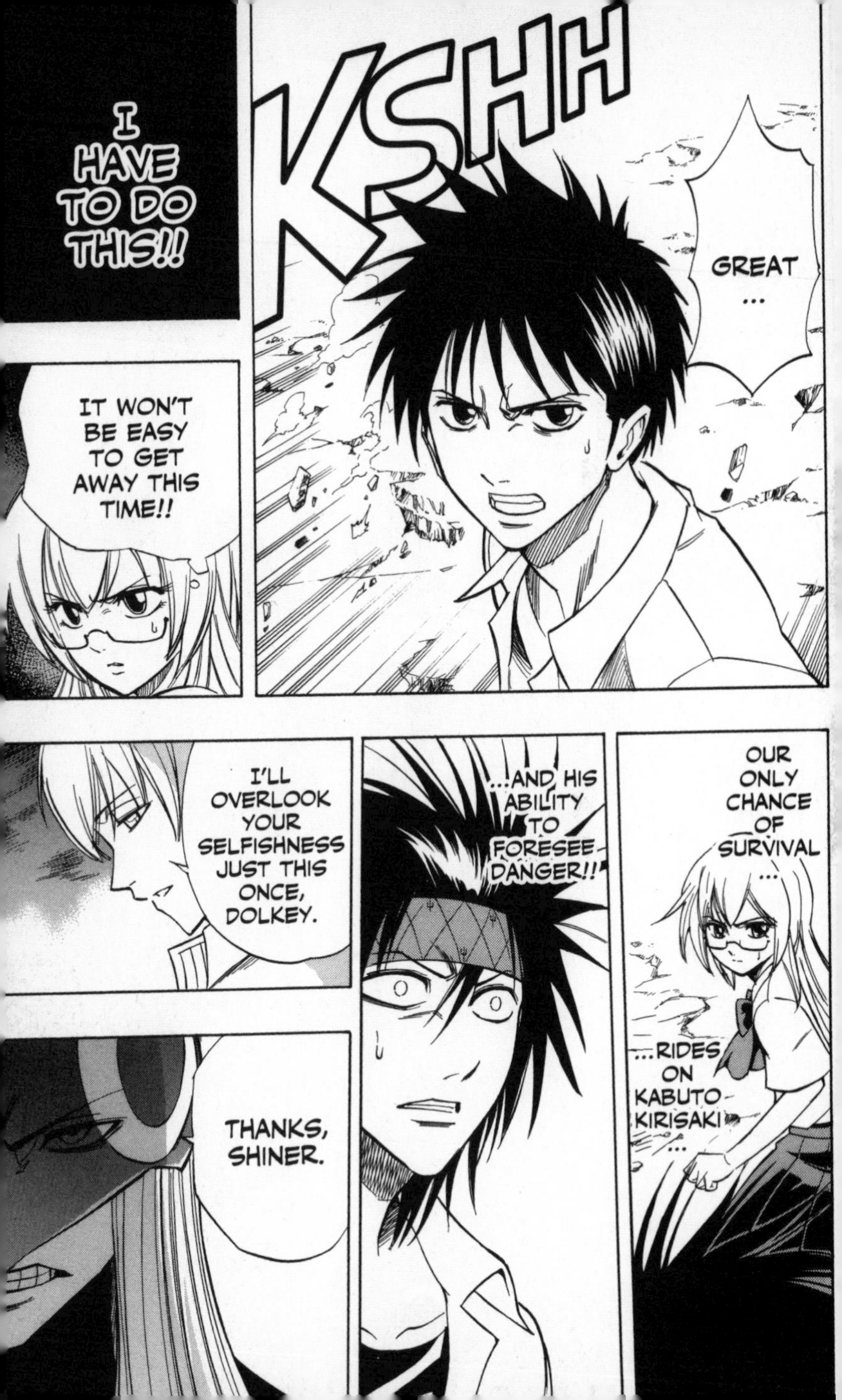
KSHH
GREAT...
I HAVE TO DO THIS!!
IT WON'T BE EASY TO GET AWAY THIS TIME!!
OUR ONLY CHANCE OF SURVIVAL...
...RIDES ON KABUTO KIRISAKI...
...AND HIS ABILITY TO FORESEE DANGER!!
I'LL OVERLOOK YOUR SELFISHNESS JUST THIS ONCE, DOLKEY.
THANKS, SHINER.

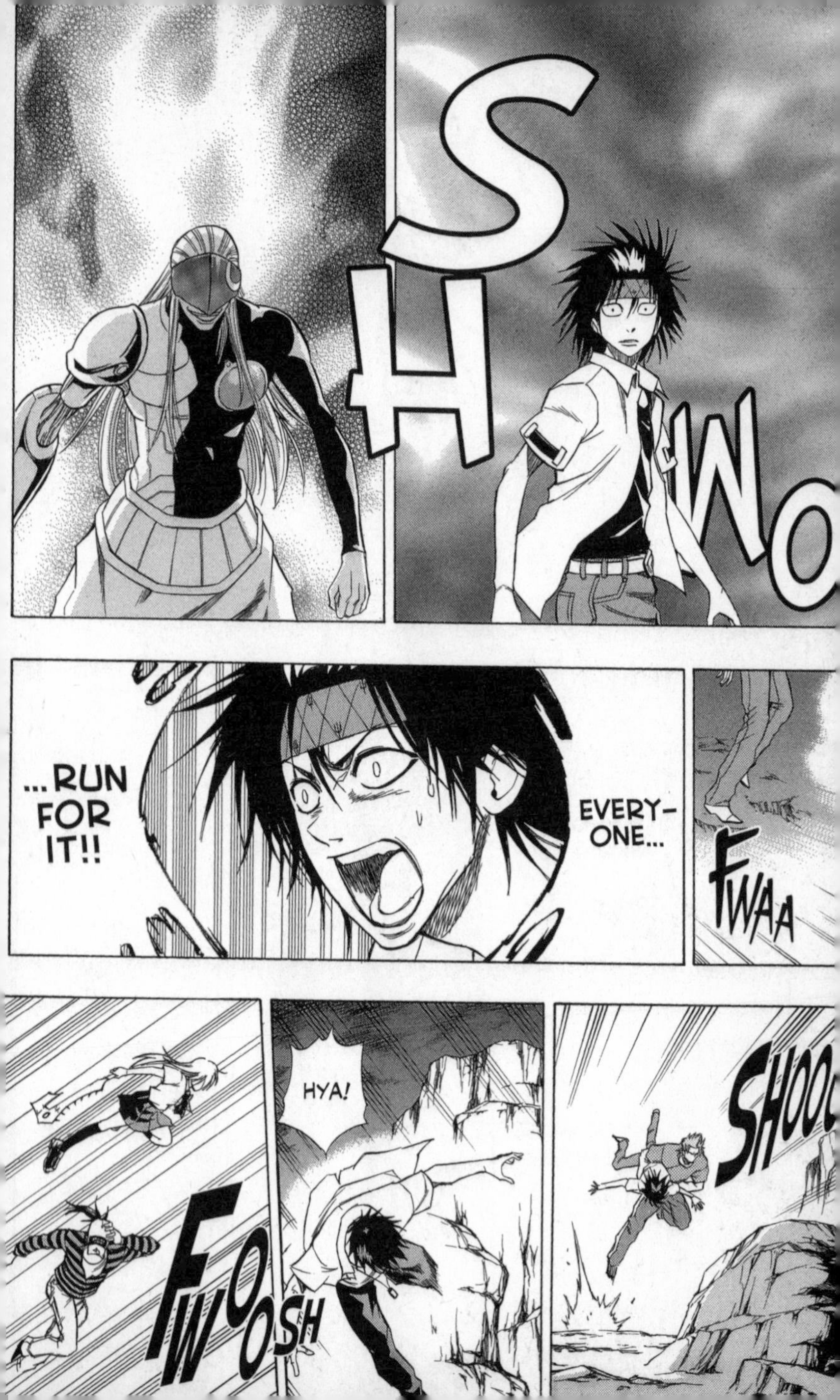
SHWO
FWAA
EVERY-ONE...
...RUN FOR IT!!
SHOO
HYA!
FWOOSH

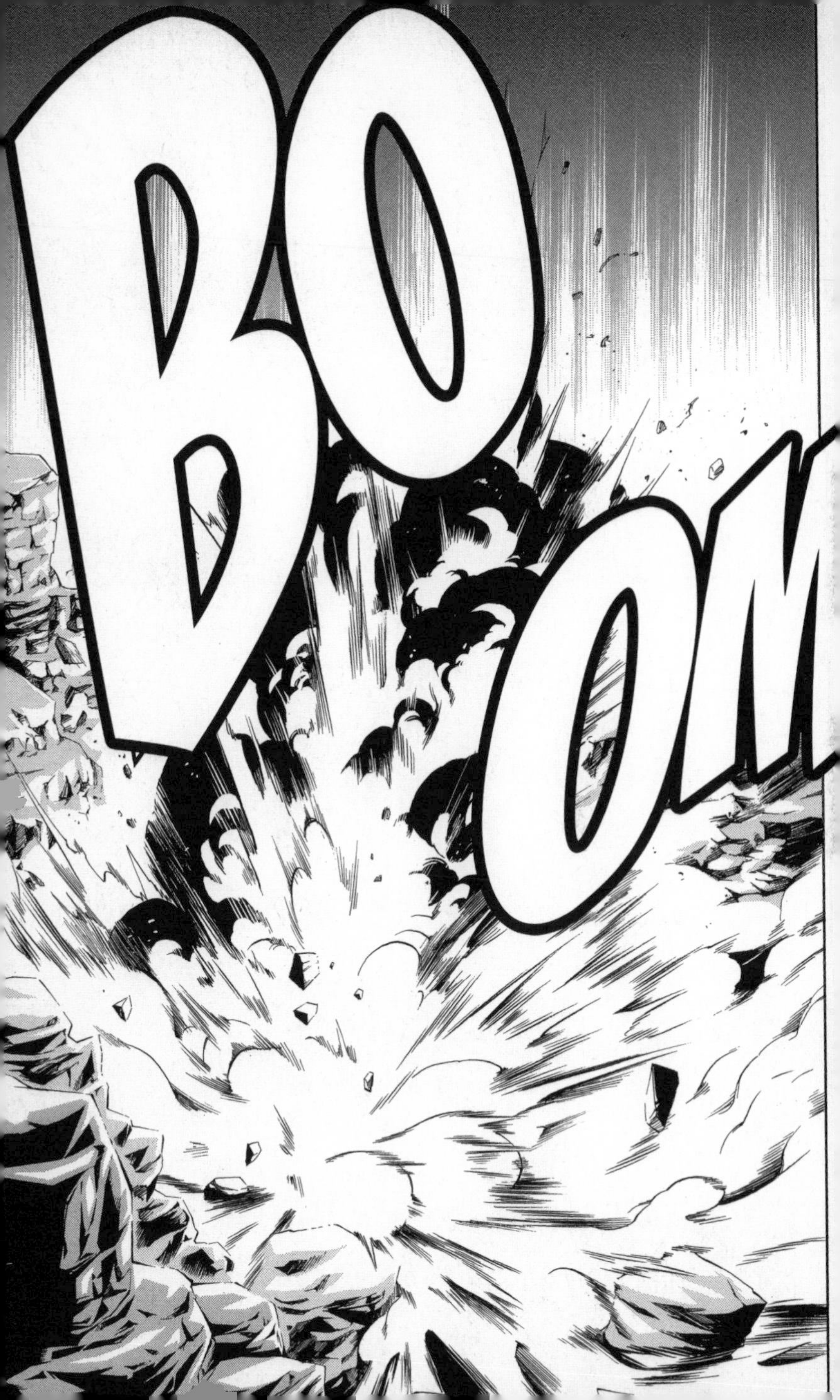
BOOM

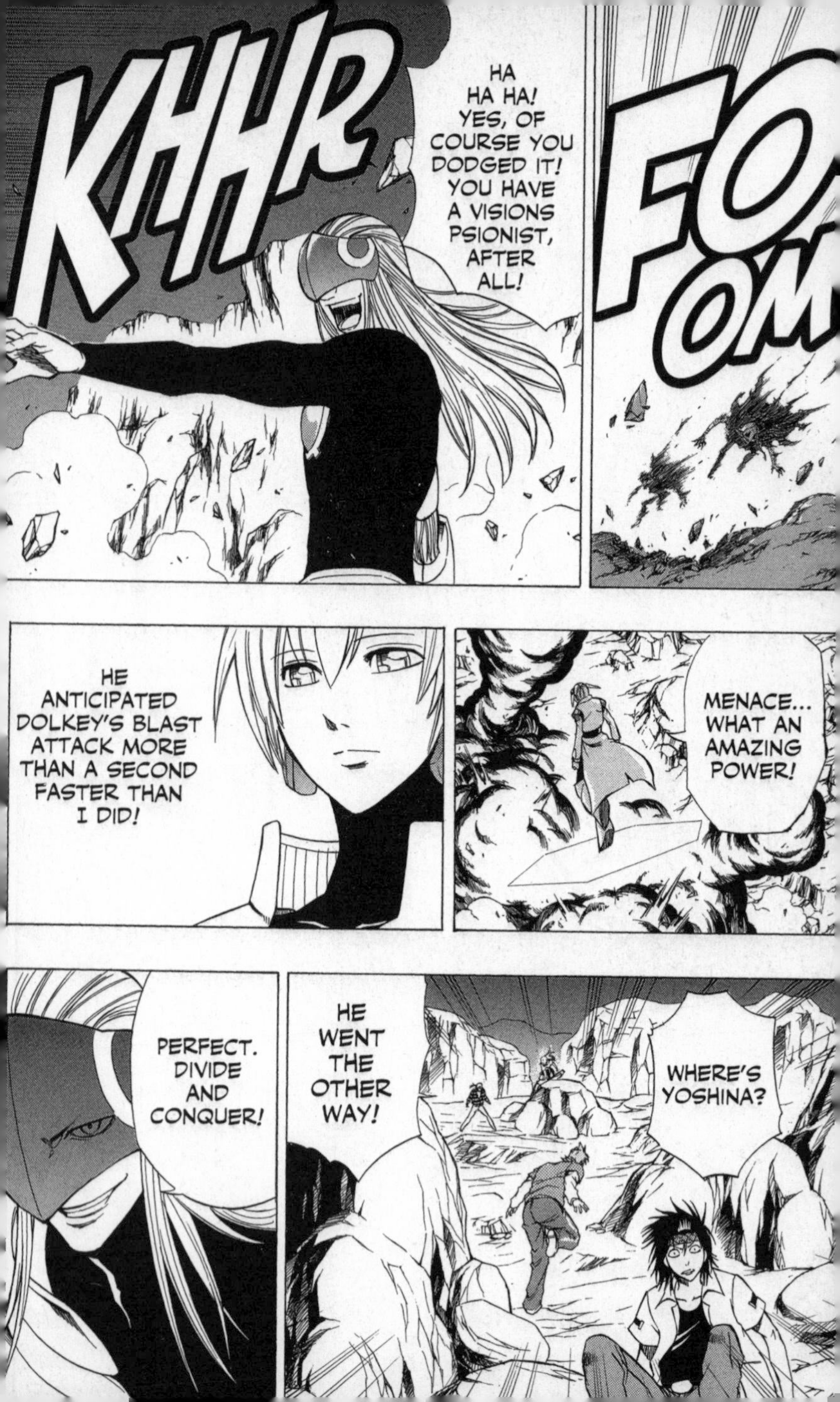
FO OM
KHR
HA HA HA! YES, OF COURSE YOU DODGED IT! YOU HAVE A VISIONS PSIONIST, AFTER ALL!
MENACE... WHAT AN AMAZING POWER!
HE ANTICIPATED DOLKEY'S BLAST ATTACK MORE THAN A SECOND FASTER THAN I DID!
WHERE'S YOSHINA?
HE WENT THE OTHER WAY!
PERFECT. DIVIDE AND CONQUER!

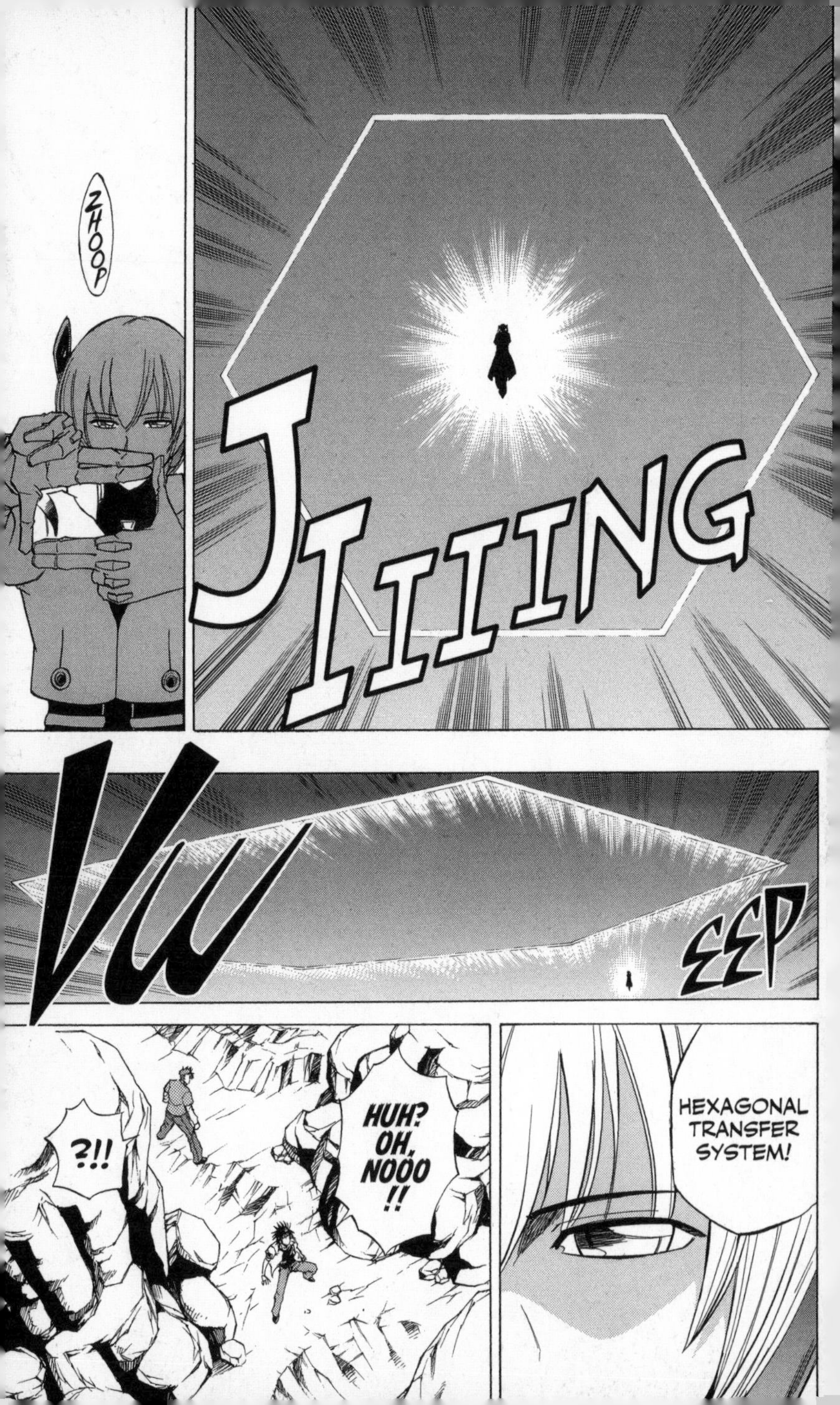
JIIIING
ZHOOP
Vu
EEP
HEXAGONAL TRANSFER SYSTEM!
HUH? OH, NOÖO !!
?!!

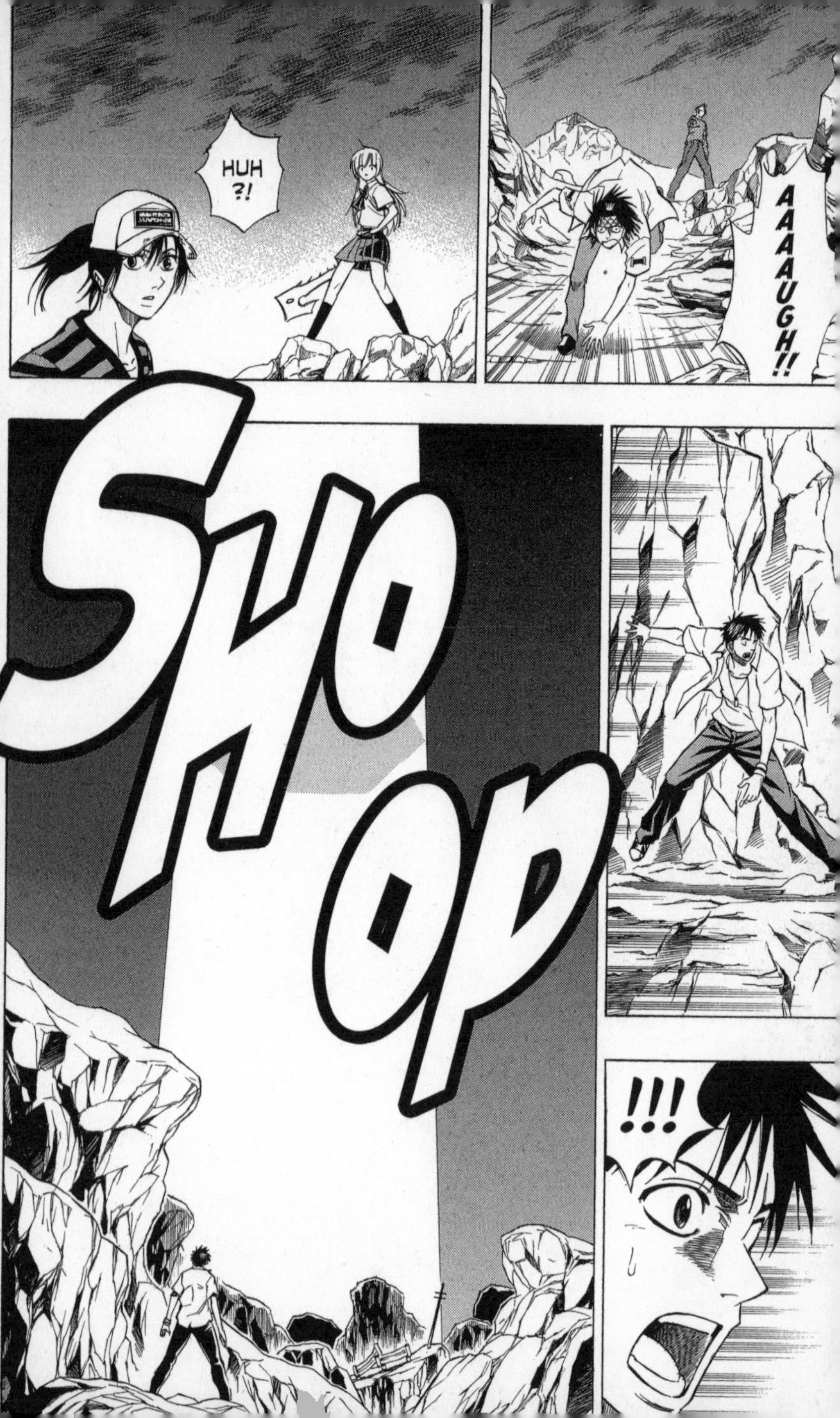
AAAAUGH!!
HUH ?!
!!!
SHOOP

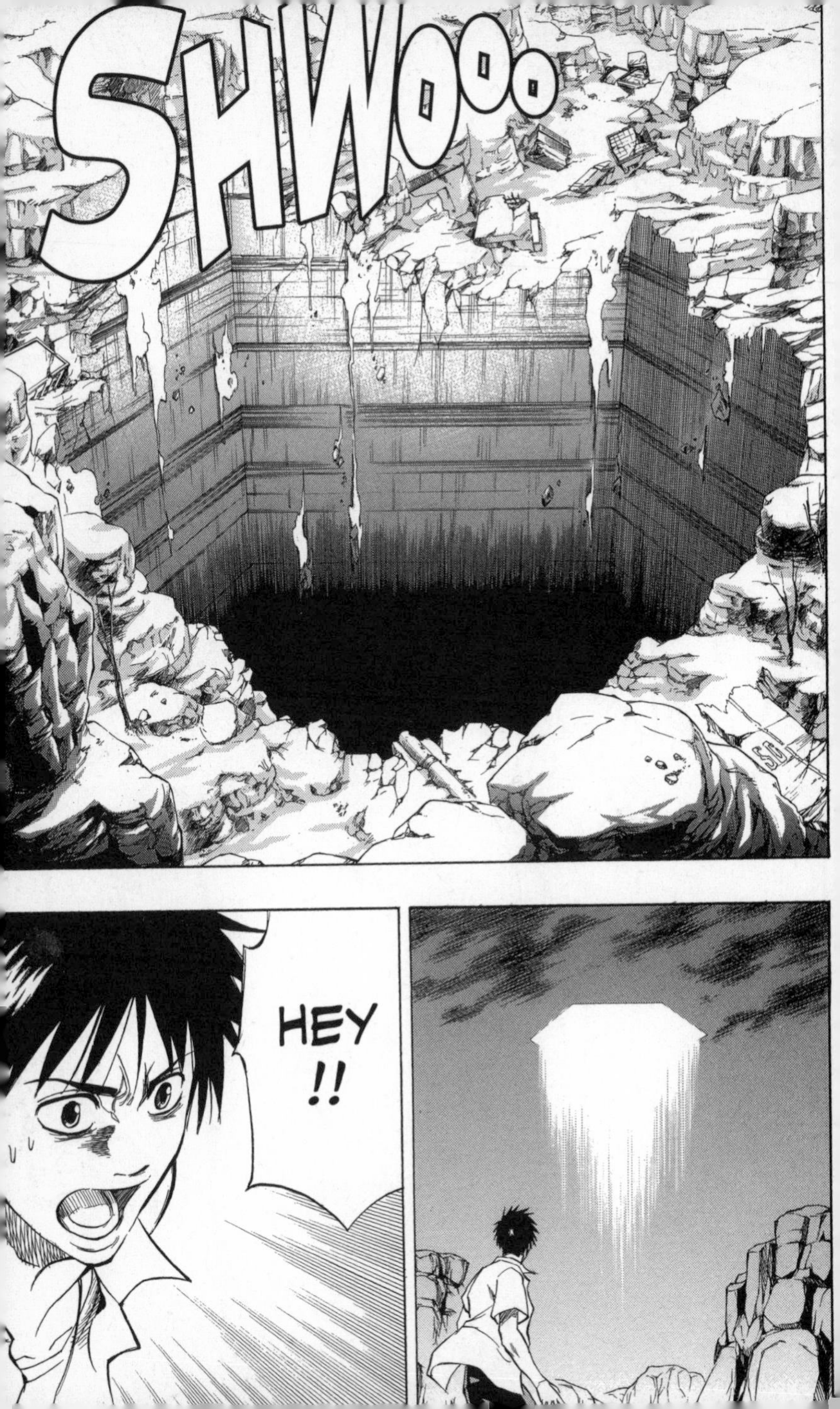
SHWOOO
HEY !!

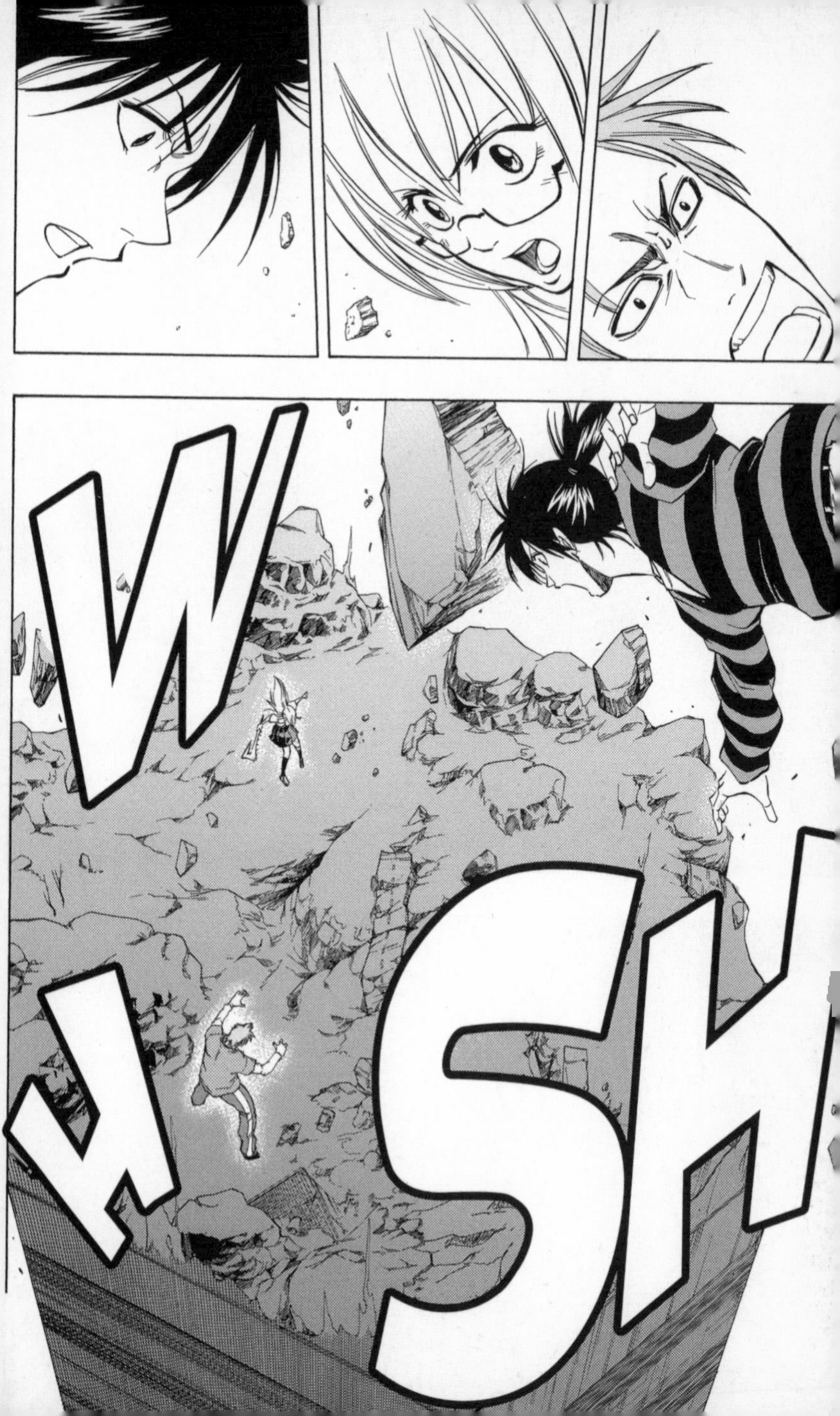
W
SH

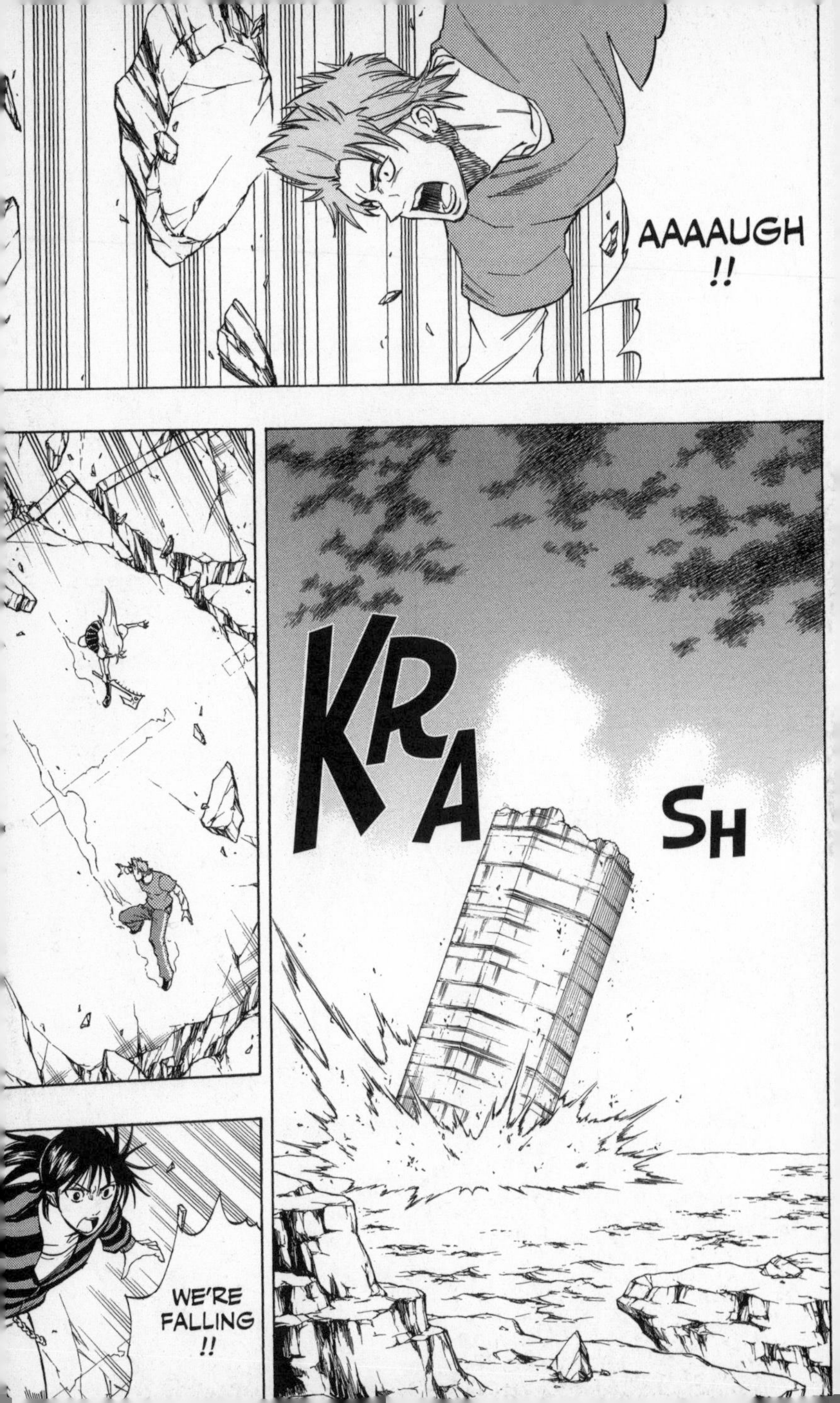
AAAAUGH!!
KRASH
WE'RE FALLING!!

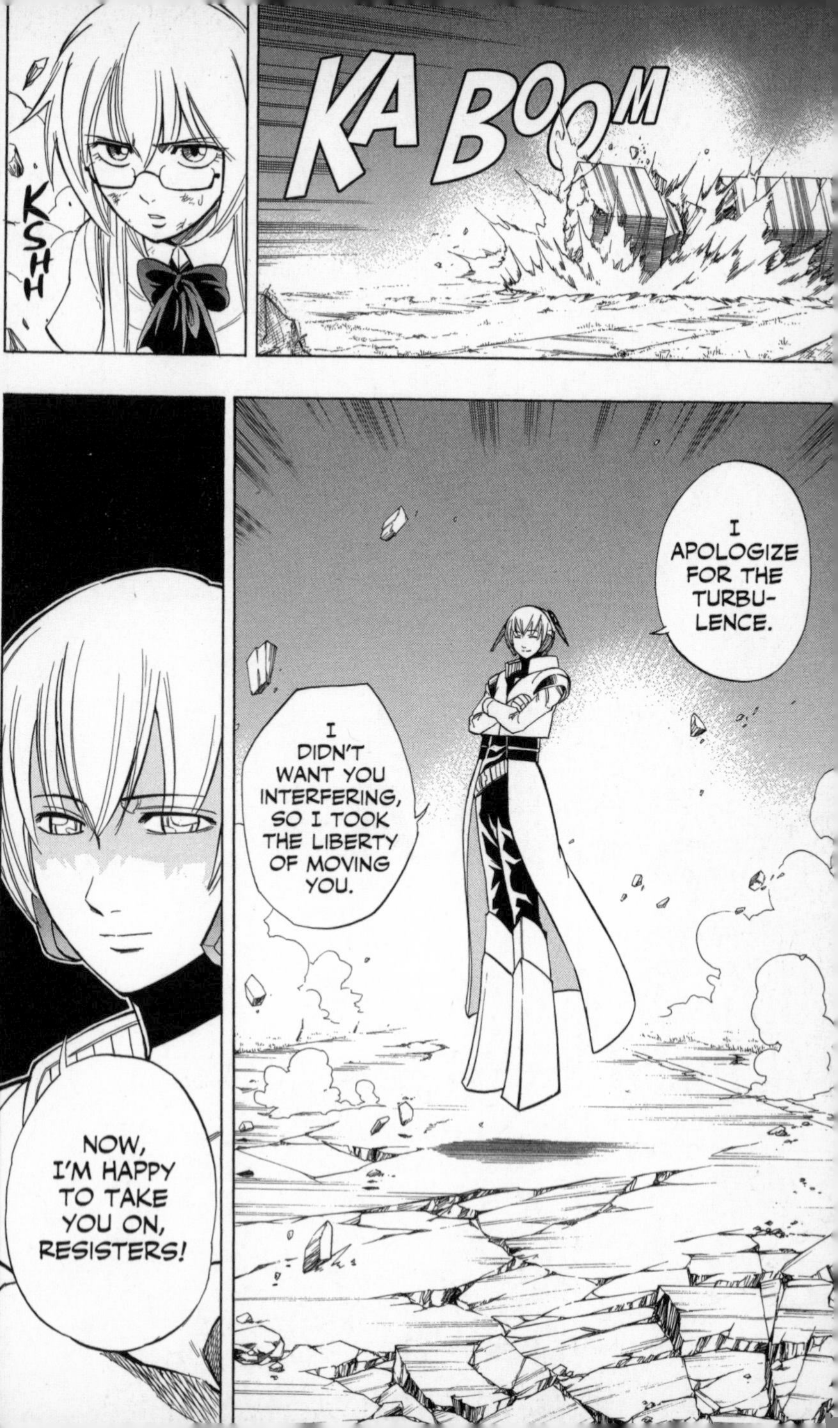
KA BOOM
KSHH
I APOLOGIZE FOR THE TURBU-LENCE.
I DIDN'T WANT YOU INTERFERING, SO I TOOK THE LIBERTY OF MOVING YOU.
NOW, I'M HAPPY TO TAKE YOU ON, RESISTERS!

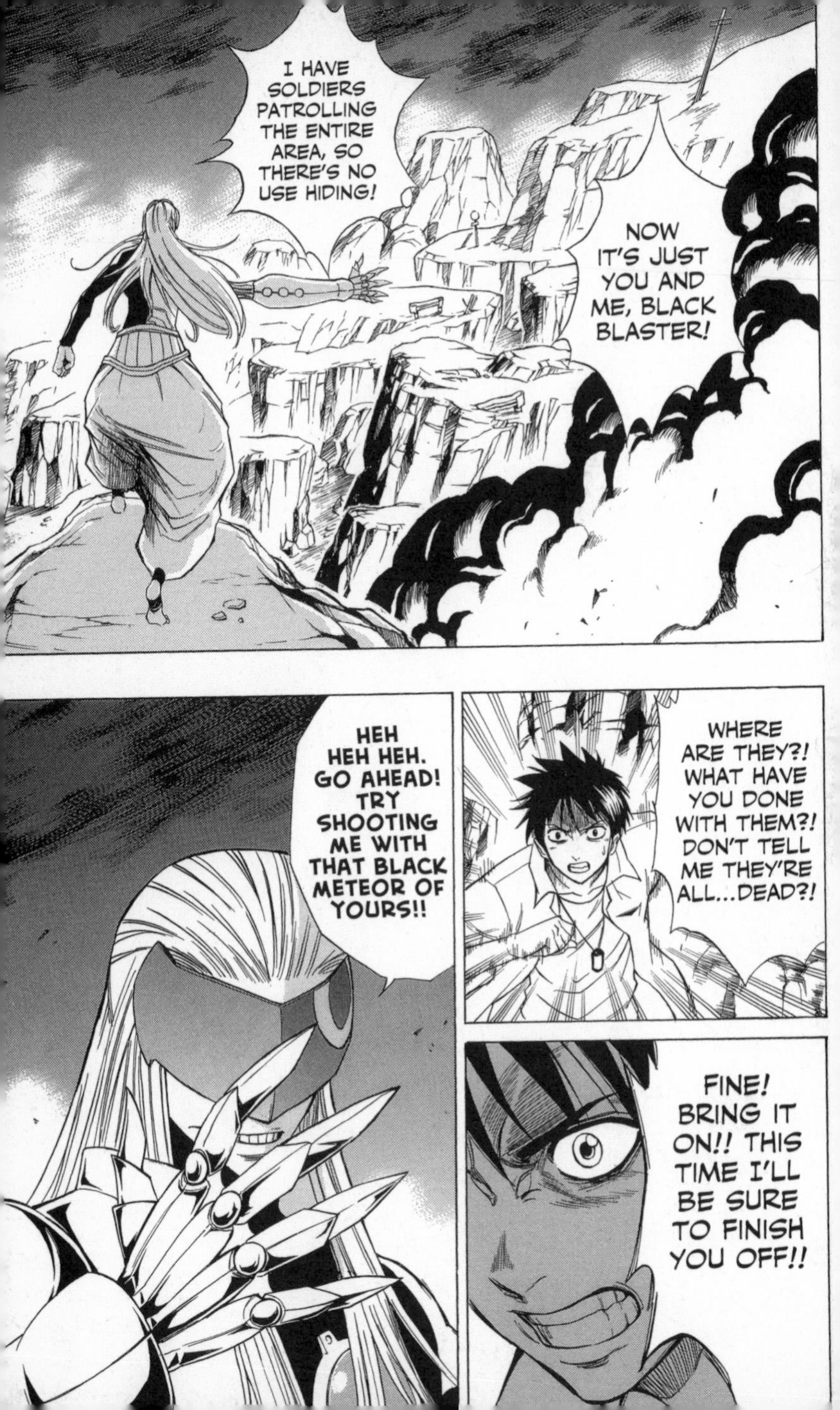
I HAVE SOLDIERS PATROLLING THE ENTIRE AREA, SO THERE'S NO USE HIDING!
NOW IT'S JUST YOU AND ME, BLACK BLASTER!
WHERE ARE THEY?! WHAT HAVE YOU DONE WITH THEM?! DON'T TELL ME THEY'RE ALL...DEAD?!
FINE! BRING IT ON!! THIS TIME I'LL BE SURE TO FINISH YOU OFF!!
HEH HEH HEH. GO AHEAD! TRY SHOOTING ME WITH THAT BLACK METEOR OF YOURS!!

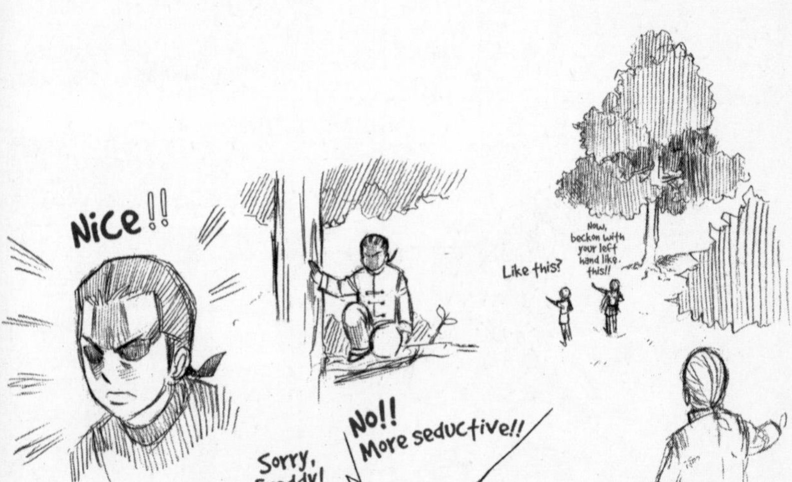
Now, beckon with your left hand like this!!
Like this?
No!! More seductive!!
Sorry, Freddy!
Nice!!

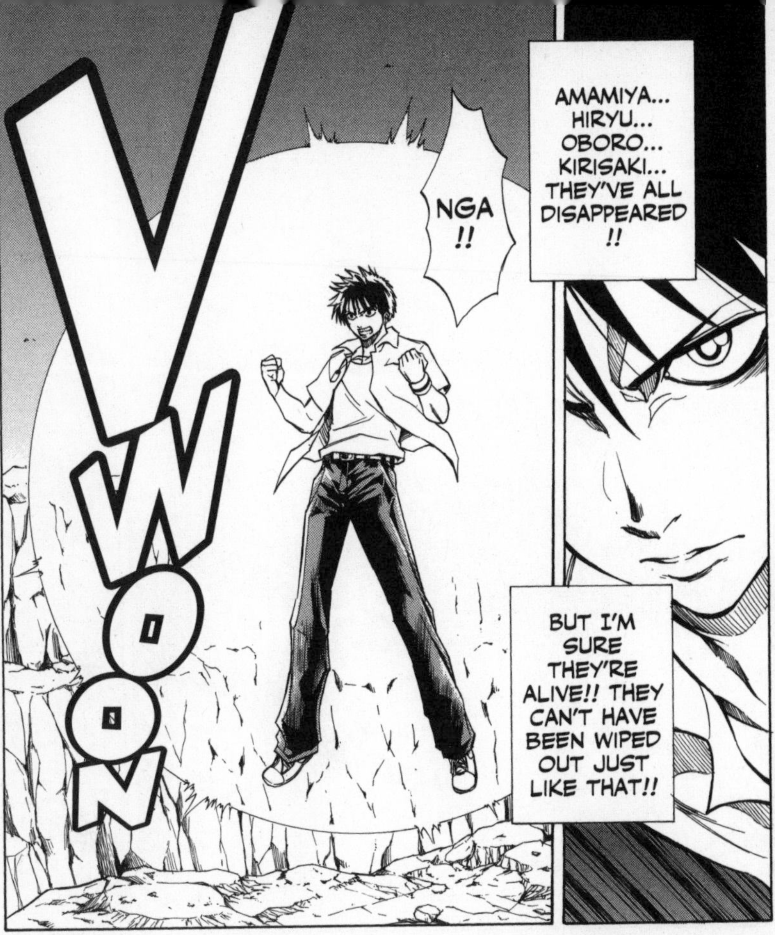
AMAMIYA... HIRYU... OBORO... KIRISAKI... THEY'VE ALL DISAPPEARED!!
BUT I'M SURE THEY'RE ALIVE!! THEY CAN'T HAVE BEEN WIPED OUT JUST LIKE THAT!!
NGA!!
VWOON

CALL.62: MUTUAL DESTRUCTION

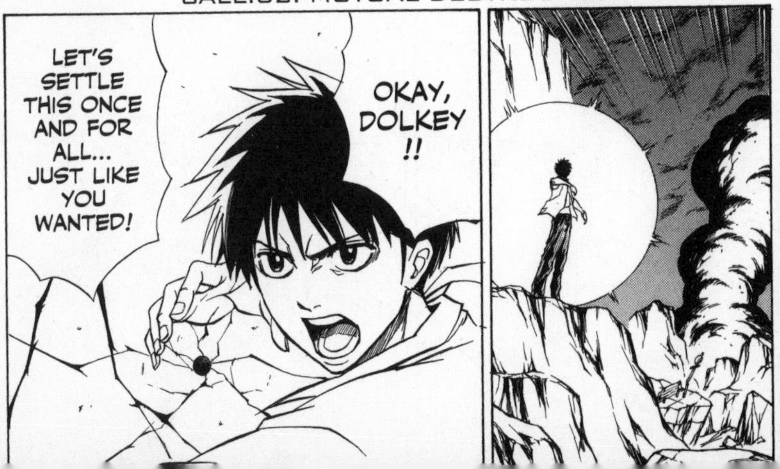
OKAY, DOLKEY!!
LET'S SETTLE THIS ONCE AND FOR ALL... JUST LIKE YOU WANTED!

Call.62: Mutual Destruction

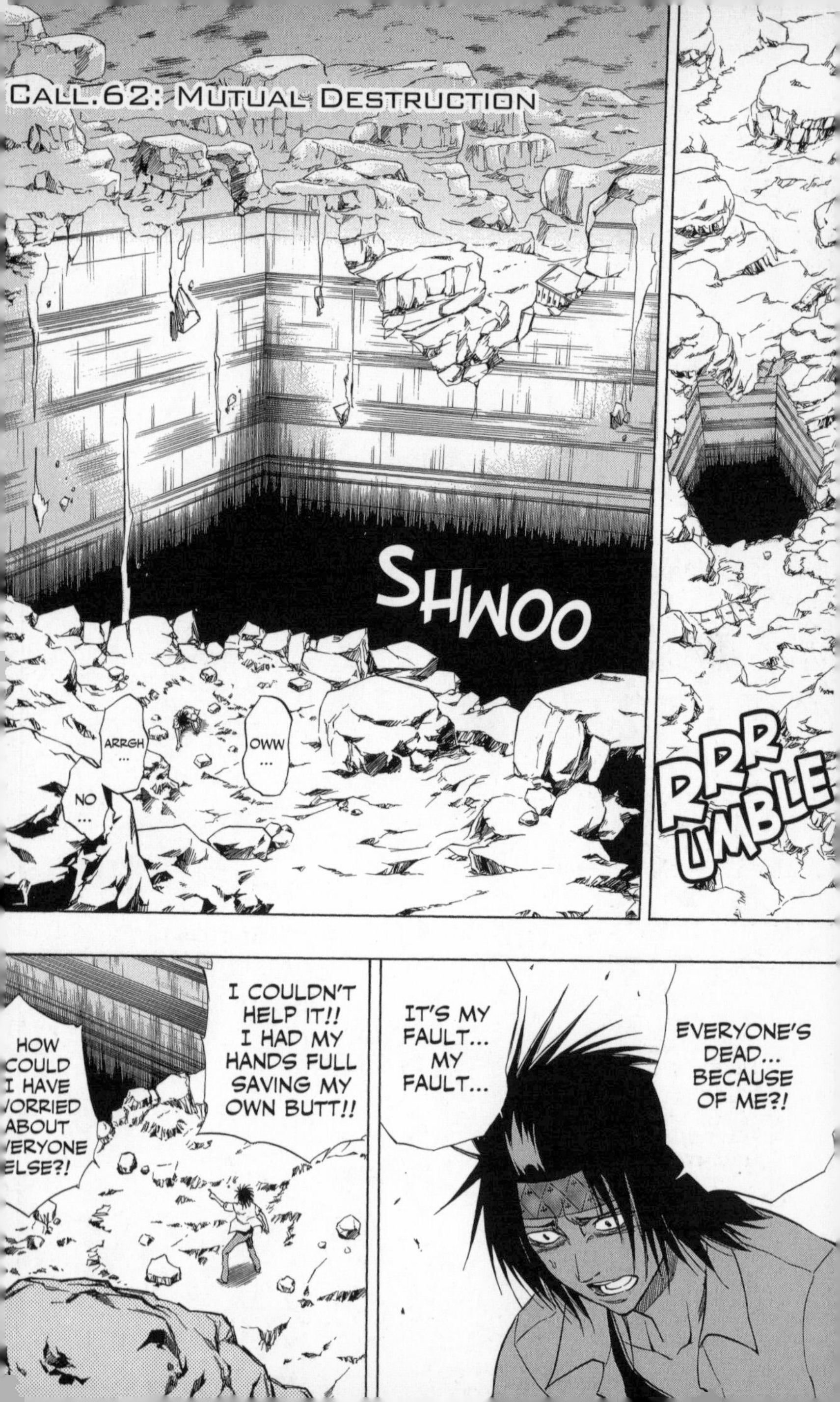

RRR UMBLE
SHWOO
OWW ...
ARRGH ...
NO ...
EVERYONE'S DEAD... BECAUSE OF ME?!
IT'S MY FAULT... MY FAULT...
I COULDN'T HELP IT!! I HAD MY HANDS FULL SAVING MY OWN BUTT!!
HOW COULD I HAVE WORRIED ABOUT EVERYONE ELSE?!

WHEE

...

I'M SORRY ...

!!

THAT'S

FOOM

AUGH !!

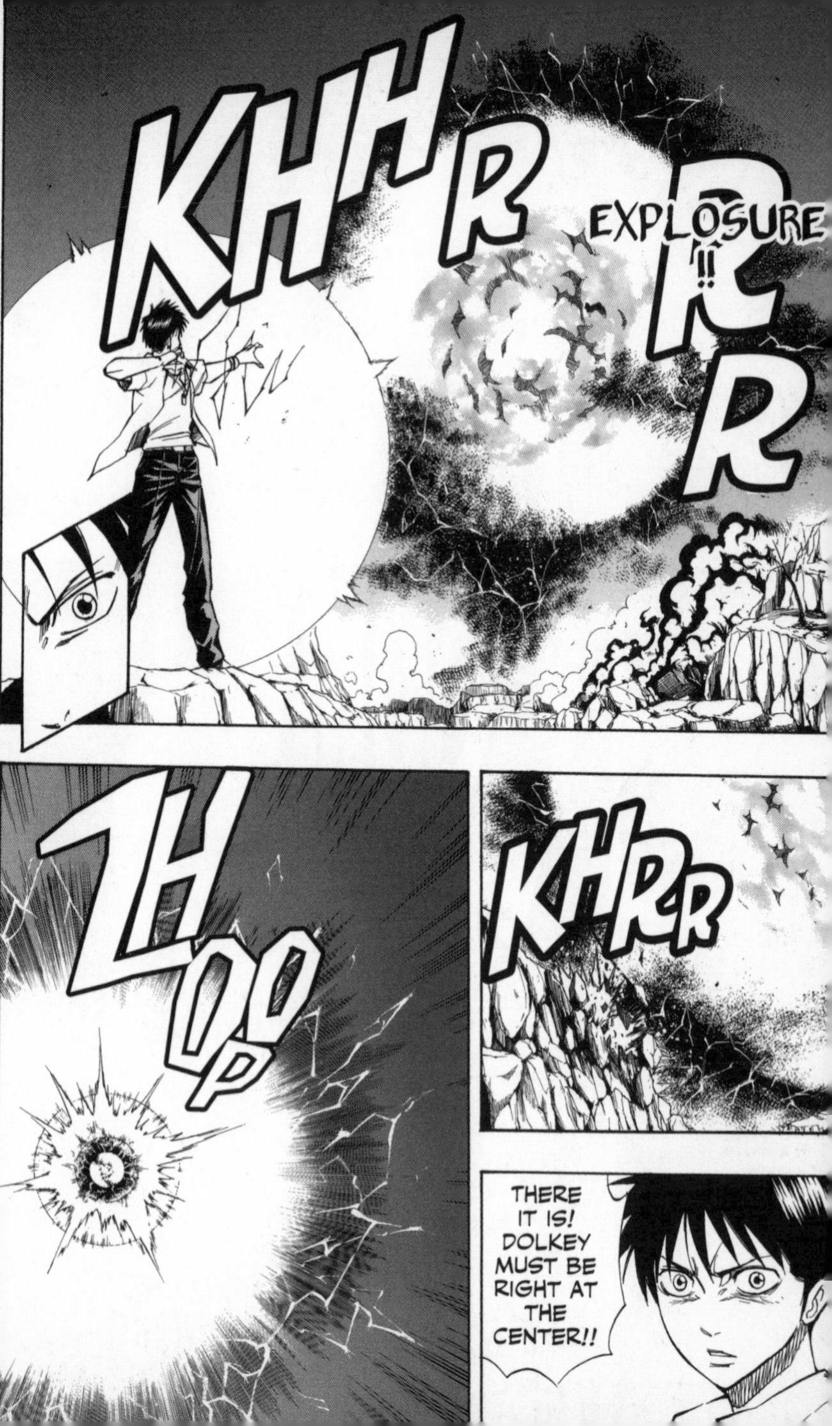
KHHRRR
EXPLOSURE!!
KHRRR
THERE IT IS! DOLKEY MUST BE RIGHT AT THE CENTER!!
ZHOOOP

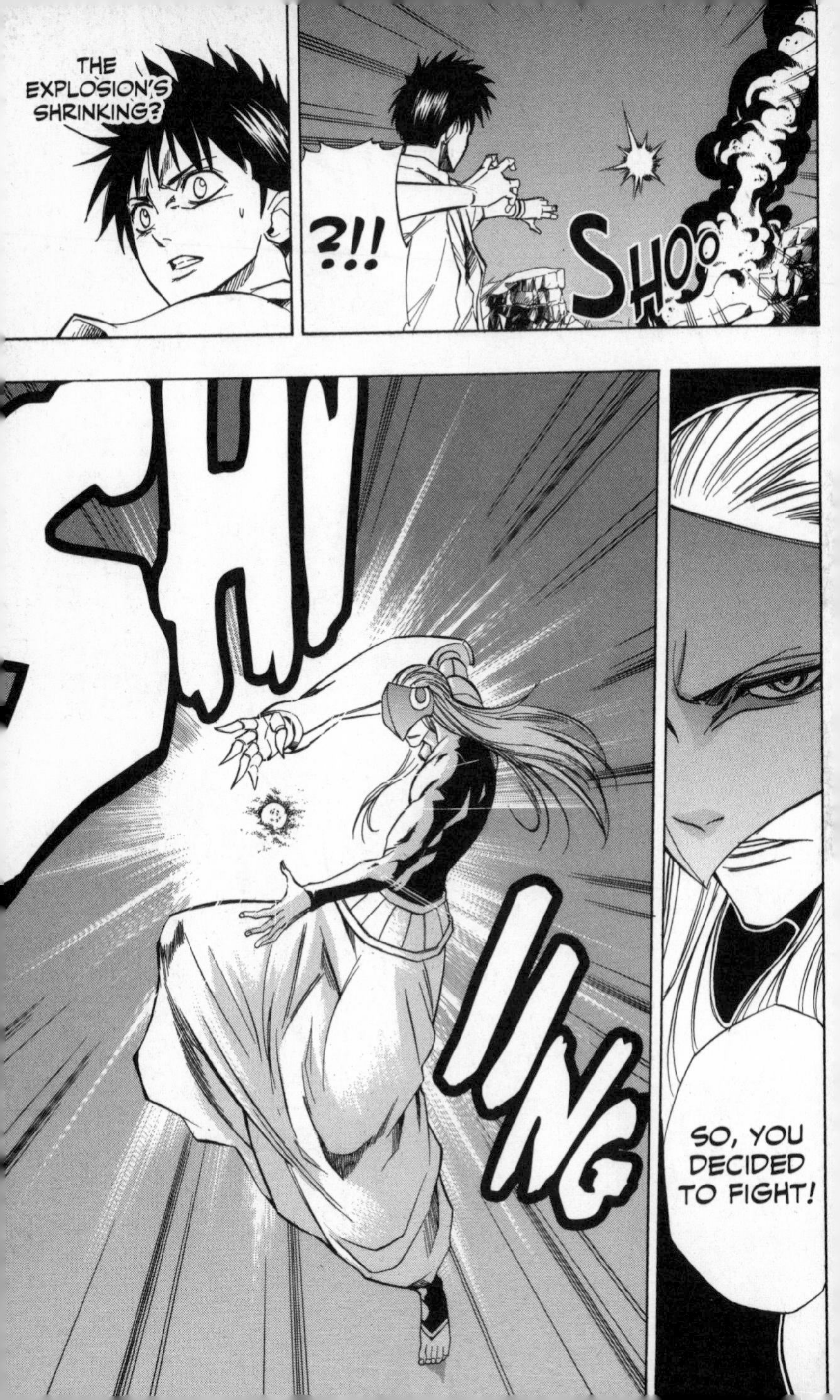
SHOO
?!!
THE EXPLOSION'S SHRINKING?
SO, YOU DECIDED TO FIGHT!
SH
ING

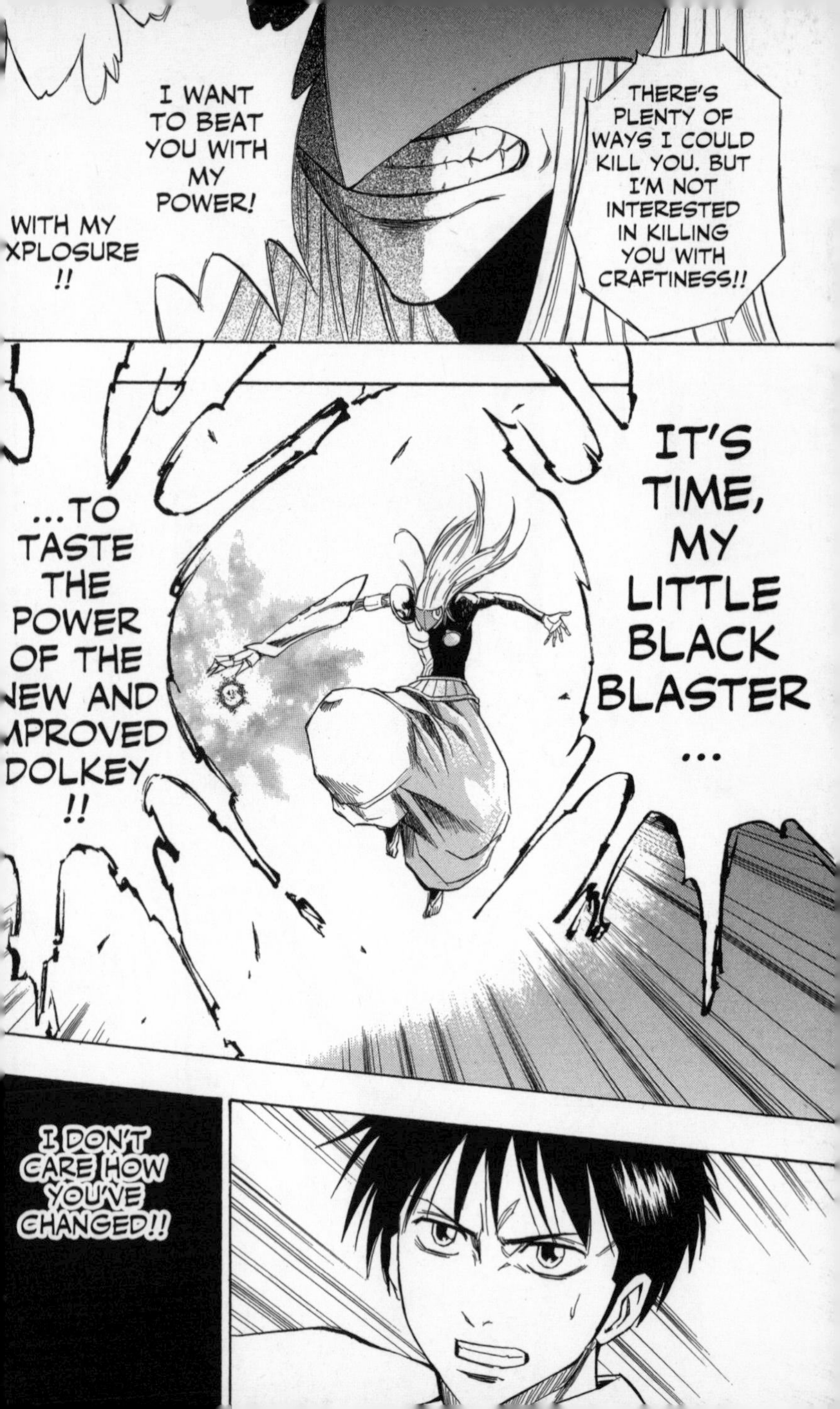
THERE'S PLENTY OF WAYS I COULD KILL YOU. BUT I'M NOT INTERESTED IN KILLING YOU WITH CRAFTINESS!!
I WANT TO BEAT YOU WITH MY POWER!
WITH MY XPLOSURE !!
IT'S TIME, MY LITTLE BLACK BLASTER ...
...TO TASTE THE POWER OF THE NEW AND MPROVED DOLKEY !!
I DON'T CARE HOW YOU'VE CHANGED!!

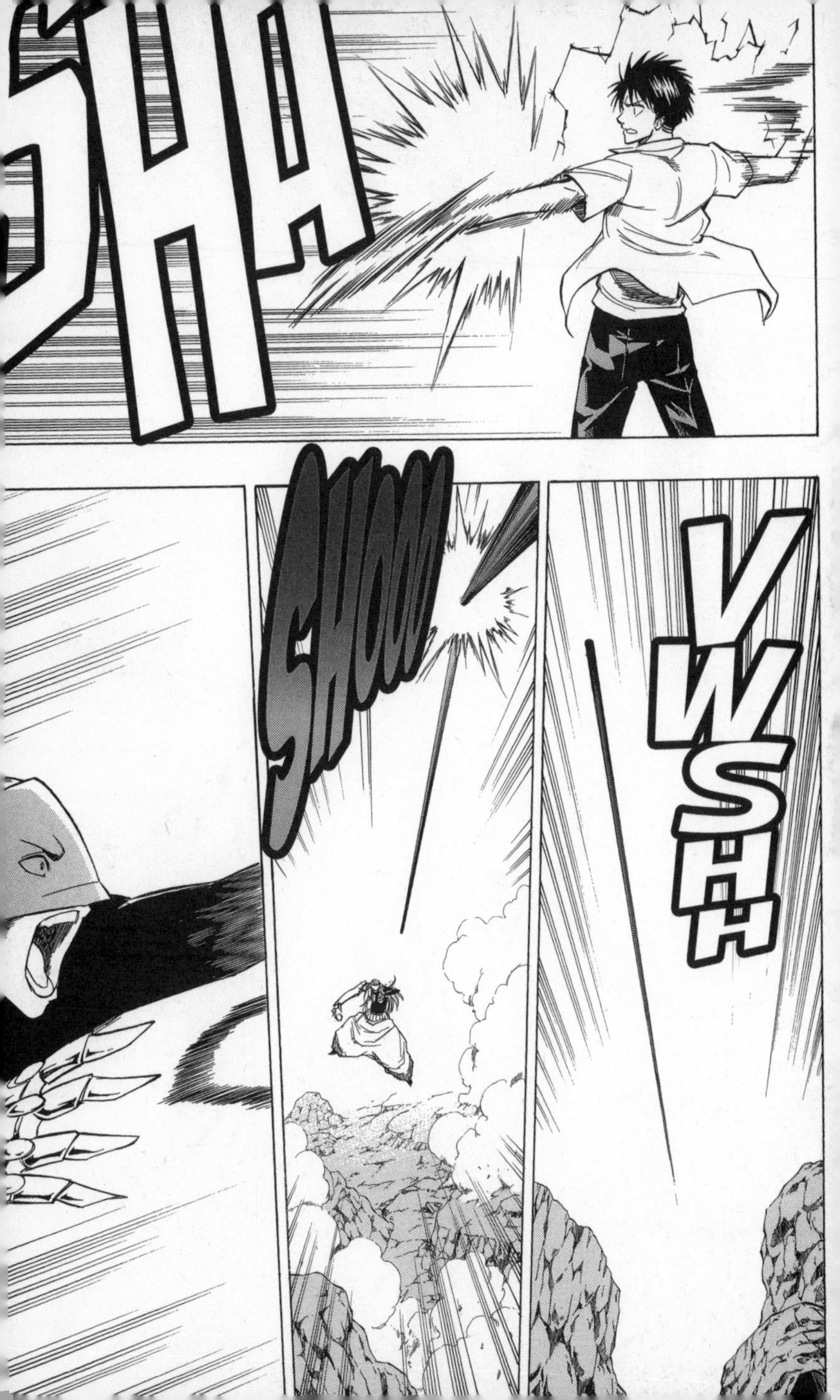
SHA
VWSHH
SHOOM

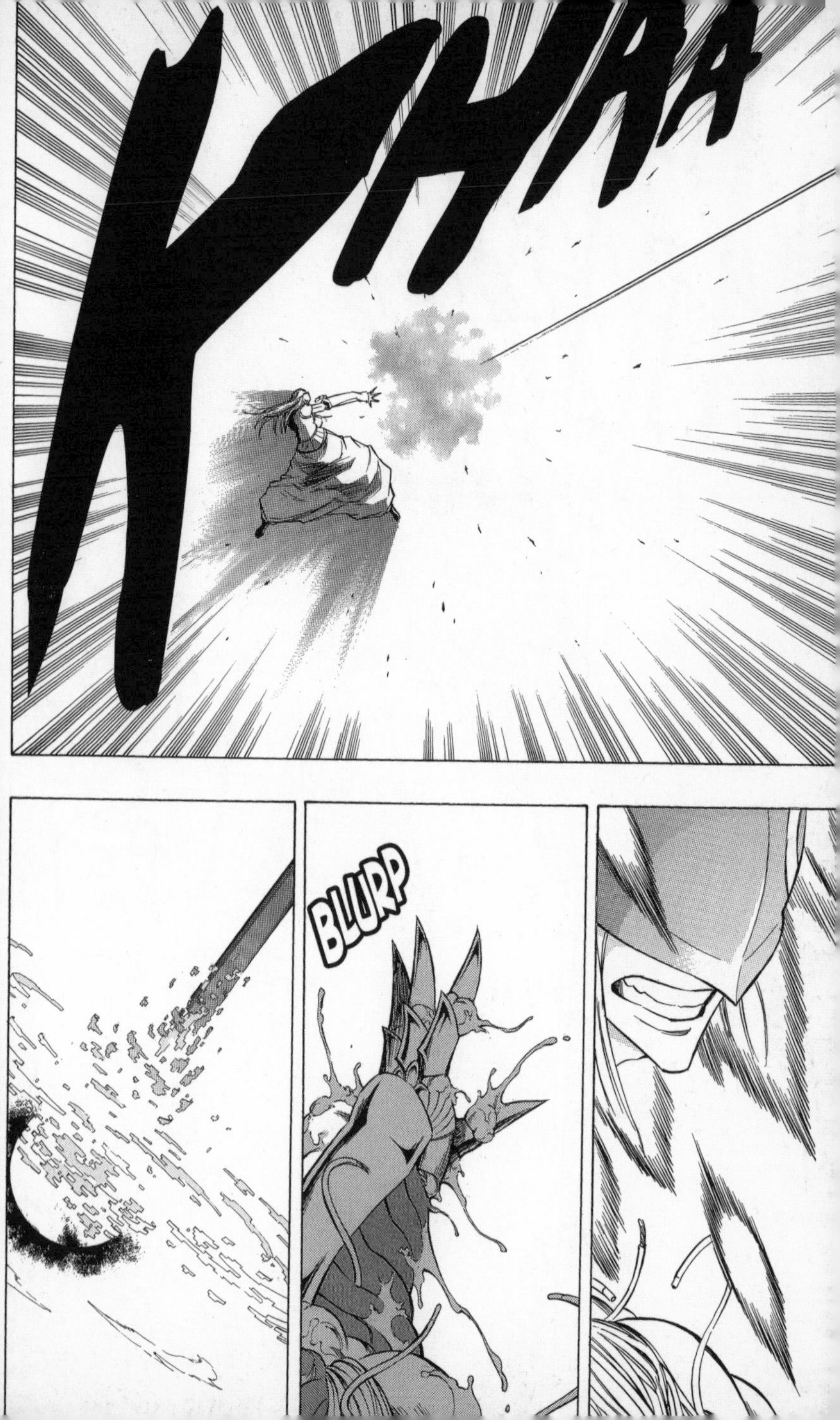
KHAA
BLURP

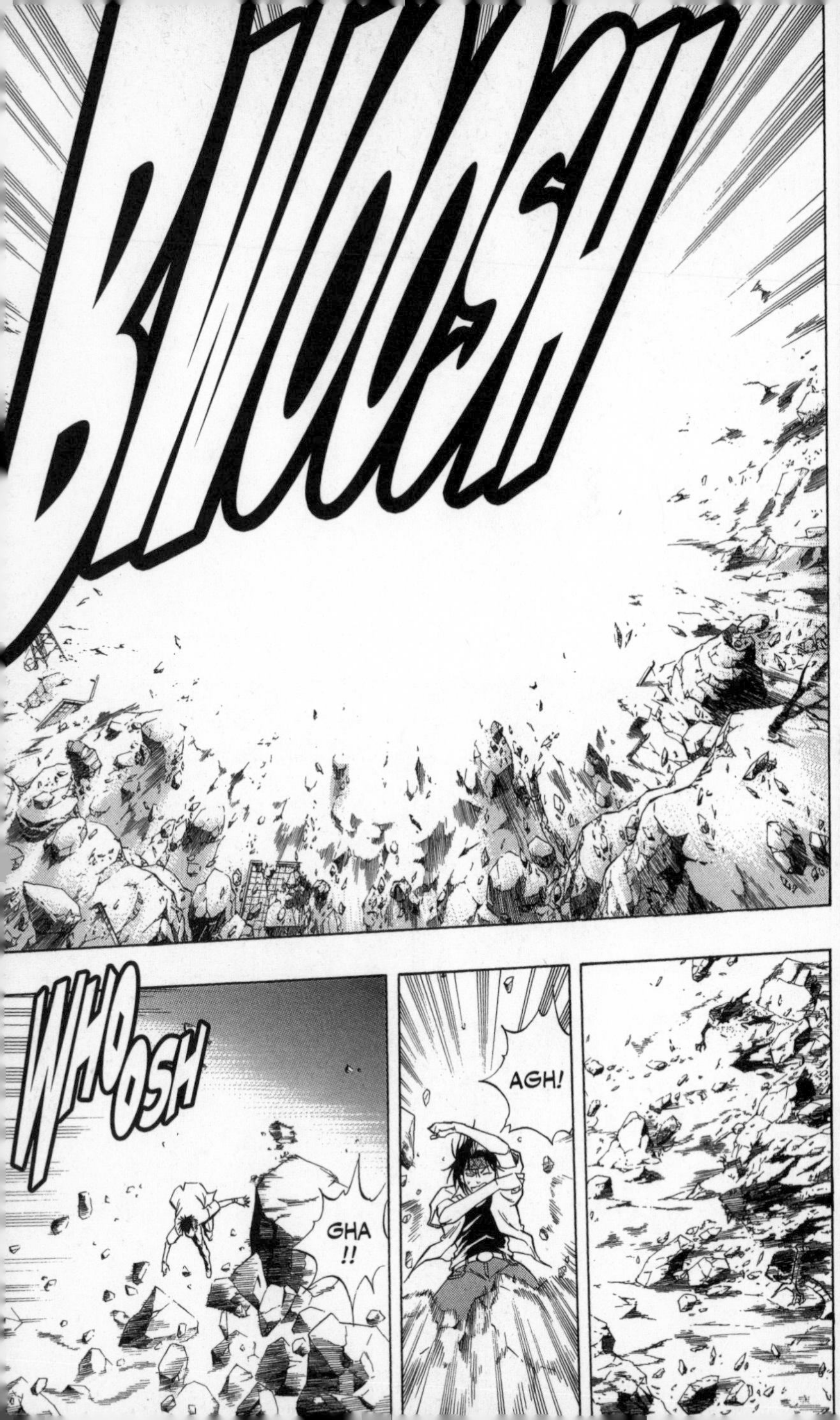
AGH!
WHOOSH
GHA !!

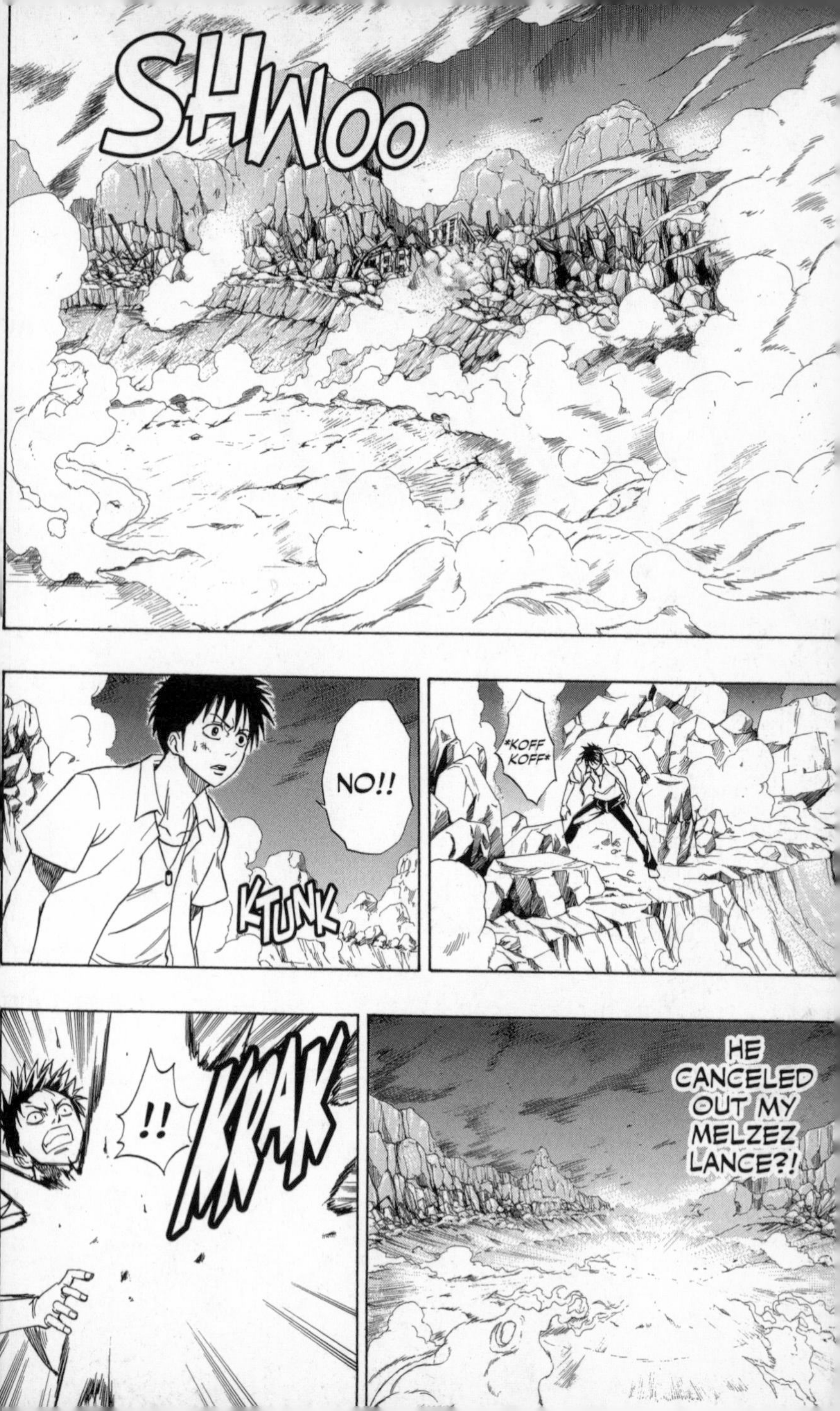
SHWOO
KOFF KOFF
NO!!
KTUNK
HE CANCELED OUT MY MELZEZ LANCE?!
!!
KRAK

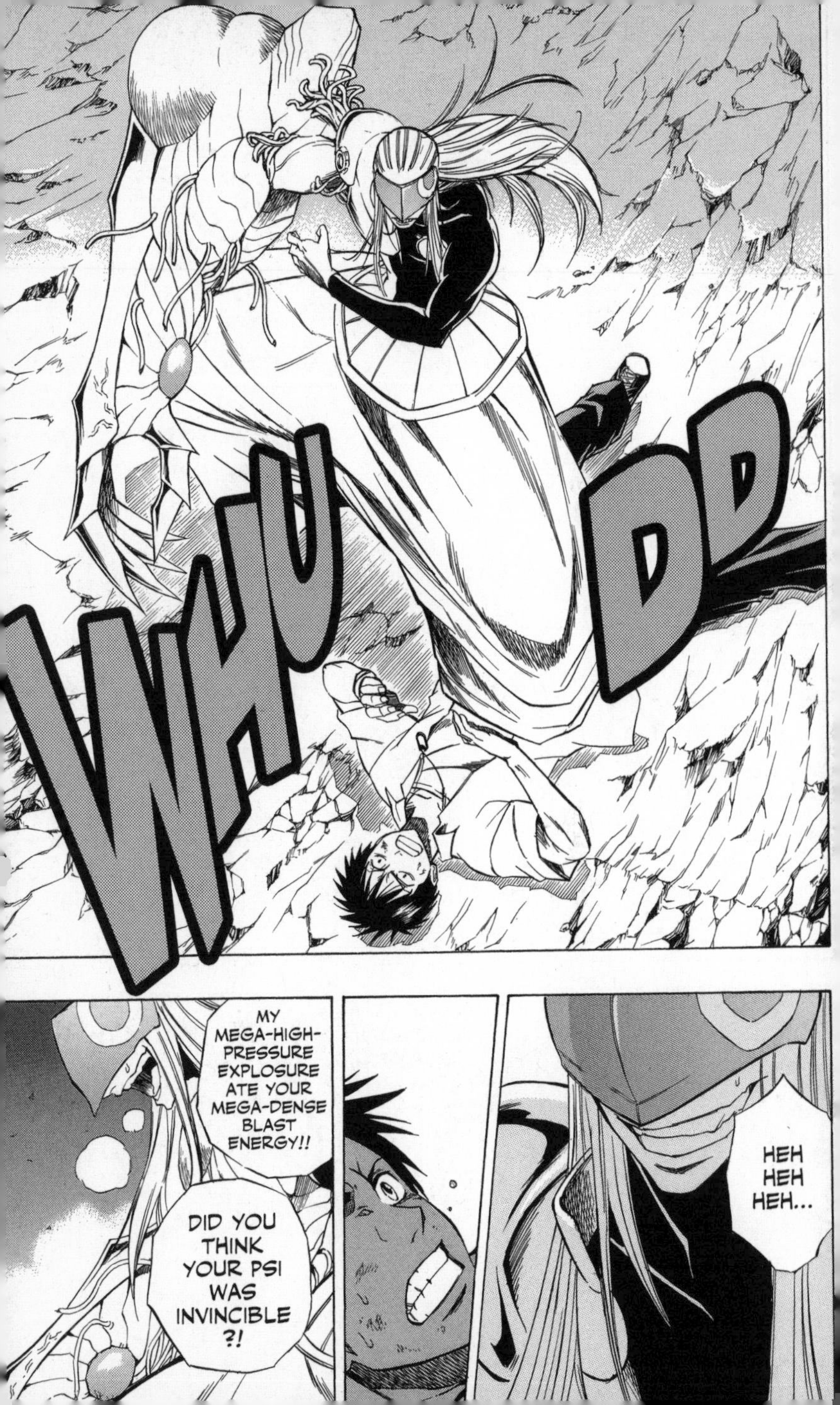
WHUDD
HEH HEH HEH...
MY MEGA-HIGH-PRESSURE EXPLOSURE ATE YOUR MEGA-DENSE BLAST ENERGY!!
DID YOU THINK YOUR PSI WAS INVINCIBLE ?!

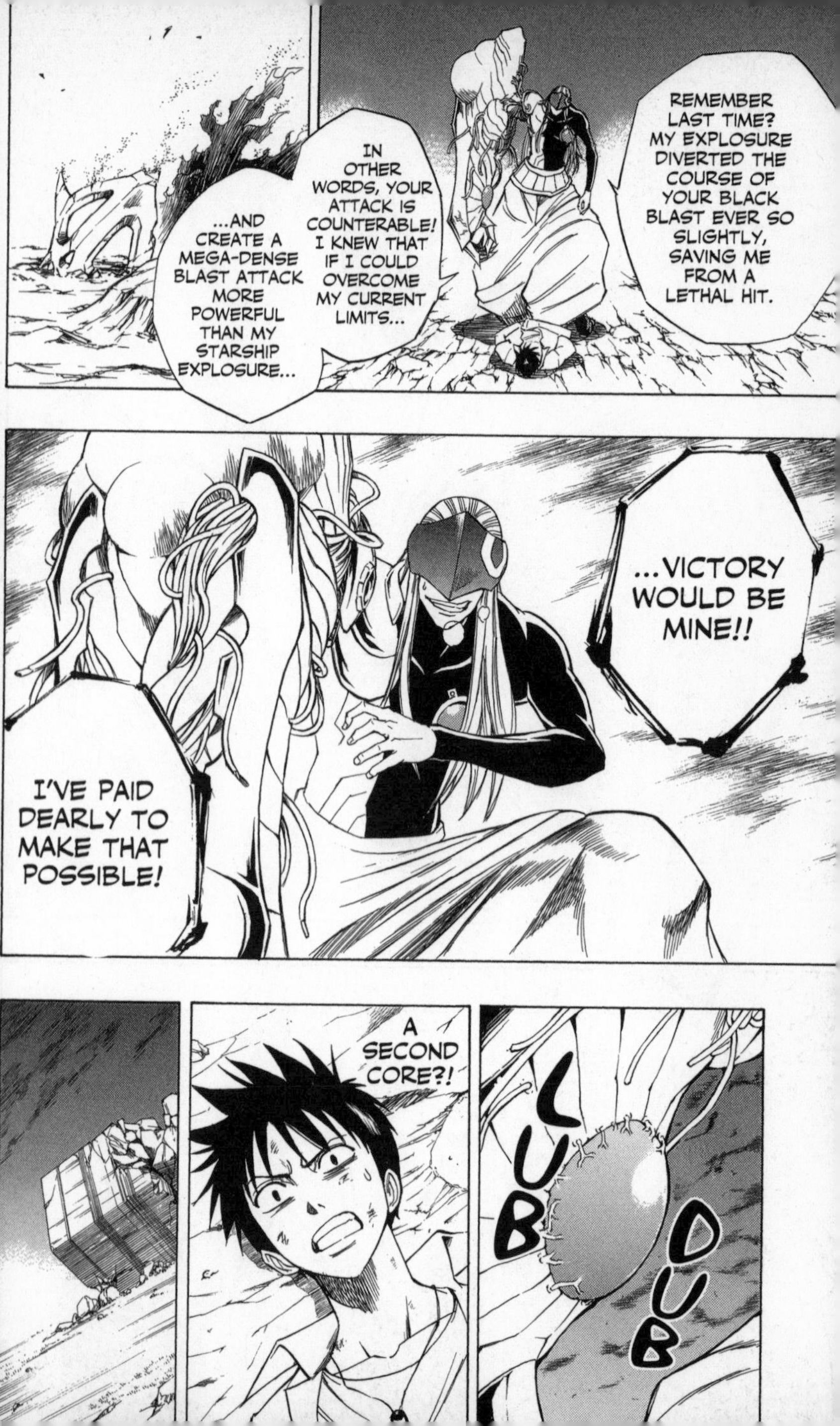
REMEMBER LAST TIME? MY EXPLOSURE DIVERTED THE COURSE OF YOUR BLACK BLAST EVER SO SLIGHTLY, SAVING ME FROM A LETHAL HIT.
IN OTHER WORDS, YOUR ATTACK IS COUNTERABLE! I KNEW THAT IF I COULD OVERCOME MY CURRENT LIMITS...
...AND CREATE A MEGA-DENSE BLAST ATTACK MORE POWERFUL THAN MY STARSHIP EXPLOSURE...
...VICTORY WOULD BE MINE!!
I'VE PAID DEARLY TO MAKE THAT POSSIBLE!
LUB
DUB
A SECOND CORE?!

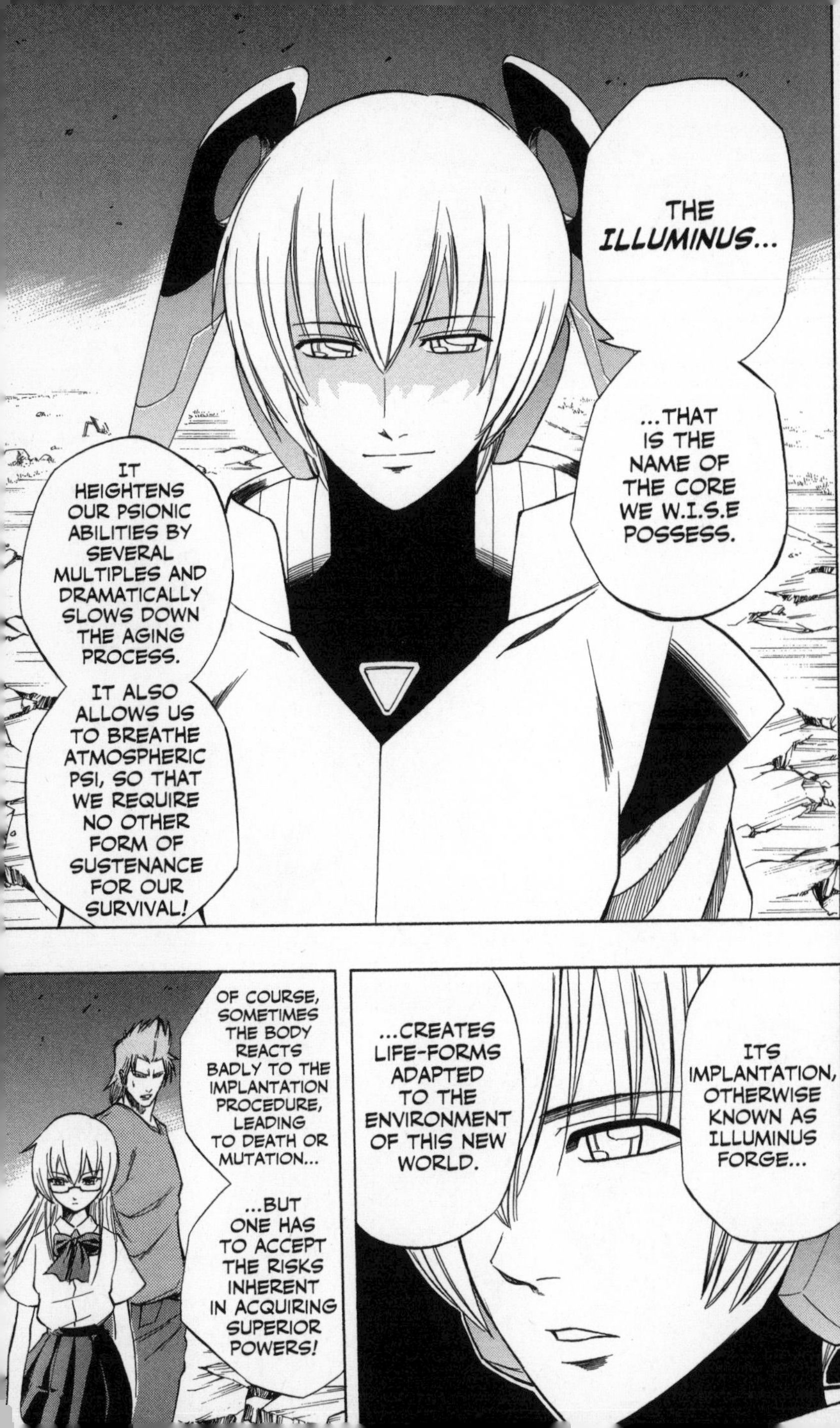
THE ILLUMINUS...
...THAT IS THE NAME OF THE CORE WE W.I.S.E POSSESS.
IT HEIGHTENS OUR PSIONIC ABILITIES BY SEVERAL MULTIPLES AND DRAMATICALLY SLOWS DOWN THE AGING PROCESS.
IT ALSO ALLOWS US TO BREATHE ATMOSPHERIC PSI, SO THAT WE REQUIRE NO OTHER FORM OF SUSTENANCE FOR OUR SURVIVAL!
ITS IMPLANTATION, OTHERWISE KNOWN AS ILLUMINUS FORGE...
...CREATES LIFE-FORMS ADAPTED TO THE ENVIRONMENT OF THIS NEW WORLD.
OF COURSE, SOMETIMES THE BODY REACTS BADLY TO THE IMPLANTATION PROCEDURE, LEADING TO DEATH OR MUTATION...
...BUT ONE HAS TO ACCEPT THE RISKS INHERENT IN ACQUIRING SUPERIOR POWERS!

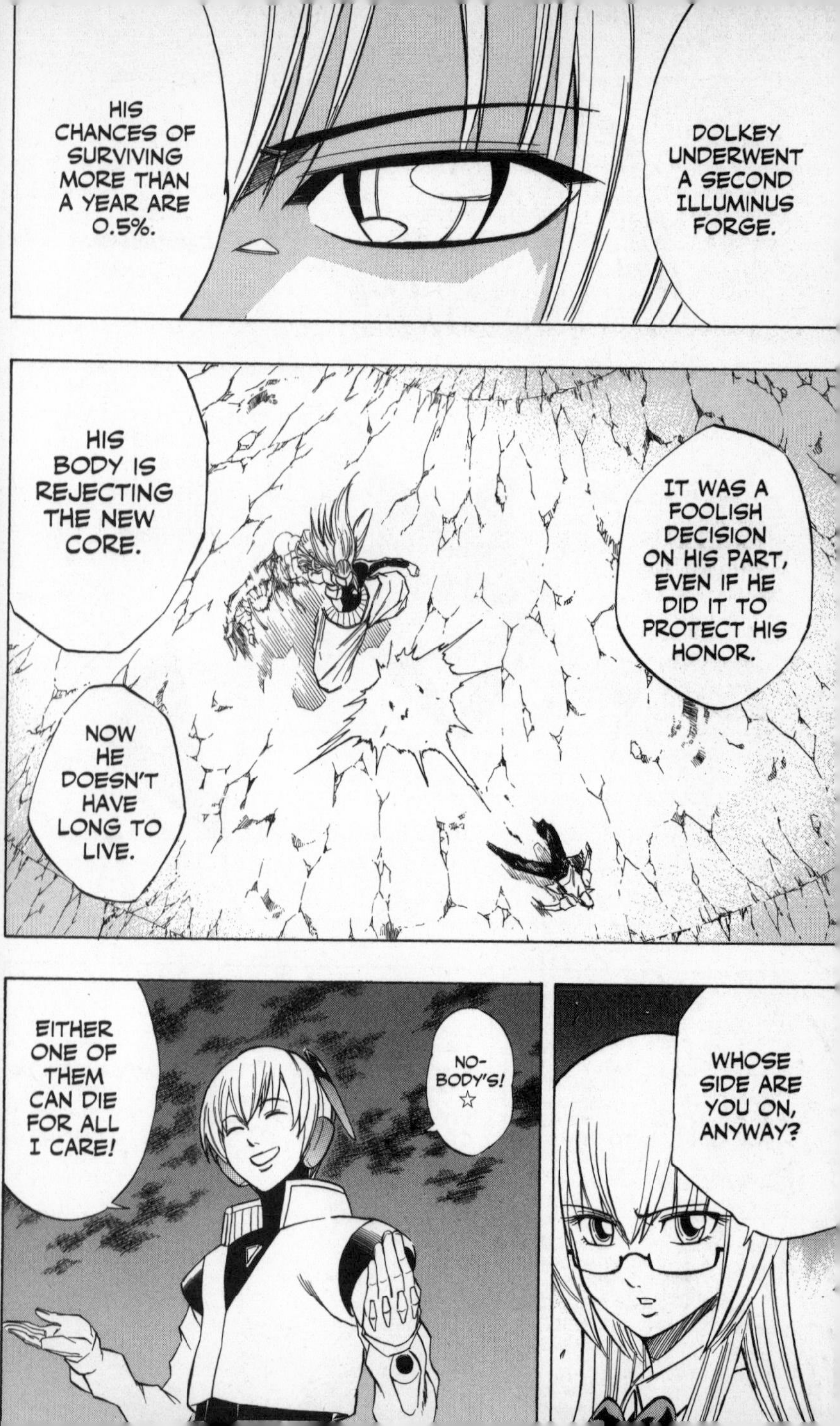
DOLKEY UNDERWENT A SECOND ILLUMINUS FORGE.
HIS CHANCES OF SURVIVING MORE THAN A YEAR ARE 0.5%.
IT WAS A FOOLISH DECISION ON HIS PART, EVEN IF HE DID IT TO PROTECT HIS HONOR.
HIS BODY IS REJECTING THE NEW CORE.
NOW HE DOESN'T HAVE LONG TO LIVE.
WHOSE SIDE ARE YOU ON, ANYWAY?
NO-BODY'S! ☆
EITHER ONE OF THEM CAN DIE FOR ALL I CARE!

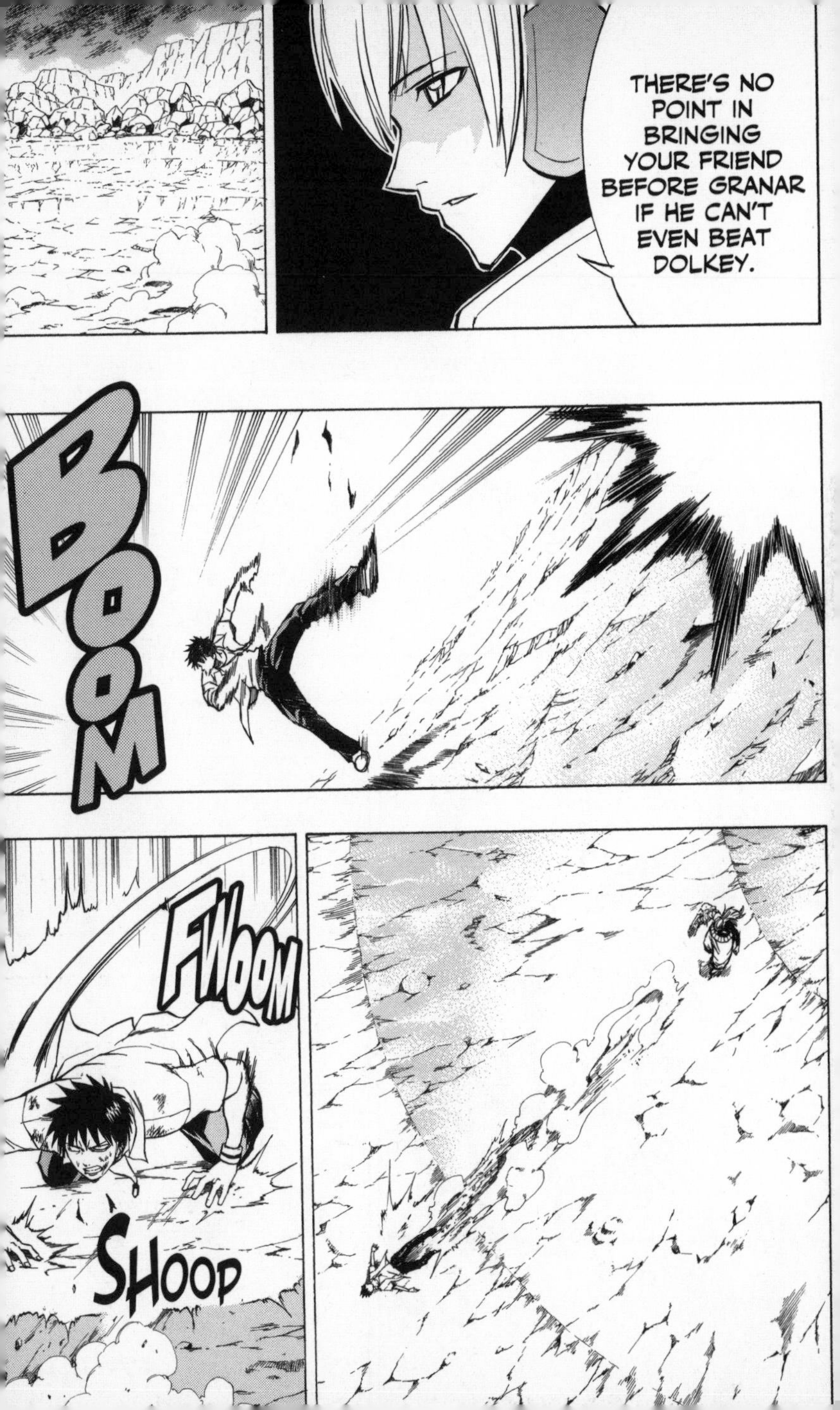
THERE'S NO POINT IN BRINGING YOUR FRIEND BEFORE GRANAR IF HE CAN'T EVEN BEAT DOLKEY.
BOOM
FWOOM
SHOOP

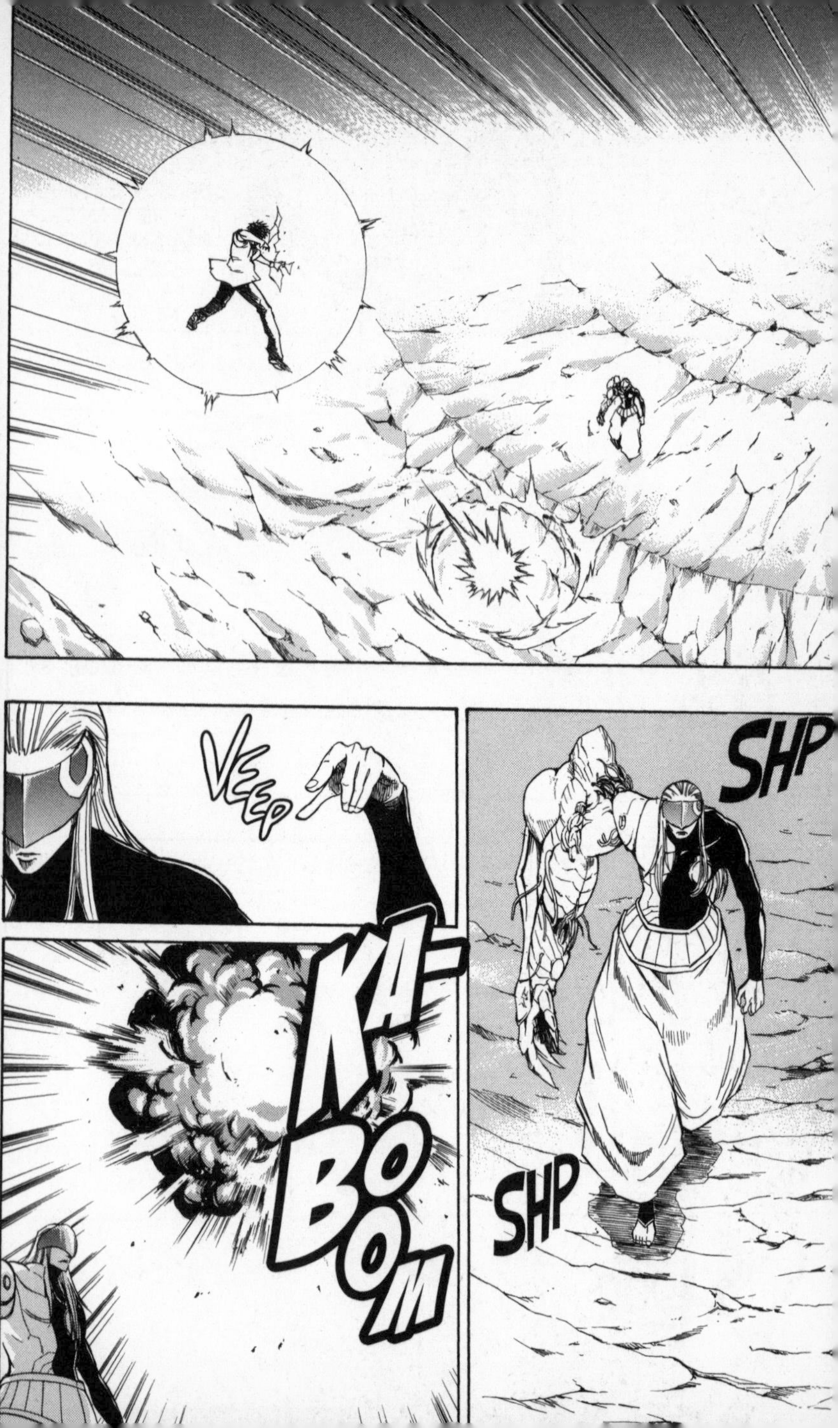
SHP
SHP
VEEP
KA-BOOM

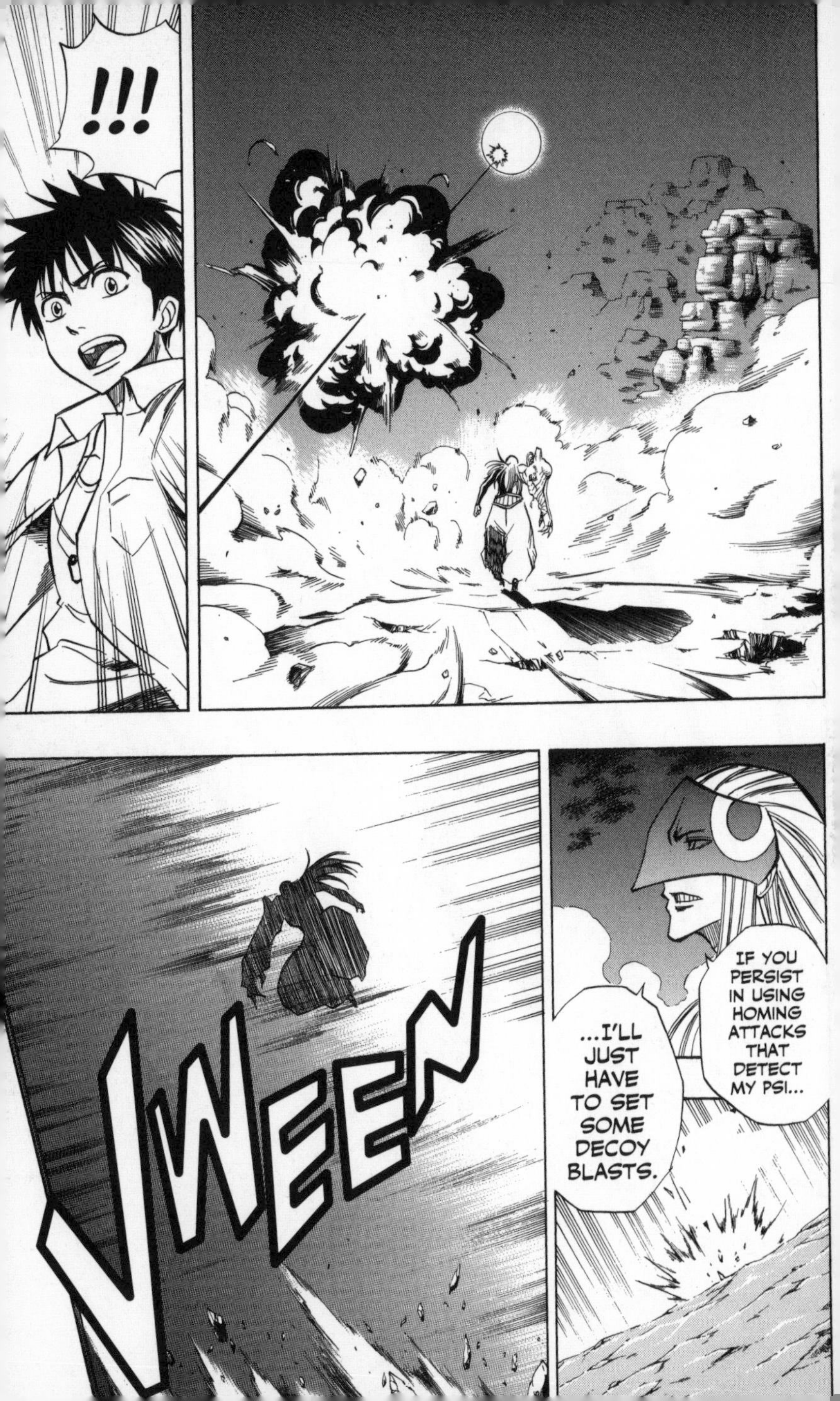
!!!
IF YOU PERSIST IN USING HOMING ATTACKS THAT DETECT MY PSI...
...I'LL JUST HAVE TO SET SOME DECOY BLASTS.
VWEEN

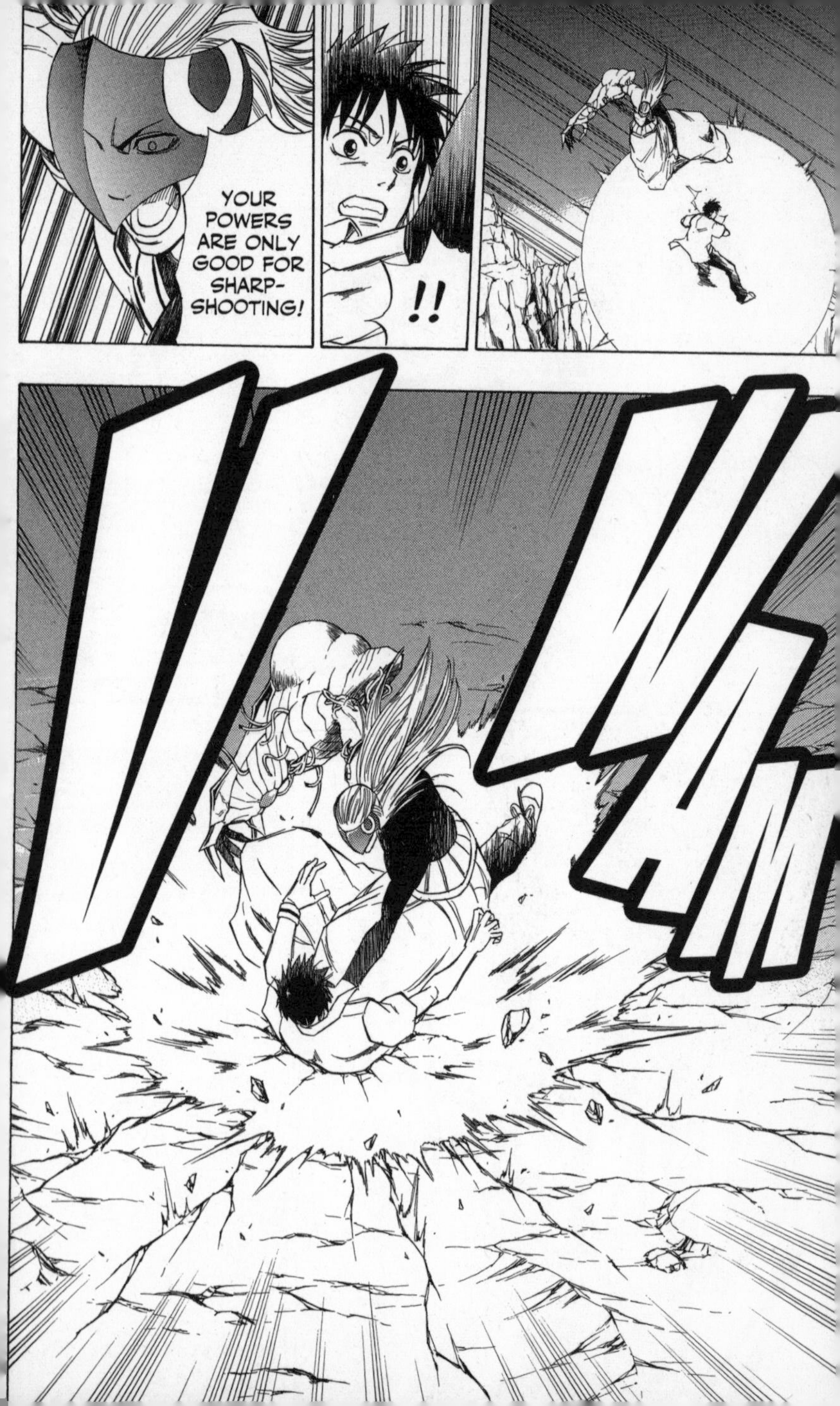
!!
YOUR POWERS ARE ONLY GOOD FOR SHARP-SHOOTING!

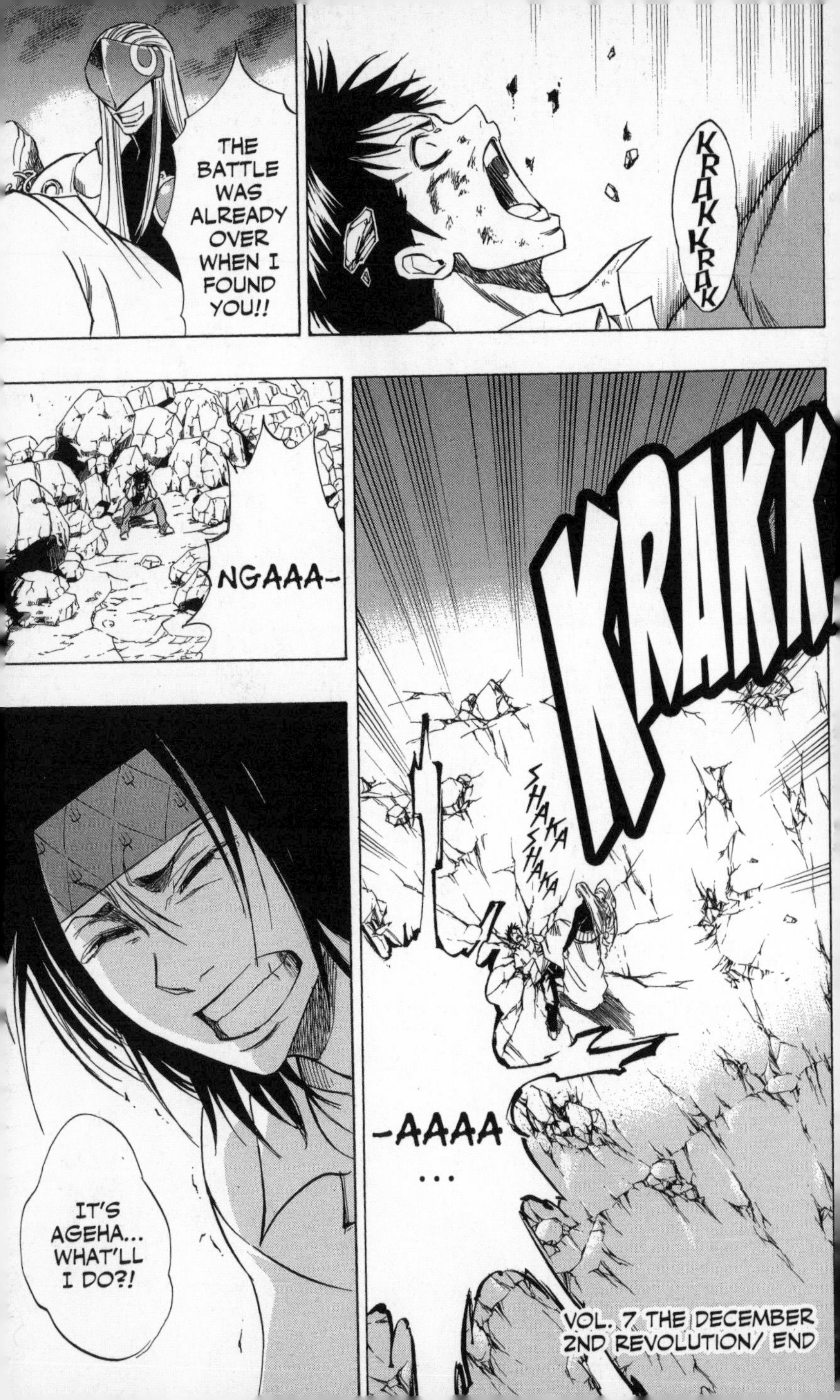
KRAKKRAK
THE BATTLE WAS ALREADY OVER WHEN I FOUND YOU!!
KRAKK
SHAKA SHAKA
-AAAA
...
VOL. 7 THE DECEMBER 2ND REVOLUTION/ END
NGAAA-
IT'S AGEHA... WHAT'LL I DO?!

HOLIDAY PSYREN 3

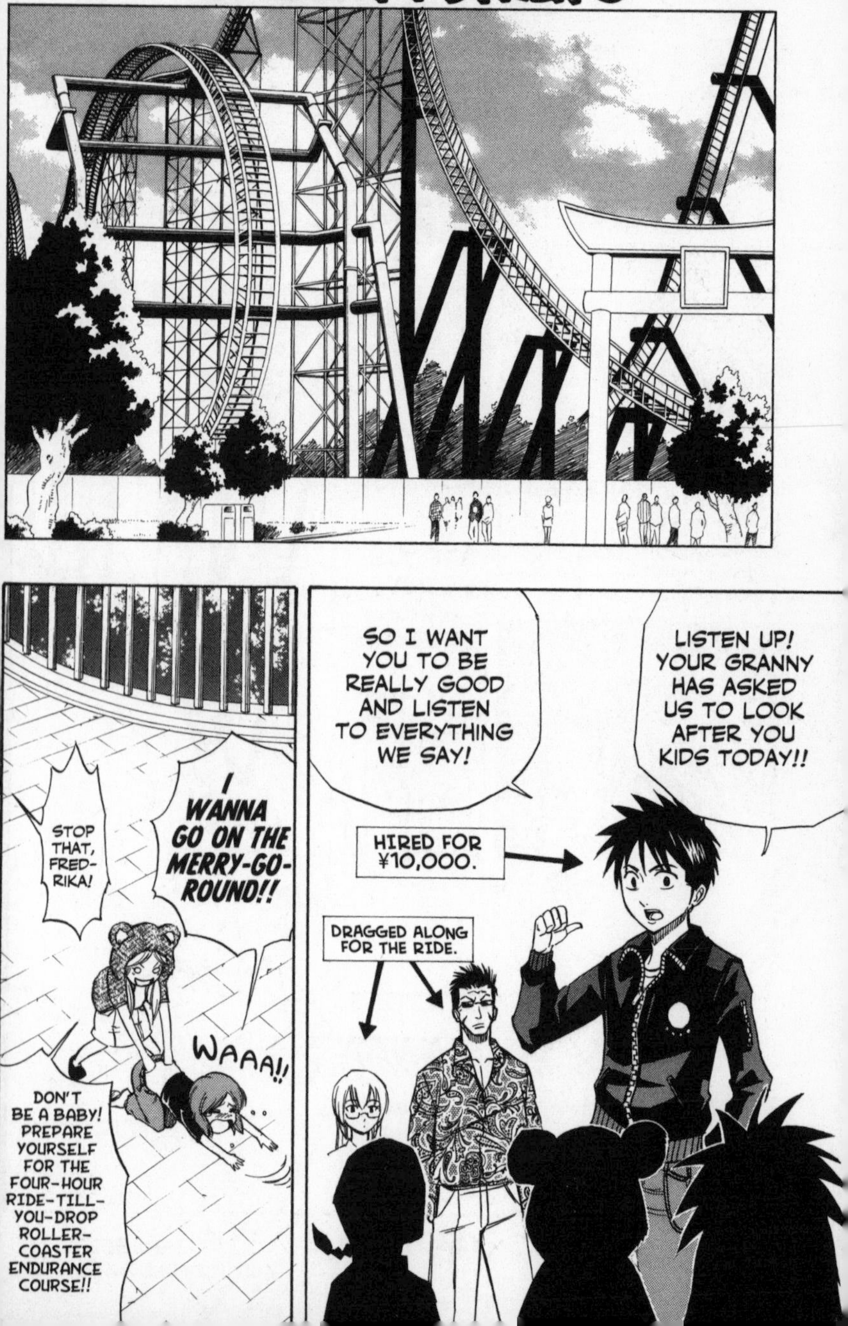

LISTEN UP! YOUR GRANNY HAS ASKED US TO LOOK AFTER YOU KIDS TODAY!!
SO I WANT YOU TO BE REALLY GOOD AND LISTEN TO EVERYTHING WE SAY!
HIRED FOR ¥10,000.
DRAGGED ALONG FOR THE RIDE.
I WANNA GO ON THE MERRY-GO-ROUND!!
STOP THAT, FRED-RIKA!
WAAAA!!
DON'T BE A BABY! PREPARE YOURSELF FOR THE FOUR-HOUR RIDE-TILL-YOU-DROP ROLLER-COASTER ENDURANCE COURSE!!

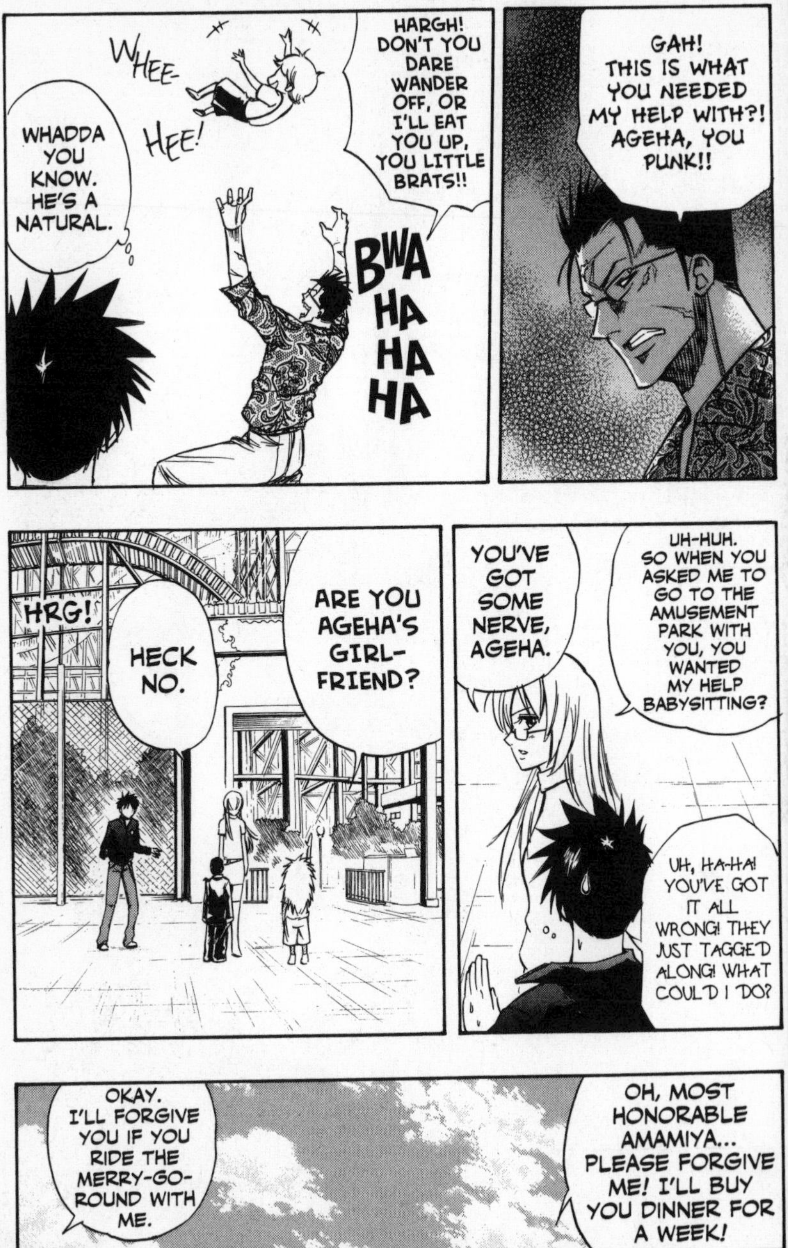
GAH! THIS IS WHAT YOU NEEDED MY HELP WITH?! AGEHA, YOU PUNK!!
HARGH! DON'T YOU DARE WANDER OFF, OR I'LL EAT YOU UP, YOU LITTLE BRATS!!
WHEE-HEE!
WHADDA YOU KNOW. HE'S A NATURAL.
BWA HA HA HA
UH-HUH. SO WHEN YOU ASKED ME TO GO TO THE AMUSEMENT PARK WITH YOU, YOU WANTED MY HELP BABYSITTING?
YOU'VE GOT SOME NERVE, AGEHA.
UH, HA-HA! YOU'VE GOT IT ALL WRONG! THEY JUST TAGGED ALONG! WHAT COULD I DO?
ARE YOU AGEHA'S GIRL-FRIEND?
HECK NO.
HRG!
OH, MOST HONORABLE AMAMIYA... PLEASE FORGIVE ME! I'LL BUY YOU DINNER FOR A WEEK!
OKAY. I'LL FORGIVE YOU IF YOU RIDE THE MERRY-GO-ROUND WITH ME.

HOLIDAY PSYREN 3 / END

PSYREN

Afterword

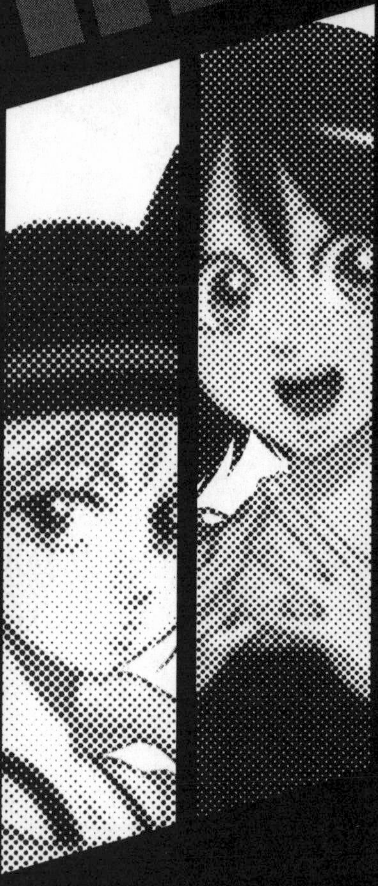

MY LAST SERIES, *MIERU HITO*, WAS SEVEN VOLUMES LONG. SO IT MAKES ME HAPPY TO HAVE FINALLY MADE IT THIS FAR WITH PSYREN TOO.

THIS TIME, WE HAVE A SPECIAL GUEST ILLUSTRATION BY RYOUHEI TAMURA, CREATOR OF *BEELZEBUB*. IT'S HILDA! WE'VE BEEN FRIENDS EVER SINCE HE WORKED AS AN ASSISTANT ON *MIERU HITO*. I CALL HIM UP EVERY NOW AND THEN AND WE HAVE CONVERSATIONS LIKE THIS:

"HEY, TAMURA! WERE YOU SLEEPING?"

"YES."

"REALLY? I'M NOT SLEEPY YET."

"OH."

"SO ANYWAY..."

THAT PRETTY MUCH SUMS UP OUR RELATIONSHIP.

JULY 2009
TOSHIAKI IWASHIRO

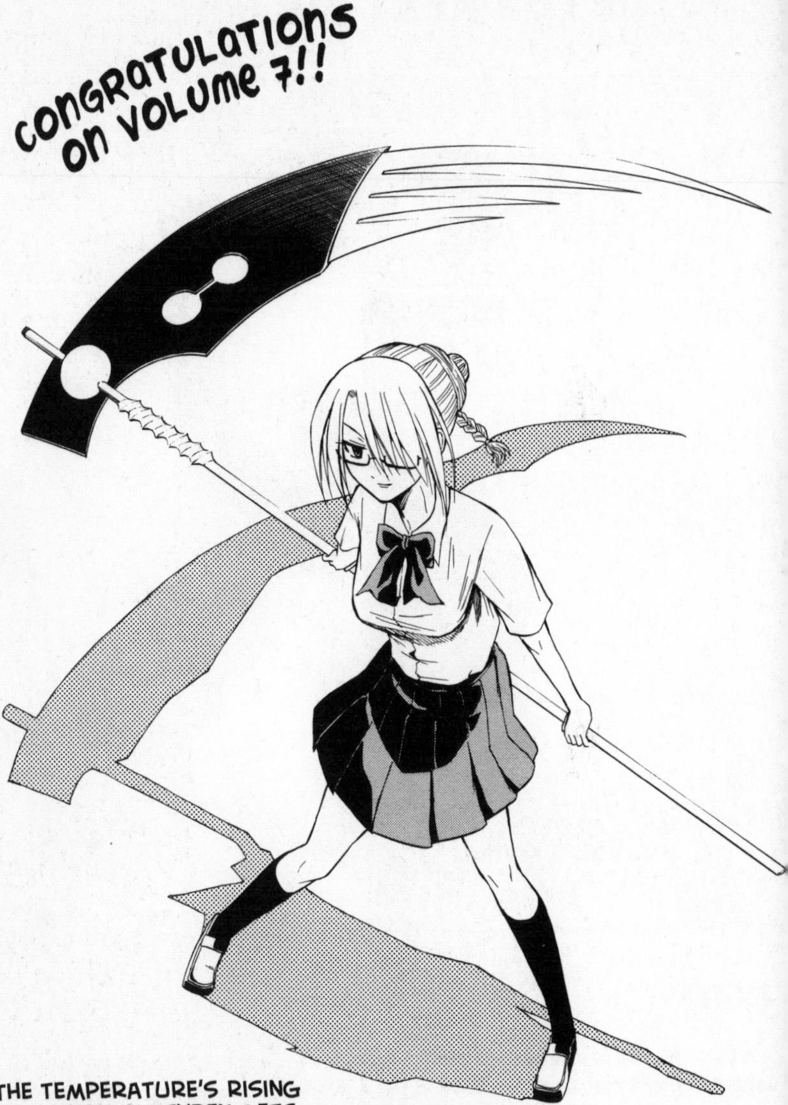
CONGRATULATIONS ON VOLUME 7!!

THE TEMPERATURE'S RISING AS ACTION IN PSYREN GETS HOTTER AND HOTTER!!

I'LL STOP BY AND CHECK IN WITH YOU EVERY SO OFTEN, SO LET'S DRAW SOME STORYBOARDS AND PLAY SOME VIDEO GAMES TOGETHER!

田村隆平
Ryouhei Tamura

IN THE NEXT VOLUME...

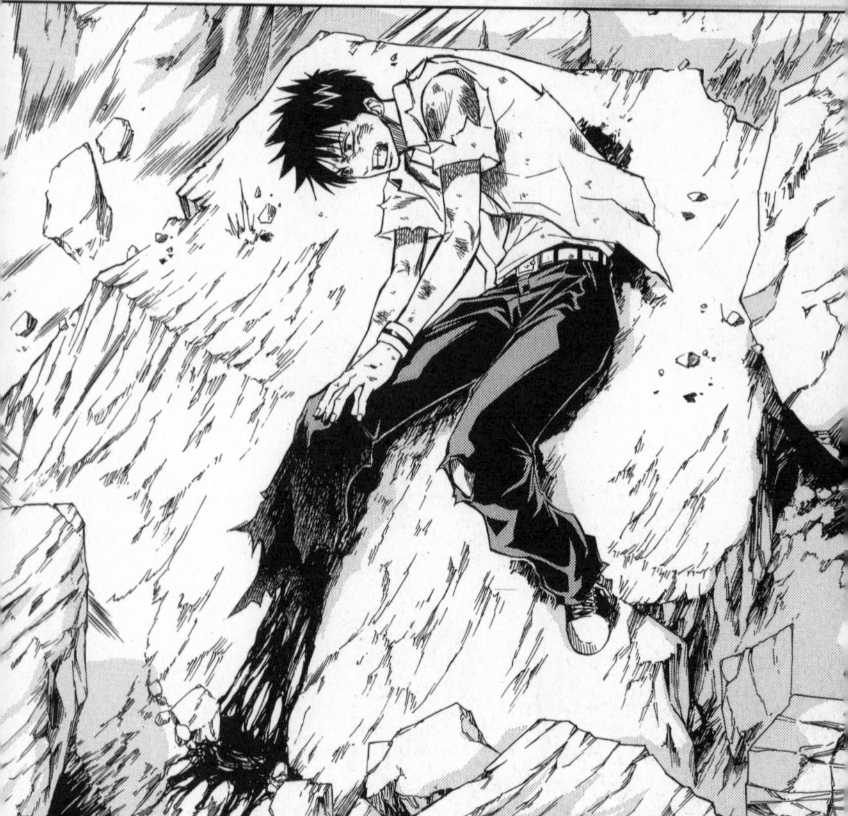

LIGHT

A trip to the future brings Ageha face-to-face with a group of friends he thought long dead, and the story they have to tell Ageha about the events of the past decade are truly shocking. The Global Rebirthday has changed everything. Not everyone Ageha cares for has survived, and the W.I.S.E organization is more powerful than ever.

Available JANUARY 2013!

You're Reading in the Wrong Direction!!

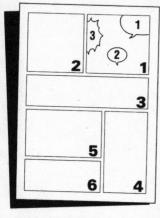

Whoops! Guess what? You're starting at the wrong end of the comic!

...It's true! In keeping with the original Japanese format, **Psyren** is meant to be read from right to left, starting in the upper-right corner.

Unlike English, which is read from left to right, Japanese is read from right to left, meaning that action, sound effects and word-balloon order are completely reversed—something which can make readers unfamiliar with Japanese feel pretty backwards themselves. For this reason, manga or Japanese comics published in the U.S. in English have sometimes been published "flopped"—that is, printed in exact reverse order, as though seen from the other side of a mirror.

By flopping pages, U.S. publishers can avoid confusing readers, but the compromise is not without its downside. For one thing, a character in a flopped manga series who once wore in the original Japanese version a T-shirt emblazoned with "M A Y" (as in "the merry month of") now wears one which reads "Y A M"! Additionally, many manga creators in Japan are themselves unhappy with the process, as some feel the mirror-imaging of their art changes their original intentions.

We are proud to bring you Toshiaki Iwashiro's **Psyren** in the original unflopped format. For now, though, turn to the other side of the book and let the fun begin...!

—Editor

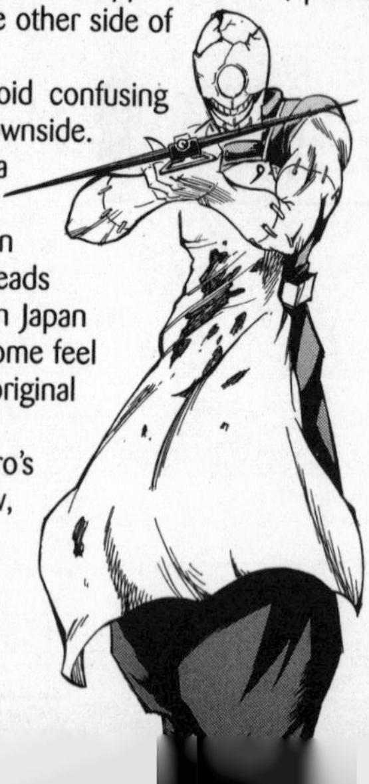